SOCIAL WORK AND SOCIAL INNOVATION

Research in Social Work series

Series Editors: Anna Gupta, Royal Holloway,
University of London, UK and John Gal,
Hebrew University of Jerusalem, Israel

Published together with The European Social Work Research Association (ESWRA), this series examines current, progressive and innovative research applications of familiar ideas and models in international social work research.

Also available in the series:

Living on the Edge
Edited by Samuel Keller, Inger Oterholm, Veronika Paulsen and Adrian van Breda

Migration and Social Work
Edited by Emilio José Gómez-Ciriano, Elena Cabiati and Sofia Dedotsi

When Social Workers Impact Policy and Don't Just Implement It
By John Gal and Idit Weiss-Gal

The Origins of Social Care and Social Work
By Mark Henrickson

Social Work Research Using Arts-Based Methods
Edited by Ephrat Huss and Eltje Bos

Critical Gerontology for Social Workers
Edited by Sandra Torres and Sarah Donnelly

Involving Service Users in Social Work Education, Research and Policy
Edited by Kristel Driessens and Vicky Lyssens-Danneboom

Adoption from Care
Edited by Tarja Pösö, Marit Skivenes and June Thoburn

Interprofessional Collaboration and Service User Participation
Edited by Kirsi Juhila, Tanja Dall, Christopher Hall and Juliet Koprowska

Find out more at:
policy.bristoluniversitypress.co.uk/research-in-social-work

Research in Social Work series

Series Editors: Anna Gupta, Royal Holloway,
University of London, UK and John Gal,
Hebrew University of Jerusalem, Israel

Forthcoming in the series:

Migration and Social Work

Edited by Emilio José Gómez-Ciriano, Elena Cabiati and Sofia Dedotsi

Find out more at:

policy.bristoluniversitypress.co.uk/
research-in-social-work

Research in Social Work series

Series Editors: Anna Gupta, Royal Holloway, University of London, UK and John Gal, Hebrew University of Jerusalem, Israel

---

International Editorial Board:

Andrés Arias Astray,
Complutense University of Madrid, Spain
Isobel Bainton, Policy Press, UK
Inge Bryderup, Aalborg University, Denmark
Tony Evans, Royal Holloway, University of London, UK
Hannele Forsberg, University of Tampere, Finland
John Gal, Hebrew University of Jerusalem, Israel
Anna Gupta, Royal Holloway, University of London, UK
Todd I. Herrenkohl, University of Michigan, US
Ephrat Huss, Ben-Gurion University of the Negev, Israel
Stefan Köngeter, Eastern Switzerland University of Applied Science (OST), Switzerland
Manohar Pawar, Charles Sturt University, Australia
Ian Shaw, National University of Singapore and University of York, UK
Karen Winter, Queen's University Belfast
Darja Zaviršek, University of Ljubljana, Slovenia

Find out more at:

policy.bristoluniversitypress.co.uk/
research-in-social-work

SOCIAL WORK AND SOCIAL INNOVATION
Emerging Trends and Challenges for Practice, Policy and Education in Europe

Edited by
Jean Pierre Wilken, Anne Parpan-Blaser,
Sarah Prosser, Suzan van der Pas and Erik Jansen

First published in Great Britain in 2026 by

Policy Press, an imprint of
Bristol University Press
University of Bristol
1–9 Old Park Hill
Bristol
BS2 8BB
UK
t: +44 (0)117 374 6645
e: bup-info@bristol.ac.uk

Details of international sales and distribution partners are available at
policy.bristoluniversitypress.co.uk

© Bristol University Press 2026

British Library Cataloguing in Publication Data
A catalogue record for this book is available from the British Library

ISBN 978-1-4473-6932-5 hardcover
ISBN 978-1-4473-6933-2 paperback
ISBN 978-1-4473-6934-9 ePub
ISBN 978-1-4473-6935-6 ePdf

The right of Jean Pierre Wilken, Anne Parpan-Blaser, Sarah Prosser, Suzan van der Pas and Erik Jansen to be identified as editors of this work has been asserted by them in accordance with the Copyright, Designs and Patents Act 1988.

All rights reserved: no part of this publication may be reproduced, stored in a retrieval system, or transmitted in any form or by any means, electronic, mechanical, photocopying, recording, or otherwise without the prior permission of Bristol University Press.

Every reasonable effort has been made to obtain permission to reproduce copyrighted material. If, however, anyone knows of an oversight, please contact the publisher.

The statements and opinions contained within this publication are solely those of the editors and contributors and not of the University of Bristol or Bristol University Press. The University of Bristol and Bristol University Press disclaim responsibility for any injury to persons or property resulting from any material published in this publication.

Bristol University Press and Policy Press work to counter discrimination on
grounds of gender, race, disability, age and sexuality.

Cover design: Bristol University Press
Front cover image: Viorika/Alamy

Bristol University Press' authorised representative in the European Union is:
Easy Access System Europe, Mustamäe tee 50, 10621 Tallinn, Estonia,
Email: gpsr.requests@easproject.com

Contents

List of figures and tables — x
List of abbreviations — xi
Notes on contributors — xiii

Introduction — 1
Jean Pierre Wilken, Anne Parpan-Blaser, Sarah Prosser, Suzan van der Pas and Erik Jansen

PART I Framing social innovation and social work

1. Social work and social innovation: how the twain can meet — 11
Jean Pierre Wilken and Anne Parpan-Blaser
2. How to change our neighbourhoods, regions and the world: using symptoms, systems and transformation as a framework for social innovation and social work — 24
Sarah Prosser and Ole Pedersen
3. Social work, social innovation, discretion and creativity: day-to-day innovation of practice — 41
Tony Evans
4. Potential for social innovation in social work: applying the capability approach — 54
Annica Brummel, Erik Jansen, Mara A. Yerkes and Jana Javornik

PART II Examples of social innovations in social work across Europe

Theme A Co-creation and co-production of social services: social innovation in practice

5. The art of co-creation: service innovation in Europe — 71
Chris Fox and Susan Baines
6. Promoting social services innovation: regional and local examples from across Europe — 84
Alfonso Lara-Montero
7. Co-creation in action: lessons from the CoSIE project — 98
Sandra Geelhoed and Eva Heijmans
8. Social innovation and service users' involvement: enhancing the knowledge of social work — 112
Kristel Driessens, Sidsel Natland and Vicky Lyssens-Danneboom
9. Moderating processes of social innovation: insights from a case study on labour market activation — 124
Koen Dortmans, Erik Jansen and Lineke van Hal

Theme B Education and learning: social innovation in social work education and learning

10 Regional learning networks in the social welfare domain: drivers of social innovation in social work — 139
Suzan van der Pas and Erik Jansen

11 Putting learning communities into practice: innovation of social work education — 150
Meike Koop, Ankie Schoenmakers, Ina Tilma, Nathalie Grahame and Henk Spies

12 Learning from innovation processes: introducing Easy Language in adult protection services — 164
Anne Parpan-Blaser

Theme C Community work, community-led innovation and collective action

13 The rediscovery of community: community development as social innovation — 179
Jean Pierre Wilken and Dagmar Narusson

14 Climate change from a green social work perspective: responding to a constantly evolving crisis challenging social work practice — 193
Lena Dominelli

15 Co-creation of nature-based solutions: guidelines for citizen engagement — 208
Nathalie Nunes, Knud Erik Hilding-Hamann and Isabel Ferreira

16 Innovating social work practices to better address homelessness: participatory action research with community services in Italy — 223
Marta Gaboardi, Sabina Licursi and Emanuela Pascuzzi

17 Challenging the power status quo: paradoxes in grassroots social innovation — 236
Luc de Droogh and Jeroen Gradener

Theme D Social entrepreneurship: inclusive and regenerative models of social business and innovation for sustainable impact

18 Social entrepreneurship as social innovation: what about social work? — 251
Leendert de Bell, Zsolt Bugarszki and Geof Cox

19 The growing rhetoric of entrepreneurship in times of crisis: future challenges of social work in the case of Portugal — 263
Antonela Jesus and Maria Inês Amaro

20	Unlimited incubators for belonging, cohesion and impact: nurturing 'what is already there' *Sarah Prosser, Ole Pedersen and Rosa Engebrigtsen Bye*	276
21	Developing the innovative power of social work: synthesis and future directions *Erik Jansen, Anne Parpan-Blaser, Suzan van der Pas, Sarah Prosser and Jean Pierre Wilken*	289
Index		298

List of figures and tables

Figures
2.1	The iceberg metaphor of symptoms, systems and mindset	26
2.2	The Problem Tree – a tool for developing a system innovation strategy	28
2.3	Three Horizon thinking	29
2.4	Three levels of innovation strategy for social change	35
4.1	Examples of Capability Cards	58
4.2	Example of a case analysed with the Person–Opportunities (PO) model	60

Tables
5.1	CoSIE sites and target populations	73
15.1	Overview of guideline categories addressing core leverages for successful citizen engagement in the co-creation of nature-based solutions	213
15.2	Learning points emerging from citizen engagement in the co-creation of nature-based solutions	215
19.1	Frequency of the word 'entrepreneur(ship)' in government programmes	267

List of abbreviations

AI	artificial intelligence
BASW	British Association of Social Workers
BWL	Bioregional Weaving Lab
CA	capability approach
CEO	chief executive officer
CoSIE	Co-creation of Service Innovation in Europe
COSMOS	Co-creation Service Modelling System
CPAR	community participatory action research
CRPD	United Nations Convention on the Rights of Persons with Disabilities
CSF	Foundation Casa San Francesco
ECSWR	European Conferences of Social Work Research
EES	European Employment Strategy
EL	Easy Language
ERSISI	Enhancing the Right to Social Inclusion Through Service Integration
ESN	European Social Network
EU	European Union
GDP	gross domestic product
GHG	greenhouse gas
GLD	grassroots-led development
GSW	green social work
HR	human resources (often used for an agency or department, or its staff)
IASSW	International Association of Schools of Social Work
ICSW	International Council of Social Welfare
ICT	information and communications technology
IFSW	International Federation of Social Workers
IPCC	Intergovernmental Panel on Climate Change
IT	information technology
KI-I	Competence Network Information Technology to Support the Integration of People with Disabilities
NBS	nature-based solutions
NGO	non-governmental organisation
NJA	Neighbourhood Job Agency
NU	Norway Unlimited
OECD	Organisation for Economic Co-operation and Development
PDF	portable document format
R&D	research and development
RNIB	Royal National Institute of Blind People

RNSWD	Regional Networks for the Social Welfare Domain
SDC	Strade di Casa
SMEs	small and medium enterprises
SSA	Social Support Act
SSD	social services department
TBBL	Tøyen boligbyggelag [Tøyen housing construction team]
UK	United Kingdom
WPPSO	Where People in Poverty Speak Out
WSF	World Social Forum

Notes on contributors

Maria Inês Amaro is Auxiliary Professor at the Instituto Universitário de Lisboa, Portugal.

Susan Baines was Professor at Manchester Metropolitan University, UK. Sadly, she passed away before this book was published.

Annica Brummel is Senior Researcher at HAN University of Applied Sciences, Netherlands.

Zsolt Bugarszki is Associate Professor at Tallinn University, Estonia.

Geof Cox is Freelance Social Enterprise Developer in the UK.

Leendert de Bell is Professor at Utrecht University of Applied Sciences, Netherlands.

Luc de Droogh is Researcher at Hogeschool Gent, Belgium.

Lena Dominelli is Professor at the University of Stirling, UK.

Koen Dortmans is Senior Researcher at HAN University of Applied Sciences, Netherlands.

Kristel Driessens is Professor at the University of Applied Sciences Karel de Grote Antwerp, Belgium.

Rosa Engebrigtsen Bye is Project Manager in Oslo Municipality, Norway.

Tony Evans is Professor at Royal Holloway University of London, UK.

Isabel Ferreira is Researcher at the University of Coimbra, Portugal.

Chris Fox is Professor at Manchester Metropolitan University, UK.

Marta Gaboardi is Postdoctoral Researcher at the University of Padua, Italy.

Sandra Geelhoed is Assistant Professor at Utrecht University of Applied Sciences, Netherlands.

Jeroen Gradener is Researcher at Amsterdam University of Applied Sciences, Netherlands.

Nathalie Grahame is Researcher at Avans University of Applied Sciences, Netherlands.

Eva Heijmans was Senior Researcher at Utrecht University of Applied Sciences, Netherlands.

Knud Erik Hilding-Hamann was Senior Specialist at the Danish Technological Institute, Denmark.

Erik Jansen is Professor at HAN University of Applied Sciences, Netherlands, and Western Norway University of Applied Sciences, Norway.

Jana Javornik is Associate Professor at the University of Leeds, UK.

Antonela Jesus is Lecturer at Universidade Católica Portuguesa, Lisbon, Portugal.

Meike Koop is Lecturer-Researcher at Avans University of Applied Sciences, Netherlands.

Alfonso Lara-Montero is Chief Executive Officer at the European Social Network, Belgium.

Sabina Licursi is Associate Professor at the University of Calabria, Italy.

Vicky Lyssens-Danneboom is Associate Professor at the University of Applied Sciences Karel de Grote Antwerp, Belgium.

Dagmar Narusson is Senior Lecturer at Tartu University, Estonia.

Sidsel Natland is Associate Lecturer at Oslo Met University, Norway.

Nathalie Nunes is Researcher at the University of Coimbra, Portugal.

Anne Parpan-Blaser is Professor at the University of Applied Sciences and Arts, Northwestern Switzerland, Switzerland.

Emanuela Pascuzzi is Professor at the University of Calabria, Italy.

Ole Pedersen is Social Entrepreneur at Nedenfra ideelt AS, Norway.

Sarah Prosser is CEO of Prosser Projects and Adjunct Associate Professor at VID Specialized University Oslo.

Ankie Schoenmakers is Lecturer at Avans University of Applied Sciences, Netherlands.

Henk Spies is Professor at Avans University of Applied Sciences, Netherlands.

Ina Tilma is Researcher at Avans University of Applied Sciences, Netherlands.

Suzan van der Pas is Professor of Social Innovation at Leiden University of Applied Sciences, Netherlands.

Lineke van Hal is Associate Professor at HAN University of Applied Sciences, Netherlands.

Jean Pierre Wilken is Professor at Utrecht University of Applied Sciences, Netherlands, Tartu University, Estonia, and Catholic University of Milan, Italy.

Mara A. Yerkes is Associate Professor at Utrecht University, Netherlands.

Introduction

*Jean Pierre Wilken, Anne Parpan-Blaser, Sarah Prosser,
Suzan van der Pas and Erik Jansen*

Background

The editors, scholars from Norway, Switzerland and the Netherlands, met and co-presented Social Innovation and Social Work themed symposia at the European Conferences of Social Work Research (ECSWR) in 2019 (Leuven, Belgium) and 2021 (online, Bucharest, Romania). The discussions around social innovation and numerous exchanges at the conferences enabled us to share insights about emerging trends and knowledge from all over Europe on a wide range of topics around innovation in social work. Our common motivation for establishing this book was therefore a shared wish for a source to turn to when looking for inspiration and a framework to ultimately ensure improved outcomes for societal challenges and to increase social quality for people and communities.

This book provides a broad collection of theoretical and practical studies about social innovation in connection to social work. The volume contains 21 chapters written by 41 experts from 11 countries all over Europe. Readers will be introduced to varied approaches and evidence-based examples that, together, allow the grasping of the concept of social innovation in the context of social work and to gain competence in relevant terms and aspects. As a result, the content will hopefully increase readers' abilities to introduce and implement social innovation in social work in a way that leads to lasting positive change for the common good.

The volume does not attempt to be either a textbook that exhaustively analyses where participatory innovations are making most impact across Europe, nor does it cover all possible kinds of innovation. It does, however, explore where social work could go in terms of social innovation in ways that are relevant and topical to the people it is intended to benefit and to develop as a discipline.

Framework

Innovation implies change. It is questionable, however, if any innovation, even of the most purely technological sort, manages to bring about its intended changes without also causing undesired and unintended side effects of some kind. Social workers, at the coalface of where change is both made and felt, are in a perfect position to oversee or act within, or upon, social innovations.

Across Europe there is a multitude of examples of inspiring innovations involving participation, collaboration and community development in teaching and practising social work. However, these examples lack a common framework to aid in comparative discourse and subsequent development. From another angle, students and practitioners are eager to make a difference, but find there is little knowledge about suitable models and strategies to be used in practice. The concept of social innovation, if well-defined within the framework of social work, can serve as a framework to answer both these challenges. The content of this book provides insights that resonate with social work practitioners, research communities, educators, citizens initiatives and decision makers in governing bodies; it also opens them up to new concepts, tools and narratives that empower them to implement change.

If learnings and research findings from the social innovation field are integrated into professional action and policies, it will strengthen the power of social work and contribute to a better and fairer future for all of our citizens, no matter what their disadvantages. A democratic and rights-based Europe needs progressive change based on foundations of inclusion and equity. Constant societal and global change drives a need for innovation based on lived experiences and human-based outcomes. Knowledge, also from indigenous and marginalised persons and groups, must therefore be recognised and woven into a new body of research for improved policy and practice.

Starting point

The book takes its framing and foundational starting point from the internationally accepted definitions of social innovation and social work. The European Commission (2013, pp 6–7) adopted a definition based on the work of Murray et al (2019), in which social innovation is viewed as the generation of new ideas in the form of products, services and models that simultaneously meet or facilitate social needs and create new relationships or collaborations. As this definition implies, the concept of social innovation is often understood as processes that spring from real-life problem-solving, but simultaneously address a basic level of capacity-building in groups, organisations or society. In addition, social innovation is deemed relevant when addressing challenges concerning societal changes (macro level), the quality of services and other resources (meso level), and needs connected to people's well-being (micro level) (Nicholls et al, 2015). Such innovations ideally also generate newer, better structures and competencies for innovation beyond the demands of the actual situation (Caulier-Grice et al, 2012). Social innovation is thus associated with social change for 'the common good', indicating that it is meant to create social value and must be experienced as useful in a particular field of practice (Mulgan, 2015).

The global definition of the social work profession defines social work as:

a practice-based profession and an academic discipline that promotes social change and development, social cohesion, and the empowerment and liberation of people. Principles of social justice, human rights, collective responsibility and respect for diversities are central to social work. Underpinned by theories of social work, social sciences, humanities and indigenous knowledges, social work engages people and structures to address life challenges and enhance wellbeing. (IFSW and IASSW, 2014)

Although both definitions are not uncontested, they may serve as a starting point for further thinking. If the goal of social work is to promote change and development, it is in fact about social innovation. Meeting social needs and strengthening social relationships is the heart of social work. In this book we explore different societal challenges and domains of innovation, and how innovation can become a reality.

Themes discussed in the individual chapters range from addressing how long-term transformation and change can be made through social innovation processes linked to social work, to concepts such as co-creation, human-centred service design, community work, neighbourhood-driven innovation, social entrepreneurship and meaningful participation in all stages of research and teaching. Many of the examples reflect upon the wider implications for future policy making and working principles for practitioners and educators across contemporary Europe.

The contributions make it clear that no one intervention, disruptive change or research project is going to radically move the whole field of social work forward. Local innovations in local practices feed the general body of knowledge of innovation in social work, and it is the collective impact of many small advances that affects the future of our field of research and practice. Any successful innovations affecting direct services with individual clients, will need to be happening in parallel with new policies for systemic change, which in turn will depend on evidence-based research and inspirational case studies. This is good reason why it is important to start building a body of literature that lays down insights, findings and experiences on the role of social work in social innovation and vice versa.

Structure of the book

The book is divided into two parts, the first framing basic concepts of social work and social innovation and the second providing more in-depth chapters about different domains, including examples from research and practice.

Part I frames the topic of social work and social innovation through European and international definitions, and in doing so includes aspects such as social cohesion, empowerment, respect for diversity, new collaborations and partnerships. It also presents an understanding of how social change can be established and approaching innovation from different conceptual directions and using different strategies.

Chapter 1, authored by Jean Pierre Wilken and Anne Parpan-Blaser, introduces concepts of social work and social innovation and explores how the notion of social innovation can be made meaningful for social work. In Chapter 2, Sarah Prosser and Ole Pedersen consider which approaches to social innovation are best suited to framing and then inducing positive change, and how these relate to social and community work in practice and as a field. Chapter 3, authored by Tony Evans, describes social innovation as a horizontal, day-to-day practice. In Chapter 4, authored by Annica Brummel, Erik Jansen, Mara A. Yerkes and Jana Javornik, the capability approach is introduced as a potential normative framework for social innovation.

Part II presents various initiatives and examples of social innovation from across Europe. The chapters in this part take up the overarching themes of public services, social entrepreneurship, neighbourhoods and education – including examples of where innovative approaches are being piloted and the research that examines their effectiveness. The chapters are divided into four thematic areas, although in these cases – as they deal with complex social challenges – there are overlaps.

Theme A focuses on co-creation and co-production as ways of putting social innovation into practice. It draws together ideas about co-creation and how it intersects with and reinforces social innovation.

In Chapter 5, Chris Fox and Susan Baines introduce principles of co-creation, drawing on experiences from the Horizon2020 project Co-creation of Service Innovation in Europe (CoSIE).

The goal of the project was to contribute to democratic renewal and social inclusion through co-creating services by engaging diverse citizen groups and stakeholders. Results inspire thinking about new roles and relationships, in particular between professionals on the front-line and citizens.

In Chapter 6, Alfonso Lara-Montero shows how social services can be innovated, using examples from the European Social Network. The author describes two sets of innovations. The first refers to innovations in social work, such as social services outreach and coordination with employment services for people farthest from the labour market or integrated services for vulnerable families. The second relates to investments in new models of social care that promote an overarching community and home-based approach particularly underpinned by technology.

Chapter 7, written by Sandra Geelhoed and Eva Heijmans, demonstrates different methods and tools that can be used in the process of co-creation. Drawing upon learnings from pilots in the CoSIE project, the authors highlight co-creation as a value-led practice. Methods that were used supporting this process include community reporting, living lab, digital tools and social hackathon.

In Chapter 8, Kristel Driessens, Sidsel Natland and Vicky Lyssens-Danneboom focus on the involvement of service users in social innovation. The authors share several examples and argue that user involvement is in itself an innovative topic, as it facilitates learning and research processes that enhance the knowledge and competences of future social workers to work in socially innovative ways. The examples show the importance of integrating experiential knowledge in social innovation, but that this requires a change in academic norms.

Chapter 9, authored by Koen Dortmans, Erik Jansen and Lineke van Hal, provides insights from a case study in labour market activation. The project that is described embraces social objectives such as well-being, job satisfaction and a more sustainable society by relating unemployed residents with (paid) jobs in the neighbourhood in a novel way. The authors demonstrate the tension between desired outcomes (sustainable labour market participation) and the open process of participation, exchange and collaboration with relevant stakeholders, including end users. They highlight the role of social workers as moderators of change and learning processes.

Theme B is about social innovation in social work education and learning. It focuses on learning processes and their role at the root of social innovation — both in active social work practice and in the education of new professionals.

In Chapter 10, Suzan van der Pas and Erik Jansen describe how decentralised regional social welfare networks can be a driver for social innovation, for instance by supporting collaborative practices, capacity-building and strategic advice. The authors illustrate how social innovation does not happen instantaneously and autonomously; it requires effort to create adequate learning situations and contexts to effectively shape the social innovation process, so that it can permeate and fundamentally change the social system.

Chapter 11, by Meike Koop, Ankie Schoenmakers, Ina Tilma, Nathalie Grahame and Henk Spies, shows how learning communities can be both helpful and challenging for higher education in social work. Structural tensions such as not-knowing versus clarity, friction versus harmony, structure versus freedom, process versus result, are recognised as characteristic of both learning communities and innovation processes. Students (and lecturers) in learning communities thus acquire innovation skills, but also contribute to the solution of so-called wicked problems and thus to the transformation of the social system.

Chapter 12, by Anne Parpan-Blaser, uses an example of introducing Easy Language into adult protection services as a case to reflect on the fact that social innovation is not only about the final result but also about the willingness of all participants to learn from each other on the way, and therefore about making explicit the process of capturing and sharing knowledge. She states that if the process of social innovation is understood as a combination of learning and problem-solving then this deserves to be weighted higher than the aimed-for final innovation.

Theme C is about community work, community-led innovation and collective action. It is a theme at the core of new ways of working for societal and environmental change, and one where emerging knowledge is opening new ways of organising and working for change in ways that include and empower the people closest to the challenges.

Chapter 13, by Jean Pierre Wilken and Dagmar Narusson, reflects on community development as a countermovement to neoliberal individualisation and its negative side effects such as loneliness and polarisation. They show how the rediscovery of the notion of community can be seen as socially innovative. They do this based on case examples from two community development projects being initiated in the Netherlands and Estonia.

Chapter 14, by Lena Dominelli, elaborates on the concept of green social work and proposes that it could be the root of a new paradigm for practice rooted in environmental justice. The chapter shows that, if social work is to meet the challenges of the 21st century around human rights, social justice and active citizenship, it will require social workers to include promoting environmental justice in and through their professional expertise, and to work transdisciplinarily with other academic disciplines.

Chapter 15, by Nathalie Nunes, Knud Erik Hilding-Hamann and Isabel Ferreira, presents the research findings on examples of co-creation of nature-based solutions in deprived urban districts in different European cities. The authors present guideline categories clustering the core leverages for successful citizen engagement in such processes. They conclude by reflecting on possible directions for further social innovation in inclusive urban regeneration settings, and on the advancement of the science, practice, policy and education of nature-based solutions.

Chapter 16, by Marta Gaboardi, Sabina Licursi and Emanuela Pascuzzi, concerns innovating social work practice with the homeless in Italy. They illustrate this through research on two local projects carried out in a context affected by national policy and a mindset of using an emergency-oriented approach to homelessness. The comparative analysis makes it possible to identify the contextual factors hindering or fostering social innovation in a given place, and to do so not only in the early experimental phase, but also when it comes to working for fundamental reform.

Chapter 17, by Luc de Droogh and Jeroen Gradener, addresses social innovation as a bottom-up process, in which social workers engage to establish an antidote to structural power disparities between market, state forces and citizens' needs. They reflect on the example of 'Where People in

Poverty Speak Out' in Flanders and on social innovations as political practice. The authors formulate lessons for practice as paradoxes at the intersection between the politicisation of individual experiences and institutional change.

Theme D takes up the topic of social entrepreneurship and its interface with inclusion, regeneration and sustainable impact. This theme is one where social innovation as a process and outcome is particularly important to differentiate from traditional commercial and effectivisation innovation approaches. The theme also addresses how social enterprise as a field for delivering positive impact to individuals and communities is relevant in social and community work.

Chapter 18, by Leendert De Bell, Zsolt Bugarszki and Geof Cox, describes social innovation from the viewpoint of social enterprises that focus on work and reintegration, in particular the role of social firms and the social-cooperative model of sheltered work. They show how social goals and social processes can go hand in hand in entrepreneurial initiatives, while also pointing out that entrepreneurial logic and values are sometimes at odds with governmental logic and values and that this can present a barrier to successful social innovation, if not consciously addressed.

Chapter 19, by Antonela Jesus and Maria Inês Amaro, uses the case of consecutive Portuguese governments that have at times used 'entrepreneurship' as a concept to conceal their own incapability to address public or social needs – and relate this to wider EU economic development policy. This approach could reflect neoliberal rationales in which entrepreneurs will either boost the economy or fill in the gaps left by the government, believing the gains will trickle down to society at large, and somehow integrate economic competitiveness with social cohesion.

Chapter 20, by Sarah Prosser, Ole Pedersen and Rosa Engebrigtsen Bye, presents the 'Unlimited' model of a community incubator as a driver of social innovation. The incubators are in neighbourhoods with untapped potential for resident participation in addressing challenges they have themselves experienced. The model combines community and social work approaches with support for founding social enterprises, and contributes to self-worth, social cohesion, inclusion and long-term vibrant communities.

Chapter 21, co-written by the editors of this book, is a synthesis of the main themes emerging from preceding chapters. It condenses reflections on where we currently stand and where the field of social innovation and social work might go. The synopsis of the contributions not only provides an overview of the richness of insights already brought to the fore by the numerous initiatives in Europe where social work and social innovation meet or are intertwined but also opens the debate for questions remaining unanswered and issues that are novel, and sometimes overarching. The latter, in particular, provide a clear sense of direction for future research and developments in the emerging shared field of social work and social innovation.

References

Caulier-Grice, J. Davies, A. Patrick, R. and Norman, W. (2012) *Defining Social Innovation: A Deliverable of the Project 'The Theoretical, Empirical and Policy Foundations for Building Social Innovation in Europe (TEPSIE)'*, European Commission – 7th Framework Programme, Brussels: European Commission, DG Research.

European Commission (2013) Guide to Social Innovation, February, Brussels: European Commission, https://ec.europa.eu/regional_policy/en/information/publications/guides/2013/guide-to-social-innovation.

IFSW and IASSW (International Federation of Social Workers and International Association of Schools of Social Work) (2014) International definition of social work, International Federation of Social Workers, July, https://www.ifsw.org/what-is-social-work/global-definition-of-social-work/.

Mulgan, G. (2015) Foreword: the study of social innovation – theory, practice and progress, in A. Nicholls, J. Simon and M. Gabriel (eds) *New Frontiers in Social Innovation Research*, Basingstoke: Palgrave Macmillan, pp x–xx.

Murray R., Caulier-Grice, J. and Mulgan, G. (2010) *The Open Book of Social Innovation*, London: Young Foundation and National Endowment for Science, Technology and the Arts.

Nicholls, A., Simon, J. and Gabriel, M. (eds) (2015) *New Frontiers in Social Innovation Research*, Basingstoke: Palgrave Macmillan.

PART I
Framing social innovation and social work

1

Social work and social innovation: how the twain can meet

Jean Pierre Wilken and Anne Parpan-Blaser

Introduction

Since the late 20th century, social innovation has become a much-debated buzzword. The term breathes progress and promising improvements, but often remains on a rather programmatic level without providing concrete indications on how societal renewal can take place, or what the actual significance is for people and communities. We choose not to entangle ourselves in debates or developments labelled as social innovation, but, after exploring the nature of the relationship between social work and social innovation more deeply propose, rather, to take a firm stand as social work community.

In this chapter, we investigate whether social innovation is a useful notion for social work and, if so, how social work can contribute to social innovation. We distinguish three dimensions. The first dimension is how social work can (co-)create innovations in the field of social services contributing to social quality and well-being. We argue that social work research has a supporting function in these processes, as it provides the empirical and theoretical basis for a critical stand and for innovation.

The second dimension is how social work can contribute to the 'social' in all kinds of innovations, meaning that social quality is put at the centre. This includes taking a critical stance towards the use of 'social' in various innovation contexts, to remain diligently focused on what the true social benefits are for people. The third dimension is to look at the innovative character of social work itself, as a profession and an academic discipline, since playing a role in social innovation means that we as professionals and researchers must be innovative ourselves. Innovation competencies therefore need to be part of the body of knowledge of social work and part of the curricula of social work education.

Based on our exploration, we conclude that if social innovation is defined properly and connected with the values expressed in the international definition of social work, it can not only be meaningful, but also strengthen the profile and practice of social work: It is part of the disciplines core mandate to further develop services and structures in line with the current state of knowledge.

Exploring the concept of social innovation

Although the word 'social' suggests that social innovation is about social relations, the concept has mostly been used since the early 2000s for other (non-relational) types of innovation. Reviewing the literature (Wilken, 2023), we see that the term appears in connection to:

- Economic and technological innovation serving 'social needs' (mostly poorly defined) (Păunescu, 2014; Aksoy et al, 2019).
- Innovation and governance structures, with the main aim of better connecting public administration and public services with the needs of the population, or better connecting local civil communities and governing bodies (Murray et al, 2010).
- Innovation and entrepreneurship, for instance developing forms of corporate social responsibility, changing human resource management, citizen engagement or developing forms of social entrepreneurship (see, for example, Adams and Hess, 2010; Weerawardena and Mort, 2012).

Social innovation as a term is used on different scales, varying from a local community or agency to a national government or a large company. More recently, social innovation is increasingly connected to challenges caused by climate change, sustainability and energy transition (Popescu et al, 2022). Several authors argue that social innovation regarding these huge challenges implies profoundly changing basic routines and beliefs (Howaldt and Schwartz, 2010). Pursuing innovations that enable profound change with respect to major global problems is important given the magnitude of the challenges and their direct relation to present social structures and behaviours (Bonnedahl, Heikkurinen and Paavola, 2022).

The adoption of social innovation in all the areas mentioned has fuelled a rapidly expanding literature, characterised by a diversity of definitions (Adams and Hess, 2010; Hochgerner, 2011; van der Have and Rubalcaba, 2016; do Adro and Fernandes, 2020; Husebø et al, 2021; Galego et al, 2022). A popular definition comes from Murray et al (2010), also adopted by the European Commission, who define social innovation as 'new ideas (products, services and models) that simultaneously meet social needs and create new social relationships or collaborations. In other words, they are innovations that are both good for society and enhance society's capacity to act' (European Commission, 2013: 3). As this definition implies, the concept of social innovation is often understood as processes that spring from real-life problem-solving, but simultaneously address a basic level of capacity-building in groups, organisations or society. In addition, social innovation is deemed relevant when addressing challenges concerning societal changes (macro level), the quality of services and other resources (meso level), and needs connected to people's well-being (micro level) (Mulgan, 2015; Nicholls et al, 2015). Such innovations ideally also generate newer, better structures and competencies for innovation beyond the demands of the actual situation (Caulier-Grice et al, 2012). Social innovation is thus associated with social change for 'the common good', indicating that it is meant to create social value and must be experienced as useful in a given field (Mulgan, 2015).

Despite the heterogeneity of the fields in which social innovation occurs and/or is promoted, shared 'core elements' do exist (van der Have and Rubalcaba, 2016). In all areas, there is the idea that social innovation comprises change in social relationships, systems or structures, although this may be approached from different levels of analysis or theoretical backgrounds. Furthermore, a shared notion also appears to be that such changes must serve human needs or should solve a social problem. It should however be noted that behind different notions and applications of social innovation, there are different discourses at play. An interesting analysis by Ilie and During (2012) identified different characteristics of these discourses. The *governmental discourse*, as adopted by the European Commission and governmental bodies, for example, is mainly concerned with making policies more efficient and more engaging for the community. It can be regarded as top-down innovation. In this discourse, it is not clear to what degree the community is involved, though it is increasingly inferred, for example through the EU Missions (European Commission, nd). In the *entrepreneurial discourse* the community becomes a more visible and active actor. It seeks for new practical solutions for pressing social demands, (re)designing enterprises and services. At the heart of this type of innovation is a 'social entrepreneur' – someone who is driving the change. A third discourse distinguished by Ilie and During (2012) is the *academic discourse*, in which social innovation is approached from a theoretical or research perspective. The academic discourse is predominantly following the governmental and entrepreneurial discourse, not only trying to define social innovation, but also attempting to discover effective factors and to measure outcomes. In this discourse, we see a large diversity in definition, causing conceptual ambiguity.

Van der Have and Rubalcaba conclude that:

> the lack of a commonly accepted comprehensive definition simultaneously reflects fragmentation of the research field and the fact that social innovation is a *complex, multi-faceted phenomenon* (emphasis by Wilken/Parpan-Blaser) that spans a wide range of activities from grassroots social innovations that respond to pressing social demands which are not commercially viable due to market failure, to novel

products and services produced by private, third sector, or public sector organisations (or a combination thereof), to new combinations of social practices, attitudes and values and to systemic innovations involving fundamental changes in strategies and policies, organisational structures and institutional frameworks. (van der Have and Rubalcaba, 2016: 1925)

Brandsen et al (2016: 5) state that social innovation can better be regarded as a *complex societal process* rather than a mere classificatory definition of an action or product. They also highlight that there is an affective component related to social innovation, since it breathes hope, expectations and progress towards something 'better' for people. With a critical lens, we could also comment that the word 'social', which is at the heart of the social work profession, is quite often used (or even abused) for economic or political purposes. Furthermore, it is remarkable that in the literature about social innovation, social work is mostly absent. This underlines the need of having a firm stand on the role and nature of social work research and practice.

Innovation and social work

Historically, innovation has a long and strong tradition in social work. One might even say that innovation is in the genes of the discipline and that social work was itself a social innovation at the time of its professionalisation. One of the historical roots of social work is its engagement with emancipatory movements, community actions and other grassroot initiatives. This has resulted in related working methods, such as anti-oppressive and strengths-based practices. Unfortunately, since the late 20th century, this activistic stream in social work has received less attention (see, for example, the debate around the social worker as 'professional' or 'street-level' bureaucrat, Trappenburg et al, 2020), although this is part of the international definition of social work that also frames innovative action in social work. It says that social work promotes social change and development, social cohesion, and the empowerment and liberation of people. It also mentions that principles of social justice, human rights, collective responsibility and respect for diversities are central to social work (IFSW and IASSW, 2014). Although the notions in this definition can be contested (they are not well defined and thereby subject to discussion; see, for example, Borrmann, 2020), they reflect values that can guide the contribution of social work and social work research to social innovation.

It becomes obvious that the orientation of social work towards its constitutive object of social problems repeatedly entails the question of how changing problems of action in the intermediate field between individual and society are to be dealt with. This goes along with the question of how knowledge of different provenance can be used for practice (Gredig et al, 2023). Moreover, as Evers et al (2014, p. 24) put it, the history of welfare can be seen as history of social innovations rejected or mainstreamed. The fact that social problems mostly have an individual as well as a structural dimension implies that innovations in social work (in the sense of novel methods, programmes and offers) not only aim at a better, more effective and precise addressing of a social problem, but at best also influence the causes of the social problem. Parpan-Blaser defines innovation in social work as new programmes, strategies, measures, procedures or concepts that (1) are based on new or newly combined knowledge, (2) aim to address social problems, respond to normative needs, (3) provide added value, notably for service users and (4) (at best) bring about changes in the social system that has induced the problem (Parpan-Blaser, 2011; Parpan-Blaser, 2020: 136–7; see also Parpan-Blaser and Hüttemann, 2019).

The social work lens puts basic human needs and human agency in the foreground. This revolves around autonomy, well-being and health, and all the conditions that are needed to ensure a good quality of life. This lens implies that social work connects the daily life of people, their social networks and communities, with the existing structures and systems in society. Social work research analyses social and societal problems and provides knowledge for solutions on micro, meso and macro levels, addressing the factors that hinder or facilitate positive change.

In the innovative approaches that social work develops, both the process and the outcome dimension in the definition of Murray et al (2010) and the European Commission (2013) can be identified. Innovation processes are about bringing together knowledge from different perspectives to look for novel ways to address identified and unsatisfactorily resolved problem situations. The outcome of such processes can then be an innovation, depending on how different it is from the previous approach. One could therefore say that the will to improve and the learning in innovation processes is more relevant than whether the result is in fact a novel solution.

Innovation in the social work discourse puts people and communities in central actor positions. Innovations are social by nature and co-production, ensuring ownership, is aimed at, to make sure that the innovation is directly addressing basic (social, economic, psychological and physical) needs. So, in order to speak meaningfully about the innovation mission of social work, we should be clear about the *social values* that are at stake. Social values have to do with normative stands, with ideas about quality of life, and with conditions that are needed for desired quality of life, as expressed for example in the capability approach (see Chapter 4 in this book).

Social quality

A framework within which several of the concepts mentioned come together is that of *social quality*.

Beck et al (1997: 3) define social quality as 'the extent to which people are able to participate in social, economic and cultural life and the development of their communities under conditions that enhance their well-being and individual potential, which enables them, in turn, to influence the conditions of their own existence'. The concept of social quality brings together the different components of human well-being on one side and the quality of social contexts as well as societal structures on the other side. In the concept of social quality four key empirical dimensions are discerned: socio-economic security, social cohesion, social inclusion and social empowerment (van der Maesen and Walker, 2012). We might translate this into four core objectives of social work as an innovative professional and academic discipline:

1. Improving socio-economic conditions – the command of adequate resources over time in the domains of financial resources, housing and the environment, health and care, work and education.
2. Contributing to social cohesion – the extent to which social relations, values and norms are shared in the domains of trust, integrative norms and values, social networks and identity.
3. Contributing to social inclusion – the ability to participate in the social, cultural and economic activities of a society in the domains of citizenship rights, labour market, public and private services, and social networks.
4. Supporting empowerment – the ability to participate in different contexts and to develop collective agency.

The social quality framework can be useful for identifying innovation needs, for monitoring the social innovation process and for identifying added value. It may help us in reflecting on and criticising existing conditions, as well as our own practices. This can be done on different levels, the micro level of services targeted at individuals and their networks, the meso level of communities and organisations, and the macro level of governments and support systems.

Typical elements of social work innovation

In summary, there are some important elements that characterise social work innovation. Many of these elements are elaborated in other chapters in this book.

Grassroots innovation

A strong asset of social work is that it works basically at a grassroots level. Innovation does not take place at the level of the individual case, because it is about methods, programmes and offers that improve and maintain networks of relationships between people or increase and strengthen social capital. But the grassroots level is where gaps in care and opportunities for improvement become most directly visible – for social workers as well as for service users.

Co-creation

Grassroots innovation requires methods of community-based work, in which the assets of a community are articulated and used as resources. Asset-based community development is an innovative approach in this regard (Russell and McKnight, 2022). Against this background, co-creation points to the fact that innovation processes are opened up and facilitated. Another aspect is developing and engaging in processes, in which citizens, social workers and other stakeholders are involved (Moulaert et al, 2013). In these processes, social work research methods like participatory action research and social design are useful (Burns et al, 2021; Tromp and Vial, 2023).

A learning process, including experiential knowledge

Since social work operates in an ever-changing, dynamic and complex reality (van Ewijk, 2018), a continuous innovation and learning process is crucial. In this process different sources of knowledge can be integrated, such as the experiential knowledge of participants, data from research and the body of knowledge of social work. Learning from the experiences of all participants are part of the innovation process (Gredig et al, 2023). Methods of experiential and cross-boundary learning are key here. Social workers can be moderators of these learning and development processes.

Connecting different forms of capital

Traditionally, social work has put social capital at the centre of attention. We believe that the value of social work can be extended if we connect social capital to other forms of capital. We can make the 'social' in all kinds of innovations tangible, finding new or better ways to put the human factor centre stage in innovations in other domains like the economy, ecology, technology, digitalisation and governance. Specifically, this requires stepping out of the silo of social work as a form of service provision, and to connect to urgent societal challenges, as expressed in the United Nations' Sustainable Development Goals. Social work is about connecting people, communities and resources, undertaking activities of 'bonding', 'bridging' and 'linking' as mentioned in theories on social capital (Bourdieu and Coleman, 1991; Putnam, 2002). Concrete examples can be found in the domains of community development, social enterprises and nature preservation.

Aligning perspectives

A big step forward in social innovation is made when different levels (micro, meso, macro) and perspectives are aligned in a bottom-up movement: the perspective of the citizen or service user, the perspective of the professional, the perspective of the service organisation, and the perspective of policy and governance (Wilken et al, 2021). The task is to align these levels and perspectives so that structures and systems, as well as structural and systemic innovations facilitate the well-being of (all) people. It starts with a perception of the 'good life' of individuals and communities, and a translation of wishes and needs about quality of life, to the support professionals may give, the way services and resources are organised, and how this is all facilitated by governmental, economic and environmental systems. Social workers in the field, social service organisations and social work researchers can make efforts to connect these different perspectives to work on alignment. Thus the implementation context of an innovation must be included in the considerations; public relations and lobbying work must be carried out, and negotiating skills and strategies for increasing civil society pressure must be developed.

Research and innovation

It is obvious that social work research is connected to the developments described earlier: social work research could be framed as 'action science', closely connected with social work practices, and meant to inform practice and policy (Joubert and Webber, 2020). Hence, in our opinion, research should fuel all kinds of social innovation and one important task for social work researchers is to demonstrate the implications of findings from micro- and meso-level studies – particularly at the policy and systems level. This may require an alliance with people who experience these problems, with social movements and social workers. That is to say, an important role of social work research, besides description and explanation, is to reveal societal wrongs and to contribute to developing solutions, really working on social innovation.

In the literature, there are many examples of social work research providing input for innovation, being part of innovation processes or showing the outcomes of innovation projects – even if this is not always made explicit. Sometimes it is referred to in the more general term of impact of research. This can range from new ways of understanding a phenomenon and arguments for investing in projects to changes in the legal framework and thematic training for practitioners.

Being part of processes of social innovation implies that the research methods should be flexible and accommodating, at the same time using standards of scientific rigour that are consistent with our epistemologies. We already mentioned participatory action research and social design research methodology being suitable for work on social innovation. These types of methodology can be tailored to a wide variety of challenges and contexts. If we are employing participatory practice research we must deal with these challenges, with the complexity and the tensions both between people and between people, systems and political, economic and environmental realities. Working on social innovation, this is inevitable. By default, this requires sound ethical standards (Banks, 2006) and appropriate strategies for both the research process as well as dissemination of results. We should be aware of dominant neoliberal discourses and the fact that social innovation is often used as a frame for improving corporate images or to revitalise bureaucracy. Social innovation can appear as a manifestation of the neoliberal order, for example when authorities are looking for improving bureaucratic procedures or aim for budget cuts in times of austerity. Researchers can be invited to make service systems more 'lean and mean'. As Ian Shaw puts it, we should consider social work research as a 'social and moral practice' (Shaw, 2018: 7). In line with the international definition, we must stick to a critical and emancipatory stand. A consequence might be that our work is disruptive in the light of current practices and policies. Stakeholders like politicians, governments or enterprises might not be pleased with the results of social work research. Still, it is important to stand by our principles and the validity of our research outcomes, and to strive for real *social* innovation.

The COVID-19 pandemic has given a boost to the use of digital technologies in social work innovations. For example, they allow social workers to reach out and stay in touch with service users and other professionals in an alternative way. This is also an example how external factors may drive innovation (Castillo de Mesa, 2021) and shows that research is needed to develop and evaluate ICT applications and new forms of e-social work (compare López Peláez et al, 2018). This could be done in co-creation with service users, neighbourhood organisations and co-designers. As in all innovations, it calls for ethical consideration, for example about exclusion and inclusion of people who do not have internet access or are lacking reading or digital abilities (Wild, 2020).

Conclusion

In this chapter we explored the relation between social work and social innovation. We distinguish between innovations in social work as a practice field, and innovations that involve actors beyond the field and the discipline, with a broad societal impact. The notion of social innovation can thus be valuable if it is well defined and contextualised. Contributions to social innovation are based on the realisation of social values and fulfilling human needs, as expressed in the international definition of social work, human rights and Sustainable Development Goals. We consider social quality to be a useful overarching concept in relation to the value orientation of social – and social work – innovations. It not only refers to central values when it comes to the conception of new programmes and services, but also clarifies the claim of social work to have a proactive influence on the framework conditions and to tackle social problems in a causal way. It can be used for clarifying objectives, and as an indicator for monitoring and for outcome evaluation.

For working on social quality, social work constantly faces challenges. Social work professionals and researchers play a vital role in identifying causes and solutions for these challenges and in initiating change and innovation. In order to effectively address societal challenges around injustice, inequality, poverty and lack of opportunities and resources, social work needs to join forces from academia and practice at the micro, meso and macro levels.

Besides the orientation towards values and knowledge, the social work perspective on social innovation implies that social work practitioners should possess the competencies to engage in transdisciplinary processes of social innovation, and that social work curricula include knowledge and skills about innovation methods, for example co-design and change theories. It requires mastering a comprehensive approach to connect different areas that are important for quality of life, like health, housing, social cohesion, security, employment, human rights and nature. Social innovation competencies should be part of social work bachelor and master programmes. In the innovation of social work itself, we see in different places around the world more and more blends of practice, research and education. The latter is one of the possible links to strengthen the transformative potential of social work. After all, collaboration and networking belong to the core competences of our discipline. Using these for innovation and change is more necessary than ever.

References

Adams, D. and Hess, M. (2010) Social innovation and why it has policy significance, *Economic and Labour Relations Review*, 21(2): 139–55.

Aksoy, L., Alkire, L., Choi, S., Kim, P.B. and Zhang, L. (2019) Social innovation in service: a conceptual framework and research agenda, *Journal of Service Management*, 30(3): 429–48.

Banks, S. (2006) *Ethics and Values in Social Work*, 3rd edn, Basingstoke: Palgrave Macmillan.

Beck, W., van der Maesen, L. and Walker, A. (eds) (1997) *The Social Quality of Europe*, The Hague: Kluwer.

Bonnedahl, K.J., Heikkurinen, P. and Paavola, J. (2022) Strongly sustainable development goals: overcoming distances constraining responsible action, *Environmental Science & Policy*, 129: 150–8.

Borrmann, S. (2020) The holistic focus of social work: the interdependence of global, national, and local perspectives in the global definition of social work, *Social Development Issues*, 42(1): 44–54.

Bourdieu, P. and Coleman, J. (eds) (1991) *Social Change for a Changing Society*, Boulder, CO: Westview Press.

Brandsen, T., Cattacin, S., Evers, A. and Zimmer, A. (eds) (2016) *Social Innovations in the Urban Context*, Cham: Springer Open.

Burns, D., Howard, J. and Ospina, S.M. (2021) *The SAGE Handbook of Participatory Research and Inquiry*, London: Sage.

Castillo de Mesa, J. (2021) Digital social work: towards digital disruption in social work, *Journal of Sociology and Social Welfare*, 48(3): 117–33.

Caulier-Grice, J., Davies, A., Patrick, R. and Norman, W. (2012) *Defining Social Innovation. A Deliverable of the Project: The Theoretical, Empirical and Policy Foundations for Building Social Innovation in Europe (TEPSIE)*, Brussels: European Commission, DG Research.

do Adro, F. and Fernandes, C.I. (2020) Social innovation: a systematic literature review and future agenda research, *International Review on Public and Nonprofit Marketing*, 17: 23–40.

European Commission (2013) Guide to Social Innovation, February, Brussels: European Commission, https://ec.europa.eu/regional_policy/en/information/publications/guides/2013/guide-to-social-innovation.

European Commission (nd) EU Missions and citizen engagement activities, European Commission: Research and Innovation, https://research-and-innovation.ec.europa.eu/funding/funding-opportunities/funding-programmes-and-open-calls/horizon-europe/eu-missions-horizon-europe/eu-missions-citizen-engagement-activities_en.

Evers, A., Ewert, B. and Brandsen, T. (eds) (2014) *Social Innovations for Social Cohesion. Transnational Patterns and Approaches from 20 European Cities*, Liege: EMES European Research Network Asbl.

Galego, D., Moulaert, F., Brans, M. and Santinha, G. (2022) Social innovation and governance: a scoping review, *European Journal of Social Science Research*, 35(2): 265–90.

Gredig, D., Schubert, L. and Parpan-Blaser, A. (2023) Pragmatism: a theoretical framework for social innovation, in P. Maeder, M. Chimienti, V. Cretton, C. Maggiori, I. Probst and S. Rullac (eds) *Innovation et intervention sociales: impacts, méthodes et mises en œuvre dans les domaines de la santé et de l'action sociale*, Zurich: Seismo, pp 29–42.

Hochgerner, J. (2011) The analysis of social innovations as social practice, *Bridges: Transatlantic Science and Technology Quarterly*, 30: 1–5.

Husebø, A.M.L., Storm, M., Ødegård, A., Wegener, Ch., Aakjær, M., Pedersen, A.L., et al (2021) Exploring social innovation (SI) within the research contexts of higher education, healthcare, and welfare services. A scoping review, *Nordic Journal of Social Research*, 72–110.

Howaldt, J. and Schwarz, M. (2010) *Social Innovation: Concepts, Research Fields and International Trends*, Aachen: IMA/ZLW.

IFSW and IASSW (International Federation of Social Workers and International Association of Schools of Social Work) (2014) International definition of social work, International Federation of Social Workers, July, https://www.ifsw.org/what-is-social-work/global-definition-of-social-work/.

Ilie, E.G. and During, R. (2012) *An Analysis of Social Innovation Discourses in Europe*, Wageningen University & Research.

Joubert, L. and Webber, M. (eds) (2020) *The Routledge Handbook of Social Work Practice Research*, Abingdon: Routledge.

López Peláez, A., Pérez García, R. and Aguilar-Tablada Massó, V. (2018) e-Social work: building a new field of specialization in social work? *European Journal of Social Work*, 21(6): 804–23.

Moulaert, F., MacCallum, D., Mehmood, A. and Hamdouch, A. (2013) *The International Handbook on Social Innovation: Collective Action, Social Learning and Transdisciplinary Research*, Cheltenham: Edward Elgar.

Mulgan, G. (2015) Foreword: the study of social innovation – theory, practice and progress, in A. Nicholls, J. Simon and M. Gabriel (eds) *New Frontiers in Social Innovation Research*, Basingstoke: Palgrave Macmillan, pp x–xx.

Murray, R., Caulier-Grice, J. and Mulgan, G. (2010) *The Open Book of Social Innovation*, London: Young Foundation and National Endowment for Science, Technology and the Arts.

Nicholls, A., Simon, J. and Gabriel, M. (eds) (2015) *New Frontiers in Social Innovation Research*, Basingstoke: Palgrave Macmillan.

Parpan-Blaser, A. (2011) *Innovation in der Sozialen Arbeit: Zur theoretischen und empirischen Grundlegung eines Konzeptes*, Wiesbaden: VS.

Parpan-Blaser, A. (2020) Soziale Innovationen im Gefüge sozialer Versorgung, in P. Brandl and T. Prinz (eds) *Innovationen bei sozialen Dienstleistungen, Band 2: Praktische Ansätze für eine innovative Zukunft*, Regensburg: Walhalla, pp 135–65.

Parpan-Blaser, A. and Hüttemann, M. (2019) Social innovation in social work, in J. Howaldt, C. Kaletka, A. Schröder and M. Zirngiebl (eds) *Atlas of Social Innovation: A World of New Practices*, Vol 2, Munich: Oekom, pp 80–3.

Păunescu, C. (2014) Current trends in social innovation research: social capital, corporate social responsibility, impact measurement, *Management & Marketing: Challenges for the Knowledge Society*, 9(2): 105–18.

Popescu, C., Hysa, E., Kruja, A. and Mansi, E. (2022) Social innovation, circularity and energy transition for Environmental, Social and Governance (ESG) practices – a comprehensive review. *Energies*, Vol. 15.

Putnam, R.D. (ed) (2002) *Democracies in Flux: The Evolution of Social Capital in Contemporary Society*, Oxford: Oxford University Press.

Russell, C. and McKnight, J. (2022) *The Connected Community: Discovering the Health, Wealth, and Power of Neighbourhoods*, Oakland, CA: Berrett-Koehler.

Shaw, I. (2018) *Research and the Social Work Picture*, Bristol: Policy Press.

Trappenburg, M., Kampen, T. and Tonkens, E. (2020) Social workers in a modernising welfare state: professionals or street-level bureaucrats?, *British Journal of Social Work*, 50(6): 1669–87.

Tromp, N. and Vial, S. (2023) Five components of social design: a unified framework to support research and practice, *Design Journal*, 26(2): 210–28.

van der Have, R.P. and Rubalcaba, L. (2016) Social innovation research: an emerging area of innovation studies?, *Research Policy*, 45(9): 1923–35.

van der Maesen, L.J.G. and Walker, A. (eds) (2012) *Social Quality: From Theory to Indicators*, Basingstoke: Palgrave Macmillan.

van Ewijk, H. (2018) *Complexity and Social Work*, Abingdon: Routledge.

Weerawardena, J. and Mort, G.S. (2012) Competitive strategy in socially entrepreneurial nonprofit organizations: innovation and differentiation, *Journal of Public Policy & Marketing*, 31(1): 91–101.

Wild, J. (2020) Digital technology and coronavirus: embedding learning for the future, 19 May, Research in Practice, https://web.archive.org/web/20200604161017/https://www.researchinpractice.org.uk/all/news-views/2020/may/digital-technology-and-coronavirus-embedding-learning-for-the-future/.

Wilken, J.P. (2023) It is all about social quality: how social work researchers can contribute to social innovation, *European Social Work Research*, 1(3): 261–74.

Wilken, J.P., Overkamp, E., Binkhorst, J. and Sprinkhuizen, A. (2021) Integraal werken en sociaal werk: vier perspectieven op een weerbarstige werkelijkheid, in J. Metz, M. Jager-Vreugdenhil, J.P. Wilken and T. Witte (eds) *Sociaal Werk Doordacht*, Amsterdam: SWP, pp 53–66.

2

How to change our neighbourhoods, regions and the world: using symptoms, systems and transformation as a framework for social innovation and social work

Sarah Prosser and Ole Pedersen

Introduction

This chapter takes its starting point in the recognition of multiple global crises that are being felt at all scales of society. There is an urgent and profound need to examine the root causes behind the complex and systemic failures that have brought these about, and to find innovative ways forward that benefit humanity and ecology for the long term.

The challenges we are facing include climate change, biodiversity loss, including the alarming rate of extinction of species (IPCC, 2022), the inequality gap with half the global population controlling only 2 per cent of global wealth and the top 1 per cent controlling 38 per cent (Chancel et al, 2021), the increasing militarisation reinforced by the war in Ukraine, and the Doomsday clock set by the Bulletin of the Atomic Scientists now hovering closer to global catastrophe than ever.[1]

Cascading down from these global trends, we find that national, regional and local communities have become entangled in complex contexts, systems and structures unfit for purpose and unsuited for times of rapid change, and multiple crises across all levels and scales. In addition to the direct implications of widespread crises, there seems to be a decrease in trust at all levels, and a weakening of a traditional sense of community, solidarity and a sense of belonging.

We need better ways of innovating for better futures – futures that rely on tangible and intangible solutions to deeply rooted problems. This chapter considers different approaches to social innovation suited to framing and then inducing positive change, and how these relate to social and community work in practice and as a field (Bagnall et al, 2023). Three case studies at different geographic scales are presented, before reflections and conclusions are made concerning how to embrace new ways of working that put research and practices from social work and community development at the very core of innovating for the futures we aspire to.

Frameworks for social innovation and social work

This book focuses on social innovation in social work, and by default also therefore on social work in social innovation. This chapter refers to, and builds from, the core understanding of these terms as defined:

- Social work – the international definition of social work (IFSW and IASSW, 2014) that encompasses a range of processes and outcomes aimed at enhancing well-being. The definition includes dimensions of change, empowerment, cohesion, collectiveness, Indigenous knowledge, and a variation of scale, from individual to regional and national.
- Social innovation – Mulgan's (2007) simple definition of social innovation as new ideas that address unmet social needs – and that work are expanded upon by others defining it as social in both process (Mumford, 2002; Westley and Antadze, 2010) and in outputs and outcome (Noya, 2011).

Various research efforts have identified and categorised different types and styles of social innovation. A common example of this is consideration of the scale of intervention and outcome, as used by Nicholls and colleagues (2015), through distinguishing micro (individual), meso (organisation) and macro (network/movement/system) levels. We note the global scale of social innovation is not usually included in the 'macro' level and that the 'size' of the innovation may be given too much weight in innovation frameworks. Other research involving categorisation of social innovation identifies a dominant actor (governmental, academic or entrepreneur, see Chapter 1) or if it is incremental or disruptive in style (Christensen et al, 2018). Again, we contend that while these categories exist and can be mapped, there is a need for a framework that allows for the complexity and deep rootedness of current and future social challenges.

In this chapter we focus on the approach used by proponents of the rapidly emerging research and practice field of systems innovation (see for example Meadows, 2015; Wilf, 2018; Birney, 2021 and free online resources such as Ashoka, 2022). In this type of framework, we consider the depth of the innovation such that visible *symptoms* of societal problems are differentiated from underlying *systems* or entrenched *mindsets*. These levels, represented in the iceberg metaphor of Figure 2.1, have different characteristics and need different innovation pathways to address them.

To understand how these different depths of innovation can be approached in social work (and other fields) we feel there is a need to clarify four more

Figure 2.1: The iceberg metaphor of symptoms, systems and mindset

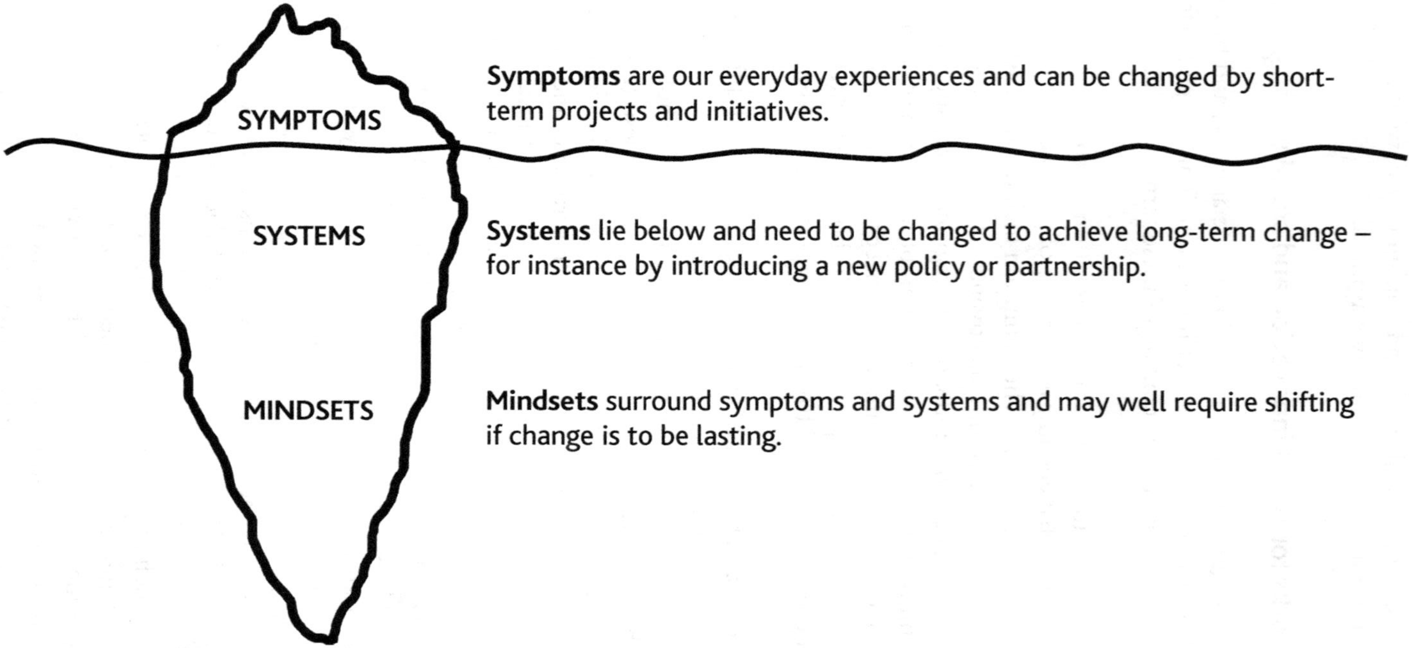

Symptoms are our everyday experiences and can be changed by short-term projects and initiatives.

Systems lie below and need to be changed to achieve long-term change – for instance by introducing a new policy or partnership.

Mindsets surround symptoms and systems and may well require shifting if change is to be lasting.

SYMPTOMS

SYSTEMS

MINDSETS

Source: Adapted from Ashoka (2022).

terms to contribute to a glossary that empowers us as practitioners and researchers to work in importantly nuanced ways – that increase our social innovation literacy and absorptive capacity of new understandings for the common good.

- *Community work*[2] *within social work* implies a bigger focus on the role of the people and place around individuals, and the importance of collective engagement. It also brings us closer to relationships, the emerging field of relational welfare (Cottam, 2011) and what happens in the spaces in between individual interventions and beyond individualistic human-centred design processes (Steen, 2011).
- *Collective impact and collaborative innovation* are the response to a social sector that is all too often stuck in isolated interventions by siloed departments. Kania and Kramer (2011) and Kania et al (2021) have become the reference research articles summarising the essential elements required for successful collective impact innovations: having a common agenda, shared measurement systems, mutually reinforcing activities, continuous communication and a backbone support organisation. See Sørensen and Torfing's research (for example, Sørensen and Torfing, 2011) for further insight on how collaborative innovation in the public sector can work for positive change.
- *Systems change*. Many social and other innovations are developed to address visible, tangible issues experienced by individuals in their daily life. This type of innovation tries to solve the visible consequences of underlying causes. Such innovation processes are often linear in nature, taking a problem and finding a solution. A systems change approach, in contrast, looks for the root causes behind the visible problems, and identifies the various systems and mindsets holding these in place, before designing innovation programmes to change these (Milligan, Zerda, and Kania, 2022). The Problem Tree (Figure 2.2) is a useful tool to understand what your innovation is targeting.
- *Transformative innovation* intentionally supports new patterns of activity suited to a changed environment where the old systems are no long working. Although anyone can disrupt a system, an alternative is needed to disrupt it with purpose. We refer here to the so-called 'third horizon', as explained in the three horizons model of building new futures we aspire by Sharpe et al (2016; see Figure 2.3). It is a tool useful for framing transformative social innovation processes.

With these innovation terms embedded in our toolbox for social innovation, we can move on to examine three cases, each taken from a different geographic scale of social change and innovation. They have the common characteristic of depending on practices associated with social and community

Figure 2.2: The Problem Tree – a tool for developing a system innovation strategy

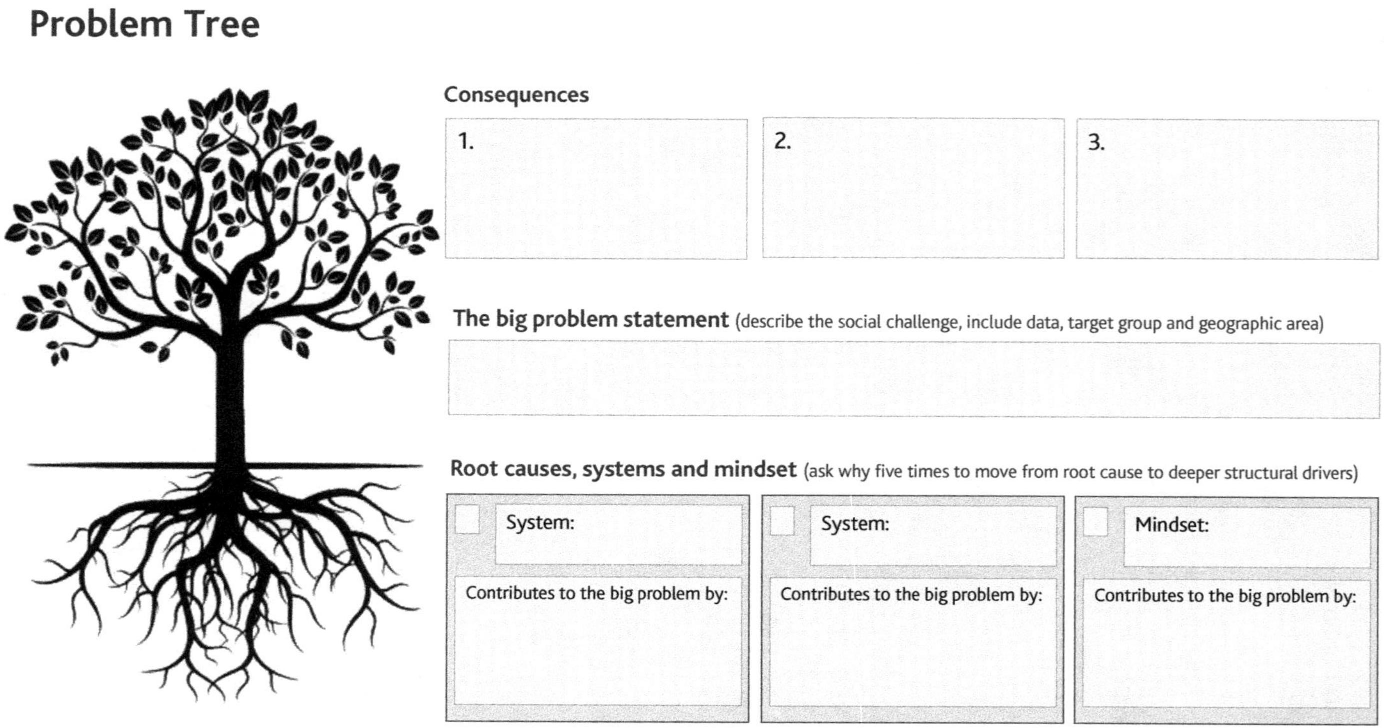

Problem Tree

Consequences

1.
2.
3.

The big problem statement (describe the social challenge, include data, target group and geographic area)

Root causes, systems and mindset (ask why five times to move from root cause to deeper structural drivers)

System:
Contributes to the big problem by:

System:
Contributes to the big problem by:

Mindset:
Contributes to the big problem by:

Note: For more details on implementation see Ashoka (2022).

Figure 2.3: Three Horizon thinking

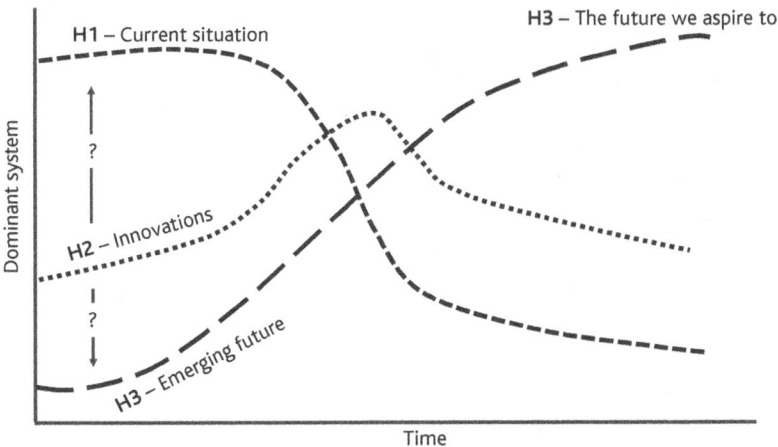

Note: For whole scale transformation we can work to lift new promising systems (H3) into the future by capturing social innovations from H2 into services and ways of being that build the future we aspire to rather than hoping they will change the broken systems of the present (H1) (Sharpe et al 2016; Raworth, 2017).

Source: www.iffpraxis.com

work, while also benefiting from consideration of the different depths of social innovation already outlined. After the case descriptions, we reflect and analyse the insights and learnings from these cases, and finally make some conclusions and recommendations for replication and mainstreaming of these ways of working in social work and social innovation practice and research.

Cases: neighbourhood, regional and global

The neighbourhood as the unit of social change

This title of this section is taken from an article by David Brooks (2018). It relates to the fact an individual may undergo positive change through traditional social work approaches but can be overwhelmed by forces in the local community to do with a sense of belonging, identity and equitable access to opportunities. The importance of this scale of change is in tune with evidence from our own research from Norwegian neighbourhoods and from the Netherlands presented by Dortmans et al in Chapter 9.

The role of social innovation community incubators can be equated to one of supporting local residents to address visible symptoms of social problems through starting social enterprises, often based on their lived experience. In the case of Norway Unlimited (NU; described in detail in Chapter 20) such incubators have been intentionally designed to also focus on catalysing social cohesion, inclusion and well-being among participating citizens and their wider neighbourhoods. This two-pronged focus can be rephrased as combining social innovation and social work to add social value at the 'symptoms level'.

NU is a national network organisation representing the collective of individual Unlimited neighbourhood incubators. NU works to change the mindsets and systemic levels of change that are needed to enable social enterprises and their local support infrastructure to become mainstreamed as part of the Norwegian landscape. This work is the level of systems and transformational innovation, and is only effective when authentically linked to working in close contact with groups addressing symptoms, that is, the individual incubators. NU activities include engaging in public debate, lobbying for changes in legal frameworks, measuring collective impact, and testing new forms of collaborative innovation between the public sector and neighbourhood incubators.

The implication of equipping a neighbourhood with a space where social work practices are combined with social enterprise support means employees in such incubators could equally come from a social work and community development background as a business innovation one. The range of skills identified from empirical observations of employees and participants in the Unlimited incubators are summarised in Prosser (2022). They are divided into two spheres: the 'human aspect' (mainly social work practices) and 'social enterprise' (social innovation tools). The 'human aspect' practices are well known in fields such as asset-based community development and relational welfare (Cottam, 2011). When these are intentionally supplemented with skills empowering participants to deliver value back to their local communities through establishing their own social enterprises, one enters the field of community development. The resulting combination for incubator participants of both feeling valued and giving value is the definition of 'mattering' (Prilleltensky, 2019) – an example of a useful concept for social work literacy within the social innovation discourse.

The bioregion as the unit of social change

A pan-European initiative established in 2022 takes the bioregion, or landscape, as the scale to design social and ecological change around. This builds on the broad empirical base of evidence accumulated in the 'backbone' organisations, Commonland and Ashoka (international NGOs working for landscape restoration and changemaking respectively). A new Bioregional Weaving Lab (BWL) initiative is now under way in eight European countries (Ashoka, 2023), and looks to local, large-scale landscapes and the communities within them as a useful scale to work for universal (social and ecological) well-being.

The scale of each bioregion corresponds to a wide landscape (typically 100,000 hectares) defined by nature (river catchments, soils and ecology) and includes the cultural heritage, towns and rural settlements within it. The working premise is that it is the relationships between the local people, their projects and their place that is core to how long-term social change can occur.

At the heart of the BWL methodology is the role of a 'weaver' employed in each of the eight bioregions. Weavers are persons mandated with the task of connecting people, place and projects in ways that can lead to systemic and transformational change. The weaver positions are hosted by local eco-social enterprises and are funded in this start-up phase by major international NGOs (Commonland, Ashoka and the Presencing Institute), though a transition to more local funding will be important to ensure local co-ownership and engagement. Prosser is currently engaged as a 'weaver' of systemic change in the BWL located in the Waterford region of south-east Ireland.

The weaver works to build trust and a sense of togetherness with local stakeholders (farmers, teachers, social entrepreneurs, municipalities, politicians and so on), through personal meetings in the landscape, and subsequently at multi-stakeholder workshops. Events and gatherings are carefully designed to build a sense of collective motivation for systemic and transformational change, in addition to the already established work on more symptomatic projects.

The weaver uses a combination of system innovation tools and relational-related methods akin to community and social work practices. Through this they uncover local passion and budding innovations that represent the futures we aspire to and create space for new collective partnerships and agency. The emerging collaborative partnerships are then able to work on system change strategies and impact scaling pathways.

Each BWL looks for local-appropriate indicators of change that show value is being created in the bioregion on four dimensions: social, natural, financial and, importantly, inspirational. One qualitative example comes from the BWL in Waterford (see box).

Return of inspiration through co-visioning

The weaver at BWL in Ireland, Prosser, has established a group of 50–60 stakeholders in the Waterford bioregion; twice that number follow progress but participate less. In the first months (April–August 2022) there was general enthusiasm for the European-scale vision (to restore 1 million hectares of land in Europe and mobilise 1 million changemakers), but there was no real co-ownership by the local communities. To address this, a workshop was held to co-write a manifesto, inspired, via the European learning platform, by the Spanish bioregion.

Some 35 diverse stakeholders from the bioregion in Ireland were led through a workshop that started in personal manifestos and moved to a group declaration of what they collectively 'know, believe and want'. The final document was worked into a 'Food Manifesto for the Waterford Bioregion'. It is almost a spoken poem in style, emotionally moving when listened to (BWL Waterford, 2022), and a powerful way of taking the collective voice of the people to direct strategy going forward.

The inspiration for the participants was tangible and feedback was universally positive – a sense of excitement, hope, belonging and collective agency was expressed. Government officials remarked that the BWL approach may be what is needed to address the mental health challenges in agricultural Ireland: Recent research (Russell et al, 2022) has shown that over 50 per cent of farmers are experiencing moderate to extremely severe forms of depression, and 23 per cent are considered at risk of suicide. No governmental directive to become organically certified, for example, will work until the farmers have a return of inspiration. Working collectively on a systemic and transformational innovation initiative can be key in returning a sense of inspiration to make change.

The case of the bioregional labs touches on social innovation in social work, and vice versa, in a number of ways. First, major funding organisations are exploring how they can make long-term impact that increases well-being at systemic and transformational scales. This is most clearly seen by a move away from transactional donations to a more trusting funding model. Second, 'weavers' as a role in creating new and stronger relationships between previously unconnected people and projects, while using a systems lens, can lead to innovation that would not have occurred without this intentional intervention on the spaces in between the people and projects in a region. Third, skills from social and community work practice, and insights from related research, are of direct relevance to the weaver and the whole BWL initiative. Weaving as a practice and profession could be an exciting area for decision makers to prioritise and introduce into different siloed departments and organisations; social and community workers would be ideal to employ in such roles.

The global community as the unit of social change

A case example of a global system innovation is the open space of the World Social Forum (WSF). The WSF, with the slogan 'Another world is possible', is a self-governing concept, having abstained from establishing any formal structures beyond a charter of principles (World Social Forum, 2001) and the International Council, where members from different countries (Pedersen is a current member) gather in order to support the process of the WSF and decide where the next event should be located.

The WSF consists of both events and processes. The main WSF event has been organised 15 times since 2001 and invites activists, networks, social movements, NGOs and others from all over the world to come together on equal footing in a semi-organised open space. It is an opportunity to share experiences and analysis across localities and thematics, and from there co-create campaigns and strategies that can be worked on at global and regional/local levels. As a process, the WSF is the resulting ongoing multilayered and interconnected activities that go on between the events.

The ambition behind the WSF is to create an open space for what Nicholls et al (2015) identify typically lies behind a disruptive style of social innovation, described as social movements and networks aiming to change power relations and alter social hierarchies. The authors go on to state that 'disruptive social innovation can be characterised by structured mass participation in political parties or formal membership schemes of social movements on the one hand, or loose coalitions of individuals and interested parties united by an evanescent issue or technology such as social media, on the other' (Nicholls et al, 2015: 3) or, in the case of the WSF, as an innovative global open space that is simultaneously an event and a process. Widespread social change is thus captured in a discourse of innovation linked to bottom-up processes that collectively manage to exert knowledge, voice and action at a global scale.

Other models of social innovation are increasingly recognising the fragmented and fractal-like nature of change (O'Brien, 2021). They recognise that whole ecosystems of frontline workers and the citizens they work with can have a collective agency that is potentially more powerful than a much smaller number of CEOs and political leaders. It is consequently interesting to consider how global movements that rely on bottom-up processes are organised and governed, since this could be key in understanding how to address systemic change with widespread impact. This in turn will influence conditions for context-specific local well-being, coordinated across territories around the world.

Examples of large-scale economic models for social innovation for the common good are becoming better known and increasingly piloted in more formalised and institutional manners at local, regional, national and international levels. Examples include the Wellbeing Economy Alliance, OECD and EU policy for supporting the social and solidarity sector, nations and cities adopting 'doughnut economics' (Raworth, 2017), and interest from major private and philanthropic organisations in movements such as regenerative economics.

As planetary consciousness increases, the WSF, as a global open space, takes part in creating the necessary conditions for humanity to move away from the patterns of extractive capitalism and systems that support destructive lifestyles, and towards one where we increasingly acknowledge that well-being comes from community, connection and stewarding of our resources for those we care about today, and for future generations.

Reflections on case examples, social innovation and social work

This chapter has taken three geographic scales of social innovation – neighbourhood, bioregion and global – and shows that all three have principles of empowering bottom-up initiatives to grow in their impact for social change and are all initiatives that depend on practices embedded in the global definition of social work, as well as those of social innovation.

Common synergies in all three cases are found in process as well as outcome. They include:

- The ways of working in each area are intentionally practice-based (and place-based) in methods and approaches that generate social cohesion and empowerment.
- They are focused on creating networks and/or spaces where collaborative innovation can be done in a decentralised and relational manner.
- Topics such as collective action, equity, relationships and respect for diversity and Indigenous/local knowledge are embedded and included in the organisations and networks.
- Well-being is the vision and mission of all the case initiatives, created through social innovation and rooted in social and community work processes.

The case studies illustrate that social work and community development approaches are relevant at any spatial scale, made possible through each case's principled stance to honour bottom-up emergence of ideas and trends, no matter how complex they may be, while also working in more vertical ways to effect that change.

A key reflection on the three case studies is that identifying the symptoms, systems and mindsets at work in any setting provides a useful starting point for designing a framework for different social innovation processes that can collectively shift society towards a more thriving context for all (Figure 2.4). These different processes are summarised next.

Symptom innovation

'Symptoms' can be acute and apparent to everyone – and this is where social workers are most often employed. Whether working directly with individuals or more widely with community work, they are skilled to listen, analyse and find solutions – this practice of deep listening is ripe for social innovation and true value creation. Frontline symptom innovation should feed back into existing services, or through tools such as service design, so they can continuously and systematically improve through feedback loops. A social work and innovation strategy facing the crises and problems outlined in the introduction to this chapter, as experienced by individuals

Figure 2.4: Three levels of innovation strategy for social change

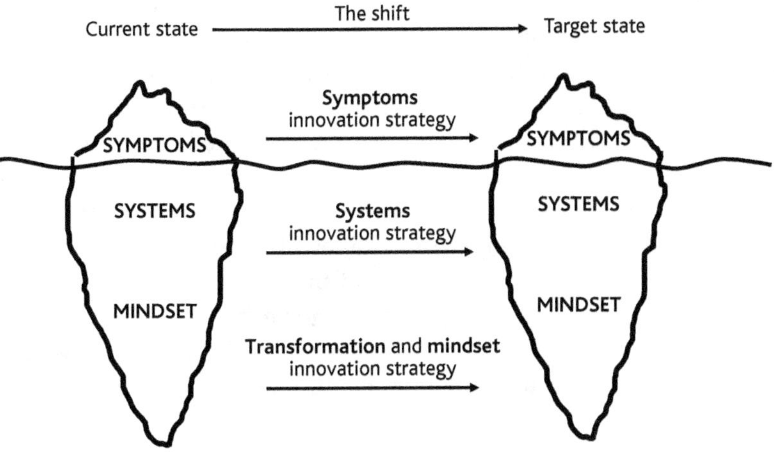

```
                          The shift
      Current state  ─────────────────▶  Target state

         /\            Symptoms              /\
        /  \        innovation strategy     /  \
   ╱SYMPTOMS╲      ─────────────────▶    ╱SYMPTOMS╲
  ────────────────                        ────────────────
  │            │         Systems          │            │
  │  SYSTEMS   │    innovation strategy   │  SYSTEMS   │
  │            │      ─────────────▶      │            │
  │            │                          │            │
  │  MINDSET   │                          │  MINDSET   │
  │            │  Transformation and mindset          │
   \          /       innovation strategy   \        /
    _____/        ─────────────▶         _____/
```

Source: Adapted from Ashoka (2022).

and communities in their daily lives, should start by listening to the citizens closest to the issue. They should then be provided with the infrastructure, both physical and human, to help solve them. The Unlimited incubators (see also Chapter 20) work at a neighbourhood scale to support establishing social enterprises by and for the local residents. The bioregional weaver works through building trust and support mechanisms for local farmers, teachers, and others who are trying new ways to build regenerative and sustainable solutions that address symptomatic challenges. The social forum activists are all working at a local, regional or national scale with territorial challenges before joining globally to make more collective impact through relational activities and deeper levels of change.

Systems innovation

The employees at the Unlimited incubators are, in addition to supporting social entrepreneurs, working with a system change strategy to build the field of social enterprise and a social economy in Norway. This systems change work requires lobbying, broad awareness raising and time for trust and understanding. A systemic approach is also core to the BWL case. The weaver role is listening and looking for patterns and root causes behind why eco-social innovations are not scaling and what systemic changes could be made to make them mainstream. The WSF is creating an open space where co-learning, co-creating and co-innovation across themes and territories have the potential for interconnected and multilayered processes to aggregate towards global system changes. These insights can be extrapolated to more general frameworks of innovation for neighbourhoods, bioregions and global movements that are out to change systems in the longer term and not limit their work to short-term solutions for the most visible symptoms.

To design a systems innovation strategy of this kind we suggest turning to research and learning undertaken by Meadows (2015) and organisations such as Ashoka (2022). These authors recognise the 'system' as any collection of related elements with a common purpose. As illustrated in the case examples, this definition means that systems innovation can be at any scale: as big as a global movement or landscape, or at the size of a local incubator.

A strategy for systems change may be different than a service-design strategy responding to alleviating symptoms and may be harder to introduce into a system with public sector departments not ready for social innovations, and who reactively want to fix visible symptoms rather than develop new systems with possibly quite different expressions than seen today.

Transformative innovation

The Three Horizons Tool developed by Sharpe and colleagues (Sharpe et al, 2016) is a useful framework for transformational thinking. With regard to the three case studies: NU is now working to create the context for a future where local neighbourhood incubators are the norm. The BWL uses this approach explicitly in multi-stakeholder gatherings and the WSF multiplies it as a whole way of being under their slogan 'Another world is possible'.

Transformational innovation can invite big-scale thinking around new paradigms – for instance the Unlimited incubators work for recognition of their position as part of a global movement for improved frameworks to support the social and solidarity economy, the bioregion works for new ways of getting whole landscapes ready for major financial flows to invest in our regenerative futures, and the WSF as a continuous process based on the premise that another world is possible.

This deepest and most fundamental level of change is perhaps less commonly visible in the strategy documents of social innovators or social workers, but it should be there at the same time as other innovation strategies if long-term sustainable change is to emerge, change that addresses global as well as local crises and issues, and that is therefore suitable for our future communities and planet. Taking the time to design a strategy for mindset change and for whole new systems to emerge is within the context of social innovation and therefore, based on our analysis in this chapter, if that innovation is to work, methodology from social and community work can be a very viable approach.

Conclusion

This chapter has presented a framework with three depths of innovation for social change (symptoms, systems and mindsets/transformation) and illustrated these at three geographic scales of change (neighbourhood, bioregion and world). It has simultaneously shown that social work and community work practices are fundamental elements of all of these – even when disguised in roles and words less commonly identified as connected to the field. Incubator support roles, weavers and global activists – they all know intrinsically that change comes when not only individuals, but also communities, networks and movements are seen, heard, believed and supported to give back in visible and structural ways: they are valued and supported to give value, thus expanding the concept of mattering (Prilleltensky, 2019) from individual to the collective.

The chapter started by asking how we might address the effects of global crises at a systemic level. The case examples, and the framework for innovation at different depths of impact and change, are part of the answer. We must now work to make sure people in power as well as practitioners and citizens are aware, willing and have the capacity to use these tools and to be bold in using their power to build a better world. If they were to set about developing some innovation strategies to achieve this, some of the findings in this chapter that they might consider implementing are as follows:

- A place-based approach to social innovation and social work is a powerful way of giving collective identity, inclusion and collective agency/empowerment. The geographic scale does not really matter with regard to innovation strategy – neighbourhoods, bioregions and the world can all be looked at through symptoms, systems and mindset lenses, and different strategies developed appropriately for these rather than geographic scale.
- Sharing and replication of analyses and strategies for change is useful, whether it occurs through networks of community incubators, bioregional weaving labs or a global social forum. Trust and relationships are at the heart of this.
- There will be fundamental diversity in the local expression of any part of a wider collective or network, or subparts thereof: spatial and cultural context is fundamental for enabling successful social change. Yet there are also major benefits to be gained from knowledge exchange that leads to a common literacy within the field of social innovation, and through this more effective replication of good practice and principles is possible.
- Multi-stakeholder ecosystems are a kind of emergent portfolio of possible social and solidaristic investments for enlightened and innovative funding alliances. Co-creation of infrastructures that support these ecosystems could provide the foundations for innovative, experience-led solutions that generate well-being for both practitioners and their target groups.
- Social work core concepts such as empowerment, cohesion and collectiveness are at the heart of any innovation framework on all levels from the local to the global. One of the main commonalities between

different actors working on different levels is a sense of weaving for relational-based networks for change, both horizontally, on a peer-to-peer basis, and vertically, weaving relationships and impact between levels, sectors and disciplines.
- There are many career and research opportunities. Weavers, local social entrepreneurs, relationship-building activists and social workers, all of whom work to unleash well-being for individuals and groups rooted in the landscapes they live in, have more overlap in their job descriptions than a search engine search would suggest. Educational institutions teaching social work should be aware of these roles in community-based social innovation and the relevance of them to their students' career options. Researchers should undertake applied research programmes to explore these roles importance in bringing about change.
- We can change the world. By implementing a framework for social work, community work and social innovation (at symptoms, systems and transformational levels, all at once), we can create shifts at local and regional levels, and at the same time build global collective capacity with the potential of transformational and systemic change and a way out of the crises we are experiencing today, towards a world of universal well-being.

Notes

[1] https://thebulletin.org/doomsday-clock/
[2] *All Ireland Standards for Community Work* (AIEB and Community Work Ireland, 2016: 7) uses the following definition: 'a developmental activity comprised of both a task and a process. The task is social change to achieve equality, social justice and human rights, and the process is the application of principles of participation, empowerment and collective decision making in a structured and co-ordinated way'.

References

AIEB (All Ireland Endorsement Body for Community Work Education and Training) and Community Work Ireland (2016) *All Ireland Standards for Community Work*, Galway: AIEB, https://www.cwi.ie/wp-content/uploads/2016/03/All-Ireland-Standards-for-Community-Work.pdf.

Ashoka (2022) Systems change masterclass, Ashoka, https://www.ashoka.org/en-nrd/systems-change-masterclass.

Ashoka (2023) Bioregional Weaving Labs, Ashoka, https://www.ashoka.org/en-nrd/program/bioregional-weaving-labs-collective.

Bagnall, A.M., Southby, K., Jones, R., Pennington, A., South, J. and Corcoran, R. (2023) Systematic Review of Community Infrastructure (Place and Space) to Boost Social Relations and Community Wellbeing: Five Year Refresh – Technical Summary Report, London: What Works Centre for Wellbeing.

Birney, A. (2021) How do we know where there is potential to intervene and leverage impact in a changing system? The practitioners perspective, *Sustainability Science*, 16: 749–65.

Brooks, D. (2018) The neighborhood is the unit of change, *New York Times*, 18 October, https://www.nytimes.com/2018/10/18/opinion/neighborhood-social-infrastructure-community.html.

BWL Waterford (2022) Bioregional Weaving Lab Waterford, Grow It Yourself, https://giy.ie/programmes/bioregional-weaving-lab/.

Chancel, L., Piketty, T., Saez, E. and Zucman, G. (eds) (2021) *World Inequality Report 2022*, Paris: World Inequality Lab, https://wir2022.wid.world/.

Christensen, C.M., McDonald, R., Altman, E. and Palmer, J.E. (2018) Disruptive innovation: an intellectual history and directions for future research, *Journal of Management Studies*, 55(7): 1043–78.

Cottam, H. (2011) Relational welfare, *Soundings*, 48: 134–44.

IFSW and IASSW (International Federation of Social Workers and International Association of Schools of Social Work) (2014) International definition of social work, International Federation of Social Workers, July, https://www.ifsw.org/what-is-social-work/global-definition-of-social-work/.

IPCC (Intergovernmental Panel on Climate Change) (2022) *Climate Change 2022: Impacts, Adaptation and Vulnerability – Contribution of Working Group II to the Sixth Assessment Report of the Intergovernmental Panel on Climate Change*, ed. H.O. Pörtner, D.C. Roberts, M. Tignor, E.S. Poloczanska, K. Mintenbeck, A. Alegría, et al, Cambridge: Cambridge University Press.

Kania, J. and Kramer, M. (2011) Collective impact, *Stanford Social Innovation Review*, 9(1): 36–41.

Kania, J., Williams, J., Schmitz, P., Brady, S., Kramer, M. and Juster, J.S. (2021) Centering equity in collective impact, *Stanford Social Innovation Review*, 20(1): 38–45.

Meadows, D.H. (2015) *Thinking in Systems: A Primer*, White River Junction, VT: Chelsea Green.

Milligan, K., Zerda, J. and Kania, J. (2022) The Relational Work of Systems Change, *Stanford Social Innovation Review*, https://doi.org/10.48558/MDBH-DA38.

Mulgan, G., with Tucker, S., Ali, R. and Sanders, B. (2007) Social Innovation: What It Is, Why It Matters and How It Can Be Accelerated, working paper, Scholl Centre for Entrepreneurship, Oxford University, London: Young Foundation.

Mumford, M.D. (2002) Social innovation: ten cases from Benjamin Franklin, *Creativity Research Journal*, 14(2): 253–66.

Nicholls, A., Simon, J. and Gabriel, M. (2015) Dimensions of social innovation, in A. Nicholls, J. Simon and M. Gabriel (eds) *New Frontiers in Social Innovation Research*, Basingstoke: Palgrave Macmillan, pp 1–26.

Noya, A. (2011) The essential perspectives of innovation: the OECD LEED Forum on Social Innovations, in OECD (ed) *Fostering Innovation to Address Societal Challenges*, Paris: OECD, pp 18–25.

O'Brien, K. (2021) *You Matter More Than You Think: Quantum Social Change for a Thriving World*, Oslo: cCHANGE Press.

Prilleltensky, I. (2019) Mattering at the intersection of psychology, philosophy, and politics, *American Journal of Community Psychology*, 65(1/2): 16–34

Prosser, S.D. (2022) Håndbok for støttespillere i Norge Unlimited, Oslo: Norge Unlimited, https://norgeunlimited.no/wp-content/uploads/2022/11/Ha%CC%8Andbok-for-stottespillere.pdf.

Raworth, K. (2017) *Doughnut Economics: Seven Ways to Think Like a 21st-Century Economist*, White River Junction, VT: Chelsea Green.

Russell, T., Stapleton, A., Markey, A. and McHugh, L. (2022) Dying to Farm: Developing a Suicide Prevention Intervention for Farmers in Ireland, https://www.teagasc.ie/media/website/rural-economy/rural-economy/farm-health-safety/Anne-Markey-UCD.pdf.

Sharpe, B., Hodgson, A., Leicester, G., Lyon, A. and Fazey, I. (2016) Three horizons: a pathways practice for transformation, *Ecology and Society*, 21(2): https://www.jstor.org/stable/26270405.

Sørensen, E. and Torfing, J. (2011) Enhancing collaborative innovation in the public sector, *Administration & Society*, 43(8): 842–68.

Steen, M. (2011) Tensions in human-centred design, *CoDesign*, 7(1): 45–60.

Westley, F. and Antadze, N. (2010) Making a difference: strategies for scaling social innovation for greater impact, *Innovation Journal*, 15(2): art 2, https://innovation.cc/document/2010-15-2-2-making-a-difference-strategies-for-scaling-social-innovation-for-greater-impact/.

Wilf, S. (2018) How Ashoka fellows create systems change: new learnings and insights from the 2018 Global Fellows Study, *Social Innovations Journal*, 52: art 2, https://socialinnovationsjournal.org/editions/issue-52/75-disruptive-innovations/2905-how-ashoka-fellows-create-systems-change-new-learnings-and-insights-from-the-2018-global-fellows-study.

World Social Forum (2001) World Social Forum Charter of Principles, http://www.universidadepopular.org/site/media/documentos/WSF_-_charter_of_Principles.pdf.

3

Social work, social innovation, discretion and creativity: day-to-day innovation of practice

Tony Evans

Introduction

The European Commission (the Commission) praises 'the innovation power of pioneer social enterprises that design successful new social services' (Borzaga et al, 2020: 125). It sees social innovation predominately as a technology to achieve efficiency, effectiveness and economy (Nicholls and Edmiston, 2019). In contrast, the argument in this chapter is that day-to-day practice in the welfare state services is inherently creative. It is a process in which there is continuous negotiation and innovation between practitioners and the people with whom they work; creativity is often seen in cumulative small gains, which are sometimes pivotal and create fundamental changes. In collaboration with service users, social workers are continuously adapting what they know and what has worked in the past to make them relevant to situations encountered. These different approaches reflect broader assumptions about the nature of knowledge and the freedom the practitioners should have to be flexible, in other words: to exercise their discretion. After distinguishing these two approaches in terms of vertical (top-down) innovation and horizontal (collective and grounded) creativity, this chapter argues that different ideas of professional knowledge and freedom are also associated with these different approaches. Vertical innovation focuses on knowledge as measurement and outcomes; about producing products, scaling them up and implementing them in practice. Associated with this is a distrust of frontline freedom of action and non-compliance. In contrast, horizontal creativity engages with the social world as a dynamic and complex environment in which knowledge is tentative and very much tied up with the social context. It is about understanding how small changes make things work better in one context, but perhaps not in another; and it presumes discretion as a framework within which to be adaptable and to work collaboratively with service users. Frontline freedom is not a threat; it is the basis of responsive service provision. The chapter argues that horizontal creativity reflects a long-standing productive approach in social work practice, based on pragmatism.

While the horizontal view of creativity and social provision is compelling, it also has to answer the criticism that the idea of fuzzy and situated knowledge limits the ability of practitioners to learn from each other and share new ways of working. Another criticism is that, because it is focused on addressing problems in their context, it cannot really engage at a strategic and structural level with social issues. The chapter addresses these criticisms in the closing section by presenting an example of an approach to sharing and disseminating situated professional knowledge that provides a good model of shared creative working and service development. The chapter also looks at the example of policy reflection as a way of challenging criticisms of horizontal development as piecemeal, by showing how it can engage with strategic and policy issues, not just individual problems.

Vertical social innovation

Social innovation is a complex idea that is open to wide and differing interpretations (Nicholls and Edmiston, 2019). In any particular setting, we must look at it carefully to ensure we know what it involves. What, for instance, does the practice of social innovation entail, and for what purpose, and in whose interest is innovation pursued? The Commission's rhetoric of social innovation as 'developing new ideas, services, and models to address social challenges' (European Commission, undated) suggests a positive social agenda but, in practice, the Commission deploys social innovation as a technology of top-down efficiency and cost-effectiveness, social investment, and activation of social agents, that sidesteps structural inequalities (Nicholls and Edmiston, 2019). The strong impression emerges of a centralised approach, driven by a managerialist agenda and technical activity of evaluation, scaling-up and implementation. This impression is reinforced when we look at the Commission's recommended 'methodological guide for social makers' – the Wrocław Guide to Social Experimentation (European Commission, 2011) – which underpins its preferred approach to the evaluation of social experiments (European Commission, 2011). The guide to social experimentation states: 'The principle of social experimentation is to test a policy intervention on a small population so as to evaluate its efficacy before deciding whether it should be scaled up' (European Commission 2011:2). It goes on to explain that: 'There are two main actors involved in social experimentation: policymakers and evaluation teams (usually made up of consultants or researchers)' (European Commission 2011:2). Innovation, from this point of view, is understood in terms of adjusting incentives, opportunities and constraints applied to a population. And in developing social innovations, innovators' concern for the people receiving intervention is to ensure 'that the targeted population will indeed be willing and able to participate' (European Commission 2011:3) in policy makers' ideas of the right intervention in their definitions of others' social needs. Social innovation, the Commission explains, is a process mediated by strategic actors, including social entrepreneurs, who '… operate at the level of new ideas and pilots, implementation and also at the level of policy making' (European Commission, 2013: 15). For the Commission, social innovation 'comes rather close to the term social entrepreneurship, in cases in which the latter is used to refer to an approach driving positive social change' (Borzaga et al, 2020: 34). In short, this is a social innovation where key actors identify and specify the nature of social (economic) problems and how to solve them. Policy makers and entrepreneurs promote solutions, which are tested and specified for replication. And once a solution is found to work, this solution should be scaled up and disseminated.

The Commission's approach to social innovation reflects the current interest of public policy actors more generally in entrepreneurialism and policy development (Cohen, 2021), which is associated with Mintrom, who uses business ideas eliding innovation and entrepreneurialism to understand policy development. He is interested in a particular group of actors he calls 'policy entrepreneurs', who 'articulate policy innovations onto government agendas and energize the diffusion process' (Mintrom, 1997: 739). He suggests their prime role is to sell and promote innovation, and their essential skill is to 'promote policy ideas' (Mintrom, 1997: 739) through identifying new problems, offering new solutions and selling them to senior policy makers.

However, Arnold (2015) criticises much of the work on entrepreneurialism for ignoring everyday entrepreneurship in service provision and tending to locate entrepreneurship outside service provision. She argues, 'street-level policy entrepreneurs seek to develop or adopt policy innovations intended to improve the implementation processes they prosecute and to entrench these innovations in the day-to-day actives of bureaucratic peers' (Arnold, 2015: 309). These entrepreneurs are not all street-level staff but a subset of frontline actors. She draws the distinction between the disorganised use of discretion, usually ascribed to street-level bureaucrats, and self-conscious innovation and entrepreneurial promotion:

> there is a substantial difference between a policy that emerges from the aggregation of piecemeal, discretionary decisions, and the policy innovations at issue here – those an entrepreneurial bureaucrat finds or creates because he perceives they will improve implementation processes in which he is enmeshed and which he then seeks to institutionalize in the practices of peers. (Arnold, 2015: 311–12)

A strength of Arnold's argument is her critique of the exclusive focus in the mainstream policy entrepreneurship literature on external agents as innovators: street-level practitioners, such as social workers, are also key innovators and entrepreneurs. However, both Arnold and policy entrepreneurial advocates put forward a view of innovation as a conscious process of problem articulation, solution discovery and dissemination, and the enforcement of a top-down service agenda beyond the world of day-to-day frontline practice that is problematic – which is a tidy but unrealistic representation, when we think of the complexity of the social world, social issues and service responses, and the world of social work practice in particular.

Horizontal social creativity

The social world is full of human agents interacting with each other, making subtle shifts and changes in their own and others' behaviours, and cumulatively these interactions shift the broader social context, adding up to a dynamic and diverse environment. Here, thinking about imaginative and responsive services, it is challenging to consider problems and solutions as either fixed or general (the assumption of vertical innovation). In any situation, it is often as difficult to see what the problem is as to see what the appropriate solution is (Evans and Hardy, 2010). This is the social world described by sociologists such as Goffman (1997); identities and relationships are rule-bound, but social rules are fluid and flexible and continually under negotiation. It can be seen in the everyday interaction of service providers and service users in human services in renegotiating roles, identifying new social resources and recognising affordances. Social experimentation is commonplace but often not dramatic. It is imaginative, reflexive and dynamic – balancing stability and change. And while creativity is often focused on instances and settings, it also has the potential to shift our shared assumptions by showing what is possible and questioning what is taken for granted (Ledan, 2022).

Foley (2012) captures this dynamic and social process in the idea of 'horizontal military innovation', which he developed in the setting of war studies.[1] This involves 'seeking out and sharing new experiences and knowledge without waiting for direction from above [where] individuals are important in moving this knowledge around, few if any claim "ownership" of new ideas or doctrine' (Foley, 2012: 802–3). He describes how combat units during the First World War had to change and adapt to new and unexpected situations. Rather than holding tight to formal doctrine or waiting for instruction, these units thought on their feet and developed new ideas and practices in response to the challenges they faced. New approaches were recorded, analysed and disseminated through 'experience reports' shared between frontline units, short-circuiting formal lines of hierarchical command and communication.

Creativity, which can be both conscious and intuitive, is perhaps a better way of capturing these social processes rather than the narrower idea of 'being innovative' (with its commercial connotation of introducing something novel or new; OED Online, nd). Creativity and creative discretion are human and humane processes, valuing collaborative interaction over proprietorial assertion, a fluid movement which is cumulative and imaginative; adaptation gives rise to creation, where new insights and practices are disseminated across services and between practitioners and communities instead of having to be exclusively transmitted up and down lines of hierarchical control (Evans, 2020; Forester et al, 2021; Visser and Kruyen, 2021).

In contrast to vertical innovation as groundbreaking and dramatic, this is a more mundane but plausible picture of marginal gains, adaptation and flexible thinking – which also occasionally generate dramatic change. Boden (1994), examining the nature of creativity, argues that the idea of innovation as exceptional historic acts is not only implausible but also unhelpful because it devalues widespread everyday creativity. She observes that describing innovations as 'historical' (or not) (Boden 1994: 76), is a judgement that is evaluative and unstable – what, at one point, looks innovative or brilliant can be seen in hindsight as unexceptional, while a small, mundane change may later be recognised as pivotal. Boden (1995) also notes that, generally, creativity is not a break from what has gone before but is cumulative, pushing and stretching our understanding and recognising affordances that are more helpful to the purpose at hand.

Importantly, Foley (2012) notes that this sort of practice requires a social context where rules and regulations are seen as advisory rather than prescriptive, where practitioner experience and judgement are valued (over formal organisational status and hierarchical roles), and there is a pragmatic culture of learning and openness to new ideas. These conditions reflect ideas of discretion as the freedom to act and the freedom to employ expertise and knowledge. The chapter now moves on to consider these two aspects of discretion and how they relate to the two approaches to innovation and creativity in the two different approaches already described.

Social innovation, creativity and approaches to discretion

Vertical social innovation and horizontal creativity entail different conceptions of discretion as room for judgement and action. For vertical innovation, discretion is a problem. The idea that new techniques are developed and evaluated by experts and promoted by policy entrepreneurs is central to the vertical approach to social innovation; freedom to exercise judgement on the ground (the core of discretion) is distrusted; discretion is deviation, a compliance challenge. However, in practice, discretion is often tolerated – adapting services to real-life situations – but often as a dirty secret that everyone knows but cannot formally acknowledge. It is a *dirty* secret because 'adaptations' question or challenge the authority of the taken-for-granted way of working. It has to be a *secret* because being seen as doing something outside the specified form of work set out by the paradigm is risky, as any adverse results are blamed on the individual (deviants), rather than considering problems with the system.

In contrast, in horizontal creativity discretion is valued. The context in which creativity operates is essential to widespread discretion: recognising a broad range of expertise and practical engagement in crafting solutions; the deployment of flexibility and imagination. This is tied to the recognition that creation is not separate from everyday life but is part of it, arising from effortful engagement with existing frameworks while also sometimes striving to move beyond them (Negus and Pickering, 2004).

Comparing vertical social innovation and horizontal creativity, discretion is not only evaluated differently but also understood differently. From the perspective of vertical social innovation, discretion is a failure of control. This approach is analogous to how paradigmatic thinking operates and is policed (Kuhn, 1970) – good practice is seen as mimetic, simply copying the right approach and setting about it with a panoply of training: there is a right way of working, which is monitored to ensure compliance. From the perspective of horizontal creativity, discretion needs to be supported to facilitate curiosity, imagination, questioning and the ability to craft situated solutions. It is a recognition that services are created 'on the hoof' and in the relationships between the service users and professionals. It is a challenge to the idea that one size fits all. Interestingly, this is a perspective that has become increasingly influential across a range of cognate disciplines such as management and economics. Critical management theorists challenge the view of human services as a form of factory production, stamping out the same service according to a set template. They argue that services are created in the context of the interaction of service providers and service users. The provider negotiates with the service user to co-create the required service (Osborne et al, 2012). In economics (Wolfson, 2019) too there is an emerging recognition of the positive role of discretion in creating new services. Discretion is seen as central to 'situational contracting', which challenges the approaches to provision as predetermined and fixed, arguing that local discretion provides the space for the expertise and imagination of both service users and professionals in the co-defining of the nature of the problem and the co-creation of solutions.

Vertical innovation assumes fixed human nature/social order – a stable problem requiring a specific intervention – but in practice, it has to acknowledge the dynamic nature of individual and social relations and the perennial challenges of application (fitting solutions to problems) and implementation (how do I adapt this 'solution' to work in this setting?). And this entails situated human judgement, strongly underpinned by respect for the ethical standing of the actors involved. Problems and their solutions are dynamic: little acts of innovation that take place within social relationships, within networks of commitments, conflicts and cooperation. This is what is often meant by the situatedness and complexity of social issues.

Innovation, creativity and forms of knowledge

While horizontal creativity's ability to engage with social reality is convincing, there is a problem with sharing innovation if all we can know is fuzzy and constantly changing. Without a body of clear and solid knowledge of how practitioners learn and identify skills to help, how can practitioners describe themselves as professionals? This argument, in a sense, has been a driving force behind the evidence-based practice movement, in its various iterations (Evans and Hardy, 2010). Are practitioners not doomed to reinvent the wheel repeatedly? Should professional expertise not be based on solid evidence that establishes a paradigm for practice? Practice should be specified in evidence-based principles; and freedom to diverge from these is unnecessary.

This sort of scientific knowledge, however, presents challenges in relating it to the messy nature of social life. In thinking about social innovation, it is useful to draw a distinction between forms of quantitative research and how these can support practice. On the one hand, descriptive research knowledge helps provides a snapshot of a context in terms of underlying structures in social arrangements. On the other hand, evaluative quantitative research seeks to identify effective interventions that can be applied to individual problems.

Quantitative descriptive research provides a time-limited picture of aspects of society such as the patterns of diversity, power, wealth and status that operate at a point in time. It provides a framework to link individual stories and needs to wider collective experiences. This sort of research knowledge underpins the sociological imagination (Mills, 2000) that enables practitioners to move beyond an individual focus on personal problems to recognise strategic issues such as social disadvantage and the power underlying them. This is discussed in the conclusion, but here the focus is on the role of quantitative evaluative research that is associated with the top-down approach to social innovation. Quantitative evaluative research breaks down social experiences into isolated phenomena that can be measured to identify their specific outcomes. The compelling claim of this sort of evaluation is that it can capture effective interventions that should direct practice (such as empirically supported treatment initiatives; see, for example, Schneider et al, 2020). In social care, for instance, evidence-based practice is concerned with identifying what works with whom in what circumstances, and once this is identified emphasises practitioners' professional and moral obligation to do 'what works', and the economic imperatives for policy makers in implementing it (Evans and Hardy, 2010). Against this idea of professional knowledge, the more local and transient nature of practice knowledge associated with horizontal creativity can seem limited and inadequate. But, as noted earlier, the claim that quantitative evaluative research provides clear and robust practice guidance is more rhetorical than reality; it is a useful theoretical device to undermine more tentative and situated knowledge as not good enough. However, as already outlined, applying and implementing the desiccated directions of quantitative evaluation is problematic in the context of significant real-life, practical problems. In fact, as a standard of good professional knowledge, it dissolves under scrutiny, and we must be careful not to allow its rhetorical pull to devalue other forms of useful knowledge (Evans and Hardy, 2010; Ziegler, 2020), particularly the tentative, grounded knowledge associated with horizontal creativity. Recognising this enables us to consider a more plausible idea of what good professional knowledge looks like – and how new practices, approaches and service ideas can be captured, shared and fed into policy development. Pragmatism underpins the approach of horizontal creativity. From a pragmatic perspective, the measure of 'good knowledge' is usefulness, rather than an abstract notion of truth. Good knowledge not only helps us solve the problems that perplex us, but it also enables us to advance our projects and realise our commitments, the opposite of vertical innovation's paradigmatic approach, which brackets off questions and privileges established theory even when it does not make sense in the circumstances. Pragmatism, as Dewey (1971 [1933]: 286) explains, is the: 'Absence of dogmatism and prejudice, presence of intellectual curiosity and flexibility ... to be interested in the unfolding of the subject on its own account, apart from any subservience to a preconceived belief or habitual aim'. When theory does not work, it is recognising that there is 'a question to be answered, an ambiguity to be resolved' (Dewey, 2011 [1910]: 9) rather than doubling down and dismissing alternatives because they do not fit a pre-established world view. This is pragmatic inquiry, a critical reflection that involves:

> Active, persistent, and careful consideration of any belief or supposed form of knowledge in the light of the grounds that support it, and the further conclusions to which it tends [and] once begun, it includes a conscious and voluntary effort to establish belief upon a firm basis of evidence and rationality. (Dewey, 2011 [1910]: 12)

Pragmatic thinking is in the genes of critical practice in social care, going back to Jane Addams – a close associate of Dewey – at the Hull House Settlement in Chicago. Addams talks about her work as an experiment in social innovation. The approach was firmly grounded in pragmatism's rejection of dogmatism: 'The one thing to be dreaded in the Settlement is that it loses its flexibility, its power of quick adaptation, its readiness to change its methods as its environment may demand' (quoted in Shields, 1999: 12). Her approach was characterised by listening to different perspectives and learning from experience. Central to this was 'not to hold preconceived ideas of what the neighbourhood ought to have, but to keep ourselves in readiness to modify and adapt our understandings as we discovered those things which the neighbourhood was ready to accept' (quoted in Shields, 1999: 12).

However, aspects of everyday creativity can be fuzzy and dynamic – they can be recognised but can be difficult to specify, especially out of context. But it is not impossible. Expressing what is new is a challenge because language alone can struggle to keep up with change. Luntley (2011), for instance, talks about the problems professionals face when sharing information about what they know and what they do. Their knowledge is dynamic, being remade and developed in a specific context of use; communication about what they are doing and how this is changing relies on shared experience, metaphor and allusion to contextual factors. Showing innovation and telling others about it cannot simply be isolated as a discrete intervention. Understanding new ideas and approaches relies not only on understanding what is new but also on the nexus of ideas and assumptions that constitute the context within which it works (Harris et al, 2015).

Horizontal creativity is liable to the criticism that, in the absence of a framework to share situational knowledge, and the ability to make links between local developments and more general issues, creativity and discretion will inevitably be on the back foot, characterised as going nowhere and continually reinventing the wheel. I want to close by offering practical responses to these criticisms by providing an example of a straightforward approach to recording and sharing local innovation and an approach to reflection that helps practitioners link local innovation to wider social needs and feed local developments into wider strategic debates.

Good Practices in Mental Health (GPMH) provides an example of how the fast-moving, tentative and context-specific nature of information that can capture horizontal social creativity can be gathered together and disseminated in a manner analogous to the 'experience reports' Foley (2012: 8) talks about. GPMH developed in the late 1970s in London and then nationally, and internationally, as a way to identify and disseminate local 'good practice' by providing practical information and ideas to support the development of innovative services (Gordon, 1986). Good practice was defined 'pragmatically on the basis of what appeared to work well' (Gordon, 1986: 6) from the point of view of those providing and receiving services. The project supported local groups (of practitioners, citizens and communities) to gather information on local service innovation. GPMH provided a loose framework within which to do this work. Contrasting its approach with time-consuming and costly full-blown research and evaluation, it promoted 'practical, flexible and inexpensive' (Gordon, 1986: 6) information generated by people on the ground. Key to this approach was structured information-gathering that described the aims, origins, operation, organisation and contact details of innovative services as 'a pool of practical information for those thinking of setting up a service' (Gordon, 1986: 13). GPMH would also act as an information exchange across localities and service areas. Key to its avowedly pragmatic approach was the recognition both that any knowledge produced needed to be contextualised to make it useful to people outside the context, and that any information was time-limited, a snapshot of a dynamic situation that would need to be revisited.

The other potential criticism of horizontal creativity is that it cannot move beyond individual problems to engage strategically with the underlying social issues. This does not have to be the case. The pragmatic perspective of horizontal creativity links well with reflection as not only a mode of inquiry but also a policy development strategy. Reflection for Dewey was both about solving individual problems and being able to make links between them and advance commitments in the social and political spheres (Dewey, 1971 [1993]). Reflection in social work has its roots in Dewey's work (Leonard, 2020) and his approach resonates with social work values (Broadhurst, 2012). He saw group reflection as a particularly powerful way of using the experience of disquiet, challenge and creativity to enable people to understand and change social situations, and to better achieve collective commitments. Group reflection provides a setting in which practice issues can be related to quantitative descriptive research, to articulate a strategic analysis of practitioner and service user disquiet and identify policy questions. This enables horizontal creativity to operate not only at the level of private problems but also at the level of public issues in addressing the broader perspective of policy and political change. Group policy reflection (Evans, 2021) draws on Dewey's approach to enable practitioners to examine practice and identify ways in which they can be involved in 'correcting unfair privilege and unfair deprivation, not to perpetuate them' (Dewey quoted in Rodgers, 2002: 847); and identify their response – 'the intelligent action' (Dewey, 1971 [1933]: 17) they can take. It is a process that entails making links between practice, policy and social conditions through concrete examples in particular situations; and doing this in a focused way, creating collective solutions that can change, or sustaining positive aspects of a policy context.

Conclusion

This chapter has distinguished between vertical social innovation and horizontal creativity. The vertical approach – which is the Commission's predominant approach – frames social innovation in terms of managerial ideas: a process and a product that is evaluated and disseminated from the centre to staff on the ground. It is an approach that is tied up with an idea of invention as exceptional, and that privileges quantitative evaluation research that valorises 'what works' and sets out models and specifications of practice. There is little space for discretion and creativity. However, in practice discretion is widespread. It bridges the abstracted world of models and specifications of practice handed down by evaluators and policy makers and the messy world of practice – What do they mean? How does this apply here? How do I change it to make it relevant here? – and so on. While practical creativity is widespread, it is liable to be denigrated as non-compliance and devalued in a rhetoric of exceptional innovation.

An alternative approach is a horizontal creativity. From this perspective, creating new responses and creative approaches to social problems is not the activity of innovators but the reality of day-to-day practice, where practitioners and service users on the ground negotiate needs and co-create responses to meet situated needs. What works for one person or community may not work for another and may not work again for the same person or community at another time. Practitioners must think on their feet and employ judgement, rather than simply following guidelines. Discretion is central to this approach – it is the context in which creativity is nurtured and can operate in practice. Reflection and networking are important tools for refining and sharing creative practice and identifying strategic as well as focused approaches.

Note

[1] Military history may seem a world away from social care, but social work has usefully drawn on some surprising sources for insights. Munro, for instance, drew on research on air crash investigation to inform her work on risk and decision-making in social work (Munro, 2009).

References

Arnold, G. (2015) Street-level policy entrepreneurship, *Public Management Review*, 17(3): 307–27.

Boden, M. (1994) What is creativity?, in M. Boden (ed) *Dimensions of Creativity*, Cambridge, MA: MIT Press, pp 75–117.

Boden, M. (1995) Creativity and unpredictability, *Stanford Electronic Humanities Review*, 4(2): 123–39.

Borzaga, C., Galera, G., Franchini, B., Chiomento, S., Nogales, R. and Carini, C. (2020) *Social Enterprises and Their Ecosystems in Europe: Comparative Synthesis Report*, Luxembourg: Publications Office of the European Union, https://ec.europa.eu/social/BlobServlet?docId=22304&langId=en.

Broadhurst, K. (2012) Moral agency in everyday safeguarding work: reclaiming hope in the 'small stories' of family support: some lessons from John Dewey, *Families, Relationships and Societies*, 1(3): 293–309.

Cohen, N. (2021) *Policy Entrepreneurship at the Street Level: Understanding the Effect of the Individual*, Cambridge: Cambridge University Press.

Dewey, J. (2011 [1910]) *How We Think: A Restatement of the Relation of Reflective Thinking to the Educative Process*, Project Guttenberg. Available at: The Project Gutenberg eBook of How We Think, by John Dewey.

European Commission (2011) Innovative Responses to the Social Impact of the Crisis, ministerial conference organised by the Polish Presidency of the European Union, Wrocław, 26 September.

European Commission (2013) Guide to Social Innovation, February, Brussels: European Commission, https://ec.europa.eu/regional_policy/en/information/publications/guides/2013/guide-to-social-innovation.

European Commission (undated) Competence Centres for Social Innovation Available at: Competence Centres for Social Innovation | European Social Fund Plus (europa.eu).

Evans, T. (2020) The art of discretion, in T. Evans and P. Hupe (eds) *Discretion and the Quest for Controlled Freedom*, Cham: Palgrave Macmillan, pp 377–92.

Evans, T. (2021) Social work and policy practice: group reflection and policy inquiry, *Social Work & Society*, 19(2), https://ejournals.bib.uni-wuppertal.de/index.php/sws/article/view/739.

Evans. T. and Hardy, M. (2010) *Evidence and Knowledge for Practice*, Cambridge: Polity Press.

Foley, R. (2012) A case study in horizontal military innovation: the German Army 1916–1918, *Journal of Strategic Studies*, 35(6): 799–827.

Forester, J., Verloo N. and Laws, D. (2021) Creative discretion and the structure of context-responsive improvising, *Journal of Urban Affairs*, 45(6): 1145–62.

Goffman, E. (1997) *The Goffman Reader*, ed. C. Lemert and A. Branaman, Malden, MA: Wiley-Blackwell.

Gordon, P. (1986) *A Guide to Organising Local Studies*, 2nd edn, London: Good Practices in Mental Health.

Harris, J., Borodkina, O., Brodtkorb, E., Evans, T., Kessl, F., Schnurr, S. and Slettebø, T. (2015) International travelling knowledge in social work: an analytical framework, *European Journal of Social Work*, 18(4): 481–94.

Kuhn, T. (1970) *The Structure of Scientific Revolutions*, 2nd edn, Chicago: University of Chicago Press.

Ledan, A. (2022) *Social Experimentation: A Practical Guide for Project Promoters*, Luxembourg: Publications Office of the European Union, https://data.europa.eu/doi/10.2767/619329.

Leonard, K. (2020) Critical Reflection as an Organisational and Professional Practice in Supervision: A Study in Two Local Authority Children and Families Social Work Teams, doctoral thesis, Egham: Royal Holloway, University of London, https://pure.royalholloway.ac.uk/en/publications/critical-reflection-as-an-organisational-and-professional-practic.

Luntley, M. (2011) What do nurses know?, *Nursing Philosophy*, 12(1): 22–33.

Mills, C.W. (2000) *The Sociological Imagination*, Oxford: Oxford University Press.

Mintrom, M. (1997) Policy entrepreneurs and the diffusion of innovation, *American Journal of Political Science*, 41(3): 738–70.

Munro, E. (2009) Beyond the blame culture, *The Guardian*, 3 November, https://www.theguardian.com/commentisfree/2009/nov/03/serious-case-review-child-protection.

Negus, K. and Pickering, M. (2004) *Creativity, Communication, and Cultural Value*, London: Sage.

Nicholls, A. and Edmiston, D. (2019) Social innovation policy in the European Union, in A. Nicholls and R. Ziegler (eds) *Creating Economic Space for Social Innovation*, Oxford: Oxford University Press, pp 268–99.

OED Online (Oxford English Dictionary Online) (nd) Innovate definition, Oxford: Oxford University Press, https://www.oed.com/view/Entry/96310 [accessed 16 January 2023].

Osborne, S., Radnor, Z. and Nasi, G. (2012) A new theory for public service management? Toward a (public) service-dominant approach, *American Review of Public Administration*, 43(2): 135–58.

Rodgers, C. (2002) Defining reflection: another look at John Dewey and reflective thinking, *Teachers College Record*, 104(4): 842–66.

Schneider, R.A., Grasso, J.R., Chen, S.Y., Chen, C., Reilly, E.D. and Kocher, B. (2020) Beyond the lab: empirically supported treatments in the real world, *Frontiers in Psychology*, 11: art 1969, https://www.frontiersin.org/articles/10.3389/fpsyg.2020.01969/full.

Shields, P.M. (1999) The Community of Inquiry: Insights for Public Administration from Jane Addams, John Dewey and Charles S. Peirce, paper presented at the Public Administration Theory Network, Portland, Oregon, 23–25 March, https://digital.library.txstate.edu/handle/10877/3979.

Visser, E.L. and Kruyen, P.M. (2021) Discretion of the future: conceptualizing everyday acts of collective creativity at the street-level, *Public Administration Review*, 81(4): 676–90.

Wolfson, D.J. (2019) Discretion from an economic perspective, in T. Evans and P. Hupe (eds) *Discretion and the Quest for Controlled Freedom*, Cham: Palgrave Macmillan, pp 143–62.

Ziegler, H. (2020) Social work and the challenge of evidence-based practice, in F. Kessl, W. Lorenz, H.U. Otto, and S. White (eds) *European Social Work: A Compendium*, Opladen: Barbara Budrich, pp 229–72.

4

Potential for social innovation in social work: applying the capability approach

Annica Brummel, Erik Jansen, Mara A. Yerkes and Jana Javornik

Introduction

Traditionally, social work deals with social structures, injustices and inequalities contributes in different ways to social change. However, social work practices are not necessarily socially innovative per se but are based on normative frameworks that guide processes of social innovation. Such frameworks allow for reflection on which social values are at stake as well as reflecting on social work as a profession. They also help to shed light on social policies and social work services by showing the interactions of individuals within specific contexts, including institutional structures. This chapter explores how the capability approach (see, for example, Sen, 2001; Nussbaum, 2011; Robeyns, 2017) herein referred to as the CA, can provide a context-rich, encompassing normative framework for social innovation in social work. It does so, first, by explaining the central notions of the CA; and second, by discussing a social work case in which we implement its key principles to enable social innovation in social work utilising a specifically developed dialogue tool: a set of cards representing several central capabilities. Based on this case, the chapter reflects on how this tool was experienced by the participants and how it relates to the central notions of the CA. The chapter concludes with a discussion on the need for social innovation in social work practices and research and the contribution of the CA.

The capability approach: central concepts

Core concepts of the CA, developed initially by Sen (2001) and later Nussbaum (2011), have been discussed at length in the growing capability literature (for example, Robeyns, 2017; Yerkes et al, 2019). Central to the approach is the notion of *capability*, that is, the real freedom to have and live a valued and dignified life. The CA does not ascribe specific values or normative expectations to any idea of a good life that a person can conceive.

Quite the opposite; drawing on Aristotle, Sen recognised that individuals desire a plurality of activities in life (Nussbaum, 1987), this plurality being fundamental to individual well-being. What matters is whether persons are realistically able to achieve what they value. The CA also recognises that individuals are situated in societies characterised by multiple inequalities and equalities that hinder or enable their real freedom to achieve well-being. Capability differs from the often-used notion of equal opportunity, with its individualist focus and insufficient attention for the context in which individuals are embedded. The emphasis on real freedom, or real opportunity (Robeyns, 2017) that goes beyond that notion of opportunity also sets the CA apart from other person-centred approaches in social work. Namely, the context in which one is situated shapes one's ability to translate resources (*means* in CA terms) into a valued life. In the CA, these contextual factors are termed *conversion factors*, which exist and interact at multiple levels.

At the macro level, one's context consists of environmental factors (the physical environment) (Robeyns, 2005) as well as social factors (such as social movements, social policies and societal norms; Robeyns, 2017; Hobson, 2014). Increasingly, it can be argued that the macro level also has global and digital dimensions, going beyond the boundaries of the physical or the country context. For example, migration and travel patterns mean that individuals can be situated in multiple social contexts (for instance, their country of origin and country of residence) or they may be active in digital online communities with their own shared practices and norms. Alongside the macro level, individuals are situated in multiple meso contexts, such as organisations (Hobson, 2014), (local) communities (Yerkes et al, 2020) and households. At the personal or individual level, factors such as one's health, cognitive abilities, age and gender similarly shape one's ability to translate resources into a valued life. These conversion factors combine to create individually unique *capability sets*, that is, the perceived alternatives from which one chooses.

While individuals may value different capability sets, or outcomes (*valued functionings* in CA terms), the functionings they actually achieve (*achieved functionings*; Robeyns, 2017) can differ because individuals differ in their *agency* to pursue valued outcomes. Agency refers to the ability to make choices from one's capability set 'through a mutually constitutive process of perceiving, interpreting and responding to one's social situation' (Yerkes et al, 2020: 520). Hvinden and Halvorsen (2018) refer to conversion factors as conversion processes, whereby conversion factors shape one's freedom to achieve valued functionings as well as their ability to change the social structures around them, thereby limiting or enhancing one's agency. One's agency therefore cannot be seen independently from one's social situation because it hinges on structural (in)equalities related to gender, race, ethnicity, class, disability and sexual orientation (Robeyns, 2017).

The capability approach and social innovation

Capability scholars are increasingly engaging with social innovation literature (Chiappero-Martinetti et al, 2017; Howaldt and Schwarz, 2017). This emerging work suggests that the combination of the CA and social innovation approaches provides a novel reflective space to consider the extent to which individuals can access and use resources in achieving a valued life (Yerkes et al, 2021). For example, social innovation may aim to rearrange social practices through the development of new public–private partnerships but may not always lead to greater capabilities or empowerment (Gallego and Maestripieri, 2022). In this reflective space, at least four key elements of the CA could help to provide a normative grounding of social innovation in social work practice and research.

First, focusing on individuals embedded in multiple, yet layered, interacting contexts, the CA enables social work research and practice to move beyond dominant person-based approaches that overlook contextual factors. An absence of attention to contextual factors can lead to societal injustice rather than justice, for example through the misrecognition of individuals or groups with less power or voice in society.

Second, the CA supports individuals to express what they value and recognises diversity in individuals' pursuit of a valued life. This perspective allows social workers to distinguish between an individual's subjective values and the implicit and/or explicit values of social workers vis-à-vis clients' normative expectations of a good life, which may or may not be reflective of societal values. Moreover, social work practitioners are themselves individuals with particular notions of a good life which may or may not be in line with the diverse values of the clients they engage with. Being aware of differing values allows social workers to reflect critically on their own preferences, preconceptions or biases, thereby avoiding a paternalistic attitude towards people they support.

A third key aspect of the CA providing a normative grounding of social innovation in social work practice and research is the distinction between capabilities and functionings. For example, *having* sufficient quality housing may be a widely shared, valued form of being (and thus, functioning) but this is not the same as *having real freedom to attain* sufficient quality housing. The recognised distinction between real freedoms to achieve a valued life and the life individuals actually achieve, enables social workers to identify patterns of deeply entrenched social inequalities, providing avenues for social change and social innovation.

Finally, the CA clearly distinguishes between pursued functionings (as desired ends) and the means individuals have at their disposal to achieve them. From a research perspective, this distinction shows the need to focus on how individuals in varying, intersectional contexts are able to mobilise means towards ends (see, for example, Javornik et al, 2019; Yerkes et al, 2019). For social work practitioners, this distinction allows for deliberating with individuals and communities about what the constitutive, substantive elements of the good life are for each individual and which elements are instrumental to individuals.

CA and social work practice and research

The CA is increasingly used by practitioners in different fields (for example, Peters and Alderliesten, 2019), including social work (for instance Brummel, 2017). Based on our earlier research with practitioners involved in social issues and social work in particular, we suggest that while practitioners find concepts from the CA inspiring, they find the approach too abstract to enable direct application in their professional practices (Javornik et al, 2019). This is unsurprising given the philosophical nature of the CA's underlying ideas; the CA as such is often considered deliberately underspecified (Robeyns, 2017). Moreover, Robeyns (2017) argues that, theoretically, the CA is to be considered an overall *approach*. Any theoretical or practical application in a given domain requires capability concepts to be translated using domain-specific knowledge, operationalising the approach into a domain-specific *theory*, *account* or *methodology*. Thus, the CA has paradigm-like qualities, rather than being a practical framework per se. Applying the abstract notions of the CA generally requires deeper understanding of the concepts, their embedded discourses, and the ethical and practical consequences of (service) design choices to maintain a steady course in the uncertainties of everyday social work practice. Thus far, only a few such examples of capability-based social work practices and practice research exist (see, for example, Beernink, 2015; Benoot, 2021).

Given its explanatory potential, it would be a loss if social work practitioners and researchers felt discouraged from employing the CA because they perceived it as too abstract and complex. We argue that the CA is an encompassing normative framework whose principles hold great potential for social innovation in the social work field. This pertains to the centrality of normative assumptions about human diversity, the meta-role of human freedom, and the emphasis placed on human agency as a function of both individual capacities and the opportunities offered by circumstances. These constitutive elements create a dynamic interplay in which justice, well-being and freedom are formed in the practices of people's everyday lives. Whereas an account of the why, the how and the what of social practices can be firmly grounded in social theories and sociological accounts, these theories generally focus on the *elements and mechanisms* of the social but lack a normative account of which distributions and outcomes should count as ethically just (Walker, 2014). A suitable *normative framework* therefore helps social workers find appropriate and innovative solutions for addressing the social problems faced by individuals they support through due processes of good professional action in social work. In other words: a normative framework inspiring and guiding socially innovative research and practice in social work should be aligned with the core values outlined in the definition of the discipline. To demonstrate how this is possible, the next section provides an example from social work practice in which we operationalised the CA in such a way that it led to innovation within the social work practice of a welfare organisation (Brummel et al, 2022).

Capability Cards as social work innovation

The case outlined here centred on the collaboration between social work practitioners at the local welfare organisation Bindkracht10 in Nijmegen, and social work researchers from the HAN University of Applied Sciences, also in the Netherlands, applying the CA in local social work practice. This collaboration started in 2013 when the welfare organisation was searching for a normative framework to underpin their social work activities. Inspired by Nussbaum's list of ten central capabilities (Nussbaum, 2011), they chose the CA as a framework. Since then, the collaboration spurred more than 35 students at HAN University of Applied Sciences to apply the CA in their research projects in the welfare service. Over these years, a conversational tool was co-created, called the Capability Cards, consisting of a set of 20 cards, each representing a capability from Nussbaum's list (see Figure 4.1).

Figure 4.1: Examples of Capability Cards

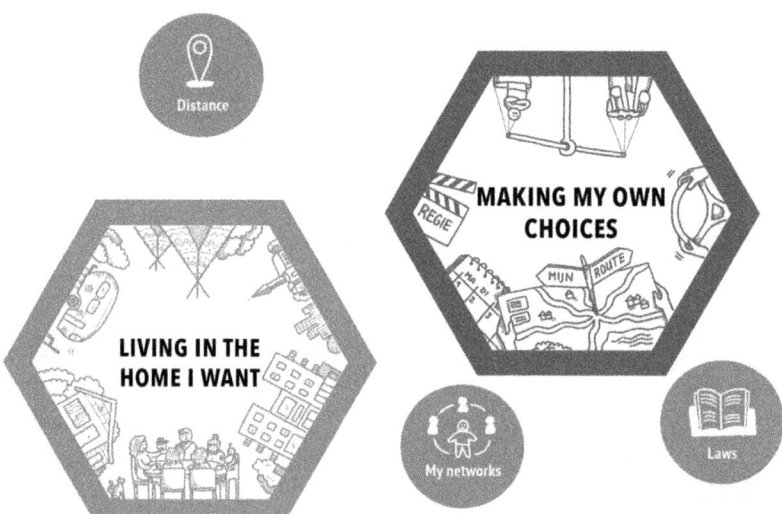

A methodology for working with the cards was then developed and studied in several social work practice pilots and investigations. As such the cards are a social innovation in their own right, but also provide a suitable method to be used in a process of social innovation.

One of these projects involved the Capability Cards in a study on the role of the neighbourhood as a capability-enhancing environment for residents in two Dutch rural municipalities (Brummel et al, 2022). The study relied on qualitative interview data with 18 individuals dealing with psycho-social vulnerabilities, identifying their individual capacities and preferences and context-dependent opportunities to live valued and dignified lives. In these interviews, the Capability Cards were used to stimulate conversation into respondents' preferences and values in relation to their environments.

Results were analysed by mapping individual responses in a conceptual model, the PO model, in which we juxtaposed expressions of the person's endowments or capacities (P) with the contextual opportunities (O) produced by the environment. The model can be depicted as a Venn diagram (see Figure 4.2) with P and O as two overlapping circles in which the overlap represents a person's actual *capability space* or capability set (that is, the choice options that are within that person's reach and therefore realistically achievable). This PO model was also later used to plot pre-existing quantitative data in a similar way using personal and neighbourhood characteristics.

The analyses with the PO model enabled us to identify patterns within the stories of the 18 respondents who were interviewed. Based on these patterns, we constructed six different anonymised stories, so-called vignettes, reflecting on both personal and contextual aspects of neighbourhood life when living with psycho-social vulnerabilities. For some respondents, the actual opportunities (O) offered by the environment appeared balanced with their personal potential (P). It was found that the neighbourhood offered those individuals actual opportunities to live the lives they value as illustrated in Rogier's vignette (Brummel et al, 2022). Rogier takes care of his wife who suffers from Alzheimer's. He enjoys life but does not take it for granted because they both suffer from health issues. Rogier gains satisfaction from caring for his wife but finds informal care demanding. Day-care activities and the support they receive at home give Rogier the opportunity to be more than "just a husband who takes care of his wife". He explained how his daily visits to a lunchroom, where he meets friends, offers distraction from being this caregiver person: "I frequently visit this place both in the morning and the afternoon. To have a talk with one person or another. You know what it is, they ask every day: how is your wife doing? You know, I feel like I belong to this, they include you within the group."

Another significant group of respondents was constrained, both on the level of personal potential (P) and opportunities (O) offered by the environment. For this group, neither their personal circumstances nor the neighbourhood

Figure 4.2: Example of a case analysed with the Person–Opportunities (PO) model

Personal potentials

Opportunities offered by environment

- Making my own choices
- Voicing my opinion
- Feeling secure
- Enjoying nature
- Living the way I want
- Enjoying life
- Being meaningful to others
- Welfare activities
- Neighbours
- Nature
- Leisure activities
- Citizens' participation

Realistic options

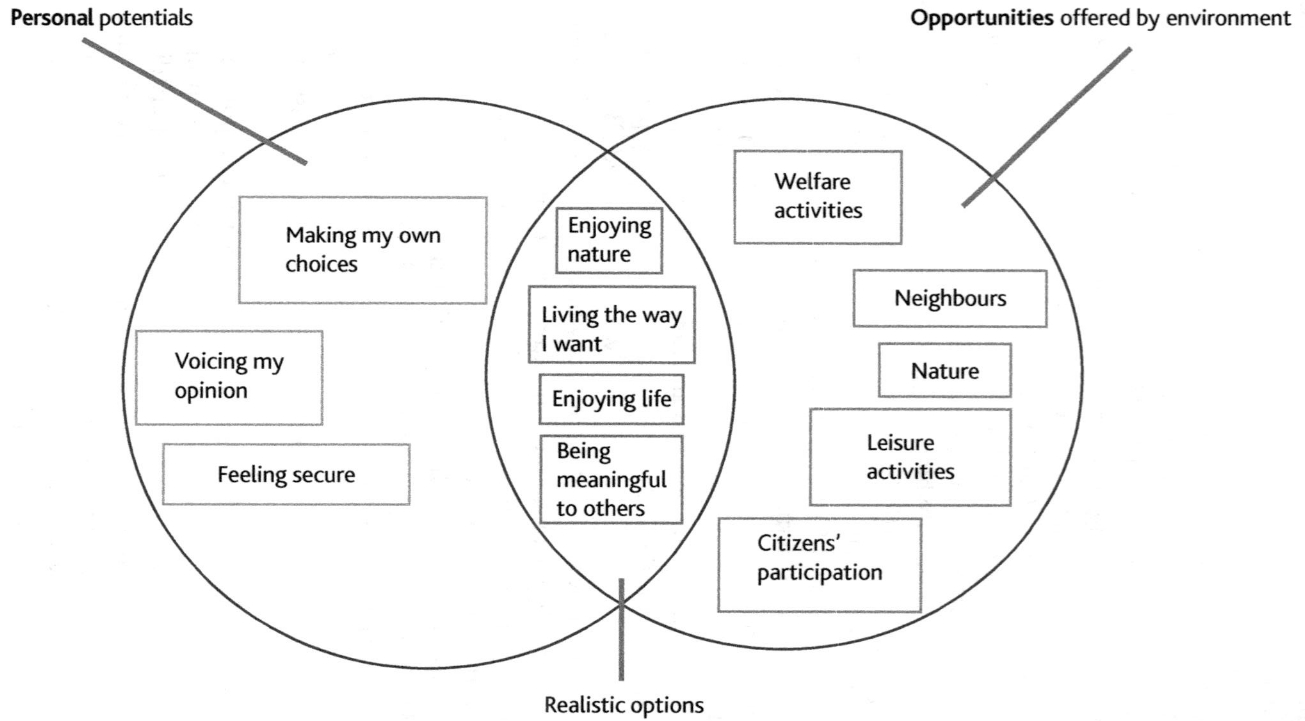

Note: Example of a case analysed with the Person–Opportunities (PO) model. The P-circle depicts the personal characteristics and potentials of the client figuring in the case example, and the O-circle demarcates the actual contextual opportunities present. The overlap between the two circles yields the realistic options or capabilities (capability space) this person (standardised vignette referred to as Rogier; see text for narrative detail) has at his disposal. Note that not all contextual opportunities (O) are relevant for the client and not all his values, desires and talents (P) can be catered for.

offered actual opportunities to live the life they value, as exemplified by Paul's vignette (Brummel et al, 2022). Paul is an adult man, living in a sheltered group home with 24-hour community support in a small village. He struggles with making his own choices, has low self-confidence and many choices are made for him in daily life. He used to have more friends, but they do not live nearby, and he does not have the financial means to visit them. To expand his social network, he could visit the only pub in the village, but he feels unwelcome there because most customers know each other well, and he supposes they are not in need of friendship with someone who lives in a group home:

> 'My entire life I have been trying to be as normal as possible, as if when I work a bit harder or when I just do a little bit better, then one day I'll be normal as well. So, if you finally get the diagnosis of autism then you know you will never be normal again. I will always be different from other people.'

These vignettes, together with the quantitative data of personal and neighbourhood characteristics plotted similarly to the PO model, were presented to a mixed group of local stakeholders (including social workers, policy officers and housing counsellors) in both municipalities. These stakeholders then engaged in a dialogue on the essence of the vignettes as potential social archetypes and how they could provide adequate support if needed. Their reflections, the outcomes of this dialogue, and insights into the process of working with tools based on the CA highlight the usefulness of the CA in guiding social innovation in social work research and practice.

Reflection on the case
Capability tools and framework

Reflecting on the case in relation to capability tools, two observations stand out. First, many participants (interviewers and respondents) noted that using the Capability Cards quickly steered the conversation towards topics that matter to the respondents and their values. Practitioners often mentioned this differed from professional–client conversations that commonly focus on requests for help, problems or specific support needs. Second, interviewers and respondents recognised that the new approach spurred a broader discussion on how they experience well-being rather than yielding a structured, professional-directed interview on life domains. This mirrors the construction of the cards that represent a broad and plural understanding of well-being based on Nussbaum's list of ten central capabilities as a basis for a dignified life. Moreover, interviewers and respondents found the cards helpful in focusing and staying centred on the client's life perspective throughout the conversation. Thus, the cards induced a broader articulation of well-being in all its plurality as experienced by the respondents. Individuals were able to use their agency to select cards which they valued. Both agency and plurality of well-being are essential elements in capability thinking.

While discussing the cards selected by the respondent, conversations were further found to expand towards discussing how personal preferences and capacities were facilitated or hindered by contextual factors. Practitioners and interviewees alike often concluded jointly that whether individuals were able to lead a valued life in many cases depended on interactions between their personal characteristics and contextual circumstances outside their control. Using the cards revealed the interaction between personal and contextual factors and enabled a reflection beyond one's opportunities. Individuals appreciated the conversation starting with what one finds valuable or important in life rather than emphasising an evaluation of their current functioning, thereby practically acknowledging the theoretical capabilities–functionings distinction. Thus, working with the cards seemed to shift the conversation towards a perspective in which human capabilities, a person's real freedoms, were the main normative anchor-points for evaluating clients' well-being.

The case thus shows how this application of the CA both as a tool (Capability Cards) and a conceptual framework (PO model) modified the interaction among the actors involved by stimulating joint deliberation and new insights on conceptions of the good life. These actors were, first of all, practitioners and clients working with the cards in their interviews, but also policy makers noticing that practitioners' views and interventions evolved into new, seemingly more productive directions. In particular, the normative stance of the CA as a framework for reviewing equity and circumstances pushed practitioners away from their former more instrumental and interventionistic ways of thinking and stimulated client empowerment in expressing what they valued. Thus, working with the Capability Cards was socially innovative in its process aspect.

Reflection on the value for practitioners

Whether working with the cards indeed leads to socially innovative outcomes, for instance by enhancing the effectiveness of interventions to the benefit of increased client well-being, is more difficult to evaluate for this case as the emphasis of the project was on doing research rather than providing actual social support. However, we noticed that the shift in the topic of the conversations appeared to feed into the professional actions of practitioners. The Capability Cards tool and associated methodical way of working spawned insight into individuals' capability sets, their conversion into actual functionings, and the variables that influence these conversion processes in daily life. Consequently, practitioners became more aware that this influenced their way of normatively evaluating whether to intervene and, if so, when and how. They noted that working with the Capability Cards provided them with a different, but collaborative, way of articulating individual preferences and contextual opportunities and their interrelationships. They also noted patterns in the six vignettes, which provided insights on not only personal, but also contextual variables. These patterns, in turn, generated awareness about deeply entrenched social inequalities, which was new for the social workers involved as an explicit and concrete topic in their work. Working with the cards indeed pushed the social workers towards new methodical approaches that could better cater to dealing with these issues. Thus, while the study progressed, the likelihood for changes in professional practice seemed to increase.

Moreover, throughout the project, the findings of the study formed a starting point for joint reflection on social policies and social work activities by social workers and social policy professionals in the municipality. These discussions led to an ensuing conceptualisation of person-in-environment being experienced as a more realistic model of well-being, both on the micro level of individuals as well as on the meso level of formal and informal support and services in the municipality. Moreover, they perceived it as providing practically useable normative considerations on how to interpret individual well-being properly.

In short, this example of applying the PO model and the Capability Cards tool shows how an operationalisation of the CA in social work can offer a normative framework for the good life in social work practice while accounting for the person within their environment. Using the Capability Cards as a conversation starter appealed to social workers, other social practitioners and the individuals they work with, and sparked deliberation both in the practitioner–client dyad and among social work and policy professionals. Furthermore, the approach taken highlights the innovative potential of the CA to bridge cross-disciplinary divides and central–local gaps between policy and practice.

Conclusion

This chapter elaborated how the CA as a broader framework can provide normative guidance for social innovation in social work given several elements inherent in the approach. On the substantive side, we see the combination of a person-centred and contextual perspective as the most important conceptual contribution of the CA to social innovation in social work. A main normative assumption of the CA pertains to diversity as a founding feature of humanity, thereby directing social work development towards diversified, person-centred service provision and support rather than advocating a standardisation of services. In essence, it is asking social workers to take a comprehensive approach to understanding the lives of their clients and their ability to change the social structures around them. This level of agency in which individuals are not only able to participate in existing practices or situations, but also to influence, change or exit them, can be referred to as navigational agency because it allows individuals to critically question and challenge existing practices and navigate beyond the status quo to a valued life (Claassen, 2018). The emphasis on such processes of agency is relevant to social work because it facilitates understanding possible effects on individual well-being over time (Hvinden and Halvorsen, 2018). Thus, applying the CA urges social workers to gain insight into a person's individual values, preferences and agency rather than just categorising persons in terms of their personal deficiencies or social problems.

Also, by introducing a distinction between capabilities and functionings, social workers are stimulated to search for patterns of deeply entrenched inequalities that significantly limit one's freedoms, in close collaboration with their clients. Such patterns represent normative indicators flagging social work interventions and agenda-setting for political action. By employing the conceptual distinction between means and ends as central to reasoning about well-being, the CA introduces a distinct form of deliberation on the 'good life', which can be implemented at all levels and with all social groups. It does so by translating concrete questions on justice and equality to consider whether the topic at hand can be framed as an instrument to an end or whether it should be viewed as an end in itself. Making these issues discursive in social work practice (as well as in research or policy making for that matter) provides an opportunity for social innovation as it sets the agenda for a deliberative process among involved actors on what should be normatively desired outcomes (Brandsen et al, 2016). Capitalising on this discursive quality of the CA, alongside the opportunity for social innovation in social work, the CA and its application offer opportunities for social innovation in policy and educational practices. While beyond the scope of this chapter, it is, for example, possible to use the CA to engage in conversations at higher levels in the policy process (such as envisioning and developing policy). Similarly, from an educational perspective, using the Capability Cards or other CA methodologies allows social work students to reflect on the contextualised lives of individuals and their role in enabling these individuals to live valued lives.

To illustrate our case in point, we propose that working with the Capability Cards can practically be laid down in a series of deliberative questions that can be asked to form a structured sequence of collaborative reasoning with clients on their conception of the good life and thereby facilitate social innovation in social work:

- What does the person regard as valuable? What are their preferences?
- What does the person need to realise these preferences?
- What is the person actually able to do or be?

- In what situation is the person involved? What barriers are there?
- Is this situation consistent with common notions of social justice?
- If not: what should or could be done to change the injustice?

Asking these questions facilitates exchange on what are to be considered the means and the ends of a valued and dignified life, which is as close to a normative discussion on the constituents of well-being as one can get. This is a firm basis for social innovation: it is collaborative, practical reasoning about what is the core of the good life (Richardson, 2015). It can guide social action to identify and work towards enabling conditions and circumstances for the groups and individuals at hand. As such, this reflects social innovation in social work in a pure form; namely, one person discussing with the other about what matters in leading a valued and dignified life as a human being and what needs to happen to facilitate it.

References

Beernink, J. (2015) *Floreren, Zoektocht naar goed leven voor mensen met ernstige verstandelijke beperking en ernstige gedragsproblemen*, Utrecht: Eburon.

Benoot, T. (2021) Autonomy in Social Work: A Search for Social Justice – The Case of Personal Budgets in the Care for People with Intellectual Disabilities, doctoral thesis, Ghent: Ghent University.

Brandsen, T., Cattacin, S., Evers, A. and Zimmer, A. (eds) (2016) *Social Innovations in the Urban Context*, Cham: Springer.

Brummel, A. (2017) *Sociale verbinding in de wijk*, Utrecht: Eburon.

Brummel, A., Jansen, E., Berkvens, J. and Leenders, J. (2022) Vignetten, Alledaagse verhalen over een goed leven van mensen in kwetsbare omstandigheden, Arnhem: HAN University Press, https://www.han.nl/projecten/2021/in-de-war-over-verwardheid/Vignetten.-Alledaagse-verhalen-over-goed-leven.pdf.

Chiappero-Martinetti, E., Houghton Budd, C. and Ziegler, R. (2017) Social innovation and the capability approach – introduction to the special issue, *Journal of Human Development and Capabilities*, 18(2): 141–7.

Claassen, R. (2018) *Capabilities in a Just Society: A Theory of Navigational Agency*, Cambridge: Cambridge University Press.

Gallego, R. and Maestripieri, L. (2022) Women's empowerment and social innovation in childcare: the case of Barcelona, Spain, *European Societies*, 24(4): 493–519.

Hobson, B. (ed) (2014) *Worklife Balance: The Agency and Capabilities Gap*, Oxford: Oxford University Press.

Howaldt, J. and Schwarz, M. (2017) Social innovation and human development – how the capabilities approach and social innovation theory mutually support each other, *Journal of Human Development and Capabilities*, 18(2): 163–80.

Hvinden, B. and Halvorsen, R. (2018) Mediating agency and structure in sociology: what role for conversion factors?, *Critical Sociology*, 44(6): 865–81.

Javornik, J., Yerkes, M. and Jansen, E. (2019) Ask rather than assume: the capability approach in the practitioner setting, in M.A. Yerkes, J. Javornik and A. Kurowska (eds) *Social Policy and the Capability Approach: Concepts, Measurements and Application*, Bristol: Policy Press, pp 107–24.

Nussbaum, M.C. (1987) Nature, Function and Capability: Aristotle on Political Distribution, working paper 31, Helsinki: World Institute for Development Economics Research, https://www.wider.unu.edu/sites/default/files/WP31.pdf.

Nussbaum, M.C. (2011) *Creating Capabilities: The Human Development Approach*, Cambridge, MA: Harvard University Press.

Peters, A. and Alderliesten, H. (2019) *Op weg naar betere ondersteuning: Intensieve mantelzorg*, Utrecht: Movisie.

Richardson, H.S. (2015) Using final ends for the sake of better policy-making, *Journal of Human Development and Capabilities*, 16(2): 161–72.

Robeyns, I. (2005) The capability approach: a theoretical survey, *Journal of Human Development*, 6(1): 93–117.

Robeyns, I. (2017) *Wellbeing, Freedom and Social Justice: The Capability Approach Re-examined*, Cambridge: Open Book Publishers.

Sen, A. (2001) *Development as Freedom*, Oxford: Oxford University Press.

Walker, G. (2014) Beyond individual responsibility: social practice, capabilities and the right to environmentally sustainable ways of living, in Y. Strengers and C. Maller (eds) *Social Practices, Intervention and Sustainability: Beyond Behaviour Change*, Abingdon: Routledge, pp 45–59.

Yerkes, M.A., Hoogenboom, M. and Javornik, J. (2020) Where's the community in community, work and family? A community-based capabilities approach, *Community, Work & Family*, 23(5): 516–33.

Yerkes, M.A., Javornik, J. and Kurowska, A. (eds) (2019) *Social Policy and the Capability Approach: Concepts Measurements and Application*, Bristol: Policy Press.

PART II

Examples of social innovations in social work across Europe

THEME A

Co-creation and co-production of social services: social innovation in practice

5

The art of co-creation: service innovation in Europe

Chris Fox and Susan Baines

Introduction

The pace of the change in contemporary societies is fast. Social work, in common with all public services across Europe, must respond to multifaceted challenges including ageing populations, mass immigration, digitalisation and the transformation of the political landscape. This chapter draws upon the Horizon 2020 project Co-creation of Service Innovation in Europe (CoSIE).[1] CoSIE built upon the idea that public sector innovations can be best achieved by creating collaborative partnerships between service providers (public sector agencies, third sector organisations, private companies) and citizens who receive services either directly or indirectly. The goal was to contribute to democratic renewal and social inclusion through co-creating services by engaging diverse citizen groups and stakeholders. This chapter draws together ideas about co-creation and how it intersects with and reinforces social innovation. It takes account of co-creation as a complex process that some fear can have adverse consequences (Steen et al, 2018; Dudau et al, 2019). Nevertheless, our overall assessment based on the CoSIE project is positive and tends to counter more sceptical voices.

The chapter sets the scene with a brief descriptive overview of the CoSIE project, who it worked with and what it set out to achieve before delving into the conceptual framework that was refined as the project progressed. It moves on to consider the policy environment in which social work practice operates and co-creation may be supported or impeded as a means of contributing to social innovation. Finally it highlights some selected results from the project to inspire thinking about new roles and relationships, in particular between professionals on the front line and citizens.

CoSIE

The CoSIE consortium was awarded funding by the European Commission Horizon 2020 under a call to advance co-creation across public services on the basis that top-down models no longer meet citizens' expectations.

CoSIE was distinguished from other projects in its ambition to advance co-creation in relational public services with citizens who are typically excluded or overlooked. It did this through real-life pilots across Europe, each working with a different service and responding with innovations to locally determined needs and priorities. Tools and resources developed through the pilots were then trialled in a test site. The participating services included, but were not confined to, social work narrowly defined, and their configurations and titles varied. All were services that address various life challenges and aim to enhance well-being. Services in the project included adult social care, youth work, children's health, older people's housing, work activation, and rehabilitation for people with criminal convictions. All the pilots took account of the interconnectedness of needs faced by individuals, families, families, groups and communities and all sought to ensure the weakest groups were part of the solutions.

Project teams in CoSIE consisted of municipalities, civil society organisations, companies and universities. Together they implemented and evaluated the pilots. The project was carried out from 2018 to 2021. Table 5.1 indicates each of the sites and its target populations.

Conceptualising co-creation

Co-creation in a public service context emphasises the rights, responsibilities and contributions of people in receipt of services, and of their family or community support networks (Brandsen and Honingh, 2018). Writing about co-creation and social innovation, Voorberg et al (2015: 1335) in a highly cited publication characterise co-creation as 'active involvement of end-users in various stages of the production process'. Although useful as a starting point, this is rather general and can accommodate different nuances and emphases. There is some scholarly debate about differences and overlaps between 'co-creation' and the longer established 'co-production' (Brandsen and Honingh, 2018). Some commentators and many practitioners use these terms interchangeably. A distinction, however, is analytically useful to avoid concept-stretching (Osborne and Strokosch, 2013; Torfing et al, 2019). 'Co-production', according to Osborne and Strokosch (2013), occurs when people who use services take on some of the work done by practitioners, whereas co-creation denotes involvement in designing and making decisions about services. Torfing et al (2019) propose a 'co-creation ladder', referencing the much older idea of a ladder of citizen participation for the enhancement of democratic influence (Arnstein, 1969). The co-creation ladder represents upward progress from lower rungs – where end users contribute only to production and delivery – towards higher rungs with co-creation involving service design, planning and decision-making (Torfing et al, 2019).

Table 5.1: CoSIE sites and target populations

Country	Pilot name	Target population
Italy	Reducing childhood obesity 'BeBa'	Families of children in Emelia Reggio diagnosed as overweight or obese
Sweden	Strengthening social services with co-creation dialogue	Residents with various needs using Jönköping's municipality personal assistance services
UK	Personalised services for people with convictions 'My Direction'	Individuals serving community sentences or released from prison on licence
Estonia	Co-designing innovative community-based services with 'Social hackathons'	People with disabilities or mental health problems in a very remote, disadvantaged rural area
Hungary	Self-sustaining villages (household economy)	Households in small, remote settlements beset by social and economic disadvantage
Spain	Empowering entrepreneurial skills 'Co-Crea-Te'	Citizens of Valencia who have been left behind by the world of work
Finland	Youth co-empowerment for health and well-being through social media	Young people not in employment, education or training
Poland	Neighbourhood meeting place for seniors 'ProPo'	Older residents of a housing estate in the city of Wrocław
Netherlands	Redesigning social services – 'No time to waste'	Residents of a socially and economically deprived neighbourhood in the municipality of Nieuwegein
Netherlands	Improving services for unemployed people	Refugees at a long distance from the labour market in the municipality of Houten
Greece	Inner-city community gardens (test site)	Residents of a suburb with high population density and lack of green space

An important line of thinking that has helped to hone understanding of co-creation is the influential body of work from public administration that presents it in terms of public service logic and value co-creation (Osborne, 2010, 2018; Osborne et al, 2016). We now examine that contribution and then explain why, despite its ubiquity and persuasiveness, we prefer to put strengths or asset-based approaches at the heart of co-creation. In doing this we are inspired by ideas that emanate from advocacy, capability, human rights and social justice.

In a series of publications Osborne and colleagues (Osborne, 2010, 2018; Osborne and Strokosch, 2013; Osborne et al, 2016; Strokosch and Osborne, 2018) invoke public management and service management theory to present a conceptualisation of co-creation around the idea of the co-creation of value through public service delivery. They position this within changing and contradictory conceptualisations of public administration. Traditional Public Administration is characterised by hierarchy, professional expertise, rule-following and standardised, often impersonal, services. It goes back to the foundation of welfare states. By the 1980s, the limitations of Traditional Public Administration were increasingly deplored (Bovaird, 2007). It was challenged and at least partially superseded (although unevenly) by New Public Management (Hood, 1991, 1998). New Public Management favours markets or market-like solutions and assumes effective public administration and management are delivered through independent service units, ideally in competition with each other. The citizen in need of public services takes on the role of a consumer empowered by purchaser choice (Slay, 2011). Osborne (2006, 2018) posits New Public Governance as a successor to New Public Management and a remedy for its perceived shortcomings. New Public Governance is much better grounded in the uncertain nature of contemporary public management with multiple governmental and non-governmental actors (Osborne, 2018). New Public Governance accommodates the 'the reality of public service management in an increasingly complex, fragmented and interdependent world' (Osborne, 2018: 225). Co-creation lies at the core of New Public Governance with an emphasis on trust, relationships and values rather than the markets and transactions (Strokosch and Osborne, 2020).

While we appreciate that the work of Osborne and colleagues has made significant advances in conceptualising co-creation within public sector governance and management, in our view it does less to elucidate what effective practice in co-creation might look like. Co-creation is essentially a moral endeavour that recognises the legitimate knowledge and lived experience of people who typically have services 'done to' them. This is perhaps somewhat implicit but not foregrounded in ideas around service logic and New Public Governance, which have little to say about the agency of citizens in receipt of services. To address this, we draw together different threads including personalisation, activism and capabilities.

From the world of public service practice, especially in social work, co-creation has much in common with the 'personalisation', at least in its more radical variants. Personalisation is an international phenomenon often linked to the struggle of disabled people for control over the support they need to live independently. At its simplest, personalisation means that public services respond to the needs of citizens who use them, rather than offering a standardised service. It encompasses a range of ways of designing and delivering services and can take what Leadbeater (2004) described as 'shallow' and 'deep' approaches. Shallow personalisation may be quite superficial and confined to more friendly interfaces and similar. Deep personalisation, in contrast 'would give users a far greater role – and also greater responsibility – for designing solutions from the ground up' (Leadbeater, 2004: 19). This sounds very close to co-creation. In social work and social care, (deep) personalisation implies a philosophy underpinned by a shift in power, responsibility and resources from state agencies to individuals (Glasby et al, 2009; Hutton and Waters, 2009). It has been argued for example, that users of personalised social services are enabled to participate more fully in society as competent citizens (Rummery, 2006), and moreover that 'community capacity' is built up as people make more use of informal support from family, peers, friends, neighbours and other sources in the community (Ayling and Cattermole, 2010). There are, however, objections to the implementation of personalisation, if not its intentions, especially the focus in the UK on individual choice in the form of cash or budgets in lieu of services. Beresford (2008: 11), for example, regretted that the 'democratising and liberating' approach originally pioneered by the independent living movement was 'reconceived by policymakers in consumerist terms'.

Social challenges today such as long-term health conditions and social isolation are increasingly complex and differ markedly from the harms that welfare states were set up to tackle in the mid-20th century. Most public services are still said to be largely deficit-based, concentrating narrowly on the presenting problems of individuals (Fox, 2018; Wilson et al, 2018). Strengths-based approaches, in contrast, start from the position that people have assets or 'strengths' and focus on their goals and resources rather than their problems (Price et al, 2020). Strengths-based working has many varieties. Price et al (2020) identified 17 different strengths-based approaches that are present within adult social care in the UK alone. What they have in common is that they support citizens' development of their capacity and opportunities to exercise agency in undertaking small acts that build meaningful relations (Cottam, 2018). These principles align well with the holistic ideals of social work that support working with rather than for people (IFSW and IASSW, 2014).

Co-creation is inextricably linked to strengths-based approaches to services. Strengths-based practice helps people to achieve their goals and live a good life. Yet laudable as this sounds there are legitimate questions to answer. Are strengths-based approaches, as argued by Gray (2011) excessively individualistic and in danger of aligning social work practice with the harsher aspects of welfare reform? How can we reconcile them with the collaborative and social dimensions of co-creation? What can be done to avoid co-creation being subverted by particular interests or producing harmful outcomes? There is after all some evidence of a 'dark side' of co-creation (Steen et al, 2018). What is needed is a normative theory of value that can help us to describe co-creation in public services in a way that explains citizens' motivations to co-create, and the balance between individual and social value in co-creation (Fox et al, 2021).

In working towards a normative theory we turn to Sen's (1990, 2009) concept of capabilities, in which assets available to the individual (or household) form the basis for capabilities, leading in turn to functioning and thereby to well-being (Oughton and Wheelock, 2003). Assets, including economic assets, are not ends in themselves but tools with which to achieve well-being, or 'flourishing living' (Nussbaum, 1988). The capabilities concept assumes that each citizen is entitled to a set of basic capabilities. Questions remain however about what the basic capabilities are. The neo-Kantian philosopher Gewirth (1978, 1996) offers a way to think through this by showing how the rational individual must invest in society and in social solutions in order to satisfy their basic needs. The starting point of his argument is that human action has two interrelated, generic features: voluntariness and purposiveness. Gewirth goes on to show that the two basic human needs or goals that are required to allow the individual to act are freedom and well-being. This leads on to the normative moral argument that if the individual claims that they have a right to freedom and well-being, they must also recognise that all prospective, purposive agents have the same rights. Claassen (2016) recognises criticisms of capabilities theory, follows the approach adopted by Gewirth and uses a conception of individual agency (instead of well-being or human flourishing) as the underlying normative ideal to select basic capabilities. This implies a conception of individual agency necessarily connected to social practices and where basic capabilities are those necessary for individuals to navigate freely and autonomously between different social practices (Claassen, 2016). Thus 'agency becomes the normative criterion for the selection of basic capabilities required for social justice [because] in a just society, each citizen is equally entitled to a set of basic capabilities' (Claassen, 2018: 1). Based on these reflections, CoSIE adopted a definition of co-creation as 'a collaborative activity that reduces power imbalances and aims to enrich and enhance the value in public service offerings' (Fox et al, 2021: 8).

Policy for co-creation and driving social innovation

In common with all public services, social work responds to and is impacted by changing policy imperatives although, of course, professional training and codes of conduct are also relevant. Co-creation (and co-production) have become orthodoxy for services in many national contexts (Bevir et al, 2019). For example, in Sweden, a legislative framework obliges state providers of disability services to design them under a co-creative method. The statutory guidance for English local authorities on social care stipulates a requirement for 'co-production', which it defines as 'when an individual influences the support and services received, or when groups of people get together to influence the way that services are designed, commissioned and delivered' (DHSC, 2023: 17). The picture is rather uneven across Europe, however, and an assessment that took place at the start of the CoSIE project showed that in some partner countries, such as Hungary and Poland, co-creation was barely recognised and they lacked concepts encouraging the involvement of stakeholders, particularly end users, in public services (Sakellariou, 2018). The European Commission has high expectations of co-creation to meet citizens' changing expectations, with many research and innovation programmes within the Horizon 2020 and Horizon Europe featuring co-creation (Timonen and Lolich, 2021). The European Economic and Social Committee, which represents civil society in the European Union, supports co-creation as one of the most effective tools for stimulating participative democracy, and thus for bolstering European integration (EESC, 2022).

Public services including social work face growing pressure to innovate (Hartley, 2014). In the contexts of industry and technology the influential concept of open innovation claims that successful innovation is not likely to emerge only from organisations' laboratories and R&D departments but from knowledge that is much more widely distributed (Chesbrough, 2011). Businesses therefore need to seek commercial success by inviting customers to co-create with them (Chesbrough, 2011). Open Innovation 2.0 places more emphasis on engagement between industry, government, universities and communities of users to solve new challenges sustainably and profitably (Curley, 2016). Empirical studies of social innovations across Europe and beyond highlight aspects of co-creation such as new provider–user relationships, revision of professional roles, collaborative forms of governance, reciprocity, cooperation and collective empowerment (Evers and Brandsen, 2016; Moulaert and MacCallum, 2019; Oosterlynck et al, 2019). Public sector and commercial variations on innovation have in common the opening of innovation processes to a broader range of people and organisations. Co-creation enables social innovation by harnessing the ideation from communities to facilitate processes of social change. New ideas, in other words, come from people and relationships (Cottam, 2018). This suggests that to foster innovation there is a strong pragmatic rationale for co-creation involving active contributions from people affected by public services.

Innovations co-created in CoSIE are presented in Chapter 6. Co-creation means everyone needs to have a voice but people on the receiving end of services and unused to being heard sometimes find it hard to participate actively. It is unsurprising that the CoSIE pilots faced this challenge, which has been quite well documented, as noted in the review undertaken for the project (Sakellariou, 2018). The next section briefly explains some of the efforts made in the pilots (in ways appropriate for local contexts) to enable often silenced voices to be heard.

Making co-creation for social innovation real

The CoSIE pilots reached people affected by public services in ten countries and engaged their participation in a very rich variety of co-creative activities. Many of these participants were from groups often seen as hard to reach and difficult to hear. CoSIE did not specify a standard way of engaging people affected by services in co-creation, and approaches were varied. All the pilots used Community Reporting as discussed in Chapter 7. Here we highlight two means of engagement employed in some but not all of the pilots: outreach activities based on principles of community development; and short, intense facilitated events.

Facilitated events (typically lasting about half a day to two days) adapted principles and methods culled from arts, industrial design and ICT for working together over a short period of intensive activity to generate, explore, prioritise and test early-stage innovative ideas. These were inspired by 'design thinking' for innovation through engagement, dialogue and learning (Liedtka, 2018). In CoSie this approach was deployed in Estonia, Finland and Poland. The participant groups were, respectively, people with disabilities or mental health problems, young people not in education, employment or training, and older residents of a housing estate.

The hackathon (utilised in Finland and Estonia) is a well-established means to facilitate innovation through intensive, fast-paced collaboration, originally by prototyping in the IT sector. The Estonian CoSIE pilot succeeded in adapting this format to mobilise people from different backgrounds in 'social hackathons' around co-defined problems. There was co-creation of some practical solutions (for example, healthier food for schoolchildren). Perhaps more importantly, there was also evidence of movement towards new local contexts where experiments and their spaces are favoured (Kangro and Lepik, 2022). This pilot and others that used methodologies from design thinking report that the fast pace is not suitable for everyone. The roots in commercial, competitive environments occasionally show rather starkly. The pace and language in some of its permutations can seem 'brutal' as, for example, when ideas enthusiastically generated are summarily 'killed'. This aspect, as well as the sheer speed and intensity, can be rather disturbing for people more accustomed to passive roles. However, practical adaptations can be made, for example in the form of welcoming venues, shorter sessions with breaks and, perhaps most of all, supportive, hands-on mentoring. From the perspective of those invited to contribute there is an important message that goes beyond such practicalities, necessary as they are. They must not only be invited to take part, but their contribution must also be seen to make a difference. If it is not, there is risk of cynicism and disillusionment. This came perilously close in the Finnish pilot when the local municipality backtracked on its original intention to implement ideas from young people's hackathons. Fortunately, the university partner and an NGO stepped in to do this. One hackathon participant in Estonia challenged the CoSIE team, "is someone really listening or are they just nodding their heads?" What she meant by this was that people with 'special needs' must not only be invited to take part, but their contributions must also be acted upon.

The pilots in the Netherlands (Nieuwegein) and Hungary used proactive outreach based on community development principles. In Nieuwegein the pilot took place in a neighbourhood consisting of four apartment buildings where residents were beset by many social problems. A multidisciplinary project group decided that 'door-to-door-talks' would be held, with professionals going to each of the homes and having an open conversation about living conditions and quality of life in general. This was initially quite successful. The amount of waste illegally discarded in the neighbourhood emerged from these conversations as a common concern and some practical steps to address it seemed to make a visible difference. Unfortunately, experiments with other activities in co-creation were stopped on the basis that inhabitants' energy for action was lacking and they expected professionals to do the planning and realisation. The project team reflected that not doing, not realising or simply stopping because of lack of energy should also be seen as part of co-creation processes.

In Hungary the pilot was situated in small settlements in rural areas where populations are in decline and household incomes low. It aimed at improving household livelihoods and local economies. Previous projects in rural Hungary had provided support for horticulture and livestock farming but the CoSIE pilot, in contrast, facilitated rural communities to co-design local projects, choosing their own economic activities and sharing their efforts and resources. The local project deliverers were part-time 'coordinators' whose main work roles included social worker, agricultural adviser, coach and lay helper. Coordinators and village mayors organised workshops with the participation of citizens and local stakeholders to discuss how the local families could activate themselves, then participants prepared plans for their activities with the support of the project. Community leaders commented in the early stages of the pilot that people in the villages had grown accustomed to a feeling of helplessness in the face of paternalistic traditions and welfare dependency (Csoba and Sipos, 2022). A key point at which they became convinced about the value of co-creative approaches was the recognition of the innovative potential of participants, that they could bring in ideas that were a better fit for the local context.

Conclusion

This chapter have introduced a Horizon 2020 project dedicated to social innovation through co-creation, and explained the conceptual thinking that underpinned it. Co-creation, we argue, has a moral foundation that goes beyond making services better and more responsive. Moreover, it aligns closely with core principles of social work. Co-creation also has a practical dimension as a driver of innovation. We have briefly reported just one aspect of the CoSIE pilots' implementation. Chapter 6 will look more deeply into the innovations and learning. Despite many enthusiastic supporters, some critics are wary of co-creation and warn of tokenism and failure to acknowledge imbalances of status and power (Dudau et al, 2019). Overall, although there were setbacks and unwanted outcomes, the CoSIE project tends to concur with the more optimistic voices.

Acknowledgement

Susan Baines passed away in 2023, when this chapter was already finished. She was a dedicated social work scholar who will be missed and remembered.

Note

[1] See https://www.cosie-project.eu.

References

Arnstein, S. (1969) A ladder of citizen participation, *Journal of the American Planning Association*, 35(4): 216–24.

Ayling, R. and Cattermole, M. (2010) Practical Approaches to Improving Productivity Through Personalisation in Adult Social Care, Egham: Social Care Institute for Excellence, https://www.puttingpeoplefirst.org.uk/_library/Practical_Approaches_doc.pdf.

Beresford, P. (2008) What future for care?, York: Joseph Rowntree Foundation, https://shapingourlives.org.uk/wp-content/uploads/2021/08/JRFViewpointonCarebyPeterBeresford.pdf.

Bevir, M., Needham, C. and Waring, J. (2019) Inside co-production: ruling, resistance, and practice, *Soc. Policy Admin.* 2019; 53: 197–202.

Bovaird, T. (2007) Beyond engagement and participation: user and community coproduction of public services, *Public Administration Review*, 67(5): 846–60.

Brandsen, T., Steen, T. and Verschuere, B. (2018) Co-creation and co-production in public services: urgent issues in practice and research, in T. Brandsen, T. Steen and B. Verschuere (eds) *Co-production and Co-creation: Definitions and Theoretical Perspectives*, New York: Routledge, pp 3–8.

Chesbrough, H. (2011) *Open Services Innovation: Rethinking Your Business to Grow and Compete in a New Era*, New York: Wiley.

Claassen, R. (2016) *Capabilities in a Just Society: A Theory of Navigational Agency*, Cambridge: Cambridge University Press.

Claassen, R. and Düwell, M. (2013) The foundations of capability theory: comparing Nussbaum and Gewirth, *Ethical Theory and Moral Practice*, 16(3): 493–510.

Cottam, H. (2018) *Radical Help: How We Can Remake the Relationships Between Us and Revolutionise the Welfare State*, London: Virago.

Csoba, J. and Sipos, F. (2022) Politically-driven public administration or co-creation? On the possibility of modernizing public services in rural Hungary, *Public Money & Management*, 42(5): 314–22.

Curley, M. (2016) Twelve principles for Open Innovation 2.0, *Nature*, 533(7603): 314–16.

DHSC (2023) *Care and Support Statutory Guidance*, London: Department of Health and Social Care.

Dudau, A., Glennon, R. and Verschuere, B. (2019) Following the yellow brick road? (Dis)enchantment with co-design, co-production and value co-creation in public services, *Public Management Review*, 21(11): 1577–94.

EESC (European Economic and Social Committee) (2022) Co-creation of services of general interest as a contribution to a more participative democracy in the EU, EESC, https://www.eesc.europa.eu/en/our-work/opinions-information-reports/opinions/co-creation-services-general-interest-contribution-more-participative-democracy-eu.

Evers, A. and Brandsen, T. (2016) Social innovations as messages: democratic experimentation in local welfare systems, in T. Bransden, S. Cattacin, A. Evers and A. Zimmer (eds) *Social Innovations in the Urban Context*, Cham: Springer, pp 161–80.

Fox, A. (2018) *A New Health and Care System: Escaping the Invisible Asylum*, Bristol: Policy Press.

Fox, C., Baines, S., Wilson, R., Jalonen, H., Aflaki, I., Prandini, R., et al (2021) A New Agenda for Co-creating Public Services, Turku: Turku University of Applied Sciences, https://julkaisut.turkuamk.fi/isbn9789522167842.pdf.

Gewirth, A. (1978) *Reason and Morality*, Chicago: University of Chicago Press.

Gewirth, A. (1996) *Community of Rights*, Chicago: University of Chicago Press.

Glasby, J., Le Grand, J. and Duffy, S. (2009) A healthy choice? Direct payments and healthcare in the English NHS, *Policy & Politics*, 37(4): 481–97.

Gray, M. (2011) Back to basics: a critique of the strengths perspective in social work, *Families in Society*, 92(1): 5–11.

Hartley, J. (2014) Eight and a half propositions to stimulate frugal innovation, *Public Money & Management*, 34(3): 227–32.

Hood, C. (1991) A public management for all seasons?, *Public Administration*, 69(3): 3–19.

Hood, C. (1998) *The Art of the State: Culture, Rhetoric and Public Management*, Oxford: Clarendon Press.

Hutton, C. and Waters, J. (2009) *Evaluation: In Control's Second Phase*, London: In Control.

IFSW and IASSW (International Federation of Social Workers and International Association of Schools of Social Work) (2014) International definition of social work, International Federation of Social Workers, July, https://www.ifsw.org/what-is-social-work/global-definition-of-social-work/.

Kangro, K. and Lepik, K.L. (2022) Co-creating public services in social hackathons: adapting the original hackathon concept, *Public Money & Management*, 42(5): 341–8.

Leadbeater, C. (2004) *Personalisation through Participation: A New Script for Public Services*, London: Demos.

Liedtka, J. (2018) Why design thinking works, *Harvard Business Review*, 2018(09/10): 72–9.

Moulaert, F. and MacCallum, D. (2019) *Advanced Introduction to Social Innovation*, Cheltenham: Edward Elgar.

Nussbaum, M.C. (1988) Nature, function and capability: Aristotle on political distribution, in J. Annas and R.H. Grimm (eds) *Oxford Studies in Ancient Philosophy: Supplementary Volume*, Oxford: Oxford University Press, pp 145–84.

Oosterlynck, S., Novy, A. and Kazepov, Y. (eds) (2019) *Local Social Innovation to Combat Poverty and Exclusion: A Critical Appraisal*, Bristol: Policy Press.

Osborne, S.P. (2006) The new public governance?, *Public Management Review*, 8(3): 377–87.

Osborne, S.P. (2010) Introduction: the (new) public governance: a suitable case for treatment?, in S.P. Osborne (ed) *The New Public Governance? Emerging Perspectives on the Theory and Practice of Public Governance*, Abingdon: Routledge, pp 1–16.

Osborne, S.P. (2018) From public service-dominant logic to public service logic: are public service organizations capable of co-production and value co-creation? *Public Management Review*, 20(2): 225–31.

Osborne, S.P., Radnor, Z. and Strokosch, K. (2016) Co-production and the co-creation of value in public services: a suitable case for treatment?, *Public Management Review*, 18(5): 639–53.

Osborne, S. and Strokosch, K. (2013) It takes two to tango? Understanding the co-production of public services by integrating the services management and public administration perspectives, *British Journal of Management*, 24: S31–47.

Oughton, E. and Wheelock, J. (2003) A capabilities approach to sustainable household livelihoods, *Review of Social Economy*, 61(1): 1–22.

Price, A., Ahuja, L., Bramwell, C., Briscoe, S., Shaw, L. and Nunns, M. (2020) Research Evidence on Different Strengths-Based Approaches Within Adult Social Work: A Systematic Review, Health Services and Delivery Research Topic Report, Southampton: National Institute of Health Research, https://njl-admin.nihr.ac.uk/document/download/2034194.

Rummery, K. (2006) Disabled citizens and social exclusion: the role of direct payments, *Policy and Politics*, 34(4): 633–50.

Sakellariou, A. (2018) *Rapid Evidence Appraisal of the Current State of Co-creation in Ten European Countries*, Turku: Turku University of Applied Sciences, https://storage.googleapis.com/turku-amk/2019/04/rapid-evidence-appraisal-of.pdf.

Sen, A. (1990) Development as capability expansion, in K. Griffin and J. Knight (eds) *Human Development and the International Development Strategy for the 1990s*, London: Palgrave Macmillan, pp 41–58.

Sen, A. (2009) *The Idea of Justice*, London: Allen Lane.

Slay, J. (2011) Budgets and Beyond: Interim Report, London: New Economics Foundation, https://www.scie.org.uk/publications/misc/budgetsandbeyond.pdf.

Steen, T., Brandsen, T. and Verschuere, B. (2018) The dark side of co-creation and co-production: seven evils, in T. Brandsen, T. Steen and B. Verschuere (eds) *Co-production and Co-creation: Definitions and Theoretical Perspectives*, New York: Routledge, pp 284–93.

Strokosch, K. and Osborne, S.P. (2018) Literature Review on Public Service Reform Models, Co-VAL Project Reference No. 770356, Deliverable D1.1, https://www.co-val.eu/download/933/.

Strokosch, K. and Osborne, S.P. (2020) Co-experience, coproduction and co-governance: an ecosystem approach to the analysis of value creation, *Policy & Politics*, 48(3): 425–42.

Timonen, V. and Lolich, L. (2021) SoCaTel White Paper, Project Deliverable D.7.3, https://ec.europa.eu/research/participants/documents/downloadPublic?documentIds=080166e5d8be332f&appId=PPGMS.

Torfing, J., Sørensen, E. and Røiseland, A. (2019) Transforming the public sector into an arena for co-creation: barriers, drivers, benefits, and ways forward, *Administration & Society*, 51(5): 795–825.

Voorberg, W.H., Bekkers, V.J.J.M. and Tummers, L.G. (2015) A systematic review of co-creation and co-production: embarking on the social innovation journey, *Public Management Review*, 17(9): 1333–57.

Wilson, R., Cornwell, C., Flanagan, E., Nielsen, N. and Khan, H. (2018) *Good and Bad Help: How Purpose and Confidence Transform Lives*, London: NESTA.

6

Promoting social services innovation: regional and local examples from across Europe

Alfonso Lara-Montero

Introduction

Theories of social innovation point to a new way of addressing a social problem that should be both transferable and sustainable. But how is social innovation promoted and implemented in social services? There are two significant approaches. The first set of innovations refers to innovations in social work, such as social services outreach and coordination with employment services for people farthest from the labour market or integrated services for vulnerable families. The second relates to investments in new models of social care that promote an overarching community and home-based approach particularly underpinned by technology. The purpose of this chapter is to describe a number of social services innovations covering both approaches based on preliminary analysis and identification of innovative social services programmes of public authorities who are members of the European Social Network (ESN). This methodology aided in developing patterns of innovation in social services, which could help identify areas for future investment. ESN is an independent network of 172 public organisations in 35 countries covering all areas of social care, social services and social work.

There are some good examples of innovative models of social services that support children and adults. However, a key challenge is to scale up these primarily small-scale successes so that as many people benefit from them as possible. Governments should be looking beyond funding to broader questions about how to develop high-quality, community-based and sustainable social services. Innovations cannot be restricted to pilot projects, instead they should be shared more effectively, adopted more widely and implemented more rapidly.

This chapter argues that innovation in social services encompasses both investments in social work including service outreach and coordination for labour and social inclusion as well as new models of social care that promote an overarching community and home-based approach underpinned by technology and digital aids. While encouraging these innovations remains important, the greater problem facing the sector is finding ways to bring to scale new models of care and support, which have been proven to work. This is at the core of driving change, not just in pockets and for the few, but across the whole of Europe.

Defining social services innovation

The modernisation of public social services is placing an increasing emphasis on innovation and evidence. At the level of service management and provision, accountable and regulated services mean ensuring that practice is based on evidence in addition to professional judgement. The imperative to spend public money efficiently is increasingly higher while at a political level, there is – at least in theory – a focus on service reform increasingly based on effectiveness rather than on a political agenda. At EU level, the European Commission has acknowledged the potential of innovation and evidence for promoting effective social interventions.

The term 'social innovation' has several definitions. For instance, the European Commission has defined social innovation as 'the development and implementation of new ideas (products, services and models) to meet social needs and create new social relationships or collaborations' (European Commission, 2020: 6). But how can we define 'social services innovation'?

There is no clear definition, but within the ESN we have had several focus groups with our members who represent social services directors and have highlighted that social services innovation should cover the three approaches of social innovation at European level, that is to say, it is directed towards vulnerable populations, addresses social challenges, and investigates systemic change. In addition, social services innovation is unique because it must encompass at least two key approaches; a set of innovations in social work aimed at promoting social inclusion, and a second set of innovations related to new models of care that promote personal autonomy (in most cases underpinned by technology).

When one opens a newspaper or tunes in to broadcast media, if the focus is on public social services, the chances are that one may come across terms like 'postcode lottery', which tends to be used negatively to refer to variation in the provision of social services, which are usually seen as a local matter (LGA, nd). Indeed, many would argue that many national programmes start from best practice at local level. However, public opinion objects to the idea of social services not being the same in different areas of one country (OECD, 2022). These objections may add to concerns about unfairness in the provision of social services across regions. Therefore, policy makers need to find a balance between national standards and local needs and wishes. Thus, for social services to be considered innovative they need to fulfil a number of criteria related to appropriateness, novelty and impact, but also how relevant they are for their local context and how transferable to a context beyond their boundaries. The combination of these factors makes a difference when compared to previous practice.

The innovative element of a social services programme should be first studied by measuring the necessity, opportunity and urgency of the specific social problem upon which it is sought to intervene (appropriateness; see Oeij et al, 2019), which in turn should be based on data (evidence). These data should be relevant and useful for improving the chances of a social services programme producing good outcomes for users and an efficient use of public money (OECD, 2014).

Social innovation also needs to include a novelty element and have the purpose to generate social benefits (Krasadakis, 2020), which links with the dimension of appropriateness. In addition, as already highlighted, an innovative practice needs to make a difference based on its possible scope on the target population, the social risks and sectors it wants to address.

Finally, an innovative social services programme needs to measure its impact, as this will allow social policy to move forward towards a more effective social welfare provision. For instance, a social practice needs to be able to prove a degree of improvement that may go from an organisational level to a financial or services level (McKinsey, 2019). In addition, it should demonstrate a degree of improvement in final outcomes (whether these are related to health improvement, preventing social problems or improving the educational level of a target group). In order for this to be properly measured, programmes need to include a number of indicators to be measured through specific evaluation mechanisms.

Key concepts in social services innovation

In the current socio-economic context, we have been witnessing how short- and long-term social demands have been growing, while there have been considerable budgetary constraints. At the same time, these social challenges may represent new growth sectors alongside acknowledgement of the need for a smart, green and inclusive growth within the EU 2020 Strategy and for socially fair green and digital transitions (Digital Europe; European Commission, 2023) in the framework of the post–COVID-19 recovery, which are also opportunities for public social services development.

Social services as a sector are committed to social change and development. In light of constantly changing and evolving social problems, social services regularly need to put in place new and novel approaches to address societal needs. Social services address the challenges brought about by new social problems and the needs of the populations with whom they work as part of their commitment to a more participatory and inclusive society. But they should also do this based on the opportunities offered by new empirical and scientific findings.

Concepts related to innovation in social services include experimentation to help in making more informed decisions about a programme, the use of data towards achieving social good and sustainable change, the relevance of an innovative programme for the professionals and the populations for whom the programme was designed, and whether the programme can be transferred beyond its specific implementation context. These concepts are discussed next.

Experimentation

A concept very much related to that of social innovation is 'social experimentation'. The European Commission defines social experimentation as 'a policy intervention that aims to provide an innovative response to social needs, implemented on a small scale and in conditions that enable its impact to be measured, prior to being implemented in other contexts including geographical and sectoral ones, or implemented on a larger scale, if the results prove to be positive' (European Commission, 2022a: 13). The result is the formulation of policy and practice based on evidence. These 'experiments' involve:

- bringing innovative answers to social needs;
- small-scale probing interventions;
- being made in conditions where their impact can be measured, for example by having a pre/post analysis, or through randomised controlled trials[1];
- being scaled up if the results prove convincing.

Data on what works (effectiveness)

As already highlighted, the appropriateness of an intervention should be based on data, which in turn should be relevant and useful for increasing the chances of an improvement in people's outcomes, which in social inclusion is measured in improving people's quality of life including their social and emotional well-being and degree of social inclusion. Data on what works (or effectiveness) is considered key in producing good evidence when innovating in the public sector (What Works Network, 2014).

Relevance

When it comes to looking for evidence of what works, policy makers and public services directors need to consider whether the programme evaluation is relevant. Elaborating on this question, outcomes are relevant depending on a particular population group and context, so evidence should identify 'what works, for whom, in what circumstances and why' (Pawson and Tilley, 1997).

Transferability

Scaling-up and transferability is another important criterion in assessing whether a programme is relevant and of good quality. This is particularly important for a European organisation like ESN, which regularly assesses practice examples and their potential implementation across borders, and also for the use of evidence by European institutions and the design of programmes under the European Structural and Investment Funds (European Commission, 2022b).

Social services innovations promoting social inclusion

The primary function of social work is to enhance people's well-being and inclusion (NASW, 2021). There is a set of innovations in social services, which are mostly related to the mission of social work. Innovation in social work has been defined as the implementation by social work professionals of actions, services or products that are novel in the context in which they are used and aim at fulfilling social needs or improving the performance of organisations responsible for addressing social needs (CGTS, 2022). This definition implies actions and the creation of tangible programmes or products that can be perceived as such by people using social services or by professionals working in social services agencies. This means that the concept of social innovation excludes the mere generation of ideas, formulation of purpose or declarations of intent. While ideas, purpose or intent are fundamental in the process of generating innovation, unless they translate into a tangible product or programme they cannot be considered as social work innovation.

However, innovating does not necessarily mean creating an actual new product, and sometimes rescuing old procedures and adapting them to new contexts is enough to be considered a social innovation (Alonso, 2016). Therefore, to determine the degree of novelty of a social services programme, it is necessary to assess it within the context in which it takes place. For example, the Housing First programme is an alternative to the traditional model of intervention with people in homelessness situations and while it first emerged in the US in 1992 as a local social innovation, it has now become an international evidence-based programme. However, if the programme is first implemented in a certain country, it becomes an innovative social service in that particular country.

Finally, social services innovation promoting social inclusion implies the implementation of innovative actions that are made available and accessible to users of social services and professionals alike. The design, prototyping and development of services and programmes must be accompanied by implementation and this is because the key focus is to address social needs and significantly improve the lives of people for whom these services were created. Improvement is very much related to the concept of efficiency and effectiveness. However, the concept of effectiveness in social services must be differentiated from innovation in other sectors, like business, where the performance improvement focus is very much linked to generating economic capital gains. This is obviously not the case in social services innovation where the primary aim is to fulfilling social needs and improving people's lives. However, making economic gains through more effective public spending has also become an objective of social services innovation (ESN, 2016).

The next sections include four local innovative social services programmes, which have been evaluated through a randomised controlled trial to establish if the evidence resulting from the experimentation programme showed positive outcomes of what works, for whom and in what circumstances; as well as their potential transferability to policy and another geographical context.

Enhancing the Right to Social Inclusion Through Service Integration (ERSISI)

This project (Gobierno de Navarra, 2020), funded with EU funding for social innovation, intended to improve the labour market integration and social inclusion of people farthest from the labour market through improved coordination between public administrations responsible for managing benefits, employment and social services. The ERSISI project did this through a social policy experiment in the Region of Navarra (Spain), a member of the ESN. The experiment consisted of a new support model for unemployed people who were farthest from the labour market, particularly minimum income beneficiaries. They selected randomly 500 unemployed persons on benefits who were provided with a tailored programme of support implemented by two case managers, one from employment and one from social services.

The programme was implemented in four municipalities and the results of the 500-intervention group were compared with standard support for the control group. The individualised package of support combined with personalised counselling for the intervention group showed positive results after the programme came to an end and was evaluated. After the intervention finished, most participants continued with their social inclusion pathway and did not drop out when compared with the control group (Grupo Alter, 2021).

Likewise, ERSISI contributed to breaking down barriers between social and employment services with improved cooperation materialising in jointly designed individualised intervention plans agreed with the beneficiaries, and the integration of the perspectives and resources of both professional profiles and services. The coordinated delivery of employment and social services produces better results for people in situations of social exclusion or vulnerability compared with standard separated services delivery. The combination of financial benefits with coordinated individualised support and counselling and the implication of participants in deciding their integration pathways impacts positively their continuation in those pathways.

The project team also developed a transferability model (Grupo Alter, 2021), which consists of putting in place the necessary measures so that the assessment and monitoring of unemployed persons who are minimum income beneficiaries is implemented through a joint team of employment and social services professionals. For this, a specific policy guideline and app were developed.

This is very much linked to a third social innovation aspect: sustainability. The app is ready to use in all social services offices and it is interoperable with the app and software used by employment agencies. Therefore, it should strengthen coordination between social services and employment services, as it allows sharing individual files (needs assessments, individual plans, and evaluations) for the purpose of putting in place joint interventions. Likewise, a training programme was developed for staff of both services. The regional government agreed to introduce the new model into its policies so that it can be extended to all the region's municipalities.

Mobile Integrated Social Services (MISSION)

Also aimed at addressing fragmentation in social services delivery, this project[2] was developed to increase the take-up of social services by families in vulnerable situations as it was felt that the large number of uncoordinated providers was preventing families from accessing services effectively.

The ESN was partner to this project developed by the city of Kortrijk (Belgium). MISSION was a new method of outreach case management, which included the creation of a new professional figure (the case manager), a digital tool for the integrated delivery of a wide range of supports and services for disadvantaged families, and the creation of a stakeholder platform to integrate the city's social services providers. The effectiveness of this integrated service delivery programme was tested through a randomised controlled trial of families who received minimum income.

After six months, initial results showed that this newly designed method of outreach support had a causal impact on the take-up and receipt of additional financial support by disadvantaged families with young children. These results also pointed out that the method is effective in increasing the share of families taking part in employment and training programmes.

As the work of outreach case managers with families intensify, the more effective they are in helping families increase their take-up of public support. However, the six months were not enough to identify structural changes in income, housing or families' living conditions. This is because there are several external conditions which impact directly the results of the programme. For instance, accessing and remaining in childcare may not be felt in several months, while accessing benefits is regulated by federal law. There are also a number of social services regulated by regional law and therefore out of the scope of local authorities' social services.

Looking at transferability and sustainability, MISSION generated opportunities for policy improvements, which have translated into policy planning for the 2020–25 policy period. For instance, the local anti-poverty plan is based at least on one of the principles of the MISSION experiment: focus on outreach work.

There has been significant interest in MISSION's outreach case work by other public centres for social welfare in local authorities in Flanders. To this purpose, the project team produced a 'how-to' manual in Flemish. The digital tool that the project generated, SIEN, also attracted interest in social welfare centres in Flanders. The Flemish government is developing, at the time of writing, a new policy to implement the concept of 'family coaches', which is based on the results of the MISSION programme and to which the MISSION team has been invited to contribute, drawing on the programme development and results.

Social services innovation promoting personal autonomy

There is a second set of innovations in social services which are mostly related to the improvement of people's quality of life through the promotion of their personal autonomy and empowerment. These innovations may be found in person-centred service design, social services commissioning with external providers, and social services delivery. But an increasingly relevant aspect is that they are progressively being underpinned by technological innovation to help people live independent lives in their own homes and communities.

Building data and digital capacity are key aspects of care innovation, as it is collaboration between professionals and organisations. Inclusive technological innovation in social care is crucial to develop and maintain the ability to control, cope and make decisions about how someone with support needs may live according to their own wishes and to help them implement their daily activities (I-Social Foundation, 2022).

Today there are many technology solutions that support people with care needs live a more autonomous life. Assisted technologies, such as electronic devices or gadgets connected to computers, smartphones or detection devices help people improve their physical, social or emotional well-being (ESN, 2021). Examples of these technologies may include social robotics that accompany older people who live alone, movement or falls sensors, and remote keys that issue warnings to social services, as well as the use of artificial intelligence (AI) to collect and use data for decision-making.

Robots fighting unwanted loneliness

Around 350,000 people over 65 currently live in the city of Barcelona (Spain), 90,000 of them on their own. Studies conducted by Barcelona city council themselves show that 90 per cent of these people want to live in their own homes for as long as possible before going to live in a nursing home or with relatives (Ayuntamiento de Barcelona, 2019). Likewise, the offer of nursing homes is limited, with just 13,000 places and a waiting list of 6,000 people, which translates to an average of three years to be able to get a place. In the meantime, more than 100,000 people need help with daily activities, of whom around 40,000 receive home care service or have a recognised family carer. Currently, people who are supported in their own homes receive an average of one hour of home care service per working day, but needs may be up to 18 hours a day (M4Social, 2022).

Therefore, the city's social services developed a robot prototype called ARI,[3] which complements the home care services that a person might be receiving and introduces adaptable AI elements according to each person's specific data held by social services.

Some of the things ARI can help with include quickly identifying sudden emergencies, such as falls and household accidents, asking for and controlling medication, or reminding people of medical visits. ARI can speak different languages, distinguish the tone of voice and personalise the user's name. The conversations that the robot is capable of holding include the possibility to discuss symptoms to be able to make pre-diagnoses, such as the quality of the person's sleep, medication or questions about the past to strengthen the person's memory.

ARI has an autonomy of eight hours and can get around every part of the home, monitor a user, identify and avoid obstacles, and act on facial and voice recognition. It has a significant capacity to be able to interact with people and can be integrated with other applications (M4Social, 2022). The initial project is now being extended to 100 homes for the next three years to consolidate the results of the initial pilot that covered ten homes and explore the possibility of introducing it into a wider range of solutions offered by social services. For instance, the council is exploring its transferability to supporting social and education services with children in preventing abuse or promoting well-being.[4]

Effective Preventive Care Supported by Artificial Intelligence

ESN member, the care department of the city of Helsingborg (Sweden) linked up with a local technology provider to implement a new tool[5] that translates the international classification of functional abilities into needs for resources from home care staff, nurses and rehabilitation staff. The model also categorises patients in target groups in both home care and nursing homes. An AI algorithm was developed to come up with possible trends in combination with the categories of functional needs and population groups. The tool is used as an intuitive interface for a continuous use of data to be able to predict trends, identify people who could be supported differently, and evaluate the support provided.[6]

The tool has had several effects. It helps staff to target individuals with the greatest potential for improvement as they did not have the means to select these individuals effectively before. Thanks to the regular use of AI, the tool allows for an ongoing evaluation of the results of its use. By using the tool, staff can identify trends sooner and ensure that people can access services at an earlier stage. This improves people's quality of life and saves municipal resources as they can intervene earlier and reach a larger number of people. Professionals are supported by the tool to make regular selections and forecasts concerning the persons they work with, including finding and selecting individuals for preventive measures, evaluating the impact of specific programmes, and learning about potential trends concerning the individuals they support.

Actual examples involving the use of this tool may include a proposal to implement a more thorough programme with older people supported in their own homes. A second example may involve supporting people with cognitive impairments. As the tool holds regular data about this population, it may advise a course of action when the early signs have been identified in someone. A third case may involve people who are supported by mainstream healthcare. Thanks to the data the system holds, it may flag concerns related to people who may not have requested home support but may have higher needs for support to be able to perform their daily activities effectively.

Conclusion

Scaling up innovative successful social services programmes is a crucial component of systemic change, whether related to social inclusion models underpinned by cooperation across sectors, or to new models of care promoting personal autonomy. Scaling up may be an increase in quantity, whether the number of sites or beneficiaries served, as well as in quality, ensuring that later iterations of the programme continuing to provide similar or improved benefits to participants.

Based on the evidence gathered and the assessed examples, we can make proposals for decision-makers about investments to continue advancing effective social services innovation, particularly in areas related to social inclusion and new models of person-centred care and support as well as how to scale them up to sustain their benefits in the longer terms.

Old-fashioned performance management and contracting systems are designed to manage the old models of care and support, not to incentivise new ones. They are institutionally based, rather than focused on people, their life pathways or local contexts. Therefore, they reinforce silos. For instance, current contracting arrangements across social care and social services promote perverse incentives as they prioritise treatment instead of prevention, and reward activity rather than outcomes.

Financial pressures may make it difficult for public authorities to fund new, innovative services while they deliver high-quality statutory services. This is where EU funding can be an enabling factor. Innovators may be able to access early-stage investment or grant funding to develop and test their early ideas, but it can be difficult to secure funding to grow and to be able to sustain their programmes in the long term. This is where new funding ideas such as linking innovation funds with structural funds is key. Likewise, when a research institute or a government body designs a social services programme as an evidence-based practice, it can quickly move up the scale, for instance due to funding availability.

However, scaling up innovative social services programmes is not just a question of money. As highlighted earlier, it implies gathering the findings about a programme to determine whether it is effective in supporting the populations for whom it was designed so that it can be transferred beyond its implementation context and possibly be sustained from practice to policy.

Across all programmes assessed, a common factor involves breaking down silos across sectors. This could take the form of professionals from two or more sectors jointly designing programmes that integrate the perspectives and resources from practitioners in both sectors and promote the provision of coordinated social services delivery. This process should be supported by investments in technological innovation to improve interoperability and data sharing to help build patterns and trends in a more effective manner. Collaborations across professionals, sectors and different types of partnerships between organisations can speed and expand the spread of effective social services programmes. Collaboration is one pathway to bring programmes to scale, but there are others, like transferring an effective programme beyond its implementation context or replicating it somewhere else with the aim of reaching more sites and benefiting more people. In all these, it is important to keep in mind the fidelity of the programme while accounting for local characteristics, ensuring that implementation is supported by guidance, while the programme is adapted as it is being implemented.

The use of technology and digital tools can also increase the number of people reached by the organisation (scaling at breadth) by tapping into new resources, creating synergies and networks, improving organisational efficiency, increasing its visibility, designing new access channels to beneficiaries and improving their outreach. Investing in user-friendly digital tools, with simple and intuitive menus and allowing immediate and regular feedback from people themselves, can certainly help the scaling-up process. Social services should take advantage of the great opportunities of digital transformation to advance community social work, promote social participation, implement new neighbouring approaches for social inclusion and new models of person-centred and community-based care.

This is certainly linked with a need to review and redefine social services portfolios to integrate innovations in social services delivery as well as new professional roles, in particular regarding the use of digital tools, whether decision-making, remote monitoring or social robotics. This implies the need to put in place the necessary professional training, including within university degrees, to increase the awareness of social services professionals towards innovative social services delivery and digitalisation. Lastly, barriers, facilitators and scaling up processes can be rather similar across social services. Hence a coordinated system of resources is useful in linking together social services leaders who are willing to scale up their programmes.

Notes

1. Randomised control trials are an experiment carried out on two or more groups where participants are randomly assigned to either an intervention group (also called a 'treatment' group) who are given the intervention, or a control group who are not. The introduction of a randomly assigned control group enables comparing the effectiveness of the new intervention against what would have happened had you changed nothing. Such trials are considered the most rigorous way of establishing if evidence resulting from an experiment shows that the outcomes have been caused by the programme or intervention (NESTA, 2016).
2. For further information on this project, please visit the official page: https://www.kortrijk.be/mission and https://missionprojectsite.wordpress.com/
3. For more information on the robot ARI, please visit: https://www.soledades.es/recursos/ari-asistente-robotico-inteligente
4. Luis Torrens, former innovation director at the department for social rights in Barcelona city council, outlined these plans at a session at the 2022 World Mobile Congress where I was also a speaker.
5. For further information on this tool, please visit the official website: https://innovation.helsingborg.se/initiativ/hogre-precision-i-insatserna-med-hjalp-av-ai/
6. The information related to this practice has been retrieved from records held at the ESN in relation to their application to the 2022 edition of the European Social Services Awards, for which they applied in the technology category.

References

Alonso, D. (2016) Trabajo social y tecnología: aceptación y uso entre profesores en formación, doctoral thesis, Madrid: Universidad Complutense de Madrid, https://eprints.ucm.es/id/eprint/36975/1/T37007.pdf.

Ayuntamiento de Barcelona (2019) Garantizar el envejecimiento activo de la población, https://ajuntament.barcelona.cat/personesgrans/es/canal/envelliment-actiu.

CGTS (Consejo General del Trabajo Social) (2022) Innovación Social y Trabajo Social, Madrid: Consejo General del Trabajo Social, https://www.cgtrabajosocial.es/files/637f447d88a95/LIBRO_INNOVACION_SOCIAL_final.pdf.

ESN (European Social Network) (2016) *Evidence-Based Social Services: Toolkit for Planning and Evaluating Social Services*, Brighton: European Social Network, https://www.esn-eu.org/sites/default/files/publications/ResearchandEvidence_Report__FINAL_1pag.pdf.

ESN (European Social Network) (2021) *Transforming Social Services Through Digitalisation*, Brussels: European Social Network, https://www.esn-eu.org/publications/transforming-social-services-through-digitalisation.

European Commission (2020) *Social Innovation: Inspirational Practices Supporting People Throughout Their Lives*, Luxembourg: Publications Office of the European Union, https://op.europa.eu/en/publication-detail/-/publication/e33b37ad-3b60-11eb-b27b-01aa75ed71a1/language-en.

European Commission (2022a) *Social Experimentation: A Practical Guide for Project Promoters*, Brussels: European Commission.

European Commission (2022b) *Scaling Up Social Innovation Toolkit: Seven Steps for Using ESF+*, Luxembourg: Publications Office of the European Union, https://op.europa.eu/en/publication-detail/-/publication/1f092971-e08c-11ec-a534-01aa75ed71a1/language-en.

European Commission (2023) Digital Europe Programme, European Commission, Shaping Europe's Digital Future, 7 November, https://digital-strategy.ec.europa.eu/en/activities/digital-programme.

Gobierno de Navarra (2020) Claves y Resultados del Modelo de Atención Integrada de ERSISI, Pamplona: ERSISI, https://ersisi.navarra.es/documents/5014040/0/1-Claves-resultados-modelo-atencion-integrada-ERSISI-EN.pdf.

Grupo Alter, Universidad Pública de Navarra (2021) Resultados de la evaluación de impacto del proyecto ERSISI: actualización a doce meses de finalizada la intervención, Pamplona: ERSISI, https://ersisi.navarra.es/documents/5014040/0/Informe+ERSISI+2021.pdf/8e13c395-0b4c-4e67-019c-812bc641d973?t=1639120452212.

I-Social Foundation (2022) Innovación tecnológica y servicios sociales, November, Barcelona: Fundación iSocial, https://isocial.cat/es/formulario-innovacion-tecnologica-y-servicios-sociales/.

Krasadakis, G. (2020) The importance of novelty for innovation, Medium, 17 May, https://medium.com/innovation-machine/how-important-is-novelty-for-innovation-f29ecf665a2b.

LGA (Local Government Association) (nd) Towards a sustainable adult social care and support system, Local Government Association, https://www.local.gov.uk/about/campaigns/lives-we-want-lead-lga-green-paper-adult-social-care/towards-sustainable-adult-0.

M4Social (2022) ARI II: el nuevo robot social ARI para la atención a las personas mayores, M4Social, 13 April, https://m4social.org/es/ari-ii-el-nuevo-robot-social-ari-para-la-atencion-a-las-personas-mayores/.

McKinsey (2019) How continuous improvement can build a competitive edge, McKinsey & Company, 6 May, https://www.mckinsey.com/capabilities/people-and-organizational-performance/our-insights/the-organization-blog/how-continuous-improvement-can-build-a-competitive-edge.

NASW (National Association of Social Workers) (2021) *Code of Ethics*, Washington DC: National Association of Social Workers, https://www.socialworkers.org/About/Ethics/Code-of-Ethics/Code-of-Ethics-English.

NESTA (2016) *Running Randomised Controlled Trials in Innovation, Entrepreneurship and Growth: An Introductory Guide*, London: NESTA, https://media.nesta.org.uk/documents/a_guide_to_rcts_-_igl_09aKzWa.pdf.

OECD (Organisation for Economic Co-operation and Development) (2014) *Effective Public Investment Across Levels of Government*, Paris: OECD Publishing, https://www.oecd.org/regional/regional-policy/Principles-Public-Investment.pdf.

OECD (Organisation for Economic Co-operation and Development) (2022) *Modernising Social Services in Spain: Designing a New National Framework*, Paris: OECD Publishing, https://doi.org/10.1787/4add887d-en.

Oeij, P.R.A., van der Torre, W., Vaas, F. and Dhondt, S. (2019) Understanding social innovation as an innovation process: applying the innovation journey model, *Journal of Business Research*, 101: 243–54.

Pawson, R. and Tilley, N. (1997) An introduction to scientific realist evaluation, in E. Chelimsky and W.R. Shadish (eds) *Evaluation for the 21st Century: A Handbook*, Thousand Oaks, CA: Sage, pp 405–18.

What Works Network (2014) What Works? Evidence for Decision Makers, GOV.UK, 25 November, https://assets.publishing.service.gov.uk/media/5a824271e5274a2e87dc1fcf/What_works_evidence_for_decision_makers_update_2018_01_12.pdf.

7

Co-creation in action: lessons from the CoSIE project

Sandra Geelhoed and Eva Heijmans

Introduction

In Chapter 5, Chris Fox and Susan Baines described the Co-creation of Service Innovation in Europe (CoSIE) project as an innovative agenda for co-creating public services. The aim was to develop more effective services in the public and social arena developed with service users and all other involved stakeholders such as social workers, policy makers and service leaders. In the project we experimented with different co-creation instruments in ten European countries. Pilots were aimed at – among others – forensic social work and probation, improvement of care services for people with disabilities (Sweden) and development of new services for disabled persons in remote areas (Estonia). Other pilots concerned young people and participation (Finland) or children and healthcare (Italy).

This chapter highlights co-creation as a value-led practice and describes the lessons learned from implementing values of co-creation in public service innovation. It starts by considering the merits of co-creation in a social work setting, followed by a description of the most important underlying values of co-creation. Through the CoSIE Roadmap to Co-creation (CoSIE Consortium, 2020d) we will show how to start and negotiate a way through a co-creation process. The tools and instruments that were used supporting this process, such as community reporting, living lab, digitalisation and social hackathon will be presented. Each instrument will be described and illustrated 'in action', through examples from different CoSIE pilots.

Co-creation as a value-led practice

What is co-creation in the setting of innovating public services? As defined in Chapter 5, co-creation is 'a collaborative activity that reduces power imbalances and aims to enrich and enhance the value in public service offerings' (Fox et al, 2021: 8). In practice, this means that service providers, citizens and other stakeholders work together with the aim of enhancing the value in public service offerings (Brandsen et al., 2018). Value may be understood in terms of increased well-being and shared visions for the common good that lead to more inclusive policies, strategies, regulatory frameworks, and services. Co-creation is explicitly not consultation of citizens or service users, nor is it a step-by-step approach to service design. It must be seen as a collaborative and value-led process (CoSIE Consortium, 2020a). The underlying values that enhance collaboration and through that, co-creation, are equal participation of all parties and working in mutual respect and trust. Awareness of existing power imbalances with the intention of reducing them is essential as power imbalance is destructive to truthful co-creation. The involvement of all stakeholders is asset-based, building on capabilities and not on deficits or problems. Empathetic listening is a key skill. Co-creation asks full commitment of all to the common journey, on the why and how of co-creation in the context of service innovation.

For these values to be put into practice in public service settings, a change in professional culture is needed, based on the attitude and skills of the reflective practitioner (Argyris and Schön, 1974; Bakker-Klein, 2019). The values lead the way in what is 'the right decision' in the process of co-creation. In the next section, the complexity of this journey in the context of public service innovation will be illustrated and the values already mentioned, and their supporting operational skills, will be elaborated upon.

Changing working routines and professional behaviour

Professionals, policy makers and politicians often work in defined hierarchical roles. Many public services are organised following the strategies of New Public Management and New Public Governance (Fox and Baines, Chapter 5 in this book). Public professionals focus on planning and control, budget and finance, and objectives and targets. Citizens depending on a public service are considered end users. This way of organising and the professional attitude coming forth from this perspective cannot lead to co-creation since it obstructs equal working relationships. A more collaborative behaviour is needed instead.

The value of equality is an essential condition to realise co-creative projects related to public service innovation. All stakeholders have an equal say in the design of the service. Not equal as in 'the same', but equal as appreciating the value of everyone's contribution regardless of their role or status in the project or society. Practising equality within a co-creation process starts with the awareness of power dynamics and power differences. Understanding that professional surroundings and habits might be intimidating to service users and a hindrance to the free contribution of ideas and opinions, is necessary. Being a good listener and having an empathetic understanding of the broader social context and the wider needs of people who depend on the service are also indispensable professional competencies.

How difficult the practice of equality and the shift in power balance are was illustrated by a CoSIE pilot partner who shared his experience at the kick-off meeting of the Co-Crea-Te project in Valencia, where policy makers, social professionals and unemployed people were exploring ideas of what service would be helpful on the road to employment.

One of the participating professionals discovered that he was thinking 'for' others. He noticed in one of the evaluation meetings:

> 'In the first co-creation meeting with service users – in this case unemployed people – I proposed a solution: a business course helping newbie entrepreneurs with their business plans. The participants were assertive and questioned the proposed solution. They also questioned the process and the power balance, having been invited to co-create, and felt "not listened to" as they were – again – doing the listening. We learned from that moment and gave them equal room to contribute. One of the (powerful) stakeholders left the room and the project, not wanting to shift this power balance at all.'

Apparently, the setting that had been created was safe enough for the service users to voice their opinion. Explicitly describing the intention of a co-creation process – and the fundamental value of equality that goes with it – at the start can be helpful to create such a safe environment. Also, though in the first instance old-school behaviour was shown, the intervention of the unemployed people was respectfully listened to, taken seriously and immediately followed up. This helped to build trust in the project – a pilot that was eventually very successful, helping more than 100 unemployed persons to start their own business.

A fundamental shift in power balance also occurred in Turku, Finland, when a group of young people in Turku who dropped out of employment or education flipped the hierarchy. It was not the professional who was in the lead, helping the young people, but the youngsters training the social workers. A participant underlined:

> 'It was difficult to find these young people, but the Turku pilot persevered and had co-creation meetings with them. These meetings resulted in young tweens developing a training, teaching social workers how they wanted to be communicated with, and what their needs were. This training was then scaled and given to more teams of social work professionals.'

This example shows the value of asset-based collaboration. First the young people were defined by what they did not have or by what they were not (no employment, no education); after that, their resources were tapped into. It is they who know their own assets and strengths and it is they who are aware of their needs.

These examples also illustrate that service innovation in the various CoSIE pilots implies a change in working routines of public services. These are based on: (1) working *with* the user and not *for* the user; (2) building mutual trust and creating power balance between stakeholders involved; (3) working on reciprocal partnerships among stakeholders; and (4) respectful of capabilities and responsibilities for each of them. To co-create, and to allow solutions to originate and accept other truths, asks for commitment to start on a common journey and to allow for trial and error. Practically, this asks of different stakeholders to understand each other's needs and possibilities, to create space and time for experimentation, to agree on a new power balance and to engage decision makers and executives in adapting work processes. This needs to be – at least partially – negotiated in advance. Even then, difficulties will occur. How to negotiate these will be addressed in the following description of the roadmap.

How to make it happen

There were three activities that were undertaken by all pilots.

In all CoSIE pilots, thorough basic assessment was conducted considering systemic questions: 'dealing with concepts affecting the broad system of delivery of public services and questions such as context, benefits and risks, resource allocation, the nature of innovation in co-creation or its relationship with technology' (CoSIE Consortium, 2020a: 7).

A second common feature was to map the core values within each co-creation activity and to operationalise these. This means: (1) define the common values together; (2) determine ways to embed these values in practice; and (3) reflect together on expected impact. By doing this, the ethical compass of the project was visualised. A Power Sharing Matrix was developed, which is useful to determine and monitor the state of power sharing within public service organisations (CoSIE Consortium, 2020a: 20).

Finally, the CoSIE project developed a set of activities and formats to get started and to keep co-creation in public services going, called catalysts, including a key-questions form visualising co-creation context and ideas, and a tool for introducing design thinking strategies. These catalysts were combined with instruments of co-creation developed later.

Hereafter we will show different co-creation practices within CoSIE and how they are interrelated. After that we will present the instruments of co-creation developed within the CoSIE project.

Roadmap: phases of co-creation

There are many different concepts and expressions commonly associated with co-creation, such as co-initiation, stakeholder engagement, co-design, co-implementation, co-evaluation, co-design, co-management, personalisation and co-management. All these involve practices of co-creation and together they can be seen as an ideal type of a co-creation journey (CoSIE Consortium, 2020a: 4–6). The journey will seldom be linear, and most likely will be a messy one. A phase in a co-creation process can fail, stakeholders can leave and trust can evaporate. In that case 'go back to start' and find a catalyst that can jumpstart the process. A catalyst can be something as simple as a telephone call, or something as complex as involving new stakeholders. Successful co-creation processes do not necessarily involve all of the described activities. It will depend on the initial situation, the stakeholders involved, the conditions and values, and how and to what extent co-creation contributes to service innovation.

Co-initiation

A co-creation process is often a common effort done by two or more organisations of different types. In the CoSIE project mainly universities, public service administrations and some NGOs played important roles as co-initiators. It is important to define a common purpose for service innovation and find out what common purpose for innovation can be.

Stakeholder engagement

Stakeholder engagement is central in the initiating phase (but not only then!) and can be the hardest part of the co-creation process. It is not one step along the co-creation path. In the CoSIE pilots, the initiators discovered that both engaging new actors and keeping original stakeholders interested need to occur throughout the process and different strategies are needed to keep all types of stakeholders on board. In the toolkit for co-creation a stakeholder mapping tool is included to reflect upon this (CoSIE Consortium, 2020a: 8).

Co-design

This part of co-creation is related to what the service should look like. The instruments of co-creation described later in this chapter were helpful in the designing of new services.

Personalisation

To meet people's individual needs, it is important that in the design (and in the execution of the service) tailoring is embedded. The CoSIE pilot in the UK provides an interesting case of personalised public service in the probation sector. One of the participants said: "The mention of peer mentoring was a light bulb moment. It made me think I can do this ... I can get into the probation service" (Baines, 2018: 3).

Co-implementation

After having designed the framework of a new service, putting the service into practice is a rewarding phase, which requires the involvement of many stakeholders, including political and financial partners. For this co-creation phase, it is necessary that all initial partners and stakeholders pull together to ensure that the service is implemented as intended.

Co-evaluation

As indicated, the co-evaluation of any co-creation process should not take place at one point in the process only, but it should occur as recurring reflective activity throughout the project, depending on the context of the public service. It is important to ensure that many stakeholders and their networks are involved, to get both formal and informal feedback on the co-creation process and steps.

Co-management

Joint management of services with citizens is not common practice, due to accountability and liability issues in public services. However, the Spanish pilot introduced a co-management structure of the newly created entrepreneur hub in Valencia. It is important to organise the facilitation of co-management well, so that it will be effective in the long run.

Instruments of co-creation

We now present the instruments of co-creation and their use in action during the processes of co-creation, purposely doing so after describing values of co-creation and phases in co-creation. The central message in using these instruments is that it is not what you do, it is how you do it. The values, not the instruments, are central when putting them into practice.

Lived experience storytelling and community reporting

Community reporting emerged in 2007 as a digital storytelling instrument developed by People's Voice Media, using video or audio, to share stories of people whose voices are not heard. It is born from community action and evolved to be a useful and innovative tool in interpretative and participatory action research schemes. Community reporting developed across Europe as a mixed methodological approach both based on community development and action on the one hand and research in and about communities on the other hand. Community reporting is not only a methodology to collect, curate and analyse stories, it also mobilises the storytellers to make a difference for change.

Lived experience storytelling can be a mechanism through which professionals from public services can truly connect with citizens (Trowbridge and Willoughby, 2020). It is a peer-to-peer dialogue interview technique and collective sense-making activity (Brown and Yule, 1983; Tummers and Karsten, 2012). It was used to evaluate services from a lived experience perspective, illustrating the impact of service delivery on the lives of people. Sharing stories of lived experience is a powerful tool to work on mutual trust. It asks for reciprocity between the storyteller and those who listen (CoSIE Consortium, 2020b).

More than 250 stories of lived experiences of people in need of services and public servants of different types of public services were collected, curated, analysed and mobilised for change. This data set gave insight into the need for fundamental system innovation. The value that a service should deliver became very evident and caused a paradigm: service providers understood the necessity of value rationality (instead of instrumental rationality) within public services (Geelhoed et al, 2021).

Evaluating the impact of service delivery from a lived experience perspective and giving people who are usually not heard a voice made participating civil servants, policy makers and managers realise that their professional efforts are perhaps not corresponding to the needs of citizens.

> 'I was used to always cut through the rambling, getting a clear view of the problem and solving it. However, despite all my good intentions, I discovered that in the end I was only fulfilling our (the municipality's) agenda, based on efficiency, and not the agenda of the citizens. In fact, I did not even know what their agenda was! I missed the broader perspective and view of the person.'

This professional discovered that her job was to connect to the situation of the citizens, instead of them adapting to the criteria and agenda of the municipality.

Analysing the system and questioning power relations: living labs and the COSMOS tool

In all pilots, living lab sessions were organised based on stakeholder analyses addressing the power positions within each of the pilots. In a living lab, stakeholders visualise and identify existing roles and responsibilities within the social service. They reflect upon powershifts related to the innovation at hand.

The living lab sessions provided awareness of these traditional power relations, and community reporting opened new conversations to engage in a common learning process to become self-reliant and sustainable communities. During these living lab conversations and systems analyses, an overview was made of the different ethical viewpoints and reflections on potential models for change.

In the Hungarian pilot, working on household economies in disadvantaged rural areas, the living lab sessions contributed to enhancing the operational mechanisms of local democracy. It created awareness about the importance of cooperation between local government, citizens, businesses and education in rural settings. Citizens in these post-socialist and traditional rural communities exchanged ideas with the mayors and local authority staff on a horizontal basis for the first time. Citizens became self-aware and confident about their contribution to the development of the local economy. The mayors discovered that the development of household economies within the Social Land Programme is not only a question of traditional paternalistic top-down leadership, inherited from the communist past. One mayor said: "I think this is important, this thinking together, working together. What we got is at least as good as what I had in mind. So, you should give them the freedom to come up with their ideas themselves, you shouldn't do the thinking for them."

The CoSIE project developed a tool, COSMOS (Co-creation Service Modelling System; Jamieson et al, 2016), based on the living lab methodology, which visualises the existing identification of roles and responsibilities within the innovation at hand (Jamieson and Martin, 2022) It also gives indications about the moral ordering of social innovation, the change models that were used by stakeholders and to get insight in existing systemic functioning.

Exploring co-creation with the use of big data with the Luuppi tool

Luuppi is a cloud-based tool that can be used to filter, visualise and analyse all kinds of social media messages, news comments, text documents and textual open data from any perspective. It is especially designed for non-technical users. The main attractions of Luuppi are the flexibility and the ease of use it offers end users. They can create their own analytical dimensions and categories.

In the CoSIE pilots all partners experimented with the use of this tool. The aim of the tool was to gather a big data set of citizens' views and opinions, of the 'silent' voices, to feed into the co-creation and innovation processes (Jalonen et al, 2021). The effectiveness of this tool depends on digital literacy. In the European Quality of Life Survey (EQLS, 2016), it is stated that people with lower income participate less in digital activities, from shopping to banking to finding jobs to using online facilities in public administration. We noticed that Luuppi was actively and successfully used in Sweden and especially in Finland where the service users were digitally skilled. The Finnish pilot, aiming at service innovation for young people, used Luuppi to collect viewpoints on the needs of young people, hard to reach through traditional (face-to-face) communication.

Social media

In the CoSIE project social media, such as LinkedIn, Facebook or other interactive communication platforms, were used as tools for co-creation or innovation, enabling citizens to create, share and comment on the innovation project at hand (CoSIE Consortium, 2020c). An overall insight from the CoSIE project was that in most instances social media added value to communications but only after a cohesive community had developed and was built on trusting relationships. A positive illustration is the pilot in Valencia, Spain, where starting entrepreneurs met and worked together in a newly created hub. They used social media to share conversations, building both online and offline communities. In a Dutch pilot, social media was perceived negatively by the main stakeholders. In fact, in both regular and social media, the image of the neighbourhood, where the project took place, was represented negatively. The stakeholders therefore strongly opposed social media use and news items about the CoSIE project in general. In these cases, use of social media and digital tools can be harmful to building trust and co-creation.

Developing digital solutions or applications

The Italian CoSIE pilot in Reggio Emilia developed a new health app as part of the innovation of public health services for children. Originally it was developed as a service for obese children, to encourage healthy behaviour. However, in one of the community reporting sessions, a young girl said that she would wear the app day and night, not to miss the steps to the bathroom at night. The Italian pilot partners realised by designing exclusively for this group of children, unforeseen new health risks occurred. They decided to develop a more inclusive healthy lifestyle app for families, teachers and other (health) professionals to make it fun to use it broadly. The app was an enormous success and was even on the national news.

In Estonia, specific applications were developed to support the communication and services for disabled people in remote areas of Estonia, where professional services are scarce and distant. The community could connect through this platform, including people with a disability themselves. In that way, people could reach and support each other with daily services.

Design thinking and social hackathon

The CoSIE pilot in Võrumaa, Estonia, offered an outstanding occasion to create together with citizens a new type of social service for people with disabilities, based on a combination of technological innovation and community building. The initiators adapted design thinking strategies and developed a series of co-creation events, based on the principles of hackathon bringing different types of expertise together in a 48-hour pressure-cooker event (Kangro and Lepik, 2022). They called it social hackathons, adapting the format to be realised for co-creative purposes involving people with disabilities (Bugarszki et al, 2020).

One of the success factors of the Estonian hackathon was the extensive preparation before the start of the actual project, also through community reporting. Even then, in their first meeting, there were no citizens with disabilities participating:

'The first pilot hackathon event occurred almost entirely without people with disabilities. We failed to involve them in our project even though we visited relevant organisations before. We changed our strategy for the second event, and we hired peer support experts from the field of community-based mental health care. We consulted with them about the design of our events and about how to make it more user-friendly for vulnerable people.'

This quotation makes visible how important a process of trial and error is. Allowing a probing phase, and work on common learnings is central to co-creation. Failure is not a reason to stop the project, but a means for progress, adapting strategies and continuing developing together, so that finally all stakeholders were contributing. A participant underlined that "making the space really comfortable" helped people to exchange personal experiences about their lives. They were enabled to speak with honesty, in a space built on mutual trust. Without honesty and trust, there is no common ground to have authentic communication about what really matters, about why services to people with disabilities are needed in the first place and how to realise change together.

Some elements of the 'original' hackathon method were tweaked: the element of competition was eliminated, so that ideas were given room to develop. It was important to pay particular attention to language – to abandon jargon and approach stakeholders with a language that people with disabilities are familiar with. Visual forms of communication – the pilot hired local artists to create design elements in a style that fit local communities – added to mutual understanding. Another participant underlined the social impact of the hackathon:

'I really liked the fact that the (blind) woman said that she also wanted to see the sights. But how does she identify the sights, how does this information reach her? What she said was very nice. I became much more aware of what it means to involve people, the importance of which came to my attention during the hackathons.'

During the follow-up process of the hackathon, the pilot connected all the ideas and proposed solutions into the local governments' development plans. Not only a new service to people with disabilities was created, but also the method of social hackathon was embraced as a new form of policy innovation. The social hackathon became an inspiration for other CoSIE pilot projects, such as in Wrocław (Poland), where design thinking strategies were used to develop a new home for elderly, and in Finland where social hackathons were held with young people about the services they need.

Conclusion

In the ten co-creation pilots, of which the CoSIE co-creation project consisted, we learned many lessons. We will summarise the most important ones.

- A co-creation process is a non-linear and unpredictable endeavour, visualised as a stellar constellation, in which stakeholders develop their own steps in the co-creation process (CoSIE Consortium, 2020d. This is an important finding, and not one that usually pleases public service bureaucrats, as messiness and unpredictability often do not fit well into management and budget cycles. It is therefore necessary to start with creating free space, meaning time and support from management and board members who believe in innovative outcomes in the long run.
- Co-creation is a bumpy road and stakeholders do not always act in a predictable way: given the many complex realities and different contexts and perspectives from which stakeholders contribute, miscommunication may develop or priorities may shift. Taking a new turn and kickstarting the co-creation process anew is then necessary, as is permanently working on trusting relationships among stakeholders. This leads to a co-creation process and innovation with endurance.
- Using the term 'hard-to-reach citizens' is principally top-down thinking and does not fit with the co-creation association of a shift in power towards citizens as a major player in the decision-making processes that surround public service provision. Due to inequalities in access to online resources and skills, the development of innovative digital tools for social service innovation are not always effective. The digital divide between high- and low-income citizens makes it very important to act responsibly when using digital means of communication or in developing digital services. For example, people who have difficulties reading or writing, or who do not have digital skills, have difficulty using offline and online information about services that are meant for them. Is it their wish to access a service

digitally, or is it a bureaucratic need (for efficiency)? Sometimes services themselves are hard to reach.
- Meaningful innovative projects are sustainable and successful when developed from shared values, horizontal decision-making and an open approach based on developmental evaluation, and constant consideration of the needs of the persons the project was meant for.
- Learning the very practice of co-creation is a major social innovation in itself. Collaborating with different stakeholders is often difficult, but a necessary part of job: together they represent the system around the service intended to be redesigned. Collaborating with the intention of practising the value 'equality' and shifting the power balance is even more difficult. However, going on this journey together, living the values and learning from mistakes lead eventually to meaningful and sustainable innovation. Social professionals, service users, public organisations and NGOs develop a relationship that is more egalitarian. Connections between policy, practice and the beneficiaries are more direct and easier to influence for all parties. In short: a collaborative and deeper understanding of the real value that a service should bring for the service user, brings forth a shift in power balance.

In the values and tools of the CoSIE project, typical social work methods and practices are recognisable, for instance community development (Phillips and Pitman, 2015; Gilchrist and Taylor, 2022) and asset-based community development (Russell, 2020; Russell and McKnight, 2021), the capability approach in social work (Sen, 1985; Nussbaum, 2011), and the use of (participatory) action research (Bradbury, 2015; Greenwood and Levin, 2007; Bihari-Elahi and Burggraaff, 2020). But what we can add as new knowledge and insights for social workers are (1) essential ingredients of a co-creation process (2) specific knowledge about the innovation of public social services and systemic change and (3) new tools and instruments for co-creation in organisations and public administration combining service design (business and marketing), policy development and IT. This knowledge provides social professionals a broader perspective as well as instruments to use in co-creative social innovation processes with citizens and services, supporting them to build bridges, at the intersection of systems and the lifeworld of people (Habermas, 1985).

References
Argyris, C. and Schön, D.A. (1974) *Theory in Practice: Increasing Professional Effectiveness*, San Francisco: Jossey-Bass.
Baines, S. (2018) Personalisation in probation services: exploring the contributors to a working culture of personalisation, December, CoSIE, https://cosie.turkuamk.fi/arkisto/uploads/2020/03/e248b5de-personalisationinprobationservicedigital-3.pdf.

Bakker-Klein, J. (2019) Anders kijken. Een zoektocht naar responsiviteit in het sociale domein/Changing Perspective: A Quest for Responsiveness in the Social Domain, doctoral thesis, Rotterdam: Erasmus University.

Bihari-Elahi, J. and Burggraaff, W. (eds) (2020) *Verandering door actieonderzoek. In stadslabs werken aan nieuwe sociale praktijken*, Assen: Koninklijke van Gorcum.

Bradbury, H. (ed.) (2015) *The Sage Handbook of Action Research*, 3rd edn, London: Sage.

Brandsen, T., Steen, T. and Verschuere, B. (eds) (2018) *Co-production and Co-creation Engaging Citizens in Public Services*, New York: Routledge.

Brown, G. and Yule, G. (1983) *Discourse Analysis*, Cambridge: Cambridge University Press.

Bugarszki, Z., Lepik, K., Kangro, K., Medar, M., Amor, K., Medar, M. and Saia, K. (2021) Guideline for Social Hackathon Events, Tallinn: Tallinn University, School of Governance, Law and Society, https://datadoi.ee/bitstream/handle/33/338/Cosie_Guidelines%20.pdf.

CoSIE Consortium (2020a) A Toolkit for Co-creation in Public Services to Accompany the CoSIE Constellations Roadmap to Co-creation, Turku: Turku University of Applied Sciences, https://cosie.turkuamk.fi/arkisto/uploads/2021/05/03f68026-toolkit-public.pdf.

CoSIE Consortium (2020b) Working with Lived Experience Storytelling as a Tool for Co-creation: Toolkit, Turku: Turku University of Applied Sciences, https://cosie.turkuamk.fi/arkisto/uploads/2021/05/412fb459-lived_experience_toolkit_final.pdf.

CoSIE Consortium (2020c) Enabling Co-creation Through Twitter: A Guidebook for Research Project Communication, Turku: Turku University of Applied Sciences, https://cosie.turkuamk.fi/julkaisut.turkuamk.fi/isbn9789522166753.pdf.

CoSIE Consortium (2020d) Roadmap to Co-creation, Turku: Turku University of Applied Sciences, https://cosie.turkuamk.fi/arkisto/roadmap/index.html.

European Quality of Life Survey (2016) European Quality of Life Survey 2016, Eurofound, https://www.eurofound.europa.eu/en/surveys/european-quality-life-surveys-eqls/european-quality-life-survey-2016,

Fox, C., Baines, S., Wilson, R., Jalonen, H., Aflaki, I.N., Prandini, R., et al (2021) A New Agenda for Co-creating Public Services, Turku: Turku University of Applied Sciences, https://cosie.turkuamk.fi/julkaisut.turkuamk.fi/isbn9789522167842.pdf.

Geelhoed, S., Trowbridge, H., Henderson, S. and Wallace-Thompson, L. (2021) Changing the story: an alternative approach to system change in public service innovation, *Polish Political Science Review*, 9(2): 52–70.

Gilchrist, A. and Taylor, M. (2022) *The Short Guide to Community Development*, 3rd edn, Bristol: Policy Press.

Greenwood, D. and Levin, M. (2007) *Introduction to Action Research: Social Research for Social Change*, Thousand Oaks, CA: Sage.

Habermas, J. (1985) *The Theory of Communicative Action, Volume 1: Reason and Rationalization of Society*, Boston, MA: Beacon Press.

Jalonen, H., Kokkola, J., Laihonen, H., Kirjavainen, H., Kaartemo, V. and Vähämaa, M. (2021) Reaching hard-to-reach people through digital means – citizens as initiators of co-creation in public services, *International Journal of Public Sector Management*, 34(7): 799–816.

Jamieson, D. and Martin, M. (2022) Supporting co-creation processes through modelling, *Public Money & Management*, 42(5): 353–5.

Jamieson, D., Martin, M. and Wilson, R. (2016) COSMOS – The Co-creation Service Modelling System, Geneva: Zenodo, https://zenodo.org/records/4058570.

Kangro, K. and Lepik, K.L. (2022) Co-creating public services in social hackathons: adapting the original hackathon concept, *Public Money & Management*, 42(5): 341–8.

Nussbaum, M. (2011) *Creating Capabilities: The Human Development Approach*, Cambridge, MA: Harvard University Press.

Phillips, R. and Pitman, R. (2015) *An Introduction to Community Development*, 2nd edn, New York: Routledge.

Russell, C. (2020) *Rekindling Democracy: A Professional's Guide to Working in Citizen Space*, Eugene, OR: Cascade Books.

Russell, C. and McKnight, J. (2021) *Looking Back to Look Forward: In Conversation with John McKnight About the Heritage of ABCD and Its Place in the World Today*, 3rd edn, independently published.

Sen, A.K. (1985) *Commodities and Capabilities*, Oxford: Elsevier Science Publishers.

Trowbridge, H. and Willoughby, M. (2020) Connecting voices, challenging perspectives and catalysing change: using storytelling as a tool for co-creation in public services across Europe, in J. Scott (ed) *CESCI Cross-Border Review Yearbook 2020*, Budapest: Central European Service For Cross-Border Initiatives, pp 59–72, https://budapest.cesci-net.eu/en/cross-border-review-2020/.

Tummers, L. and Karsten, N. (2012) Reflecting on the role of literature in qualitative public administration research: learning from grounded theory, *Administration & Society*, 44(1): 64–86.

8

Social innovation and service users' involvement: enhancing the knowledge of social work

Kristel Driessens, Sidsel Natland and Vicky Lyssens-Danneboom

Introduction

In the first chapter of this book, Wilken and Parpan-Blaser related the concepts of social innovation and social work. This chapter focuses on the involvement of service users in the education of professional social workers and in social work research. Our aim is to discuss whether and how this cooperation with service users in education and in research is 'socially innovative'. We explicate the choice of concepts and theoretical frameworks needed to conduct a systematic analysis of our selected examples. We explore the core elements of social innovation in relation to social work and service user involvement.

Our analyses of social innovation through service user involvement in social work education and research are guided by Parpan-Blaser's (2011: 242) definition of innovation in social work as:

> new programmes, strategies, measures, procedures or concepts that
>
> a. are based on new or newly combined knowledge
> b. that aim to address social problems, meet normative needs
> c. add value, in particular to service users, and
> d. (at best) produce changes in the social system that created the problem

This framework combines the structural perspective on social innovation, focusing on social structures and organisation, with the agency perspective, which focuses on individual agents and communities as determinants of social innovation.

An important point of departure for our analysis is that user involvement is in itself an innovative topic, as it facilitates learning and research processes that enhance the knowledge and competences of future social workers to work in socially innovative ways. In this chapter, we present and discuss these different aspects of social innovation.

The involvement of service users in education

Service user involvement has become increasingly common in research and education, especially in medical education, mental health nursing and social work. The UK is the only country where service user involvement is a mandatory part of the social work curriculum. But innovative collaborative practices are also emerging in many countries in Europe, mostly on an experimental basis. The book *Involving Service Users in Social Work Education, Research and Policy: A Comparative European Analysis* brings together a collection of models of collaboration with service users in social work education (Driessens and Lyssens-Danneboom, 2022). For this chapter, we select three different models to analyse their nature of social innovation:

1. the mobilisation course that works with a mix of students and service users;
2. teachers and service users working together in tandem;
3. the community of development.

These examples of social innovation were developed in experimental projects and are now structurally embedded in their institutional context of social work departments at universities (of applied sciences).

Three models of cooperation with service users in social work education

The mobilisation course is a gap-mending course developed at Lund University in Sweden in which social work students and service users study together. It seeks to create more reciprocal relationships between social work students, teachers and service users, in joint development projects. Marginalised and discriminated groups are invited to study together with social work students. The external students (called commission students) are recruited from different service user organisations and have backgrounds of substance abuse, mental health problems, homelessness, physical disabilities or a combination of these problems. The course lasts six weeks. In enabling niches where different students have equal status and share common goals, they work together in a co-productive manner of dialogue and trust, encouraged to bring forward their own resources and strengths and develop a joint project of community development (Heule et al, 2022).

Co-teaching in tandem with service users is a collaborative practice in social work education that is similarly applied in several European educational institutions. In Flanders and the Netherlands, lecturers prefer to use the term 'experts by experience' to emphasise that service users are actors with vulnerabilities and strengths, and with experiences as clients or patients. They have gained experiential knowledge as collective knowledge, by reflecting on their own experiences and by sharing experiences with others. The experiential knowledge is linked to a context of exclusion and disruption and combined with sufficient distance and abstraction. The experts by experience are co-educators in theoretical courses, in workshops, in training programmes and in supervision. By teaching and training alongside a lecturer, the expert by experience introduces openness and courage to discuss and share life experiences in an atmosphere of equality, respect and reciprocity. Human-to-human encounters emerge, and participants release their prejudices or stigmas (Driessens et al, 2022).

In a community of development, professionals, service users, researchers and other stakeholders engage in a process of learning, action and reflection for the specific purpose of improving a professional practice. It is a learning community in which services users participate as co-researchers and co-designers. Based on the community of practice model (Wenger, 1998), members engage in the domain of interest, in a community of joint activities and discussions, and share a practice or resources, such as experiences, stories, tools and methods. Additional is an increased focus on learning (including learning to work with a diversity of people with multiple perspectives), focus on research and development (academic researchers participate to help shape innovations) and the combination of different types of knowledge. Every voice and all sources of knowledge are of equal value, essential to the co-creation process. The group consists of 5 to 15 members: social workers, service users, researchers and possibly formal and informal network members, managers of services or municipality workers, coached by a facilitator who provides guidance and acts as a role model by highlighting participants' strengths, talents and passions. Service users' experiences help to improve practices from their perspective. This requires a safe and open atmosphere, collaboration on equal terms and eagerness to develop innovation (Wilken et al, 2022).

The involvement of service users in research

Social work research must also be innovative to secure knowledge that can contribute to improving and facilitating social innovative practice. We define an innovative research project as research that involves users in innovative ways – as co-researchers – and recognises experiential knowledge. We will present experiences from research that used a methodology that was deemed well suited to involving service users as co-researchers, and where users' experiential knowledge was recognised to be consistent with and complementary to theoretical and professional knowledge (Natland and Hansen, 2016; Natland et al, 2019).

Social work operates in a complex context with regard to recognising users and providing them with high-quality and effective services. Many social workers report the increase of users with diverse and interrelated problems, such as health, work, education and social networks. This places high demands on how social work can be carried out effectively and in line with the principles of social work, which again calls for research that can improve social work practice. This section will provide an example from the research project 'Contradictory institutional logics in interaction? The interface between the education system and field of health and welfare services' (Natland et al, 2019). The project call required the involvement of service users.

As the project progressed, user representatives in the group argued that the project needed to explore methodologies suitable for capturing service users' experiences of their encounters with social services. The background for this was their experiential knowledge of follow-up work focused on long-term users: the goal of social services is to enable service users to be self-sufficient, for example, in terms of employment, income and/or other activities to improve their life quality. However, there may be shortcomings between what is offered and service users' expectations and needs. Therefore, the user representatives asked for a study with the aim of exploring a methodology suitable for capturing users' experiences and views. They proposed dialogue seminars to produce that knowledge. The hypothesis was that the users' experiences and desires can produce knowledge that can be used to improve social work in practice, because it can identify what practitioner competences are needed to meet users' expectations and needs.

Dialogue seminars have their origins in participatory action research and the idea that knowledge about a phenomenon should be sought from different sources, not least those who have first-hand/subjective experience and knowledge of the subject. Dialogue seminar is a method of establishing an equal dialogue between different parties. What these parties have in common is that they are in a relationship with each other in which they must work together toward a goal, face challenges and find solutions. The method can help develop conditions for more equal cooperation. The method not only follows a special model for implementation but is also suitable for facilitating user participation. In dialogue seminars in which both users and employees participate, the meetings are intended to erase distinctions between different positions of power. Everyone is given space to speak, and everyone's voice should be heard.

The user representatives' initiative on dialogue seminars was approved by the project leader (representing the university), and the user representatives were given the responsibility of planning and moderating such seminars. They had experience with this from previous research projects (Natland and Hansen, 2016). Some 51 long-term users (dependent on benefits from 4 to 20 years) of social services from a rural municipality were invited to participate in the dialogue seminars. Their ages ranged from 25 to 65, and they represented different gender and ethnic backgrounds. User representatives in the research group moderated the seminars. The other researchers in the group attended, helped with practical tasks and documented the process.

Participants were asked to discuss what had helped them most in their encounters with social services, and why. The results of the dialogue seminars were collected and analysed in collaboration between user representatives and one conventional researcher (Natland) using the two questions 'what' and 'why'. The data were then analysed to identify common themes inspired by thematic analysis (Braun and Clarke, 2006). The findings were interpreted theoretically within the framework of the philosopher Kierkegaard's concept of 'useful help'. Three categories of what users perceived as 'useful help' were identified: (1) the working relationship of counsellor-user, (2) knowledge of opportunities in the labour market, as it was not helpful if the counsellor lacked knowledge and competences regarding return-to-work processes to get closer to job and income, and, closely related to this, (3) the importance of interprofessional collaboration (Natland et al, 2019).

These findings were then further developed in a new dialogue seminar. This time, both service providers (13) and social workers and managers (48) attended. The service users' representatives presented the findings, and the brief for the dialogue this time was to identify what professional competences a social worker should have in order to perform 'helpful assistance', and what they saw as drivers and barriers to providing it.

The municipality's management asked for enhanced collaboration to develop a local 'implementation guide' to ensure the involvement of users in service development. This guide was developed and written in collaboration with one researcher (Natland) and the user representatives, but municipality users were also involved in this work.

Discussion

To search for the characteristics of social innovation in models of collaboration with service users in social work education and research, we analyse how these four key elements are visible in the selected educational models and research methodology: the development of new or newly combined knowledge, the aim to address social problems, the added value for people, groups and organisations involved, and the transformation of social relations and change in social systems

The development and use of new or newly combined knowledge

Kowalk and Wetterling, both experts by experience involved in social work education, argue that intrinsic to involving experts by experience is the integration of different knowledge and perspectives (Kowalk and Wetterling, 2022).

In the three models from education, there is the recognition of experiential knowledge as equivalent to academic knowledge. The tandems bring analyses of economic and social inequality in society, of the causes of social problems and the impact of these structural mechanisms on individual lives. Through the experiential stories, students feel the effects of exclusion and policies and discover how social services can lead to negative reinforcement or positive change (Driessens et al, 2022). Students explore their own lived experiences and their impact on their thinking and actions as social workers. The mutual exchange of personal stories brings greater understanding of the impact of living conditions. It breaks down prejudices and brings relationship building in equality. In the mobilisation course and the development community, the integration of academic, professional and experiential knowledge leads to new projects and products for better social work practice.

In relation to research too, recognition of experiential knowledge is crucial and should be recognised as a form of knowledge in the same way as theoretical knowledge and knowledge from practice. The use of dialogue seminars had a double effect that should be emphasised: (1) the importance of recognising users' ideas and initiatives within the research group and (2) the dialogue seminars themselves provide data and findings from the users' perspective. The knowledge created from their perspectives and from their local context can then be combined with existing research, and such exploratory projects can also identify new and emerging topics for further research. Phillips and Shaw (2011) argue that research can be defined as innovative when innovative methods are used within the specific project and when researchers with no proven track record in the field of the proposed research are involved. The dialogue seminar is an innovative method that revealed new data on what service users perceive as useful services. This research also benefited from the recognition of service users' experiential knowledge as a different track from academic knowledge.

The education models and research can be contextualised as modus 2 knowledge production (Nowotny et al, 2001). In the context of innovation, the findings from both education and research align with Windrum's (2008) concept of systematic innovation; a concept aimed at catching up with new and improved ways of collaborating with other organisations or knowledge bases.

Boschma's (2005) concept of 'cognitive proximity' marks the extent to which two or more people share the same knowledge. At the micro level, it may be professional social workers working together, researchers or educators – they share communication codes, jargon, academic or professional standards. However, too much proximity can hinder new learning and innovation, also known as the 'competence trap' (Levitt and March, 1988). Therefore, a certain cognitive distance is needed to access new, different and complementary knowledge. Such new sources can give life to new ideas and creativity. User involvement in both education and research can be approached as a means of creating cognitive distance, renewing both research methods for social work and models for teaching.

The goal of addressing social problems, responding to normative needs

All three educational models and the case study from the research focus on social problems in society. Service users are not seen as people with individual problems, but as individuals suffering from social mechanisms and processes and fighting against this social exclusion and discrimination. They experience barriers in society that prevent them from achieving justice. Service users can also identify how a paternalistic, controlling or sanctioning basic attitude of a social worker can trap and harm them. In courses, workshops and training programmes, they argue for an open, listening, supportive and empowered attitude, for strength-based social work. Their need for a dignified life, for tailored support, for respectful dialogue and relationship leading to partnership guide their interventions and discussions with students.

The use of participatory research methods, such as the dialogue seminar, allows service users to come together in a 'neutral' space to share and communicate their life stories, their experiences of shame, guilt and hopelessness. In terms of methodology, the project's user representatives, who played the role of moderators, were instrumental in building trust and giving voice to the participating local users. As moderators, they were clear about the agenda of the dialogue seminar: that the focus should be on what can be done to improve services, and that participants should therefore focus on their positive experiences, and not be 'trapped' in previous negative and unhelpful relationships with services. It was perceived as stimulating and as a source of relevant knowledge.

Provision of added value for education, research, the profession and service users

The cases presented in this chapter show how collaboration with service users contributes to improving the quality of both education and research. It is a meaningful action where all stakeholders feel taken seriously.

In education, this collaboration helps lecturers reflect on their own role in an education system and places them in a different role: that of stimulator, facilitator and mediator. The lecturer believes in the power of dialogue and learns from users' experiential knowledge as a strong complementary source of knowledge.

For students, it is a taste of reality. They see the whole person with strengths and weaknesses and do not focus on the problem. They hear about helpful and harmful aspects of social and mental health care and become aware of alternative solutions and approaches. Working with service users helps students think about their future role as social workers, supporting people and standing up for people's rights. Service users feel respected because they are seen and recognised as competent, credible and equal. They are often silenced and have lost dignity and confidence in their abilities. But in the models described, they are able to use their lived experiences to restore both (Kowalk and Wetterling, 2022). They create a new support network and develop new competences, inviting them to further study or work.

There is empowerment for all involved. Service users develop as actors, as attentive parents, as people with talents and strengths, as valuable contributors. All involved develop interpersonal skills in a co-production that requires mutual respect, patience, dialogue and the ability to listen to each other. The models speak of deep learning, identification of unconscious biases, understanding of structural relations of inequality and processes of awareness and critical self-reflection.

Similar experiences of empowerment occurred during the dialogue seminars. Users were recognised as equal partners; they were given responsibility for facilitating the dialogue seminar project. Involving users in research can be promising because their involvement potentially enables them to produce knowledge (co-researchers) and they develop competences within the research. However, this requires conventional researchers to share power and involve users as more than mere advisers in research.

Transformation of social relations and changes in the social system or structures in the line of fight against injustice, inequality and inaccessibility

This collaboration in both education and research leads to a transformation of social relations. Differences, similarities and the impact of the social context are analysed. A deeper dialogue and genuine human-to-human connection emerge.

Participants develop an awareness about the maintenance of power relations through the language we use. By working together in a mixed group, people speak in a different, more respectful way to each other and to people experiencing social exclusion. By becoming aware of oppression at interconnected structural, cultural and personal levels, all models explore and discuss unequal power relations and transcend stereotypical roles in social work. We discover the breakdown of stigma, in which opportunities for change emerge. In these cooperative models, social workers see vulnerable and disadvantaged groups as their allies in mutual efforts to change and improve society (Beresford and Croft, 2001; Krumer-Nevo, 2020). There is the potential to contribute to reducing power differences and promoting collaborative partnership. Reciprocal relationships and recognition of each other's knowledge are seen as a strength, as key elements for this innovative co-production in which people in teams develop into change agents. In the dialogue seminars, social workers and users agreed on barriers and facilitators to implementing services that users perceive as helpful and respectful. Social workers seemed surprised that users showed understanding of their organisational context that may hinder them from acting in the desired way to meet the individual user's needs. Power relations were reduced and a mutual understanding of their position as users and professionals emerged.

Framing social work education within a discourse of social justice, inclusion and anti-oppression practice leads to models taking an active role in shaping an inclusive society.

The mobilisation course produces ambassadors of co-production with service users. Some projects were realised in local community practices, new organisations of service users were created. Many alumni remain involved in producing alternative practices in civil society organisations and community development. Working in tandem forms more reflective practitioners, with a sensitivity to work in partnership with service users for cultural and structural change, to make services more accessible, to combat social isolation and polarisation, to improve support systems and reduce social injustice. The communities of development create meaningful and sustainable projects, products that can be used for reflection, evaluation and service delivery, working methods, guidelines, e-learning modules and manuals, which are also used in education.

Service users participating in the study may also benefit more than just on a personal level. They may develop new networks and/or feel more competent and empowered to continue with education, work or other meaningful activities, such as working in user organisations or creating such networks. Some of the local users who participated in the seminars became more empowered and they were later involved in developing a user council in their local municipality.

Furthermore, innovative methods can result in socially innovative research themes and findings useful for social innovation of services.

Conclusion

Social work supports the most vulnerable groups in society, for whom rights, goals and opportunities are often the most difficult to achieve. For working towards empowerment and bridging the gap between desires and possibilities, social work as a profession and social services face constant challenges. Research, education and practice take place in a broader social and political environment and therefore need to ensure that they are consistent with the values of social work.

In this chapter, we have shown that service user involvement in education and research meets the key dimensions of social innovation in social work and can lead to increased quality in research, education and social work.

Different models of service user involvement in social work education are good practices of social innovation. But to realise them in a qualitative and ethical way, the core elements of social innovation need to be constantly kept in mind. And the most challenging goal is to embed those promising practices into the mainstream structures of our social work education, because of their potential for the further development of social work as a discipline.

Social work research plays an important role in innovation, choosing appropriate methods such as participatory action research and design-based research. In this chapter, we encourage social work researchers to develop new frameworks for social innovation research based on the involvement of service users as co-researchers. Our examples show how, to succeed, this requires the recognition of knowledge as a tripartite concept consisting of academic, theoretical knowledge, practice-based knowledge and experiential knowledge. This is crucial for avoiding epistemic challenges or epistemic injustices related to power relations between stakeholders in new and innovative collaborative projects (Natland and Hansen, 2016; Natland, 2020).

The focus on positive and promising experiences in this chapter does not remove the fact that there can also be conflicts and disagreements in the implementation of educational models and research projects in which users play an active role. The fair payment of users' contribution, the protective attitude of lecturers, the dominance of academic knowledge and lack of support from managers are important barriers in education. With regard to research, there is a tension between innovation and impact. The pursuit of socially innovative research methods may risk not being able to meet traditional academic requirements for dissemination and output. Sometimes the process itself should be recognised as an important outcome, for example in terms of improved communication and relationships. But this requires a change in academic norms. These conflicts and thresholds can be interpreted as signals of empowerment (Natland, 2020) and a call for continued social innovation.

References

Beresford, P. and Croft, S. (2001) Service users' knowledges and the social construction of social work, *Journal of Social Work*, 1(3): 295–316.

Boschma, R. (2005) Proximity and innovation: a critical assessment, *Regional Studies*, 3(1): 61–74.

Braun, V. and Clarke, V. (2006) Using thematic analysis in psychology, *Qualitative Research in Psychology*, 3(2): 77–101.

Driessens, K. and Lyssens-Danneboom, V. (2022) Involving service users in social work education and research: is this structural social work?, in K. Driessens and V. Lyssens-Danneboom (eds) *Involving Service Users in Social Work Education, Research and Policy: A Comparative European Analysis*, Bristol: Policy Press, pp 224–37.

Driessens, K., Lyssens-Danneboom, V., Peeters, W., Van Geldorp, C., Vandenhende, P., Bloemen, H., et al (2022) Service users as tandem partners in social work education, in K. Driessens and V. Lyssens-Danneboom (eds) *Involving Service Users in Social Work Education, Research and Policy: A Comparative European Analysis*, Bristol: Policy Press, pp 35–48.

Heule, C., Knutagård, M. and Kristiansen, A. (2022) The gap-mending concept: theory and practice, in K. Driessens and V. Lyssens-Danneboom (eds) *Involving Service Users in Social Work Education, Research and Policy: A Comparative European Analysis*, Bristol: Policy Press, pp 11–22.

Kowalk, H. and Wetterling, J. (2022) Experiences matter equally, in K. Driessens and V. Lyssens-Danneboom (eds) *Involving Service Users in Social Work Education, Research and Policy: A Comparative European Analysis*, Bristol: Policy Press, pp 199–208.

Krumer-Nevo, M. (2020) *Radical Hope: Poverty-Aware Practice for Social Work*, Bristol: Policy Press.

Levitt, B. and March, J.G. (1988) Organizational learning, *Annual Review of Sociology*, 14: 319–38.

Natland, S. (2020) 'Recently, I have felt like a service user again': conflicts in collaborative research, a case from Norway, in H. McLaughlin, P. Beresford, C. Cameron, H. Casey, and J. Duffy (eds) *The Routledge Handbook of Service User Involvement in Human Services Research and Education*, Abingdon: Routledge, pp 467–76.

Natland, S. and Hansen, R. (2016) Conflicts and empowerment – a processual perspective on the development of a partnership, *European Journal of Social Work*, 20(4): 497–508.

Natland, S., Bjerke, E. and Torstenssen, T.B. (2019) 'Jeg fikk blankpusset håpet om at jeg hadde en framtid': Opplevelser av god hjelp i møter med Nav, *Fontene forskning*, 12(1): 17–29.

Nowotny, H., Scott, P.B. Scott and Gibbons, M.T. (2001) *Re-Thinking Science: Knowledge and the Public in an Age of Uncertainty*, Cambridge: Polity Press.

Parpan-Blaser, A. (2011) *Innovation in der Sozialen Arbeit: Zur theoretischen und empirischen Grundlegung eines Konzeptes*, Wiesbaden: VS.

Phillips, C. and Shaw, I. (2011) Innovation and the practice of social work research, *British Journal of Social Work*, 41(4): 609–24.

Wenger, E. (1998) *Communities of Practice: Learning, Meaning, and Identity*, Cambridge: Cambridge University Press.

Wilken, J.P., Witteveen, E., van Slagmaat, C., Van Gijzel, S., Knevel, J., Loeffen, T. and Overkamp, E. (2022) Community of development: a model for inclusive learning, research and innovation, in K. Driessens and V. Lyssens-Danneboom (eds) *Involving Service Users in Social Work Education, Research and Policy: A Comparative European Analysis*, Bristol: Policy Press, pp 145–57.

Windrum, P. (2008) Innovation and entrepreneurship in public services, in P. Windrum and P. Koch (eds) *Innovation in Public Sector. Entrepreneurship, Creativity and Management*, Cheltenham: Edward Elgar, pp 3–20.

9

Moderating processes of social innovation: insights from a case study on labour market activation

Koen Dortmans, Erik Jansen and Lineke van Hal

Introduction

A glance at the autumn 2022 unemployment rates in Europe quickly leads to optimism (Eurostat, 2023). In the Netherlands alone, there are 121 jobs for every 100 jobseekers (CBS, 2023). Upon closer inspection, however, serious labour market issues arise. In some sectors there is a dire shortage of staff and the quality of the jobs is poor: irregular hours and low wages. Furthermore, a significant group of people still remain unemployed, despite labour market policy. In 2015, the Participation Act was introduced in the Netherlands aiming for 'allowing as many people as possible to participate in the labour process' preferably with a regular employer, also people 'for whom participating in the labour process is not self-evident' (Van Echtelt et al, 2019: 8; all translations in this chapter are ours). After all, work provides satisfaction and financial security, prevents social isolation and offers opportunities for personal development. Moreover, the social security system needed to remain affordable in times of austerity. The Dutch Participation Act was therefore primarily intended to simplify the complex system of regulations hoping that employment rates would increase. However, an evaluation of the Act in 2019 showed that these objectives had only been achieved to a very limited extent. While chances to find work for young people with disabilities and work capacity increased from 29 to 38 per cent, their income position worsened due to temporary part-time contracts which 'does not outweigh the fact that they are often no longer entitled to benefits' (Van Echtelt et al, 2019: 10). The situation for welfare recipients is similar: hardly any more opportunities and poor job quality. Furthermore, assisted work opportunities for people with limited work capacity decreased.

When intractable social problems such as unemployment appear difficult to solve within established (public, private, civil) systems and mainstream solutions, social innovation can emerge. As Nicholls and colleagues put it:

The rise of social innovation demonstrates a collapse in trust in the status quo – as established models and social relations have increasingly failed to deliver well-being for many. In this context, intractable problems are seen as highlighting the failure of conventional solutions and established paradigms, entrenched in institutional settings across all three conventional sectors of society. This is evident through private sector market failures, public sector siloed thinking and a lack of scale in and fragmentation across civil society. (Nicholls et al, 2015: 7)

Although social innovation may not always and exclusively be motivated by a decline in trust, discontent with how municipalities and executive agencies succeeded in guiding people to work they value was the key driver for a group of social entrepreneurs to develop the Neighbourhood Job Agency (hereafter: NJA; in Dutch: Buurtbaanbureau), central in this chapter. The NJA is a social innovation initiative that aims to connect people and employment opportunities within their own neighbourhood. As social work researchers, the authors studied this initiative by way of an action research project during the first two years of its development.

In this chapter we critically assess NJA as a social innovation using the definition of Voorberg et al (2015: 1334): 'the creation of long-lasting outcomes that aim to address societal needs by fundamentally changing the relationships, positions and rules between the involved stakeholders, through an open process of participation, exchange and collaboration with relevant stakeholders, including end-users, thereby crossing organizational boundaries and jurisdictions'. Like other well-known definitions of social innovation (see Chapter 1), these authors emphasise the importance of both social outcomes and process, the open collaboration with stakeholders, particularly end users of products and services. NJA embraces social objectives such as well-being, job satisfaction and a more sustainable society by relating unemployed residents with (paid) jobs in the neighbourhood in a novel way. Although innovative from a labour market perspective, we argue that the process of achieving those results with NJA could have been more social in nature. First, we present how we performed a responsive evaluation study and participated in the social innovation process of NJA as researchers from a social work perspective. Next, we describe NJA in its context and juxtapose its objectives with experiences of end users. Finally, we reflect and draw conclusions about what makes social innovation such as with NJA social and how social workers can relate to such innovation as social change moderators.

Methodology: responsive evaluation

We have followed NJA for two years, from its inception in September 2019 until August 2021, in a neighbourhood of Arnhem, a middle-sized city in the Netherlands with 165,000 inhabitants, conducting a responsive evaluation (Abma and Widdershoven, 2005). Instead of merely measuring outcome effectiveness, responsive evaluation aims at facilitating a learning process for all stakeholders by actively involving them (participatory), being open to the plurality of their perspectives on quality and success (pluralistic), recording and relating their stories and experiences (interpretive) and initiating a mutual conversation (dialogical). Responsive evaluation is appropriate for the (mid-term) evaluation of unique and small-scale social innovations such as NJA because of their complexity: the many actors involved, the broad spectrum of activities and possible effects or outcomes are usually unpredictable in advance. Moreover, NJA is context-specific as it is rooted in a specific social and political environment, and is constantly evolving and ambiguous, reminiscent of the idea that social innovation is always fluid and contextual. Responsive evaluation creates space for all perspectives, including those of end users. It therefore fits well with the social development process that characterises social innovation.

Abma and Widdershoven emphasise the importance of recording lived experiences of – in our case – participants in NJA's employment services in the form of stories for producing thick descriptions (Geertz, 1973); quantitative research methods are complementary. To obtain the stakeholders' stories, we conducted focus groups with both participants and developers, we interviewed participants who decided to stop using NJA's services (that is, non-users) who, as is common in the social science of technology, are considered a valuable source of information (Oudshoorn and Pinch, 2003). Moreover, two researchers (first and second authors) conducted participant observation (such as team meetings and design sessions). We also used an instrument developed to help articulate the impact of social innovations based on stakeholder dialogue (the so-called effect calculator) and questionnaires to measure capability well-being (ICECAP-A; Al-Janabi et al, 2012) and worker capabilities (Abma et al, 2016).

Because responsive evaluation focuses on understanding instead of explaining, researchers take a role as interpreter of the various stakeholders' stories as well as facilitator by exchanging these accounts among those involved. This requires explicating our own normative framework. We take the capability approach as a starting point (see Chapter 4) and it is suited for several reasons. First, capability scholars have already applied this framework to labour market activation, work and careers (Bonvin and Orton, 2009; Robertson, 2015; Egdell and McQuaid, 2016; Van der Klink et al, 2016). Further, these authors stress the success of active labour market policies and programmes in terms of enhancing the broader well-being of their beneficiaries, that is, to allow them to lead the life and perform the job they have reason to value (Bonvin and Orton, 2009). Finally, this also includes enhancing the 'capability of voice', allowing end users to have a say in the development, implementation and evaluation of employment services (Egdell and McQuaid, 2016). Before explicating the experiences of NJA's (non)participants, we briefly describe the social innovation of NJA, its development and its objectives.

NJA as a new practice for job activation

NJA originates from a citizen initiative – called Blue Neighbourhood Economy – that aspires to contribute to 'a more sustainable living environment with more well-being, solidarity and an eye for nature' (Hoogenbosch, 2019). As NJA's co-developer Philip (all names are pseudonyms) describes it: "Put somewhat bluntly, we need [work] capacity for realising the circular, inclusive neighbourhood we aspire. Hopefully, NJA will provide that". Apart from new jobs from small, circular start-up companies (for example, one cultivating oyster mushrooms using coffee grounds), NJA hopes to realise a new neighbourhood economy by establishing social enterprises such as a greening company and a care company. These enterprises can take over the work now done by companies and workers who commonly reside outside the neighbourhood.

So, NJA aims to address social needs: enhancing local residents' personal capabilities (working skills) and letting them (re)discover their 'dream job' they have reason to value (ambition 1), matching them with durable locally based, paid work (ambition 2) contributing to a more sustainable neighbourhood (ambition 3). Second, NJA aims to fundamentally change relationships, positions and rules between stakeholders by making residents' aspirations and capabilities a starting point in new job mediation practices, redefining work and creating jobs at a neighbourhood level and matching these two. NJA can be considered as a social enterprise, 'a hybrid organization that represents sites for social innovation as a boundary-blurring activity', operating between 'state (municipality responsible for social benefits and labour market activation), civil society (local residents), private sector (employers and entrepreneurs)' and combining 'social objectives with business models' (Nicholls et al, 2015: 9) resulting from the reduction of social security costs. In its own words, NJA takes:

> a wide perspective and concrete action [that] exceeds existing frameworks and practices enabling *really new solutions* to some wicked social issues. For example, with regard to labour participation of 'people distanced from the labour market' [quotation marks added, compare Kampen and Tonkens, 2019], issues of loneliness, liveability and sustainability in the neighbourhood or people who experience insufficient pleasure or meaning in their (working) lives. (Van der Haak, 2021: 20, emphasis added)

Furthermore, NJA can be considered a user-driven innovation (Von Hippel, 1986) since a group of professional trainers who are themselves experts by experience in getting stuck in their working lives and switching to their 'dream' jobs (trainer) jointly developed the labour participation services of the NJA with welfare recipients as the intended primary end users. The municipality was involved as a co-developer of the NJA and a 'supplier' of possible participants. Specific social work expertise was not structurally present in the development team; the authors as social researchers were asked to bring in a social perspective as part of the participatory action research. In the conclusion we reflect upon this absence of social workers in relation to social innovation.

The NJA works as follows. After an unemployed local resident expresses interest in participating in the programme to their job coach at the unemployment organisation, an extensive intake interview follows. A trainer maps the candidate's work experience, ideas of future work, education level and learning needs, and assesses suitability based on personal circumstances, ability to reflect, motivation, language skills, social abilities and availability. When the assessment is positive, the participant can start an intensive group-based job training of 14 weekly meetings. Trainers promote self-understanding among the participants (talents, drives, obstacles), by using a personal assessment method and by sharing everyday experiences of success and disappointment (at work and beyond). Role play and assignments are to help participants to discover their talents and pitfalls ('dragons'). Participants also develop personal 'business models' which they present to local employers including new start-up businesses arising from the citizen initiative. The goal is to help participants to find valuable work, acquire work experience or to start their own enterprise. The workshops, coaching and peer supervision sessions during the programme are aimed at supporting this.

During the two years we followed NJA, two groups of in total 35 residents have participated in the programme, 21 women and 14 men, aged between 20 and 62. They received benefits from different sources, had diverse work experience and education levels. Most participants completed the programme, some of whom found paid work ($n = 5$), started their own business ($n = 4$), engaged in volunteer work, mostly in the neighbourhood ($n = 10$), others started an education, internship or work placement ($n = 6$). Some participants stopped the programme early ('non-users') because they found work elsewhere, started education or because the programme did not meet their expectations. Two people continued job mediation at other agencies. Of seven, the outcome was unknown.

The voice of users and non-users of NJA's employment programme

The first ambition of NJA was to develop the talents of local welfare recipients, to enhance their job skills and to let them (re)discover their 'dream jobs'. The interest of local residents in participating in the programme showed

NJA responds to a need. Judging from the evaluation forms, participants experienced the group-based training as positive because self-confidence, self-knowledge and insight increased. However, our observations also revealed some adverse effects that did not emerge from the developers' own evaluation.

First, we observed an issue of freedom of choice, a main principle in labour market activation as capability approach scholars contend. Participation should be voluntary, termination without sanctions, work or work placements freely selectable and the programme tailored to individual needs (Bonvin and Orton, 2009). Although participation in NJA's activation programme was not mandatory, some participants experienced it this way. Ralph: "If you refused then they [civil servants of the municipality] would have looked for something else". Abraham: "I had to come here because of social services". Pete felt glad "to be free from social services for a while. [Now, I] don't have to report every six weeks that I haven't found a job again and feel worse and worse". Except for Pete, motivation of most participants increased considerably during the training.

Second, the programme raised some issues concerning inclusion. The programme is selective by nature since trainers assess participants' 'suitability' during the intake interview. Some residents could not enrol because they 'lacked self-reflection', according to the trainers' perspective. Moreover, having particular cognitive abilities (or not) appeared to be a subtle exclusion mechanism. The assignments during the group training evoked negative feelings. Pete believed the training was depressing and complicated: "as if I was doing things wrong". Nevertheless, he completed the training. This was not the case for 'non-user' Iris, for whom a drug addiction prevented her from continuing to work as a nurse. Despite her initial enthusiasm for the training, she quitted before its completion.

> 'I fell into old patterns: fear of failure. I felt like a lot was expected of me that I couldn't achieve. I thought: "Oh here we go again." I have tried so many trainings for seven years, but I keep running into the same thing. I should not have a stomach ache all week every time I have group training.'

The training team, however, had no clue of Iris' motivation for quitting, let alone an alternative to the assignments. For her the training was not empowering. What is more, it sparked old experiences of failure while a lack of self-confidence is generally viewed a major stumbling block in finding work, especially for people with a (former) drug addiction (Banerjee and Damman, 2013). It hindered Iris's ability to find work "in a completely different direction" that she so desperately wanted after her addiction. This raises some questions: is the programme equally accessible to all local residents? What alternatives has NJA to offer when its services do not seem to fit the participants' abilities and needs?

Third, the programme was not effective for all participants. For some, increasing self-determination resulted in a more critical perspective towards job opportunities. Why settle for just any job? Steven: "Trainers teach you exactly this: 'Please, be one hundred per cent yourself!' I have become more critical. Do you want a job to reflect only forty per cent of who you are? In a sense, the training makes it more difficult to find the right job".

For others however, confusion arose. Jessy reported being "more stuck" than at the start, which evoked "feelings of helplessness". For Eileen, the training stirred up existential questions: "The training triggered an inner process, about who I am [hesitates because of emotion]. I have to take some other steps first before I come to work". Each participant went through an individual, sometimes emotional, process that was not necessarily in sync with the programme schedule but needed to be passed before successfully moving towards a new job.

The NJA's second ambition is to match participants' talents to local, or locally created, paid work. Working in one's own neighbourhood appealed to participants. Some called it the main reason for participating. It should allow them to combine work and care responsibilities at home. Cath: "I have animals and a daughter at home". For others, it could prevent an unpleasant, long commute. John: "In my sector [IT], commuting one and a half, two hours is common. Even UWV [government agency retaining people to employment] thinks it's very normal. I said: 'I don't do that anymore. I'm too old, too tired for that.' A ten-minute walk to work sounds very appealing".

Besides participants like Iris who prefer working as a volunteer, most participants regarded local paid work as a necessary condition in order to become or remain financially independent. As John expressed it: "I want to wipe my bum with paper I bought myself". However, the work available to participants was mostly voluntary work. John: "The promise of local paid work is not correct. The NJA should keep this promise". He felt the work placements at local entrepreneurs were unfair: "These people earn a living with it. Why can't I be paid for my effort?". Moreover, he perceived the voluntary work the citizen initiative had to offer, as stigmatising. "Have we as a society fallen that far, that maintaining a neighbourhood's liveability has to be done on a voluntary basis? Let everybody work part-time and additionally do voluntary work for the community. Then it is evenly distributed and not just for suckers who cannot get a paid job."

Here, John articulated his desire for normality: combining a job in addition to volunteering like 'normal' neighbours. Now, voluntary work in the neighbourhood during office times shows that you are a "sucker without a paid job".

The local businesses as part of the new local economy that the citizen initiative is working on were still in their preconceptual stages of development. It was expected to take considerable time before these companies would provide new jobs or any jobs at all, while the participants' need for paid work was urgent. Jessy: "The new businesses NJA is working on are beautiful concepts the neighbourhood can benefit from in time, but they are not yet concrete. Our need [for paid work] is. I believe NJA needs to shift its focus".

Building a vital network of existing employers should be NJA's top priority, some participants believe. Ralph who was able to obtain a job as a concierge at a local hotel proved the success of the concept. But the quality of the current network was 'really disappointing', according to some participants. Jessy:

'When we presented our personal business models only two people [potential employers] outside our own inner circle attended. "Is this it?" I thought. The place should be packed with companies, recruiters and the municipality's HR. Trainers urge us to find a company that suits us. Where on earth to start? I see NJA's role in building a network of companies open to participants without having the label "distance to labour market".'

Participants were particularly struck by the fact that no manager of the municipality attended the presentations while, as a major welfare agency, it directly benefits from participants finding paid work. Steven: "If I were a municipality manager, I would make connections at the end of such a job training, saying: 'Now you have discovered your dream job, let us explore if we can make the connection.' Now, the municipality seems to think: 'Nice programme, good luck with it'".

In the focus group conversations, participants suggested additions to NJA's current services. Steven proposed job coaches, Danny a job fair, comparable to temp agencies: "Every jobseeker can present her profile, tell something about the organizational culture she prefers. Temp agency workers know the job market, the cultures of employers".

Iris came up with the idea of a voluntary job board, to show local residents the available volunteer work to see what they value. In the present situation, the citizen initiative provided work placements and voluntary jobs, mostly arising from their sustainability projects that did not suit everyone. Steven: "The opportunities NJA creates just coincidentally need to be what you are looking for."

In addition to the adverse effects of the programme and the generally broken promise of local paid work, the ambition of enhancing the neighbourhood's liveability, increasing its resident's well-being and realising a more sustainable living environment did not align with participants' preferences. In its philosophy, NJA regards the neighbourhood as a social community where people care for the environment and for each other. Within this view, doing paid work for the benefit of one's own 'household' makes it more rewarding, valuable and attractive. Although participants regarded local work appealing, for only a few participants it appeared crucial to employ one's capacities as a local community member to improve one's own living environment. Some identified themselves more with being a fellow town-dweller rather than a resident of the neighbourhood. Jessy: "What I like about working in Arnhem is that it is for the benefit of the people who live here". The same goes for Eileen: "For me, the neighbourhood can also just be Arnhem. It would be nice if you can find work in the city where you live".

Moreover, most participants were not primarily interested in contributing to a circular and sustainable community, which is incompatible with the efforts of NJA to create jobs in this area. As one participant put it: "If you are not interested in worm hotels, it pretty much ends here". The presentations at the end of the job training also revealed interests diverging from the ambitions of NJA's developers. Further, the programme did not produce new social entrepreneurship and businesses in that particular field as the developers' team had hoped. Whereas some participants of the second cohort felt attracted to the activities of the citizen initiative, the majority did not sign up, to the disappointment of the NJA team of developers who indeed noticed that commitment to sustainability projects was limited. They thought a higher response to neighbourhood activities could result from embedding the programme in the initiative's activities. As one of NJA's working documents stated: 'The current training is too solitary and will need to be better embedded in what is already there: the various initiatives, the projects, joint lunch sessions'.

The results of our responsive evaluation, however, seemed to suggest a different problem framing: not the mere lack of embeddedness, but the discrepancy between participants' aspirations and those of the developers appeared to explain the low response to community activities.

Conclusion

In the capability approach literature on labour market activation, the success of social innovations like NJA depends on the extent to which the capabilities of jobseekers have been enhanced, the real freedom they have to find the work they have reason to value. To that end, jobseekers as end users of labour market activation services and programmes must not only be free to choose ('exit' and 'choice') but also be able to articulate their opinions, thoughts and experiences and to make them count in the development of innovative products and services, that is, to have 'capability of voice', during design, implementation, delivery and evaluation. In our responsive evaluation we attempted to enhance the capability of voice of NJA participants and to show what remained unarticulated when these voices are barely expressed and heard.

What these voices tell us, is first that the needs of end users should be leading – not the developers' own desires to generating work capacity to enhance sustainability of the neighbourhood tomorrow, but the urgent needs of participants who wish valuable paid work today. Moreover, they teach us that these needs are very diverse, which calls for an approach that allows for customisation, since nothing simply works for everyone.

Second, like technological innovations, social innovations almost always have unintended consequences such as subtle exclusion mechanisms and potentially detrimental psychological effects. What does NJA have to offer for people whose confusion increased, or who stopped because of triggered fear of failure or perhaps who did not even have a chance of starting the programme? Moreover, NJA seemed to have created overstated expectations – locally based, paid work – among participants who can be expected to have had previous negative experiences with job mediation and training. This makes them vulnerable to new disappointments and feelings of failure.

Third, commitment to NJA resonates in the voices of participants as they generate new ideas for improvement that provide valuable input for the maturation of NJA. Some participants even explicated their willingness to take these ideas forward themselves as a form of user-driven innovation. Thus, the perspective of NJA participants as end users forms a valuable resource for innovation.

Moreover, in the development of NJA the pursuit of undeniably social outcomes that benefit society as a whole – sustainability, labour market activation – seems to have prevailed over 'an open process of participation, exchange and collaboration with relevant stakeholders, including end-users' (Voorberg et al, 2015: 1334). In other words: outcomes were given priority over process which poses the question of the truly social character of NJA as an innovation. Moreover, it underlines the inextricable link between product and process in social innovation since the developers of NJA could have benefited from these ideas and experiences to improve their services.

Of course, these conclusions must be seen in light of NJA's early stages of development in which a small group of inspired entrepreneurial citizens dared to challenge existing systemic practices of labour market activation that often enough appear to have fallen short. Social innovation often, if not always begins with the courage of the few to put forward a new idea. Nevertheless, amid the heat of development it is fairly easy to merely focus on outcomes and neglect process, reflecting an attitude of well-intended paternalism as if to say: *we* know what is good for these people.

What do we learn from the case of NJA as regards the role of social workers in social innovation processes? First, our findings draw the attention of social work practitioners and researchers to the social dimensions of the innovation process and its characteristics. These entail particularly: (1) the importance of enhancing the capability of voice of end users, (2) acknowledging the diversity of needs and experiences of joint stakeholders, primarily end users, (3) monitoring, averting or mitigating the unintended effects of innovation, and (4) preventing well-intended paternalism of innovators striving for (radical) social change to develop a blind spot for the systemic partnerships necessary to sustainably embed their social innovations.

Second, this creates a significant position for social workers in the social innovation landscape. Apart from being potential social innovators themselves, they can act as moderators of change as initiated by other societal change agents, such as social entrepreneurs. Performing this role adequately requires, on the one hand, that social workers be aware where and by whom social innovation initiatives take place within their local working practices. On the other hand, they need to relate to the stakeholders involved and position themselves as moderators of the innovation process to influence the course of development, as it is taking place, in accordance with public and democratic values. Such a role as change moderator would enable social workers to create or safeguard space for end users to enact their capability of voice in social innovation.

Third and finally, social workers can guide and support the societal learning process that (social) innovation ultimately is. The methodological principles of responsive evaluation as we applied in the present study – participatory, pluralistic, interpretive and dialogical – fit well with the underpinnings of social work methodology. These principles enable social workers to facilitate social innovation processes that indeed enhance the opportunities of persons to lead the valued and dignified lives they have reason to pursue.

References

Abma, F.I., Brouwer, S., de Vries, H.J., Arends, I., Robroek, S.J.W., Cuijpers, M.P.J., et al (2016) The capability set for work: development and validation of a new questionnaire, *Scandinavian Journal of Work, Environment & Health*, 42(1): 34–42.

Abma, T.A. and Widdershoven, G.A. (2005) Sharing stories: narrative and dialogue in responsive nursing evaluation, *Evaluation & the Health Professions*, 28(1): 90–109.

Al-Janabi, H., Flynn, T.N. and Coast, J. (2012) Development of a self-report measure of capability wellbeing for adults: the ICECAP-A, *Quality of Life Research*, 21(1): 167–76.

Banerjee, M.M. and Damman, J.L. (2013) The capabilities approach: a framework to understand and enhance TANF recipients' employability, *Journal of Poverty*, 17(4): 414–36.

Bonvin, J.M. and Orton, M. (2009) Activation policies and organisational innovation: the added value of the capability approach, *International Journal of Sociology and Social Policy*, 29(11/12): 565–74.

CBS (Centraal Bureau voor de Statistiek) (2023) Dashboard labour market, https://www.cbs.nl/nl-nl/visualisaties/dashboard-arbeidsmarkt [accessed 27 January 2023].

Egdell, V. and McQuaid, R. (2016) Supporting disadvantaged young people into work: insights from the capability approach, *Social Policy & Administration*, 50(1): 1–18.

Eurostat (2023) Unemployment rates, EU and EA, seasonally adjusted January 2008–December 2022, https://ec.europa.eu/eurostat/statistics-explained/index.php?title=Unemployment_statistics [accessed 27 January 2023].

Geertz, C. (1973) Thick description: toward an interpretative theory of culture, in *The Interpretation of Cultures: Selected Essays*, New York: Basic Books, pp 3–30.

Hoogenbosch, P. (2019) De Blauwe Wij(k)Economie [The Blue Neighbourhood Economy]. Presentation at Spark Spijkerkwartier Arnhem, June 11.

Kampen, T. and Tonkens, E. (2019) A personalised approach in activation: workfare volunteers' experiences with activation practitioners, *European Journal of Social Work*, 22(6): 1038–49.

Nicholls, A., Simon, J. and Gabriel, M. (2015) Introduction: dimensions of social innovation, in A. Nicholls, J. Simon and M. Gabriel (eds) *New Frontiers in Social Innovation Research*, Basingstoke: Palgrave Macmillan, pp 1–26.

Oudshoorn, N. and Pinch, T. (eds) (2003) *How Users Matter: The Co-construction of Users and Technology*, Cambridge, MA: MIT Press.

Robertson, P.J. (2015) Towards a capability approach to careers: applying Amartya Sen's thinking to career guidance and development, *International Journal for Educational and Vocational Guidance*, 15: 75–88.

Van der Haak, P. (2021) BuurtBaanBureau: Theoretisch kader en concept [internal document].

Van der Klink, J.J., Bültmann, U., Burdorf, A., Schaufeli, W.B., Zijlstra, F.R.H., Abma, F.I., et al (2016) Sustainable employability: definition, conceptualization, and implications – a perspective based on the capability approach, *Scandinavian Journal of Work, Environment & Health*, 42(1): 71–9.

Van Echtelt, P., Sadiraj, K., Hoff, S., Muns, S., Karpinska, K., Das, D. and Versantvoort, M. with Putman, L. (2019) *Eindevaluatie van de Participatiewet*, Den Haag: Sociaal en Cultureel Planbureau.

Von Hippel, E. (1986) Lead users: a source of novel product concepts, *Management Science*, 32(7): 791–805.

Voorberg, W.H., Bekkers, V.J. and Tummers, L.G. (2015) A systematic review of co-creation and co-production: embarking on the social innovation journey, *Public Management Review*, 17(9): 1333–57.

THEME B

Education and learning: social innovation in social work education and learning

10

Regional learning networks in the social welfare domain: drivers of social innovation in social work

Suzan van der Pas and Erik Jansen

Introduction

Since 2015, the Netherlands has undergone a major welfare system transformation which has impacted healthcare governance and the redistribution of responsibilities and austerity measures. Key to this is the devolution of formerly centralised responsibilities, services and support in the social domain to the municipalities, which in turn necessitates a strategy for social innovation in which local partners and municipalities develop new practices for social care and support. Regional learning networks were established as a channel of knowledge distribution, to address wicked problems and encourage innovation in the social welfare domain.

Although the Regional Networks for the Social Welfare Domain (RNSWD) are highly diverse in structure and approach, they do share a common transformative rationale for their approach. Learning facilitators hold key, preconditional roles, often being (politically neutral) action-researchers from the affiliated RNSWD, but sometimes also boundary workers from (stakeholder) practice organisations. Agenda formation was generally determined collaboratively by network members, comprising themes such as collaborative issues and new conceptions of care and well-being practices. All networks apply peer supervision or deliberative procedures.

The learning networks are defined as a group of people who learn together through various forms of learning to improve a particular practice, in this case in the social domain (Jansen et al, 2020). The core of such a group consists of professionals working in the social domain, but as the principle of multi-perspective or multi-actor learning is applied, other people can also be members of the network (for example local residents, volunteers and healthcare professionals). Researchers and students also often participate. Such a learning network can be organised at a local district level, or at municipal or regional level.

In this chapter, we focus on the role of these regional learning networks for innovation in the social welfare domain. We discuss how these regional learning networks can be drivers of social innovation in social work practice and education. We draw on our experiences from these RNSWDs and give two examples from diverse social work practices. We also reflect on which learning and design processes are involved in social work practice.

Regional learning networks in the social welfare domain

As part of an ongoing trend throughout Europe to decentralise care and social policies towards lower levels of organisation, developments in the social domain in the Netherlands have occurred, anchored on the introduction of new legislation for the supply of social support services. In 2007 the so-called Social Support Act (SSA) was implemented in which central social policy tasks and responsibilities were transferred to the municipal level, along with the accompanying budgets. The SSA is often called the 'participation law' (Verhoeven and Tonkens, 2013). The main objectives of the SSA are to promote participation in society, to support people who have limitations to living independently, to advance active engagement in society for all citizens and to promote social cohesion (De Klerk et al, 2010: 28–33). The objectives of the SSA are implemented at a local level of municipalities who have the autonomy to determine their own tasks and priorities within the frameworks set by law (Dijkhoff, 2014). In 2015 a new revised SSA[1] was implemented in which changes were framed more in terms of major systems transformation. As such it not only pertained to substantive social restructuring, but also to changes in the governance and collaborative structures. It also acknowledged the characteristics of the transformation as a collection of wicked problems involving many different stakeholders and their respective perspectives, visions and interests (van der Steen et al, 2010). Moreover, the SSA also included a redistribution of responsibilities across local social services and, quite problematically, came with an austerity regime in which budgets transferred to lower levels were severely cut by 25 per cent compared to the former central budgets. One reason behind this rationale was the notion that locally collaborating actors would be able to do things more effectively and at lower costs (Dutch Parliament, 2012). Similar developments have taken place in other countries, notably in the UK (Newman and Tonkens, 2011; Verhoeven and Tonkens, 2013) and Sweden (Minas et al, 2012).

Considering these developments, the Ministry of Health, Welfare and Sports already recognised in 2008 that the policy transition would imply grave changes in the local professional and policy practices of practitioners and policy makers. Therefore, to support the practice development in the field, they set up a programme to fund 14 RNSWD with a key role for universities of applied sciences as facilitators. The tasks of these networks are: (1) to innovate local professional and collaborative practices for social and policy professionals; (2) to support municipalities and their local partners with applied research on these changes in the field and with competence building of practitioners; and (3) to give strategic advice to policy makers. Further, an important aspect of the regional learning networks was collaboration and knowledge-sharing between the participating partners.

Within the universities of applied sciences, the network coordination was primarily positioned in departments of social work education and research. This was partly substantively informed, as the SSAs were focused on the social domain rather than the healthcare domains, although they had tangential overlaps. However, it was also strategically important as it allowed social work research and education of social workers to claim a stronger role in the collaborative practices in social support and welfare. This was noticeable in, among other ways, that whereas participating practitioners were from both healthcare and social disciplines, the demand-driven competence building programmes placed heavy emphasis on community building and transdisciplinary collaboration skills, in other words on typical social work and community development competences. A key development was that the majority of municipalities decided to set up multidisciplinary social support teams (Kooiman et al, 2015; Trappenburg and van Beek, 2019), that worked integrally around clients or families and were neighbourhood-based. Consequently, working in a neighbourhood-based team became an important topic in social work educational curricula across the country.

Further developments regarding the devolution of welfare, the Social Support Acts and social support teams is reported on elsewhere (see for instance Kooiman et al, 2015; Jansen et al, 2021). For this chapter it is important to note that the close collaboration between the work field, education and research led to emergent learning approaches with action research as the dominant mode of research. Wicked challenges are most often tackled best by applying a constructivist method allowing stakeholders to deliberate and discuss various approaches to the issue and to search for co-creative solutions or ways forward. Examples of questions relating to these wicked challenges are: how can different sectoral systems of financing be combined for establishing a joint multidisciplinary team? What is good integral method of client support across these sectors? How can team members deal with conflicts of interest between organisations? The involvement of other stakeholders, including students of social work and professionals from other disciplines, allowed for fruitful sources of practice-based education and place-based learning, though this was not always easy, as is described in more detail in Chapter 11. Common to all approaches, however, appeared to be the fact that questions on learning and innovation were collectively taken up by local stakeholders in an integrated way. Because of these commonalities the RNSWD decided to join forces and set up a national working group to study these learning and innovation processes in their own right.

In this chapter we report on a study conducted by the national working group with the purpose of developing models for interdisciplinary collaboration and learning, based on emerging practices and experiences in the different regional RNSWD. The research focus was to gain an overview on how learning approaches are currently operationalised in the RNSWD, how the networks devise and support local learning processes as a form of networked social innovation, and how that in turn can lead towards transformation of the field of social services. To derive these insights an exploratory survey was set up to examine current working practices within the networks, which could then be used to yield practical frames and tools for further development.

Survey

A survey was constructed consisting of open and closed questions on the themes, structures, processes and overall vision the respondents considered essential to the learning networks in which they operated. The survey was disseminated online across coordinators and contact persons within the 14 networks using the web-based data collection tool Qualtrics. In total 17 learning networks were described, with some RNSWD reporting more than one thematic learning network within their RNSWD. The patterns discovered in the collected data were then interpreted and employed to develop practical frames and tools for networked learning as a social innovation approach.

To indicate the variations between the RNSWDs we provide an illustration of two quite different set-ups of learning networks. In the first example, the regional learning network focused primarily on organising interactive symposia, workshops and expert meetings on various themes (content-based programming). The aim of the network is to exchange and develop knowledge on how to approach social transformation with regional municipalities, social enterprises, universities of applied sciences and voluntary organisations/volunteer initiatives. The question that this learning network dealt with varied by theme and activity.

The organisation of the learning network is rather informal with an open form of collaboration, although there are collaborative agreements with the stakeholders. Social professionals (social workers, civil servants, volunteers, social entrepreneurs), researchers, social work teachers and social work students took part in the various activities and meetings of the learning network. It is a light form of cooperation based on iterative evolution.

The second example of a RNSWD focused on developing practical tools and activities that help to improve the articulation of social care and support needs of citizens, develop (more suitable) solutions and monitor the results. In some of these more planned local learning networks in different municipalities, the social professionals, citizens, researchers and students worked together to improve and further refine already established practical tools and activities. Under the guidance of a facilitator (from a service user organisation), each learning network formulated a description of the bottlenecks, change goals and an action plan. Subsequently the learning network applied action research to improve the social care and support needs of citizens via a step-by-step process of testing, evaluation and implementation.

The learning process was based on two formal models: best practice unit (BPU) model (see Wilken et al, 2013) and an integrated process supervision of groups (IPG) model (Goossens, 2009). The BPU model is characterised by interaction between individual and collective learning processes, the development of new or improved working methods, and the implementation of these methods in daily practice. Multiple knowledge resources are used, including experiential knowledge, professional knowledge and scientific knowledge. The learning process takes place via six phases: (1) formulating the sense of ambition; (2) selecting the participating members; (3) conducting a baseline assessment; (4) formulating goals and a plan of action; (5) conducting a plan–do–check–act cycle to realise the plan of action; and (6) producing outcomes, products and other forms of dissemination.

The core of the IPG model (Goossens, 2009) is an integrated approach in which the individual group dynamics are connected in order to arrive at a unified group process. The IPG model seeks a connection between four core elements: (1) group development, (2) communication levels, (3) leadership and (4) the context of the group.

Using these models, knowledge and experiences were exchanged in a systematic way between the different learning networks so that a collaborative regional learning process is made possible. The interaction between citizens and social professionals was initially difficult (learning to understand each other's language), but it yielded new insights for the social professionals in their support and care for citizens in need. Creating safety and learning to understand each other took time, but eventually citizens felt empowered and became more vocal towards social professionals. Citizens played an important role in the translation and explanation of activities within their local network of fellow citizens. Second, the dynamic local context of social work practice had an impact on the learning process and the results achieved. Also, the role of the process facilitator was crucial, giving enough attention and time to the process and outcome. Shared ownership was important for the process of the learning network.

Findings

The patterns in the survey results can be summarised as follows. The regional networks reveal great diversity in approaches and practices employed, as well as in the characteristics of the participants. The latter may be positioned at different strategic levels and come from a variety of disciplines affiliated to the learning networks. Local or regional choices are made depending on the aims and specific focus of the network. We also see many differences in the openness or closedness of the networks, in the sense that some function as ever-growing and evolving learning groups, whereas others work based on more formal participant designation and specific aims for impact or results.

In all networks much thought is given to what is being done and how it should be done. Respondents of the networks were able to provide a conscious rationale for the learning process entailing some sort of methodological approach, even though it may be an emergent and responsive approach rather than a planned or top-down method. The key figure initiating and facilitating the learning network is often also the one propagating this process vision or learning strategy. They usually also have an active role in protecting the joint learning process from external policy or contextual pressures to solidify it into instrumental services programming. Learning generally involves reflective space for deliberation and exchanging uncertainties while tolerating the not-knowing, but municipal policy and politics often ask for concretisation and action in advance. The extent to which facilitators were able to shield the learning process seems to have a great impact on engagement and support of network participants.

Regarding the type of persons performing the role of network facilitator, these were often local boundary workers who were able to gather support and arouse innovative capacity with others, including by connecting disciplines and operating transversally. According to respondents they seem almost an essential prerequisite for a good learning process and for involvement from local parties. Learning facilitators mainly originate from (practice-based) research or education, notably in the field of social work. This is not surprising as the RNSWDs were set up from within departments of social work education with the regional universities of applied sciences. As these universities are not competing parties in local service delivery practices for the social and welfare domain, educators and researchers are considered neutral, allowing them to fulfil their role as facilitators with trust and unburdened by substantive or economic interests. Also, when the learning facilitators are linked to social work education, they stimulate both the linkage between social work practice and education, and between social work competence and the social support teams.

Agenda-setting in the networks can arise from a central question from one of the participating partners in the learning network such as a municipality or organisation (as a so-called closed approach) or is developed from the bottom up based on local issues that cooperating parties decide to work on (vice versa, as an open approach). In almost all learning networks, once an agenda is set, some form of peer review or substantive deliberation is organised as the main constituent mode of learning.

In short, the survey revealed that despite the diversity in process and method approaches between and within the learning network and also regionally, the respondents considered the mere setting up of the learning networks helped them to gain a grip on the development of the local social domain and foster innovation with the groups of participating partners.

Deliberation and emancipation as learning: towards a conceptual framework

Reflection on the results of the survey by the working group Learning Practices yields several relevant conclusions.

First, regarding the relevance of the RNSWD for social innovation we note that the objective of the regional networks lies within the purpose for which they were initially set up: facilitating the societal transformation for practice and policy professionals in the social and welfare domain. Because of the learning approach through applying action research in practically every network, the resulting innovation is highly focused on a participatory process by all relevant actors thereby enhancing a constructivist approach to innovation. Moreover, the innovation itself focuses on enhancing the social support for citizens by way of the vision articulated in the SSA and its consecutive iterations and specifications. One important observation in many of the learning networks was that further operationalisation of the principles of the SSA actually required dialogue and supervision on how these principles could and should be put into practice in the local setting and which forms of action by social workers and other stakeholders is necessary. In fact, the function of the deliberation appeared to be that time and space should be created for reflection on issues arising from the instrumental interventions involved in transitioning towards a new system, such as issues on ethical dilemmas and professional and role identities. A concrete example is that somewhere along the way social support team members generally experienced an identity tension or even loyalty conflicts between being an employee within their own social service organisation and being outsourced in a multidisciplinary team, with different roles and tasks. Such issues pertain to the so-called transformative questions rather than the simple instrumental 'how-to' issues and can thus be labelled as 'slow' questions, as opposed to 'quick' fixes and the actions social workers are used to in everyday hurried professional practice (see for instance van Doren et al, 2020). Therefore, the RNSWD form a nice example of a programme approach that in some instances indeed spurred large-scale social innovation and systems change, particularly for the social and welfare domain. Another example, at a more macro level, is innovation focusing on the governance of healthcare and well-being and more inclusive participation in society.

Second, to further grasp how the social innovation processes as described lead to durable social change in professional practice, the working group wanted to adequately describe the embedding conditions under which learning occurs. This yielded a practice-based framework in which seven aspects, which can be described as a systemic configuration of the learning practices, are outlined. These aspects (formulated as questions) are:

- Intentions: what are the aims of the learning practices and what are the various participants trying to achieve?
- Activities: what is being done as purposeful or opportunistic action, including rituals and formal or informal sense-making routines?
- Normativity: what conceptions, norms and values are leading and inform the actions of participants, and what themes or issues are considered important?
- Actants: what are the relevant forces or key players in the learning practices, persons or objects such as documents, artefacts, events or developments having causal effects?
- Context: how does the global (narrative) context provide a background or setting for the events and actions taking place, and how does it help to understand them?
- Space and place: in what abstract physical dimensions (space) do the learning networks and their participants operate, such as at the town hall office, at the university or in the neighbourhood centre, and how are these dimensions perceived psychologically (place), for example, the town hall can suggest a dominant role for the municipality, while the neighbourhood feels closer to the clients and dwellers?
- Outcomes: what is the impact or consequence of the learning both individually and collectively, and is that intentional or unintentional? How does that compare to if there was no learning network?

With this framework the deeper insights as to how learning and innovation can occur and can be stimulated becomes tangible and transferable. To date, testing and iterative revising of the framework in practice is taking place in different contexts, with different stakeholders and various wicked challenges.

Third, the social transformation was spurred particularly by external pressure from the ministry and national policies. Thus, the transformation of the social and welfare domain pertains to innovation on several aggregate levels ranging from the macro level of national policies, meso level of local social policies to the micro level of client service provision. This brings with it a central–local tension in policy making, as the rather abstract guidance from legislation and national policies was impossible to apply directly in local practice of social care and support, but required extensive deliberation among local stakeholders, the time and space for which could not always be found, as happens in such processes (Jansen et al, 2021). We found support for this in our survey as respondents stated that they put a lot of effort into organising the reflective space and time for local stakeholders to deliberate what needed to be done and how, albeit that network facilitators chose various methods for this. All networks employed some kind of peer supervision or reflection sessions. Also, it should be noted that the funding of the networks was organised in such a way that the ministry covered one third of the costs of the learning networks, the local partners covered one third as in-kind contribution, and the universities of applied sciences the remaining one third of the costs.

Finally, the substantive aims of the national policies underlying the social transformation in which these regional networks operate are very much in line with the aims of social work, notably: working integrally and neighbourhood-based, and working holistically and needs-based from the client's perspective. This, as already noted in the introduction, legitimised and put forward a central role for the social worker. However, local practices at the municipal level and developments in the learning networks indicate that many more disciplines were practically involved than only social workers, even though a major part of the transformation was dedicated towards social work competence by the whole network system involved. Interestingly, team members from other disciplines such as community nurses and housing consultants were stimulated to work and act more like social workers. This culminated in the importance of neighbourhood-based teams being developed everywhere in the country. This suggests a shift towards a conception of 'social work' as a collective capability of the system rather than it being conceived as an exclusively disciplinary task of social work professionals. In other words: the network-based social innovation taking place, partly but not solely spurred by the learning networks, in fact pertains to collaborative developments in implementing social work as a collective capacity of the system, rather than that it innovates specific social workers' methods and practices. Based on these reflections we now turn to the broader relevance of the learning networks for social innovation in social work.

Conclusion

In this chapter we reported on the experiences of actors involved in the RNSWD in the Netherlands as social innovation networks. Based on the survey responses we gained an overview on the large-scale social innovation capacities of these networks. This overview yielded a conceptual framework for social innovation and learning in social work practice and education.

One conclusion is that for such large-scale social innovation processes to take place in the social work field, it is imperative that participant stakeholders are actually capable of engaging in the innovation process. This entails (1) that competence in organising deliberative reflection and innovation is present and (2) that participants have the actual time and space to engage in these collaborative reflection sessions. Social innovation does not happen instantaneously and autonomously, it requires effort to create adequate learning situations and contexts to effectively shape the social innovation process. This requires slowing down and being able to take the time to develop the learning network and recognise the influence of the local context and other external processes. Moreover, particularly for the social domain, such deliberation involves making sense of the deeper values of the innovation for social care and support of clients in need. As can be seen in the collaboration in the regional learning networks this sense-making is not only among social workers but among stakeholders across all disciplines involved in the social domain.

Moreover, our analyses and reflection suggest that the large-scale social innovation these learning networks aim for are in a sense unbound: they may have initially been focused on social work but came to involve much more in terms of disciplines and participants and learning processes. The result is that the scope of the social innovation becomes more pervasive systemically thereby also fostering broader sense-making across on the holistic view on persons and social work values and methods. Although networks differ in the extent to which they seemed to have succeeded in implementing real systemic change, one perspective stands out: social innovation should be considered a collective capability of the system and requires cross-disciplinary collaboration as much as it requires changes and innovation in methods and instruments.

Our main conclusion is that processes of liberation and empowerment of network professionals are fundamentally intertwined with a learning approach to social innovation: dialogue and supervision create a space for reflection on existential questions regarding (the organisation of) care and social support, and what this means for professional and personal identities. However, this requires active facilitation of the time and space needed for reflection.

Acknowledgements
The authors wish to acknowledge the support of the members of the working group Learning Practices of the RNSWD: Ina Tilma, Renate Werkman, Annelies Kooiman, Renske Schamhart, Marjolanda Hendriksen, Iris Middendorp, Sabrina Keinemans and Huub Purmer.

Note
[1] http://wetten.overheid.nl/BWBR0035362/2016-08-01

References

De Klerk, M., Gilsing, R. and Timmermans, J. (eds) (2010) *Op weg met de Wmo: Evaluatie van de Wet maatschappelijke ondersteuning 2007–2009*, Den Haag: Sociaal en Cultureel Planbureau.

Dijkhoff, T. (2014) The Dutch Social Support Act in the shadow of the decentralization dream, *Journal of Social Welfare and Family Law*, 36(3): 276–94.

Dutch Parliament (2012) Bruggen slaan: Regeerakkoord VVD – PvdA, 29 October, http://www.parlement.com/9291000/d/regeerakkoord2012.pdf.

Goossens, W. (2009) Integrale procesbegeleiding van groepen: een basismodel voor groeps- en teamcoaching, *Tijdschrift Voor Coaching*, 4: 28–31.

Jansen, E., Javornik, J., Brummel, A. and Yerkes, M.A. (2021) Central–local tensions in the decentralization of social policies: street-level bureaucrats and social practices in the Netherlands, *Social Policy & Administration*, 55(7): 1262–75.

Jansen, E., Pas, S. van der and Tilma, I. (2020) Sociaal transformeren kan alleen lerend, *Journal of Social Intervention: Theory and Practice*, 29(7): 18–24.

Kooiman, A., Wilken, J.P., Stam, M., Jansen, E. and Van Biene, M. (2015) *Leren transformeren: Hoe faciliteer je praktijkinnovatie in tijden van transitie?*, Utrecht: Movisie.

Minas, R., Wright, S. and van Berkel, R. (2012) Decentralization and centralization: governing the activation of social assistance recipients in Europe, *International Journal of Sociology and Social Policy*, 32(5/6): 286–98.

Newman, J. and Tonkens, E. (eds) (2011) *Participation, Responsibility and Choice: Summoning the Active Citizen in Western European Welfare States*, Amsterdam: Amsterdam University Press.

Trappenburg, M. and van Beek, G. (2019) 'My profession is gone': how social workers experience de-professionalization in the Netherlands, *European Journal of Social Work*, 22(4): 676–89.

van der Steen, M., Peeters, R. and van Twist, M. (2010) *De boom en het rizoom: Overheidssturing in een netwerksamenleving*, Den Haag: MinVROM.

van Doren, D., Driessen, P., Runhaar, H. and Giezen, M. (2020) Learning within local government to promote the scaling-up of low-carbon initiatives: a case study in the City of Copenhagen, *Energy Policy*, 136: art 111030, https://doi.org/10.1016/j.enpol.2019.111030

Verhoeven, I. and Tonkens, E. (2013) Talking active citizenship: framing welfare state reform in England and the Netherlands, *Social Policy and Society*, 12(3): 415–26.

Wilken, J.P., van Slagmaat, C. and van Gijzel, S. (2013) The best practice unit: a model for learning, research and development, *Journal of Social Intervention: Theory and Practice*, 22(2): 131–48.

11

Putting learning communities into practice: innovation of social work education

Meike Koop, Ankie Schoenmakers, Ina Tilma, Nathalie Grahame and Henk Spies

Introduction

In this chapter it will be argued that learning communities are both helpful and challenging for higher education in social work. When learning communities are part of the obligatory curriculum of social work students, they may contribute to building up the identity and skills of (young) professionals and their educators in dealing with wicked problems from a social work perspective. We offer several sensitising concepts as a tool for reflection and action in learning communities to improve participants' agency.

First, we contextualise our learning communities as emerging in the field of social work and in higher education in the Netherlands, specifically Avans University of Applied Sciences. Second, we offer the concrete principles our learning communities are built upon and explain how those principles have been innovative for education in social work. Third, we introduce four stages and several dualities at work in learning communities. The chapter is based on the longitudinal action research project Learning from Learning Communities, financed by Avans University of Applied Sciences and Regional Network Social Welfare Domain Noord-Brabant, the Netherlands.

Learning communities as an emerging model

The transformation of the social service system and changing perspectives on wicked problems in the Netherlands have inspired social work education at Avans University of Applied Sciences to bring about social innovation in process and outcome (see European Commission, 2013) by starting to work with informal open-ended education in learning communities focusing on wicked problems.

Transformation of the welfare state as a wicked problem

Social work in the Netherlands had to reinvent itself in response to the introduction of new legislation transforming the welfare state. Those changes and other developments were understood as wicked problems reflecting a paradigm shift for social work (Stam et al, 2015). The term 'wicked problems' refers to societal problems that cannot be described in definite detail as the problems can only be identified in the perspective of a prospective solution. Consequently, a wicked problem can be explained in different ways. Or, to tell it in the founding words of Rittel and Webber: 'The information needed to understand the problem depends upon one's idea for solving it' (1973: 161).

Wicked problems in social work were identified and newly defined in the perspective of this transformation. Social workers were supposed to methodologically intensify support by the informal social network of citizens in need, instead of organising formal professional help (Bredewold et al, 2018). Also, organisations were challenged to intensify cooperation with other organisations setting up cross-organisational, interprofessional teams inventing and arranging their work (de Waal, 2018). It also involved a disruption in financing social work. The money flow to pay for cure and care was decentralised and new structures for annual contracting and financing were developed by municipalities and their partners. This development was followed by new systems for justifying social work to their new financiers (De Rijk, 2018). The field of social work seemed to be continuously evolving and social workers had to cooperate with various and constantly changing stakeholders. At present, social work is challenged by wicked problems and recent crises, for instance those related to the COVID-19 pandemic and the war in Ukraine, increasing polarisation and inequality, and ambitions related to the United Nations' Sustainable Development Goals (Kromhout, 2020; VHSS, 2022).

Learning communities at institutions of higher education

Due to this transformation of the welfare state, social workers longed for a learning zone, a way for organising social innovation. As an answer to this and other developments, an increasing amount of learning communities are set up in the Netherlands since the early 2010s (Stam and Wilken, 2015; De Waal, 2018). It can be understood as a strategy for the attempt to address wicked problems (Beckmann, 2017). The term 'learning communities' refers to a more or less self-organised group of participants who collaboratively engage with each other in order to learn together, to utilise knowledge and social innovation in dealing with wicked problems. There are many different versions of learning communities with names like communities of practice, learning networks, field labs and so on (Wenger, 1998; De Waal, 2018; Zestor, 2018; Emanuel et al, 2022).

Institutions of higher education have become an important player for initiating and participating in learning communities (VHSS, 2022). This effort contributes to the ambition to intensify cooperation and co-creation within the threshold education, research and practice. Furthermore, learning communities are supposed to stimulate just-in-time education and informal and lifelong learning. Educators and professionals from various fields expected learning communities to fundamentally and sustainably change the way higher education is organised in the Netherlands and other countries (WRR, 2013). Many universities of applied sciences started to transform themselves into more flexible organisations, intensified co-creation and searched for matching pedagogical and didactic strategies in order to help students and professionals develop competences for dealing with wicked problems and reach innovative learning (see, for example Taylor, 2017; Hoeve et al, 2021).

Working with learning communities in higher education matches with the paradigm shifts Biesta (2016) describes as a shift from the instruction paradigm to a learning paradigm, and the education paradigm to a paradigm of life-long learning. Instead of students following bounded education programmes in a demarcated period of time, the will to learn is increasingly becoming part of the identity of professionals and citizens in general. Life-long learning becomes a constant part of the basic attitude and there is a wide range of actors engaged in learning and appearances of learning. A recent example of this development is the advice by a commission to social work higher education, to invest in interprofessional approaches of life-long learning and connect different levels of education in arrangements combining learning and working (VHSS, 2022).

Starting with learning communities in social work education

The educational programme for social work at Avans University of Applied Sciences started bottom-up experiments with learning communities in 2014. At first, educators pioneered on a small scale with learning communities with students, professionals from the field and educators. All participants engaged in those experiments voluntarily.

Educators dreamed that learning communities might offer a learning zone in which students, social workers and educators could cooperate, innovate and learn based on experienced urgency. And, not unimportantly, be intrinsically motivated to engage. They wished for participants to contribute to the necessary innovations in social work in the Netherlands, and to develop a professional identity prospering in a very dynamic social work field, and ready to constructively tolerate uncertainty. Other social work educators commented critically that education must not be all about attitude. They wished to guarantee that students would still be learning about theorising social work, incorporating working methodically and thinking in an evidence-based way. Quite unique for the Netherlands in that period, learning communities became part of the mandatory curriculum of first- and second-year students in social work in 2017 instead of an elective programme. The curriculum leaders succeeded in enthusing service providers, resulting in actively hosting learning communities and enabling social workers in their organisation to participate.

Learning communities put into practice

As all participants were new to learning communities in social work higher education, during the first five years this social innovation was supported by action research. A group of researchers from Avans University of Applied Sciences focused on helping participants putting the initial idea into practice. The action research contained focus and reflection groups, interviews with overall 60 participants, participant observation, and various interventions like the development of a reflection and action game. In evaluations, educators reported that the action research contributed to a better understanding of their role in learning communities and helped them develop their pedagogic and didactic repertoire. Next, we describe the principles and experiences with the concept.

Principles of learning communities

A learning community consists of at least one social worker, one educator and a mix of first- and second-year social work students. The learning community is embedded in the professional field of the social worker. For one year, the learning community explores and defines itself as a group of (young) professionals and works on innovations dedicated to wicked problems in the field of the participating social worker. Students or professionals from other fields may participate incidentally or for the full year. Some learning communities exist for several years in the same professional field with a turnover of students (and sometimes educators and social workers).

Every student participates in two learning communities during two consecutive years. Examination in learning communities is constructed on principles of assessment as learning. Formative and summative examination takes place usually three or four times a year. Mostly, the exams take place in an oral setting and have similarities with appreciative performance reviews. In many learning communities, performance reviews focus not only on students, but also on the educator and social worker. Participants of learning communities evaluated those exams as a booster for the process of learning and innovating.

The learning community is scheduled weekly, offering around four hours to meet and work. The exact focus of a learning community depends on the agenda of the learning community itself. Many learning communities work flexibly in subgroups, individually and as a whole group. There is no predefined exact objective. The learning community must negotiate about nearly everything, such as what mission(s) to engage with, how to cooperate, what exactly to learn, how exactly to innovate, and whether and how to connect with stakeholders outside the learning community. Also, who is taking which role when is decided through mutual negotiation, and is consequently part of the group dynamics.

As part of the arrangement in learning communities, all participants are understood to be equal to each other. Educators are supposed not to dominate the learning community. Instead, they are asked to positively influence bottom-up processes of constructive cooperation in learning, working and innovating around wicked problems. Some participants criticised equality as a false construct of egalitarianism: educators were in the position to pass or fail a student at the exam while students were not. Also, a certain seniority of educators and social workers makes a great difference between them and students, leading to more power of interpretation and definition for example. Over the years, this critique has changed the arrangements in learning communities. Many educators work with notions of equality to constructively influence group dynamics instead of understanding themselves as completely equal. Also, educators as well as social workers make their seniority productive for learning communities by sharing their experiences.

Examples of learning communities

Around 80 learning communities with 160 educators and social workers and 1,200 students are active every academic year at Avans University of Applied Sciences. All learning communities are unique and consequently differ from each other on a multiplicity of contextual and structural factors, the combination of the participants' individual effort, available resources and the interplay of all together at specific, mutable moments. In the two examples of learning communities introduced in this chapter, participants had to deal with the differing and changing intensity of client contact, embeddedness of the social worker in a professional network of cooperation, variety in ambitions by the hosting organisation, the personality of all individual participants, and the unfolding group dynamics.

One of the learning communities is based at a centre for psychiatric treatment, with many clients on the autism spectrum. This learning community has been active since 2018. It is situated on the premises of the institution, and the students have contact with the clients. Wicked problems addressed in this learning community are, for instance, related to the physical health of clients. The learning community designed a route across the grounds of the centre where the clients could take a walk and do some exercise. Another issue they were working on was related to acquiring more volunteers for the centre, especially volunteers operating as buddies for the clients. All students in this learning community also became buddies for part of the time. This helped them to understand what it means to be a buddy, thus getting new input and ideas on how to attract new volunteer buddies.

Another learning community was set up in 2019 in cooperation with a municipality. The learning community was situated at the offices of the municipality. There was no contact with citizens at first. The municipality had various social work–related issues the students could work on. It was organised around themes like youth, senior citizens and illiteracy. Once the students started working on the chosen topics, they were introduced to other relevant professionals who could put them in touch with other organisations and citizens. The learning community worked on making information material more suitable for citizens with lower language skills. During the COVID-19 crisis they also worked on the issue of how to stay in touch with the senior citizens and keep them connected to the community. They let children make and write postcards for the senior citizens, and worked on introducing senior citizens to simply operated tablets for video calls to their relatives and friends.

Positioning educators in learning communities

Especially during the first two years of working with learning communities, educators were puzzled by the role expectations of the new approach. They indicated that role expectations in learning communities differed from more traditional forms of education, impacting their identity and position in group dynamics. Traditional educators expect to be in control of group dynamics, follow a goal-oriented and content-related programme based on social-constructivism, and position themselves as an expert.

In reflection groups, educators often referred to 'what is not', when talking about the new-to-develop didactic and pedagogic repertoire and their new-to-develop professional identity. They had incorporated a strong professional language for coaching students in project work, for instance (see Bos and Harting, 2006), and compared learning communities with it. They said things like: "In project work I could support students in goal-oriented working and was convinced they did and learned what they had to". Educators sometimes had sleepless nights as they experienced their learning communities to be out of their control. They questioned their own positioning in learning communities and felt responsible for frustrations among students. One of the often-asked questions by that time had been when to intervene and when to sit on one's hands.

Stages and dualities as sensitising concepts

The reflection groups have helped to develop sensitising concepts as a tool for reflection on the complex dynamic in learning communities and to identify options for action acknowledging contextual and structural factors, the strategy and personality of individual participants and the interplay of all together. The sensitising concepts refer to stages and dualities at work in learning communities.

Stages

Learning communities can be conceptualised to develop along four different stages. Those stages do not chronologically follow one another. Depending on the purpose of understanding learning communities in terms of stages, the stages can be used as sensitising concepts applied to a short-term period like one session, and to a long-term period of several months or the full year. It is useful to understand that the learning community can locate itself in a specific stage, but also subgroups within the learning community can differ from each other in relation to the stages.

With those stages, the focus is not exclusively on defining stages of group dynamics like the stages of the Orman model by Tuckman or the model by Levine do (Bekker, 2020). The specific Learning Community Stages are helpful in acknowledging the intertwined condition of group dynamics with everybody's individual agency and the actual focus on wicked problems. The stages we named are: (1) Testing the Waters, (2) Digging Deeper, (3) Blue Monday and (4) Reaping the Harvest.

Testing the Waters refers to the condition that participants question, such as their own position and ambition in the learning community, the quality of others and the group, and the meaning of wicked problems. Activities in the learning community are related to bonding, surface explorations of wicked problems, and negotiations about everyone's place.

In Digging Deeper, participants are engaged with each other and the wicked problem. Many participants experience basic needs according to the self-determination theory (Ryan and Deci, 2018) to be met at its optimum. Things seem to work out smoothly, challenges are welcomed, expectations have become clearer and participants are ready to individually and collectively delve into wicked problems by, for example, research and cooperation. In relation to group dynamics, there can be a positive flow, but also conflicts about leadership or focus might arise.

Blue Monday comes up if the individual and collective holding space for setback is subverted. Whatever factors related to individual and group dynamics, wicked problems, or the interplay of all together, might induce this condition. Lack of motivation, panic zone instead of learning zone, and experienced stagnation predominate. This is a tough time for a learning community and its individual members.

When Reaping the Harvest, participants experience urgency to accomplish and leave things behind. The learning community evaluates its own performance in relation to individual progress, group dynamics and innovations to work on wicked problems. Some go for a sprint in order to excel, search for possibilities to display what they are proud of, transmit things, accept what is not achieved and make new plans.

Dualities

Several dualities pop up within the named stages. Where to best position oneself within a duality depends on the stage and what exactly is at stake within the stage and in relation to other dualities influencing the condition of the learning community.

Not-knowing versus clarity

In a learning community, often participants long for clarity in focus about positions, perspectives, possibilities, ways out. As part of the same reality, learning communities often do not know what to do, and if they do know, how to get things done. Not-knowing can be experienced as frustrating, irritating or paralysing, as a threat, failure or insult, and it might inflict anger and powerlessness. There is a great temptation to jump to solutions in order not to tolerate the discomfort of not-knowing and to reach clarity.

Somewhere in between not-knowing and clarity, another condition is located: uncertainty. Stam and Wilken (2018) invite people to appreciate uncertainty and make it productive instead of giving it a negative perspective. Learning communities may learn to understand the condition of uncertainty as a chance, an open space for what is yet undisclosed. This condition can be understood as a source of knowledge, although there is a thin line between exploiting uncertainty and suffering not-knowing. To make uncertainty productive, it is helpful to invest in patience and trust in order to create a holding space.

The students at the centre for psychiatric treatment experienced the discomfort of not-knowing when they first met their client buddies. They were afraid not to know what to do, what to say and what to expect. They longed for clarity and asked the educator and social worker for a clear instruction about what to do at their first meeting. They did not get an instruction however; instead they were encouraged to just go and see what would happen if they entered the situation with an open heart and mind. Therefore, students were helped not to enter a panic zone of not-knowing, but were encouraged to benefit from the open space of uncertainty.

Afterwards the students were very positive. They experienced the feeling that they would be more confident in similar situations in the future.

Friction versus harmony

Participants may enjoy their learning community most when there is harmony in the group dynamics. A learning community experiences harmony when there is enough trust, a feeding structure and a nice process flow. If chaos dominates instead of structure, stagnation instead of process and distrust instead of trust, there is much potential for friction in group dynamics. Like uncertainty, friction is also associated with negativity.

Therefore, if friction dominates, a learning community is in search of a formal or informal leader to stand up and bring back harmony (Löhmer and Standhardt, 2015). There is a great temptation for educators to take this role, as they are good at ascertaining the needs of groups and individuals, feel highly responsible for the dynamics in learning communities, and other participants prefer the educator to take leadership instead of others, due to role expectations mentioned earlier. Nevertheless, standing up as leader often is not the best way to remove friction in learning communities.

A learning community may benefit most from whatever friction, if all participants take responsibility instead of leaning back on individual leaders. If searching together for everyone's will and ability to develop solutions, friction becomes constructive (Löhmer and Standhardt, 2015). Learning communities benefit from developing a holding space for tolerating friction like argued for tolerating uncertainty. If the learning community as a group learns to restore harmony, this might have a positive influence on individual participants, group dynamics and the innovative potential in relation to wicked problems.

> The learning community of the municipality experienced friction between the subgroup responsible for activities and the group responsible for the public relations. The activities group had been very busy organising a meet-up for the local youth. The date of the activity was approaching, but the public relations group had not made any flyers, yet. The activity group did not want to wait any longer and decided to make the flyers themselves. When they presented the flyers at the next meeting, the public relations group became angry. It was their task to make the flyers. The emotions between the groups flared up. At that moment, the students seemed not ready to make the friction constructive. The educator did not come up with a solution bringing back harmony, but took the role of mediator as the groups discussed the causes of the friction from both sides. Students came to see responsibility for the friction and agreed on how to deal with a comparable situation in the future.

Structure versus freedom

One of the challenges educators encounter is trying to find the right balance between offering the students sufficient structure, while at the same time giving them the space to explore and learn, make mistakes and figure things out on their own. Students ask for structure, and look to the educator and the professional for guidance, just as new groups need direction and look to their leader to offer them clarity and purpose (Remmerswaal, 2013; Bekker, 2020). Therefore, at the start of a learning community some structure may help. Too much structure and guidance, though, can make students become dependent on the educator and professional. When the educator works hard, and does the most structuring, students tend to do less and lean back. In the process, they need enough freedom to be able to make choices, feel autonomous, and able to contribute and share their ideas (Ryan and Deci, 2018).

> In the example of the centre for psychiatric treatment, in the stage of Testing the Waters, the educator is trying to create a safe environment for the students. The professional wants a clear structure for the students. The students also ask for this. They struggle with their freedom and the uncertainty of the exact purpose of the learning community. The structure is given by an introductory programme in which the students get a tour of the premises, meet clients, and are divided into groups to work on some specific issues the centre has proposed the students to work on. Besides that, all students are matched with a client of the centre. Some freedom was also given: the students were invited to work on their own ideas for the centre next to the given specified issues. Students appreciated this structure as a holding space and came up with their own fresh ideas.

Process versus results

Process and results are two sides of the same coin. Attention for one side can boost the other. Nevertheless, too much or too little attention for one side can also cause stagnation. Process aspects are about the quality of relationships, creating the safe environment needed for learning on individual and collective level. Result aspects are about the task at hand, planning, goals and who does what. Strong alliances on mutual agreements, the tasks and the relationship aspects may positively influence learning communities (Bordin, 1983).

Both students and professionals are usually more focused on achieving results, while focus on the process helps in reflection and learning. Making mistakes, figuring out how things work instead of being told what to do.

When there is too much focus on the result, the quality of the process may recede into the background. When relation issues are not properly addressed, they may start to fester under the surface and may also infect the results. At the same time, too much focus on the relationship may result in a group where hardly anything gets done.

> In the learning community at the municipality, the professional organised a meeting with the mayor and some other professionals. The students could choose which themes they wanted to address, and the students were invited to first acquaint themselves with the various themes. Students were left completely free in how to organise themselves as a group, leading to some students in the lead and others keeping passive and silent. At a certain point, the leading students complained about this dynamic. The silent students said that they would feel more safe learning to work on wicked problems in small groups, first. They planned to let their voice be heard in the bigger group in a later stage. By first organising cooperation in small groups, everybody could develop skills needed in cooperation and simultaneously better focus on results.

Group versus individual(s)

In the learning communities all participants work together on the wicked problems, thus learning together and from each other. At the same time everyone has their talents, strengths and challenges, leading to individual learning processes and personal growth. When there is no room in a group for each member's needs, the existence of the group may be at risk (Remmerswaal, 2013). This requires the learning community to support both the group process and the individual processes. Finding a connection between the goals of the group and the goals of the individual members may be supportive in combining both processes successfully. This also entails knowledge of the roles the members of a group can take on, communication issues, levels of interaction and various leadership styles. This goes for the educator, social worker and students involved. Knowledge about group dynamics and individual basic needs enables participants to better recognise what is at stake, making possible to intervene in an appropriate manner.

> The learning community of the centre for psychiatric treatment started with activities to get to know each other, working on creating alliances and a safe environment for learning. At the same time, all members were asked to formulate individual learning goals and how to realise them. Therefore, there was room for both: the group and the individual processes. A few weeks later, there was stagnation in the group process

focusing on addressing wicked problems. In a reflection in small groups, individual students said they felt too insecure about what to do, and were struggling with their role in the group. The individual insecurities stood in the way of a good cooperation. A second-year student suggested using a game focusing on roles in a group, everyone's qualities, pitfalls and ambitions. Playing this game helped the learning community in bonding, offering feedback and making a concrete plan for cooperation and how to hold each other accountable individually.

Conclusion

When social work educators of Avans University of Applied Sciences developed the idea of working with learning communities, they got enthusiastic about the transforming potential. They understood learning communities to be a social innovation answering wicked problems related to the transformations in the field of social work and higher education in the Netherlands.

By putting learning communities into practice on a large scale, educators experienced becoming part and parcel of the transforming process. Educators had to enter a learning zone and reinvent their roles as participants in learning communities instead of positioning themselves as educators leading groups of students. In this way, education through learning communities has turned to be socially innovative in process and outcome.

In the beginning, educators relied on concepts belonging to traditional forms of education. Also, they came up with vague questions about whether to intervene or sit on one's hands. In this way, educators tried to overcome not-knowing. However, in reflection groups, educators learned to use uncertainty in search for new concepts for education offering clarity about process and result in learning communities. In this chapter we introduced those sensitising concepts in terms of stages and dualities.

The concepts help to understand how just-in-time education and informal learning unfold. These reflect the condition of open-ended education by naming what is at stake and offering perspectives for action, but no clear-cut solutions. In this way, the concepts sensitise for dealing with uncertainty in a constructive and productive way and contribute to the ambition to keep learning and innovating.

Students participating in learning communities were indeed challenged to enter a learning zone in which they deepen their understanding of wicked problems and work on skills needed when dealing with uncertainty in relation to their own role, expectations by others and group dynamics, as well as developing solutions. In our examples, students were able to reflect on dynamics, come up with ideas for interventions, based on their own practice complemented with theoretical insights. Nevertheless, complex answers to wicked problems, taking multiple perspectives and professions into account, turned out to be too ambitious. This shows that the model is well suited for the education of future professionals, but that the relevance for practice will be even stronger when the model is embedded in the quality system of service organisations, as a tool for continuous learning and innovation.

References

Beckmann, E.A. (2017) Forums, fellowship and wicked problems in teaching, in J. McDonald and A. Cater-Steel (eds) *Communities of Practice. Facilitating Social Learning in Higher Education*, Singapore: Springer, pp 545–66.

Bekker, M. (2020) *Groepsdynamica: Werken in en met groepen*, 2nd edn, Amsterdam: Boom.

Biesta, G.J.J. (2016) *The Beautiful Risk of Education*, Abingdon: Routledge.

Bordin, E.S. (1983) A working alliance based model of supervision, *Counseling Psychologist*, 11(1): 35–42.

Bos, J. and Harting, E. (2006) *Projectmatig creëren 2.0*, revised edn, Schiedam: Scriptum.

Bredewold, F., Verplanke, L. and Tonkens, E. (2018) Tussen begrip en vernedering: Sociale Netwerk Versterking in de praktijk, in F. Bredewold, J.W. Duyvendak, T. Kampen, E. Tonkens and L. Verplanke (eds) *De verhuizing van de verzorgingsstaat: Hoe de overheid nabij komt*, Amsterdam: Tijdschrift voor sociale vraagstukken/Van Gennep, pp 129–57.

De Rijk, M. (2018) Zorg en geld: Hoe onbetaalbaar is de verzorgingsstaat?, in F. Bredewold, J.W. Duyvendak, T. Kampen, E. Tonkens and L. Verplanke (eds) *De verhuizing van de verzorgingsstaat: Hoe de overheid nabij komt*, Amsterdam: Tijdschrift voor sociale vraagstukken/Van Gennep, pp 211–29.

De Waal, V. (2018) De opkomst en betekenis van interprofessionele teams: Introductie, in V. de Waal (ed) *Interprofessioneel werken en innoveren in teams: Samenwerking in nieuwe praktijken*, Bussum: Coutinho, pp 21–44.

Emanuel, E.S., Sijbom, R.B.L., Koen, J. and Baas, M. (2022) Learning communities: Een begripsbepaling en verkenning van leerprocessen en kennisbenutting, *Gedrag & Organisatie*, 35(3): 289–315.

European Commission (2013) *Social Innovation Research in the European Union: Approaches, Findings and Future Directions* – Policy Review, Brussels: European Commission, https://data.europa.eu/doi/10.2777/12639.

Hoeve, A., Nieuwenhuis, L., Verhoef, M. and Van der Werf, W. (2021) *Prepareren voor innoveren: Open eind leeromgevingen als hefboom voor toekomstbestendig beroepsonderwijs*, white paper, Arnhem: HAN University of Applied Sciences, https://www.han.nl/onderzoek/lectoraten/lectoraat-responsief-beroepsonderwijs/onze-kennis/211108-whitepaper-prepareren-voor-innoveren.pdf.

Kromhout, M., Van Echtelt, P. and Feijten, P. (2020) *Sociaal domein op koers? Verwachtingen en resultaten van vijf jaar decentraal beleid*, Den Haag: Sociaal en Cultureel Planbureau, https://www.scp.nl/publicaties/publicaties/2020/11/16/sociaal-domein-op-koers.

Löhmer, C. and Standhardt, R. (2015) *TZI – Die Kunst, sich selbst und eine Gruppe zu leiten: Einführung in die Themenzentriete Interaktion: Mit einem Gespräch zwischen Ruth C. Cohn und Friedemann Schulz von Thun*, Stuttgart: Klett-Cotta.

Remmerswaal, J. (2013) *Handboek groepsdynamica: Een inleiding op theorie en praktijk*, Amsterdam: Boom.

Rittel, H.W.J. and Webber, M.M. (1973) Dilemmas in a general theory of planning, *Policy Sciences*, 4: 155–69.

Ryan, R.M. and Deci, E.L. (2018) *Self-Determination Theory: Basic Psychological Needs in Motivation, Development, and Wellness*, New York: Guilford Press.

Stam, M. and Wilken, J.P. (2015) Zeven principes van transformatieleren, in A. Kooiman, J.P. Wilken, M. Stam, E. Jansen and M. Van Biene (eds) *Leren transformeren: Hoe faciliteer je praktijkinnovatie in tijden van transitie?*, Utrecht: Movisie, pp 108–24.

Stam, M. and Wilken, J.P. (2018) Transformatieleren: Hoe onzeker weten tot innovatie kan leiden, in V. de Waal (ed) *Interprofessioneel werken en innoveren in teams: Samenwerking in nieuwe praktijken*, Bussum: Coutinho, pp 135–48.

Stam, M., Wilken, J.P., Kooiman, A., Jansen, E. and Van Biene, M. (2015) Inleiding: Transformeren kun je leren, in A. Kooiman, J. Wilken, M. Stam, E. Jansen and M. van Biene (eds) *Leren transformeren: Hoe faciliteer je praktijkinnovatie in tijden van transitie?*, Utrecht: Movisie, pp 3–8.

Taylor, M. (2017) Wicked problems and social professional competence, in P. Share, T. Cavaliero and B. McTaggart (eds) *Wicked Problems and Young People: Co-creative Teaching for the Social Professions*, Sligo: Institute of Technology, pp 9–20.

VHSS (Verkenningscommissie Hogere Sociale Studies) (2022) *Sociaal in beweging. Empowerment van de sociaal professional als fundament: Advies van de verkenningscommissie Hogere Sociale Studies*, Den Haag: Vereniging Hogescholen, https://www.vereniginghogescholen.nl/system/knowledge_base/attachments/files/000/001/340/original/Sociaal_in_beweging_-_Advies_verkenningscie._HSS_-_def..pdf.

Wenger, E. (1998) *Communities of Practice: Learning, Meaning, and Identity*, Cambridge: Cambridge University Press.

WRR (Wetenschappelijke Raad voor Regeringsbeleid) (2013) *Naar een lerende economie*, Amsterdam: Amsterdam University Press, https://www.wrr.nl/publicaties/rapporten/2013/11/04/naar-een-lerende-economie.

Zestor (2018) *Leergemeenschappen van hogescholen met het werkveld*, Den Haag: Zestor, https://zestor.nl/leergemeenschappen-van-hogescholen-met-het-werkveld.

12

Learning from innovation processes: introducing Easy Language in adult protection services

Anne Parpan-Blaser

Introduction

In many areas information access is not yet fully realised. Therefore, the United Nations' Convention on the Rights of Persons with Disabilities (CRPD) holds considerable potential for innovation in this regard – namely in social work. This chapter reflects on introducing Easy Language (EL) in adult protection service as an innovation and learning process. More specifically, the framework conditions, success factors and emerging challenges will be highlighted allowing conclusions to be drawn for similar innovation processes in cooperation with practice. A key finding is that innovative results in the form of concepts, tools or media are not yet sufficient to bring about innovation, but that it depends on the intensity of the engagement in the process of development whether (new) knowledge can be integrated so that it leads to a fundamental change in social work practice.

In 2015, the project 'Einfach leicht verständlich' [Just Easy to Understand] was the first R&D project in Switzerland to address questions relating to the transfer of official texts into EL (Parpan-Blaser et al, 2021). While EL as a language variety is an innovation in itself, the project encompassed various aspects of innovation and learning. Three important changes have contributed to its emergence: a new understanding of social participation of people with disabilities, increased awareness for the accessibility of communication and information, and the revised adult protection law in Switzerland. Although the project broke new ground in many areas, it was not systematically approached or implemented as an innovation process. This chapter now allows reflection on the core of the project, that is, the process of creating and introducing EL texts in the context of adult protection, from an innovation-specific perspective.[1] By examining framework conditions, success factors and learning effects from this perspective, conclusions can be drawn for similar innovation processes in cooperation with practice. For this purpose, first the central basics and then the project 'Just Easy to

Understand', including some results, are presented. Subsequently, central findings from each work package are discussed from an innovation-specific perspective. The chapter concludes with some fundamental considerations and further questions in the sense of an outlook.

The innovation potential emanating from the UN Convention on the Rights of Persons with Disabilities

The CRPD, adopted on 13 December 2006, specifies existing human rights obligations with regard to persons with disabilities along the guiding principle of an inclusive society. This was already lived up to in the process of its creation under the motto 'Nothing about us without us' and with the participation of 469 NGOs at the last session of the 2006 conference. Among them were many people with disabilities who contributed their experiences, their political and sociopolitical ideas and visions to the consultation process. One of the central postulates of the CRPD calls for equal access to information in order to participate and make informed decisions in relevant areas of life. Article 9 of the CRPD refers to the obligation to remove barriers and explicitly emphasises that this also means barriers to access to information and communication (United Nations, 2006).

Switzerland ratified the CRPD only in 2014. Implementing the CRPD means addressing the question of what participation opportunities for people with disabilities look like in various social areas and what learning processes need to be set in motion in society, in organisations and among professionals in this regard. The period since ratification shows that Switzerland lacks a national disability policy. The CRPD Committee therefore advised Switzerland in 2019 to create enforceable accessibility standards for public and private facilities in the field of communication and information. Thus, the CRPD still holds considerable potential for innovation – including in social work. In this context, the project at hand focused on lowering communication barriers for people with poor literacy in the field of adult protection.

Easy Language as an innovation in practice

The barriers can be sensory (perception of text and sound are impeded), subject-related (thematic background information is missing) or technical language barriers (specific terms are too complex for laypersons), which make it difficult to comprehend texts in standard language (Schubert, 2016). Added to this is the varying level of reading competence and comprehension skills in the population: the *OECD Skills Outlook 2013*, for example, shows that between 4.9 per cent and 27.7 per cent of adults across the countries involved in the study have only the lowest levels of literacy proficiency

(OECD, 2013). This leads to the fact that communicative objectives of authorities or administrative bodies (such as inform, communicate decisions, instruct) are often not achieved when using standard language.

EL is a language variety dedicated to simplifying written and oral communication linguistically (and as required, in terms of content), adapting it to the reading competence and prior knowledge of the persons addressed. Modifications of the text refer to the word, sentence and text level, as well as to design elements. In terms of text accessibility, EL can be described as an innovation that has spread to many different areas of life, such as administrative websites, patient information in the health system, news portals and media, election and voting documents, museum catalogues and much more (Kellermann, 2014). EL is one tool among others, such as Braille, sign language or audio description to make communication accessible.

The target group of EL is broad and heterogeneous: it includes people with intellectual disabilities or functional illiteracy, persons with the onset of dementia or with temporary impairments (for example, aphasia after a stroke) or second-language learners. They all benefit from having direct access to information because it is in a language they can understand and that has a layout that supports untrained readers. Texts in EL are marked with a label, such as the European Easy-Reading logo of Inclusion Europe (2017).[2] This makes the text recognisable and its special features comprehensible for readers.

EL has its origins, on the one hand, in cultural policy movements (for instance, 'Culture for All' in 1964 in Sweden) and, on the other, in self-advocacy efforts by people with intellectual disability (for example, 'People First', 1996 in the US). Lindholm and Vanhatalo (2021), in the introduction to the *European Handbook on Easy Languages*, show how the concept has developed from practice in different places in Europe. In Switzerland it was only in 2014 that the first translation agency and training initiative was started (Parpan-Blaser et al, 2021). Although much has been done in the field of EL in recent years, there is still a long way to go before professionals – especially in the social, administrative and communication sectors – are sensitised and that all information relevant to active citizenship is available in EL. The project 'Just Easy to Understand' represents a step in this direction.

Another important reference point for the project at hand was that in 2013 the new Child and Adult Protection Act came into force in Switzerland, which brought about some fundamental changes: it provides for tailor-made measures in individual cases and, at the organisational level the communal militia and lay authorities were replaced by interdisciplinary specialist authorities with members from law, social work, education and psychology.[3] As Häfeli (2013: 3) puts it 'the new right is intended to guarantee the human dignity of people with temporary or permanent states of weakness and a resulting need for protection, and to preserve and foster the right to self-determination as far as possible' (all translations in this chapter are by the author). Experts emphasise that the assessment of the personal and social resources of a person with a state of weakness relevant to adult protection law and the resulting need for help and protection is highly demanding, and the importance of comprehensible communication at various levels is growing. Affected persons often receive adequate verbal explanations from social workers and members of the authorities. However, these are ephemeral and no longer tangible after the meeting. Apart from that, the right to self-determination is contradicted by official letters and administrative forms often written in such a complex way that the addressees do not understand crucial information for their decisions and an essential basis to assert their rights.

These three developments have opened a window of opportunity for the 'Just Easy to Understand' project. Its results allow us to reflect on the extent to which the project has succeeded in acting as a catalyst for structural changes. For this purpose, the project is first presented in its broad outlines.

The project 'Just Easy to Understand'

'Just Easy to Understand' investigated and evaluated the potential as well as the challenges of the creation and implementation of texts in EL. This entailed training validators, evaluating text creation, training and examination of practitioners, evaluating the results and sharing the insights. The overall aim of the project was to contribute to a basis for high-quality processes for the development of EL texts with the involvement of all relevant stakeholders.

The project was implemented between 2015 and 2017 in cooperation with an adult protection authority. It was funded by the Federal Office for the Equality of People with Disabilities. At the beginning, five central texts of adult protection procedures were identified and transferred into EL. The text production process was thus cyclical, with phases of writing the texts in EL, feedback from authority members and test subjects, and revision. From June 2016 onwards, the documents were used by the protection authority. Starting in September 2016, the perception of the texts and their influence on cooperation were investigated in a qualitative approach. For this purpose, persons affected by adult protection proceedings, case managers and persons from the assessment units as well as private and professional holders of an adult protection mandate were interviewed by means of guided interviews.

The project from an innovation-specific point of view

This chapter reflects on our project on EL in adult protection with a focus on social innovation with the aim of: (1) showing which innovation-specific aspects become apparent, (2) establishing links to learning processes and (3) drawing conclusions that allow further refinement the concept of social innovation. To this end, a central result from each project phase is presented and discussed under innovation-specific aspects.

Creating texts in EL – needs-orientation and unexpected results

The five central documents selected for transfer to EL would have needed much explanation of specific terms or procedural steps, which would have made them too long. It was decided to produce an information brochure on the adult protection law to complement the documents. The brochure, an unplanned additional product of the project, not only became the most used document in the authority we worked with, but also aroused the interest of the specialist public. This led us to revise the brochure later and within a more comprehensive project in cooperation with two more regional administrations, to give it a professional layout and, at the same time, to produce a similar brochure for child protection, again with the participation of target-group representatives.

Both information brochures have been published in German as PDFs on the websites of the services and have later also been made available in French. The topic of comprehensible communication from adult and child protection authorities was further supported by the fact that KOKES (the national Conference for Child and Adult Protection) took up the topic of communication and invited us to speak at their annual conference.

The creation of the information brochure, and what further emerged from it, shows how little innovation processes can be planned and what unexpected turns they can take when favourable circumstances coincide. Innovation processes are rarely linear – not least because they bring together a wide variety of actors whose different knowledge bases stimulate each other so that the unexpected can emerge (Huq, 2019; Nandan et al, 2020). Accordingly, it is not only about the final result but also about the willingness of all participants to learn from each other. 'The cognitive operations ... in innovation processes can also be understood as a combination of learning and problem solving' (Hüttemann and Solèr, 2018: 232). New perspectives develop through interactions between the carriers of knowledge, 'which corresponds to the process of variation that is central to innovation' (Hüttemann and Solèr, 2018: 246).

Training validators – knowledge base and initial development

Texts in EL are usually validated and checked for comprehensibility by members of the target group in moderated review sessions (Inclusion Europe, n.d.: 9). At the time of the project, no standardised procedure was known. We therefore developed one based on available knowledge. Due to the lack of possibilities in Switzerland, we sought professional exchange on validation with the KI-I in Linz (Competence Network Information Technology to Support the Integration of People with Disabilities: https://www.ki-i.at/), which already had proven expertise and experience at that time.

We adapted the procedure for the text validation to the local conditions and worked with three organisations where people with intellectual disabilities live or work. Because we wanted to evaluate different procedures for the comprehensibility check, we set up our own group of validators on the one hand (internal text review) and used the services of the first provider of plain language in Switzerland on the other (external text review). To set up the project's internal validation group, validators were recruited and then trained.

In this part of the project designing an entirely new process we certainly did not get everything right the first time and we learned a lot – as is typically the case in innovation processes. We worked here on a topic in which the (empirical) knowledge base was lacking at the time: what we developed on the basis of the then tangible state of knowledge and on the basis of proper and pragmatic considerations has proven itself in many situations. On the other hand, a research gap became apparent on the topic of validating texts in EL. This shows various factors relevant to a successful innovation process: the space to try things out and make mistakes, applying foresight to avoid too serious risks, secure knowledge from research and evaluations as a basis for making decisions (Parpan-Blaser, 2018).

Evaluating the processes – capture and share knowledge

We documented and evaluated the whole process of transferring the texts into EL and implementing them in practice. The analysis of data (written feedback after review meetings, telephone interviews with key actors from the adult protection agency, research logs) has allowed us to compile recommendations. They provide important guidance in the field of EL and have been published (Parpan-Blaser et al, 2019) and used for capacity building in training programmes in organisations that want to address the issue of communication and EL and to sensitise their staff.

The evaluation has shown that implementing EL materials in practice is as significant as the products developed, because it is about increasing the acceptance of EL. The parties involved thereby gain a feeling for the necessity and possibilities of EL and change their (written) communication beyond the texts produced. On the one hand this is about issues at the interface between innovative methods, programmes and/or services and regular operation, which typically arise with innovations in social work. It is important to carefully inform and get on board those who are not directly involved in an innovation process. We addressed the practical use of the documents in EL in two training sessions. In the second, an exemplary text validation was conducted with people from the target group. Some of the authority members only realised on this occasion how little their clients had understood so far. On the other hand, it is about questions of diffusion: how can newly developed things be adopted elsewhere? What considerations does a takeover need? What can be adopted unchanged? What needs to go through a learning process again?

Innovations typically question what has been done so far and thus contain criticism that can have an unsettling effect. Irritations and adversarial frictions (Jaskyte and Kisieliene, 2006) are part of learning processes, because they have an opening effect breaking up cognitive structures if they are socially appropriately framed. As a counterweight to the uncertainty of an innovation process, a stabilising orientation framework is needed, for example through shared visions or appropriate structuring (Albury, 2005). It is also about how to make the results of an innovation process accessible so that they can be taken up elsewhere and stimulate learning.

Evaluating the effects – added value and fundamental change?

One of the research questions of the project related to the practice of the adult protection authority after some months of working with the texts in EL. For this purpose, we conducted guideline interviews with clients and authority members. Data were analysed based on the coding steps of Grounded Theory (Corbin and Strauss, 1999).

On the clients' side, the attitude conveyed via the documents made them feel basically addressed and welcome: "You have the feeling that you are in good hands". The texts in EL also succeeded in reducing their fears and mistrust. This had less to do with the content of the documents than with the visible effort of the authority to communicate at eye level. They reported that they had understood unexpectedly well what the authority wanted to convey them: "So I find it … great. No, this is the first time I would know that I can clearly look up things and read". Clients also reported that the documents have helped them to become aware of their own rights and to exercise them (by inspecting files, for example). On the other hand, the documents also raised expectations. Clients were disappointed when the authority staff did not succeed in communicating as clearly in oral exchanges as in writing.

Authority members agreed that comprehensible information prepared the ground for good cooperation in the procedure, as stated by one of them: "So I already have the impression that with this leaflet, this brochure, they are of course at a level where they can talk to us at all. And the conversation is already simplified in that sense". There were fewer enquiries, fewer angry telephone calls and questions on "what it is all about". The letters in EL and in particular the brochure allowed the clients (often together with relatives) to take note in advance and without stress of what to expect in the interviews.

Various forms of use developed around the brochure in EL: while some authority members distributed it widely, others used it mainly in discussions to explain specific aspects of the procedure. Sometimes clients were asked to make notes in it, so that the brochure took on the function of a reminder. Staff were also able to rely on the comprehensible formulations from the EL documents in oral exchanges.

EL proved to be an appropriate way of reducing barriers to (written) communication in an area of social work where legal aspects, technical language and administrative logic stand in the way of genuine participation by those affected. Equally, the project has also clearly shown where habitual inertia makes fundamental change difficult and only a thorough additional qualification of the staff would pave the way.

A result of the project was an increased awareness of communication barriers within the authority. Overall, however, there has certainly been no radical rethinking nor a 'comprehensive, profound and lasting change in practice' (Moore et al, 1997: 276) characteristic of innovation. The comparison with the province of Upper Austria, where the Office of Social Affairs, in cooperation with the KI-I, managed a changeover to EL in written communication in 2014, shows the main difference. While in Switzerland further steps would have depended on committed individuals, in Upper Austria there was a clear political will to introduce and implement the adjustment from the top down. In 2014, the Upper Austrian Equal Opportunities Act legally anchored the obligation to issue notifications of benefits paid to persons with disabilities in EL.

Disseminating the results – effects beyond the project

Various factors within and outside the field of social work were decisive for the emergence of the present project and the progress of the topic of EL in Switzerland. In addition to the three important developments described at the beginning, these were, on the research and research funding side, funding priorities that allowed for project submission to the Federal Office for the Equality of Persons with Disabilities, a generally increased tendency towards user participation in social work research, and a considerable gap in research on EL. On the practice side the project team had received numerous inquiries on the topic of EL (for example, to contribute to the conception and publication of an accessible magazine, to speak at conferences and events about the topic of EL or to do translations into EL), that we were unable to fulfil. All in all, the preliminary work showed that there was a great need for research on and the use of EL in Switzerland and that it was necessary to begin to develop a knowledge base, so that good-quality offers are made available for text production with the involvement of the target groups.

Subsequently, the response from various areas of social work was gratifying, which is partly due to the fact that pressure from civil society with regard to accessibility had increased since the start of the project. After the project ended, we decided to continue the specialised seminar on EL launched in the context of the project and to expand it into a certificate of advanced studies on addressee-oriented and accessible communication. Based on the initial situation at the time and the findings of the project, we saw it as our task to disseminate knowledge about EL and make it accessible to interested parties.

Overall, the project has allowed us to increase the visibility of the topic of EL and to strive for broad networking. In addition to various publications that reached a wide range of fields for which EL is relevant, an example of this is a meeting of the project team with the representative for EL of the Federal Chancellery. The aim was to explore the possibilities of using EL in the documents of the Federal Chancellery and in the various federal offices. Subsequently, coordinated by the Federal Office for the Equality of Persons with Disabilities, work was started on a concept for plain language in the federal administration.

This shows the need-orientation of innovations in social work: developments come about above all when social change, new or changed social problems or new findings from science and practice make this necessary or possible. It also shows how valuable it is to make development results known in a form that allows them to be referred to elsewhere and to find allies for a topic with transformative potential.

Conclusion

In summary, I would like to take up three points that became visible through the project 'Just Easy to Understand' and which are of further relevance for the discussion on social innovation.

While the project involved a process in which the most diverse knowledge of researchers, professionals, service users and other stakeholders was integrated, its outcome cannot be considered an innovation in the strict sense. The adult protection brochure, while still valid and in use, has not led to such significant changes (that is, comprehensive, profound, lasting) in practice which, according to Moore et al (1997), is essential to be labelled as innovative. This would be the case if they were used within the framework of a comprehensive communication concept. Accordingly, there is no continuous added value for the social work target groups (Parpan-Blaser, 2011). Essential things happened – one could say – beside or beyond the project. What was developed at a micro level of a client-centred project with one organisation has resonated to the meso level (Van Wijk et al, 2018) and made new developments possible. This is comparable to the stone thrown into the water disappearing under the surface and the ripples becoming wider and wider and remaining visible for a long time. The stone we threw into the water was not very big, but the ripples that stretched across the water's surface grew large – perhaps also and precisely because it had laid very still beforehand.

In a broad understanding of innovation (especially at the micro or meso social level), it therefore seems to be more important to get things going and maintain an attitude that takes advantage of opportunities than to be able to call the result an innovation. Learning in innovation processes in the sense of revising or expanding one's own schemata often goes beyond what is available as an immediate development result. Therefore, the process of innovation is to be weighted higher than the innovative concept, tool or media that emerge (or are to emerge) from it.

In my understanding, (empirical) insights are at the core of innovation and it is about making them relevant for a practical context. These can be new or newly combined findings. Accordingly, innovation processes in human services are primarily about bringing together carriers of knowledge and about how to process knowledge in (planned) interactions. When it comes to that, social work service users have an important role to play as they can bring a very specific perspective. User participation in innovation processes is therefore highly desirable and often essential for an outcome tailored to their needs (see, for example, Chesbrough and Di Minin, 2014; Stougaard, 2021; Driessens and Lyssens-Danneboom, 2022). However, user participation is not unconditional and needs to be carefully considered. The project at hand shows where challenges can lie and that the effort should be realistically assessed. However, this was probably the most important aspect for the professionals involved: perceiving from a different perspective who their counterpart is and what language is needed to really reach them. Not only did we notice a change in the attitude of the individuals, but also an astonishment that it is possible with profit, to break away from a legalistic language, to set the bar differently in terms of comprehensibility and to emphasise by doing so the granted right to be heard.

What we succeeded in only to a limited extent was the networking that would have been necessary for the further promotion of the topic at meso and macro level. This is all the more regrettable because, in a federal system, forces have to be pooled in order to be able to apply the lever effectively. Since the conclusion of the project, there have been numerous individual initiatives on EL in Switzerland (for example, the online news magazine *infoeasy*,[4] teaching material for general education classes in vocational training, a label and a charter for inclusive culture). However, these have so far remained unconnected and with mostly regional reach. In order to further exploit the potential of EL, however, political will is needed so that it is no longer just committed individuals or organisations that become active because they consider participation important, but that (legal) requirements facilitate and enable adoption of EL on a large scale. This raises the question of the political work that is required in the context of social innovation and whether profound change is possible without changing the structural conditions that underlie the need for change.

Notes

1. This chapter takes up some thoughts from the presentation 'Innovation through accessible information' given online at the European Congress of Social Work Research in 2021.
2. https://www.inclusion-europe.eu/easy-to-read/
3. https://www.historyofsocialsecurity.ch/institutions/cantonal-local-and-private-institutions/child-and-adult-protection
4. https://infoeasy-news.ch/info/

References

Albury, D. (2005) Fostering innovation in public service, *Public Money & Management*, 25(1): 51–6.

Chesbrough, H. and Di Minin, A. (2014) Open social innovation, in H. Chesbrough, W. Vanhaverbeke and J. West (eds) *New Frontiers in Open Innovation*, Oxford: Oxford University Press, pp 169–88.

Corbin, J.M. and Strauss, A. (1990) Grounded theory research: procedures, canons and evaluative criteria, *Zeitschrift für Soziologie*, 19(6): 418–27.

Driessens, K. and Lyssens-Danneboom, V. (eds) (2022) *Involving Service Users in Social Work Education, Research and Policy: A Comparative European Analysis*, Bristol: Policy Press.

Häfeli, C. (2013) Das neue Kindes- und Erwachsenenschutzrecht: Eine Zwischenbilanz und Perspektiven, *Jusletter*, 9 December, https://vbbrb.ch/files/files_vbbrb/newsarchiv/Jusletter_Haefeli_Erwachsenenschutzrecht_Zwischenbilanz_20131209.pdf.

Huq, J.L. (2019) Conditioning a professional exchange field for social innovation, *Business & Society*, 58(5): 1047–82.

Hüttemann, M. and Solèr, M. (2018) Zur Relevanz und 'Relevierung' von Wissen im Innovationsprozess, in J. Eurich, M. Glatz-Schmallegger and A. Parpan-Blaser (eds) *Gestaltung von Innovationen in Organisationen des Sozialwesens*, Wiesbaden: Springer, pp 225–51.

Inclusion Europe (2017) *Information For All: European Standards for Making Information Easy to Read and Understand*, Brussels: Inclusion Europe, https://www.inclusion-europe.eu/wp-content/uploads/2017/06/EN_Information_for_all.pdf.

Inclusion Europe (n.d.) *Do Not Write For Us Without Us: Involving People with Intellectual Disabilities in the Writing of Texts that Are Easy to Read and Understand*, Brussels: Inclusion Europe, https://sid-inico.usal.es/idocs/F8/FDO23139/write_for_us.pdf.

Jaskyte, K. and Kisieliene, A. (2006) Organizational innovation: a comparison of nonprofit human-service organizations in Lithuania and the United States, *International Social Work*, 4(2): 165–76.

Kellerman, G. (2014) Leichte und Einfache Sprache: Versuch einer Definition, *Politik und Zeitgeschichte (APuZ)*, 64(9/11): 7–10.

Lindholm, C. and Vanhatalo, U. (2021) Introduction, in C. Lindholm and U. Vanhatalo (eds) *Handbook of Easy Languages in Europe*, Berlin: Frank & Timme, pp 11–26.

Moore, M.H., Sparrow, M. and Spelman, W. (1997) Innovation in policing: from production line to jobs shops, in A. Altshuler, A. and R.D. Behn (eds) *Innovation in American Government*, Washington, DC: Brookings Institution, pp 274–98.

Nandan, M., Jaskyte, K. and Mandayam, G. (2020) Human centered design as a new approach to creative problem solving: its usefulness and applicability for social work practice, *Human Service Organizations: Management, Leadership & Governance*, 44(4): 310–16.

OECD (Organisation for Economic Co-operation and Development) (2013) *OECD Skills Outlook 2013: First Results from the Survey of Adult Skills*, Paris: OECD Publishing, http://dx.doi.org/10.1787/9789264204256-en.

Parpan-Blaser, A. (2011) *Innovation in der Sozialen Arbeit: Zur theoretischen und empirischen Grundlegung eines Konzepts*, Wiesbaden: VS.

Parpan-Blaser, A. (2018) Organisationen des Sozialwesens als Ort von Innovation, in J. Eurich, M. Glatz-Schmallegger and A. Parpan-Blaser (eds) *Gestaltung von Innovationen in Organisationen des Sozialwesens*, Wiesbaden: Springer, pp 31–53.

Parpan-Blaser, A., Girard-Groeber, S., von Fellenberg, M., Antener, G. and Lichtenauer, A. (2019) Behördenkommunikation leicht verständlich und inhaltlich korrekt, Soziale Sicherheit, 6 September, z /.

Parpan-Blaser, A., Girard-Groeber, S., Antener, G., Arn, C., Baumann, R., Caplazi, A., et al (2021) Easy Language in Switzerland, in C. Lindholm and U. Vanhatalo (eds) *Handbook of Easy Languages in Europe*, Berlin: Frank & Timme, pp 573–622.

Schubert, K. (2016) Barriereabbau durch optimierte Kommunikationsmittel: Versuch einer Systematisierung, in N. Mälzer (ed) *Barrierefreie Kommunikation – Perspektiven aus Theorie und Praxis*, Berlin: Frank & Timme, pp 15–33.

Stougaard, M.S. (2021) Co-producing public welfare services with vulnerable citizens: a case study of a Danish-Somali women's association coproducing crime prevention with the local authorities, *Voluntas: International Journal of Voluntary and Nonprofit Organizations*, 32(10): 1389–407.

United Nations (2006) Convention on the Rights of Persons with Disabilities, United Nations, https://www.un.org/development/desa/disabilities/convention-on-the-rights-of-persons-with-disabilities/convention-on-the-rights-of-persons-with-disabilities-2.html.

Van Wijk, J., Zietsma, C., Dorado, S., de Bakker, F.G.A. and Marti, I. (2018) Social innovation: integrating micro, meso and macro level insights from institutional theory, *Business & Society*, 58(5): 887–918.

THEME C

Community work, community-led innovation and collective action

13

The rediscovery of community: community development as social innovation

Jean Pierre Wilken and Dagmar Narusson

Introduction

The field of community development is rapidly gaining interest as it comes to social work and social innovation. Community-building can be regarded as a countermovement to neoliberal individualisation and its negative side effects like loneliness and polarisation. The notion of community is rediscovered and reinstalled. Social workers can play an important role in supporting communities to find their own strengths and to revitalise. Although social work already has a long history when it comes to community development, since the 1990s it was a neglected field. Also, the nature of communities has changed considerably. Therefore, the profession of the community worker also needs innovation. In Europe, Utrecht University of Applied Sciences (Netherlands) and Tartu University (Estonia) are doing community development research and have initiated master programmes in community development. Both authors are affiliated with these programmes. This chapter, first, introduces some general notions about community, then reviews recent insights regarding community-building in relation to social innovation and social work. With examples from community programmes in Estonia and the Netherlands, we illustrate how processes of community innovation can be constructed, what the necessary conditions are and how they can lead to the desired outcomes.

Notions of community

A community can generally be described as a network of people organised in an informal or more formal way. The way a community is shaped depends on the nature of the social ties among people and the way a community is structured demographically, geographically and institutionally. Another type of community is formed by a shared culture or religion, or by shared interests, for example around climate activism. Communities have both a subjective and an objective dimension. The subjective dimension is formed by how members perceive the community, their 'sense of belonging'. The objective dimension is formed, for example, by physical characteristics and resources like public facilities, enterprises and natural assets. From Robert Putnam's work we learn about the notion of social capital, and how working on bridging and bonding can strengthen community life. 'Bonding' refers to the quality of the connections community members have, that give a sense of belonging and help them get by. 'Bridging' refers to the connections that community members have that help them expand opportunities (Putnam, 2000). The third concept Putnam introduced was 'linking', which refers to the connections a community has with resources provided by institutions and systems. Nowadays, there is a growing awareness that our natural resources like water, air and land are also of utmost importance. Ecological or 'green' social work is a growing field of innovation (see Chapter 14 in this volume).

Communities fulfil basic human needs and are thereby important for well-being. For our well-being we need informal networks and connections with community members. Social connections, beyond the immediate circle of family, help to access resources and opportunities. A range of qualitative and quantitative studies show that personal networks and social relations are important for maintaining well-being (Harrison et al, 2016; Bagnall et al, 2018). Relational networks established through community activities bring considerable benefits, like social support, and generally improve people's quality of life (Phillipson et al, 2004; Helliwell et al, 2009; Ross et al, 2019).

Rediscovering community is an answer to the negative effects of neoliberal society, with its emphasis on individual performances, self-reliance and autonomy, neglecting the value of social relationships. Realising that we are all connected and depending on each other, this implies that we have a collective responsibility to care for each other and our environment. The COVID-19 pandemic, the energy and climate crises make us aware of our interdependency in terms of health and our reliance on natural resources. This awareness also becomes apparent in a change of institutional views and governance. Personal freedom and autonomy are still essential human values, but these are always related to, and dependent on, the quality of communities and their resources, locally, nationally and globally.

The local community is the place where people live their daily lives, where children are born and raised, where people care for one another. It is also the place where lack of safety and of opportunities are the most felt. Research shows that all kinds of programmes aimed at fighting criminality (like the neighbourhood watch and the neighbourhood police officer), creating local enterprises, organising cultural and sport events, redesigning housing blocks, including public meeting spaces like parks and playgrounds, all contribute to a higher satisfaction, well-being and health. Places in the community are relational and spatial contexts in which people establish their daily routines, form emotional bonds, develop feelings of belonging, and shape relationships and their meanings (Bromley et al, 2013). In modern times, where we are facing a large degree of individualism and 'liquidity' (Bauman, 2000), the composition and cohesion in communities can change fast. This may lead to tensions between people of different cultures and backgrounds. People often seem to lack the ability to 'socialise'. Therefore, professional 'community builders' are needed to act as facilitators to promote bonding and bridging. We are on the turn of reinventing the local community (Van Ewijk, 2010) and well-trained social workers are most welcome to help (re)building community life, to re-create caring and flourishing communities.

Although community development is traditionally a social sciences and social work field, the challenges of our times demand innovative answers because of the fluid and complex character of today's society. On the one hand we can speak about renovation instead of innovation: regenerating all kinds of community life. On the other hand, community practices require innovation of the social work profession. Knowledge is needed to engage in co-creation and co-production processes, which aim, in line with the definition of Murray et al (2010) and the European Commission (2013), to improve social relationships as well as generate concrete solutions to the problems a community is facing. It is important to generate solutions for these problems and also to see vital communities as places of inclusion for people in marginalised positions.

Community co-creation

Community development focuses on increasing the quality (or 'capital') of communities. This primarily concerns social capital (Putman, 2000), but in contemporary community development this is closely connected to economic, physical, cultural and ecological capital. These resources are indispensable for well-being (Argyle, 1996). People need an income, decent housing, healthy air, water and food, a safe and friendly environment, opportunities to move around and to enjoy nature. Globalisation is having a strong effect on local communities. Any crisis that is affecting a large part or even the whole community can also be an opportunity to join forces. Putnam (2000) mentions three key elements that are important. These are engagement, trust and efficacy. The quality of social capital is increased if members with a common social background, but also those with different social backgrounds, engage with each other and have a good connection with organisations and systems. It becomes even stronger if there is mutual trust. This can be quite a challenge if the community has a loose structure ('weak ties') or is composed of people with a large diversity of backgrounds. The challenge is then to oppose polarisation and to embrace diversity. A third element is efficacy. This is the shared belief that change is possible and that the community is able to achieve this.

The notion of social capital is not uncontested. While Putnam's view of social capital is quite positive, Pierre Bourdieu, for instance, argues that social capital may also be used for the benefit of a privileged group and may even reproduce inequality, for instance if people gain access to powerful positions through the direct or indirect employment of social connections (Bourdieu and Wacquant, 1992). Without 'bridging', bonding communities can become isolated and disenfranchised from the rest of society. Others point at structural socio-economic conditions of the society which may strengthen or hinder social capital in communities (DeFilippis, 2001). Later studies by Putnam show that, in societies where immigration or ethnic heterogeneity is high, citizens lack both kinds of social capital and are overall far less trusting of others than members of homogenous communities were found to be. Lack of homogeneity led to people withdrawing from even their closest groups and relationships, creating an atomised society as opposed to a cohesive community. These findings show that it is not self-evident that exposure to diversity strengthens social capital. It may need a lot of bridging efforts (Putnam, 2007).

Practice

We consider social innovation to be a process enhancing social cohesion and empowerment. This can be achieved through specific activities, like local enterprise: neighbours that work in a communal garden, take care of clean streets and parks, and do voluntary care work for people in their neighbourhood who need assistance related to a disability or a disease. These activities are often linked to assets that are available in the community, such as natural resources (woods, gardens, parks) and public facilities (like libraries, museums, sport halls and community centres). An adjacent trend is the development of urban and rural 'commons', land, buildings or services that are commonly owned and managed (Villamayor-Tomas and García-López, 2021).

Community social workers can assist communities where the ties are not so strong, and social capital is weak or underused, to build bridges between community members. Often, the work of social workers is directed by a problem-solving policy of the local authority, meaning that the explicit or implicit assignment is to solve problems. Research shows, however, that a strengths-based approach is more successful and leads to more sustainable outcomes (Harrison et al, 2019). An example of a strengths-based approach to community-building is asset-based community development (Kretzmann and McKnight, 1993; Russell and McKnight, 2022). Asset-based community development is built on five foundations (Russell, 2020):

- it is citizen-led and community driven, 'building communities from the inside out';
- it is relationship oriented: quality and power of relationships;
- it focuses on community assets and strengths rather than problems and needs: it identifies and mobilises individual and community assets, skills and passions;
- it is place-based: the neighbourhood as the primary unit of change;
- it is inclusion-focused: everybody has certain capacities, to be discovered and used for productive reciprocal relationships and actions.

The discovery and articulation of the qualities of the community and community members is already empowering. Using, connecting and strengthening assets for facing challenges and improving the quality of community life is even more empowering (Gilchrist, 2019). Mapping the community will already build or (re)activate relationships, involving many community members not only serving as a source of information but also including them in articulating common interests and generating ideas for new community initiatives. From the viewpoint of research, methods of participatory action research match well with community development, and especially community-based participatory research (Hacker, 2013). During this process, ambitions can arise, goals can be set and plans can be made. In these stages, the community worker can fulfil the role of facilitator or adviser. In the phase of executing community action plans, the worker can take up different roles, like facilitator, adviser or 'community organiser'. Sometimes they might act as 'change agent' or 'mediator'. Evaluation is important since it is connected to 'community learning'. The community worker can help to collect data for this purpose or to facilitate reflection and learning sessions. Throughout all phases the role of 'community connector' is always present. The main task is to connect people and their strengths, to enhance social cohesion and inclusion, and to optimise the availability and use of resources. Both the social capital theory and the capability approach (described in Chapter 4 in this volume), offer appropriate theoretical frameworks for community work.

Working on social inclusion

We give two examples of community development starting from the perspective of people in marginalised positions, one from Estonia and one from the Netherlands.

The Estonian example is a project that aims to find out community inclusion options for people using long-term mental health services. The study is a joint work of the University of Tartu and AS Hoolekandeteenused, an organisation that provides support to manage daily activities of people with mental health difficulties in supported-housing homes across Estonia. Both authors of this chapter are involved in the research part of this project. The research is novel in two aspects: 19 persons with mental health difficulties participated as co-researchers; and, for data collection, creative methods were used. Co-researchers are living in apartment buildings in ordinary neighbourhoods in three Estonian cities. This project also shows how researchers, students of a master's programme in community development and social well-being, service users and care workers can work together using an asset innovative-based action research methodology.

Empowering niches

The research addresses the issue that deinstitutionalisation has improved the living situation of people with mental health difficulties, but we do not know about their level of participation in the community and the quality of connections to other local community members. Goscha (2020) explains that people do not recover inside the walls of the organisation's physical facilities; they recover in the community. The question is, according to him, how to recognise empowering environmental niches and opportunities enabling individuals to move from entrapping environmental niches towards empowering environmental niches. According to Goscha, these niches are points in space where people experience reciprocity and meaningful engagement with the community. By entering these niches, in interactions with other people, they develop strengths they already possessed (Goscha, 2020). Doroud et al (2018) demonstrate that community places and spaces, as potential contexts for becoming, doing, belonging and being, are niches in which people can become themselves, act, experience feelings of belonging or simply 'being there'. The meaning of a place, like a neighbourhood where someone is living, is shaped by the interpretation of the experience with that place and interactions with other people that occur there (Doroud et al, 2018). According to Doroud et al, certain places (corners, places in the neighbourhood, parts of the landscape) can have a therapeutic effect on physical, mental or spiritual health. They distinguish between objective and subjective perspectives to the place. The objective view of the place includes physical and social attributes such as other people, spaces and objects. The subjective perspectives consist of 'meanings, experiences, social interactions, viewing places as fluid, dynamic, experiential and relational' (Doroud et al, 2018: 111). Our study explored both aspects of the view of a place, with emphasis on the subjective view. People with mental health difficulties need experiences of real connections with community members, being perceived by them as agents and being able to develop an adaptive sense of agency (Narusson and Wilken, 2018). To do this, they need to find their niches – places where they feel connected to people in the community, where they feel respected and hence feel stronger.

Discovering connections

The focus of the first part of the research was to explore experiences with reciprocal connections and community spaces. We assessed the desires of people with mental health difficulties to visit neighbourhood places, to establish connections with community members and to participate in community events and outdoor activities. Data collection and analysis took place in 2021 and 2022.

The analysis of the data revealed that three topics were important for the residents: the importance of undemanding neighbourhood sociality; opportunities for reciprocal relationships between members of the broader community and people with mental health difficulties; and links with groups whose members share common interests (communities of interests).

Results show that people with mental health difficulties pay considerable attention to their neighbourhood and surroundings. They prefer to visit streets and neighbourhood areas with gardens and parks where local people spend their time. They like to watch fishers at the riverside. They like to go swimming and visit the city centre or old town parks, walk in the woods or botanic gardens – places generally considered suitable for walking. Libraries and bookshops are open spaces where people with mental health difficulties feel comfortable. The same applies to summer outdoor events. These are places for being and doing. We believe that these are also places that Doroud et al (2018) refer to as spaces suitable for 'undemanding sociality'. Public parks, public spaces and neighbourhood places are spaces where private and social life can intersect, and thus they provide opportunities for the previously mentioned undemanding sociality. If a person with mental health difficulties is in a park, for example, with other people walking by, they meet without necessarily being forced to talk to each other. If they speak to each other, it may (initially) be more of an exchange of gestures (such as nods, greetings, mutual acknowledgement of positive feelings about something that is around), rather than a complex conversation. Such situations provide opportunities for the development of a person's identity as a distinct individual who expresses their authentic feelings, rather than feeling like a being who is defined only by their mental health difficulties. This indicates that these places could be considered as 'places for becoming' based on Doroud et al's (2018) notions.

Reciprocity

Another important quality of community relationships is reciprocity. The co-researchers' experience is in line with the aforementioned assumptions of Doroud et al (2018: 117) and described that in their spontaneous contacts with locals they appreciated being able to talk to them about nature, their surroundings and everyday life. If in these non-intentional contacts both parties were sharing information, ideas, friendly gestures or visiting neighbourhood people's homes and sharing food the reciprocity occurred, and it was considered very valuable by people with mental health difficulties. They experienced themselves as givers (not just receivers). Some of the residents found opportunities to establish friendly longer-term reciprocal connections with their neighbours. Results showed that many participants practise hobbies (playing music instruments, writing poetry, collecting model cars) and would be interested in having connections with interest-based communities, which would allow the building of more reciprocity.

Our study delivered important insights about relational trajectories of people with mental health difficulties:

- through reciprocal relationships, they develop bonds with people who live in close proximity;
- through undemanding sociality in local community spaces, they develop bridging;
- bridging expands opportunities in communities and reduces isolation and polarisation.

The results will be used to improve community connections, thereby increasing the quality of life of people with a mental health vulnerability. The mental health agency has developed a new strategy, emphasising the importance of community involvement. It also realises that workers need more knowledge and skills to support residents.

The example from Estonia shows that participatory action research involving people with lived experiences as co-researchers reveals wishes and opportunities for bonding and bridging. By involving all stakeholders in this process, mutual understanding is increased. The data from the research provide insights how the quality of community places can be improved. The project is an example of bottom-up or horizontal social innovation (see Part I of this book).

Integrating formerly homeless people in the community

An example from the Netherlands concerns the integration of homeless people in a local community. This community project 'First a Home', revolves around a housing project for homeless people in the city of Utrecht. The aim was not only to provide a home, but also to support the new residents to create relationships with the community, enhancing participation. The project is a 'living lab', in which all parties involved were learning to create a social infrastructure for homeless people. Parties included service users, the municipality, the university of applied sciences, homeless services and the housing corporation. Between March 2021 and June 2023, more than 200 people were being given a home in various housing projects in the city of Utrecht and its surroundings. Some live individually in a neighbourhood, but most were got a place in so-called communal housing complexes, where they live together with socially motivated regular tenants, with the specific intent of being 'good neighbours'. One of our researchers was involved in this project using a participatory research design (Van Ewijk, 2022). She played an active role in connecting the different actors and organisations, bridging different positions and perspectives. Among other things she co-organised interactive sessions and inspiration visits to similar projects elsewhere. Van Ewijk states: 'The interests and perspectives of municipalities, service providers, housing cooperations and homeless people can differ considerably, even though all underline the same goal: increasing the well-being of homeless. I navigate constantly between all these actors and try to bring people closer together' (2022: 5, translation by editors).

Building bridges

In this example we see that bonding refers in fact to two types of communities: the community of the people getting a home in the housing project, and the broader community of the neighbourhood. Before they entered the project, the former homeless people often experienced a lack of respect and human compassion, which made them feel invisible (Van Ewijk, 2022). 'By having a house of your own, taking direction over your own life and paying attention to how to become part of the neighbourhood, hopefully a sense of belonging will develop' (Van Ewijk, 2022: 7). The challenge is to build bridges, overcoming fixed images about homeless people that hinder social inclusion. This turns out to be a process that takes time and requires different types of bridge-building activities. Examples are inviting neighbours to have a cup of coffee, and creating a magazine about the project that was distributed in the neighbourhood. Our research shows that it is quite complicated to develop an inside community in the housing project at the same time as working on bonding with the neighbourhood. Being a project that was initiated top-down with a large degree of involvement of institutions hindered the developments from the bottom up. More time and effort are needed to empower the people living in different housing facilities around the city, and to create 'natural' connections in the broader community, using an asset-based approach. Creating mutual relationships between people is an important condition for the sense of belonging and for bridging, using the resources that the community has to expand opportunities. An interesting element in this example is that Putnam's notion of linking was used in a reverse way, in the sense that resources (like houses for the homeless people, and professional support) were provided by institutions and systems, and that bonding and bridging followed afterwards. This shows that a dynamic interplay of all the elements of social capital is important. Having institutions in the lead creates the danger that the voices of the affected citizens are neglected or suppressed. In this example, the people entering the housing facility had little opportunity to really participate in decision-making, and were even confronted with demands and reproaches (such as: "you have been living here now for three months and still don't have a job"). Our research shows that it is important to put this voice at centre stage, and to create a safe and open dialogical space. Working at a grassroots community level requires a common vision on inclusion, and translating this vision into practice.

The example from the Netherlands shows that in processes of social innovation, in this case integration of people with a history of homelessness in the neighbourhood, social workers have to deal with old patterns of 'taking care of' instead of 'taking care with', and with mechanisms of exclusion. The project also shows that in innovative community development we must connect different forms of capital: in this case, the experiential knowledge of 'new' residents; the professional knowledge of social workers and services; and the expertise and physical resources of housing cooperations. Innovative community development requires to be able to work transdisciplinary with a diversity of actors.

Tensions and challenges

A community worker is in a way a public servant whose main task is to support the well-being of the community, and to help to increase the quality of community life. It concerns the well-being of the whole community, not just certain parts of the community or individual members. Community workers are striving for social inclusion, which means that all people in the community count, and that the opportunities that the community has, or that will be created, are opportunities for all. Knowledge about mechanisms of inclusion and exclusion is important. We have to deal here with what is called the inclusion paradox, which illustrates the natural tension between individual freedom and the need to make room for diversity, to accept others to be part of the community (Kramer, 2019). For 'bonding', a community needs certain boundaries, which are important for internal trust and safety. But this also means that people are excluded. Also, internally, there will always be mechanisms of exclusion at play, which often turn around power, for example about who can make decisions. Power can be related to a particular status in the community, such as being a business owner, a lawyer or a politician. Power and wealth can be distributed unequally, creating gaps between people that might not be easy to overcome. For the social worker, this means that a sound ethical framework is important (Banks et al, 2023).

As mentioned earlier, the political and institutional context of the community may facilitate or hinder community development. Community workers might be faced with directives of the local authority or funding agency that are contrary to their professional standards and the mission of social work. They might, for example, be asked to control a group of young people hanging around in the streets and causing a nuisance. It might be valuable then to show that a strength-based community approach is producing the same or even better results. In this example, this approach includes connecting to the youngsters, asking about their talents, wishes and needs, and taking these as a starting point for a meaningful contribution to the community. Setting examples and showcasing these can even be part of innovating local or national social policy. Community workers often have to mediate between the 'system world' of authorities and institutions and the 'life world' of the community. It is important to keep a firm position in order not to be the victim of a tug of war. A good back-up by a strong community association or the community service organisation can be very helpful.

Another challenge community workers have to face, but at the same time underlining how important their work is, concerns the polarisation in many European countries, both on a national and a local level. In local communities this can lead to tensions and social exclusion. These can be hard to counter, to preserve a neutral position, and at the same time continuing to work on dialogue and mutual understanding, to look for what binds people instead of dividing them. Bringing people together and creating places where people could listen to each other safely counteracts aggression and a culture of othering. Well-connected communities could handle better the polyphony of views and counteract polarisation and exclusion.

Finally, we mention the challenge of mobility. The stability of a community is constituted by people who are part of the community for a longer time. A large degree of fluidity makes it difficult to work on sustainable developments. Nowadays we are also facing the great influx of newcomers from Ukraine and other countries. This means even more that we have to overcome cultural and language barriers. This further emphasises the importance of a strong core network, a basic social infrastructure that is resilient enough to cope with changes in the population. A strong 'community heart' has a great absorption potential, allowing newcomers to integrate and become part of community life.

Conclusion

Community development is needed more than ever. We consider this as a process of social innovation because it is aimed at improving human relations and increasing social quality. Community agency workers can play an important role in supporting communities to revitalise, to use and increase social capital, as a form of horizontal or grassroots innovation. Social workers in the community are especially needed to support the social inclusion of people in marginalised positions.

Considering the – often complex – interplay between community members, institutions, systems and the impact of global developments, this work needs great sensitivity, creativity and courage, beside bonding, bridging and linking skills. Since the quality of social relations is key to using and strengthening assets, social workers trained in community-building can play an important role. Methods like action learning and community-based participatory action research are suitable for engaging in a process of co-creation. By working collaboratively on common goals, the quality of relationships in the community can be increased, and thereby individual and collective well-being.

Modern community work requires a sound ethical basis (focus on human well-being and inclusion) and the skills to understand and connect people with different perspectives. Strengthening social quality should connect communities with all the resources that are important for health and well-being, such as decent employment and income, good-quality services and physical as well as natural resources.

References

Argyle, M. (1996) Subjective well-being, in A. Offer (ed) *In Pursuit of the Quality of Life*, Oxford: Clarendon Press, pp 18–45.

Bagnall, A., South, J., Di Martino, S., Southby, K., Pilkington, G., Mitchell, B., et al (2018) *A Systematic Review of Interventions to Boost Social Relations Through Improvements in Community Infrastructure (Places and Spaces)*, London: What Works Centre for Wellbeing.

Banks, S., Shevellar, L. and Narayanan, P. (2023) Ethical issues in community development: setting the scene, *Community Development Journal*, 58(1): 1–18.

Bauman, Z. (2000) *Liquid Modernity*, Cambridge: Polity Press.

Bromley, E., Gabrielian, S., Brekke, B., Pahwa, R., Daly, K.A., Brekke, J.S. and Braslow, J.T. (2013) Experiencing community: perspectives of individuals diagnosed as having serious mental illness, *Psychiatric Services*, 64(7): 672–9.

Bourdieu, P. and Wacquant. L. (1992) *An Invitation to Reflexive Sociology*, Chicago: University of Chicago Press.

DeFilippis, J. (2001) The myth of social capital in community development, *Housing Policy Debate*, 12(4): 781–806.

Doroud, N., Fossey, E. and Fortune, T. (2018) Place for being, doing, becoming and belonging: a meta-synthesis exploring the role of place in mental health recovery, *Health & Place*, 52: 110–20.

European Commission (2013) Guide to Social Innovation, February, Brussels: European Commission, https://ec.europa.eu/regional_policy/en/information/publications/guides/2013/guide-to-social-innovation.

Gilchrist, A. (2019) *The Well-Connected Community: A Networking Approach to Community Development*, 3rd edn, Bristol: Policy Press.

Goscha, R.J. (2020) Strengths model case management: moving strengths from concept to action, in: A.N. Mendenhall and M.M. Carney (eds) *Rooted in Strengths: Celebrating the Strengths Perspective in Social Work*, Lawrence, KS: University of Kansas Libraries, pp 165–86.

Hacker, K. (2013) *Community-Based Participatory Research*, Thousand Oaks, CA: Sage.

Harrison, E., Quick, A. and Abdallah, S. (eds) (2016) *Looking Through the Wellbeing Kaleidoscope: Results from the European Social Survey*, London: New Economics Foundation.

Harrison, R., Blickem, C., Lamb, J., Kirk, S. and Vassilev, I. (2019) Asset-based community development: narratives, practice, and conditions of possibility – a qualitative study with community practitioners, *SAGE Open*, 9(1), https://doi.org/10.1177/2158244018823081.

Helliwell, J., Barrington-Leigh, C.P., Harris, A. and Huang, H. (2009) International Evidence on the Social Context of Well-Being, NBER Working Paper No. 14720, Cambridge, MA: National Bureau of Economic Research, https://www.nber.org/papers/w14720.

Kramer, J. (2019) *Jam Cultures – Over inclusie: meedoen, meepraten, meebeslissen*, Deventer: Management Impact.

Kretzmann, J. and McKnight, J. (1993) *Building Communities from the Inside Out: A Path Toward Finding and Mobilizing a Community's Assets*, 3rd edn, Chicago: ACTA Publications.

Murray, R., Caulier-Grice, J. and Mulgan, G. (2010) *The Open Book of Social Innovation*, London: Young Foundation and National Endowment for Science, Technology and the Arts.

Narusson, D. and Wilken, J.P. (2018) Recovery in the community: relational and cultural sensitivity, *Journal of Recovery in Mental Health*, 2(1): 68–81.

Phillipson, C., Allan, G. and Morgan, D. (eds) (2004) *Social Networks and Social Exclusion: Sociological and Policy Perspectives*, Farnham: Ashgate.

Putnam, R.D. (2000) *Bowling Alone: The Collapse and Revival of American Community*, New York: Simon & Schuster.

Putnam, R.D. (2007) 'E Pluribus Unum: Diversity and community in the twenty-first century, the 2006 Johan Skytte Prize lecture', *Scandinavian Political Studies*, 30: 137–174. https://doi.org/10.1111/j.1467-9477.2007.00176.x

Ross, A., Talmage, C.A. and Searle, M. (2019) Toward a flourishing neighborhood: the association of happiness and sense of community, *Applied Research in Quality of Life*, 14(5): 1333–52.

Harrison, E., Quick, A. and Abdallah, S. (eds) (2016) *Looking Through the Wellbeing Kaleidoscope: Results from the European Social Survey*, London: New Economics Foundation.

Russell, C. (2020) *Rekindling Democracy: A Professional's Guide to Working in Citizen Space*, Eugene, OR: Cascade Books.

Russell, C. and McKnight, J. (2022) *The Connected Community: Discovering the Health, Wealth, and Power of Neighborhoods*, Oakland, CA: Berrett-Koehler.

Van Ewijk, D. (2022) *Eerst een Thuis, Verbinding en kennisdeling binnen het living lab*, Utrecht: Utrecht University of Applied Sciences.

Van Ewijk, H. (2010) *European Social Policy and Social Work: Citizenship-Based Social Work*, Abingdon: Routledge.

Villamayor-Tomas, S. and García-López, G.A. (2021) Commons movements: old and new trends in rural and urban contexts, *Annual Review of Environment and Resources*, 46: 511–43.

14

Climate change from a green social work perspective: responding to a constantly evolving crisis challenging social work practice

Lena Dominelli

Introduction

Contemporary social work presents practitioners with myriad challenges. Upholding human rights and social justice and obtaining recognition of social work as a research-led profession have guided practitioners for decades. This chapter examines urgent global challenges including climate-induced disasters and their non-existent coverage in qualifying curricula. I argue that such gaps must be rectified to affirm environmental justice and care for planet Earth in and through professional practice. Green social work (GSW), a new paradigm for theory and practice, provides a model for addressing these. GSW argues that social workers can include environmental justice in their daily engagement with service users, and when assisting in disasters. Very few qualifying social work programmes teach social work students to practise within disaster settings except for the Tata Institute of Social Sciences that has covered disasters since the 1947 Gujarat earthquake. Innovative approaches are necessary to address climate change–induced disasters since they will occur with greater frequency and intensity than previously. New approaches rooted in transdisciplinarity carry extensive scientific expertise for engaging complexity in contemporary disasters. Another innovation is encouraging service users to acknowledge the social vulnerabilities and social dimensions of disasters and co-produce new solutions (Alexander, 1993; Cutter, 1996; Dominelli, 2012).

Interaction between a hazard and society through people's behaviour exacerbates vulnerabilities to produce a disaster. For example, a flood plain is a natural hazard that provides space for a river to overflow its banks during periods of heavy rain. It becomes a disaster when people build housing on it without flood-proofing the houses. When the overflowing water ingresses people's houses, a disaster occurs because the risks posed by the vulnerability of building on a flood plain was not mitigated through preventative action (de Lange, 2018). The United Nations defines a disaster as an event of a magnitude wherein the resources available are insufficient to address it and require external assistance. The COVID-19 pandemic exposed the social dimensions of disasters because the coronavirus harboured by animals in their own habitat reached humans. Once brought into society through a host animal having regular contact with people in the domesticated arena, the 'new' coronavirus, SARS-COV-2, could wreak havoc upon a humanity that lacked natural immunity (WWF, 2020). Innovations for tackling this social problem required scientists to develop vaccines to protect people from the virus's worst effects. The scientific advances entailed in this discovery encouraged people opposing vaccinations to spread fake news and misinformation to discourage their use. Their views cannot be ignored. Social workers can facilitate community-based dialogues for people to explore such issues together. Participation and co-production can address new fears stemming from challenges to existing social relations, including mistrusting official or scientific information (Chou and Budenz, 2020).

Innovation encourages doing things differently to produce better processes and outcomes. Promoting intergenerational leisure groups bringing elders and younger people together to appreciate nature and its wonders is innovative because it encourages dialogues that enable young people to experience older people as assets, not burdens.

Existing generic skills in qualifying training, supplemented by transdisciplinarity among diverse disciplines and co-engagement with community stakeholders provide useful transferable skills for intervening in disaster contexts. Transdisciplinarity is central to GSW, a novel paradigm to facilitate innovations in social work practice by preparing practitioners to 'do science differently' (Lane et al, 2011) when responding to disasters like climate change, a critical, constantly evolving disaster. In this instance, practitioners addressing flooding events can learn from flood experts like Lane et al (2011), who have worked with flooded communities to enhance resilience. Their working with residents has meant valuing their local knowledge and skills, and provides a way of working that social workers can build upon in their engagement with communities across a range of issues, social and environmental. Tackling environmental degradation and injustice impacts all disasters including poverty, which aggravates any disaster's seriousness (Dominelli, 2012, 2018) and is an area of routine practice in social work. 'Doing science differently' brings a new perspective, that is, transdisciplinarity, or the practice of working across academic divides to bring the physical sciences into their work. War, another environmental disaster, emits copious amounts of greenhouse gas emissions (GHGs), and heavy metals that degrade soils, water and air. Wars also adversely affect people's physical and mental health and well-being.

In this chapter, social workers are asked to address these issues as a strong, united profession working alongside dispossessed and marginalised peoples whose voices are seldom heard, who lack access to global resources and bear the brunt of ecological degradation despite having small ecological footprints. To assist practitioners, GSW, a new paradigm for practice, is presented. GSW practice is embedded in an environmental justice that enhances the well-being of people, flora, fauna and ecosystems that sustain and support all living things. I propose that GSW for disasters be included in the social work curriculum to equip practitioners to meet the complex demands occasioned by climatic and other disasters. The 2022 heatwave, accompanying drought and wildfires, clarified the necessity for climate action globally (Ahmad et al, 2022).

Defining climate change

No agreed definition of climate change exists (Werndl, 2016). The Intergovernmental Panel on Climate Change (IPCC) definition is (IPCC, 2007):

> Climate in a narrow sense is usually defined as the average weather, or more rigorously, as the statistical description in terms of the mean and variability of relevant quantities over a time period ranging from months to thousands or millions of years … The relevant quantities are most often surface variables such as temperature, precipitation, and wind. Climate in a wider sense is the state, including a statistical description, of the climate system.

The 2022 heatwave in the UK and elsewhere caused high numbers of deaths through droughts and floods that displaced millions, as exemplified in Pakistan. These extreme weather events compelled people to heed extensive warnings on climate change. Despite generalised notifications, only limited action on the climate crisis has occurred. I refer to a climate crisis rather than climate change because the time remaining on the clock for humanity to take radical action to end human-induced contributions to climate change is rapidly disappearing (IPCC, 2021). Putin's War Against Ukraine is adding significantly to GHGs, as is Netanyahu's constant bombardment of Gaza. However, the environmental costs imposed through the discharge of military ordinances, the destruction of built infrastructures including homes, hospitals, schools, power and communications systems, and in rebuilding everything that has been demolished, are poorly understood (Dominelli, 2023).

The snail's pace of climate action continues to degrade nature and stress people and other sentient beings, especially those contributing least to climate change but suffering the climate crisis's worst consequences. Deleteriously affected are low-lying countries like Bangladesh, and small island developing states like Kiribati, Tuvalu and the Maldives that are sinking into the sea. Their plight demands urgent action now, not by 2050, the date the United

Nations Framework Convention on Climate Change set for reaching 'net zero' globally. This mid-century date is becoming increasingly inadequate, given that the IPCC (2019) argues that all countries must limit rises in global warming to 1.5°C by 2030. Yet, agreements reached during COP26 to limit use of methane gas for a quick reduction in GHGs, have not materialised. The presidents of China and Russia, among the largest emitters, did not attend either COP 26 or COP 27. Moreover, the dates for the top four emitters reaching 'net zero' – in order of emissions, China, the US, India and Russia are disheartening: 2060, 2050, 2070 and 2060, respectively. This is worrying because they comprise 50 per cent of the world's population, located mainly in urban centres that consume disproportionate amounts of fossil fuels compared to their rural compatriots and countries with small populations. Ensuring that each person in every country can lead a comfortable, decent life requires transfers of renewable energy technologies to realise each person's right to development without costing the Earth. Disagreement on equitable transfers of renewable, green technologies to all countries requiring them is a political failure that highlights a social dimension of disasters.

Moreover, huge inequalities in fossil fuel consumption exist within countries. Rural peoples in the Global South, and marginalised groups like homeless people in the Global North consuming small amounts of fossil fuels suffer disproportionately. Rich people within and between countries, consume the bulk of fossil fuels through luxurious lifestyles. The top 10 per cent of the income scale globally uses 20 times more energy than the lowest 10 per cent (Vogel et al, 2021). Their consumption of luxury items results in the top 10 per cent of the income spectrum spending 187 times more on transportation than the lowest 10 per cent (Vogel et al, 2021). Furthermore, without energy efficiency measures, those adopting middle-class lifestyles dependent on high levels of fossil fuel usage are likely to consume ever more energy as their numbers increase globally. Currently, the middle classes of India and China are anticipated to account for half the global increase in energy use by 2050 (Vogel et al, 2021).

Of the world's four largest emitters, only the US has a historical debt to account for. But casting the arguments solely in terms of past consumption is inadequate. Current consumption must be included in the equation for reducing GHGs. Both sources of environmental stress – historical and current additions to GHGs – must be addressed to ensure that changing demands arising from industrialised and emerging economies are combined to calculate the overall GHGs emitted today. The Earth is indifferent to who produces the increasing amounts of GHGs that it has to eliminate through slow natural processes of carbon storage. Their combined data are essential to calculating the relationship between what humanity is contributing to GHGs and what the planet can absorb within its capacity to store carbon in the air, waters, soils and trees. The IPCC (2021), in its *Sixth Assessment*

Report, provided evidence for drastic reductions in GHGs now, alongside worrying scenarios of not reaching overall limits for controlling rises to 1.5°C, or 2.0°C. As CO_2 (carbon dioxide) lasts in the air for 100 years, today's emissions will prevail for generations. Additionally, the moral issue of reducing all GHGs while ensuring economic development for inhabitants of the Global South and preventing small island developing states sinking into the sea requires urgent attention.

Sharing green technologies freely globally requires everyone to eliminate fossil fuel usage for production and consumption purposes. Transfers of green technologies will promote decent standards of living for everyone. Dialogue on tackling climate change necessitates boldness presently absent among global leaders. Green social workers can mobilise communities to co-develop renewable energy policies and lobby politicians to provide financial resources, technology and expertise for achieving net zero by 2030. They can also use data gathered in daily practice from individuals and households suffering hardship and disruption from climate change to argue that governments act to end today's climate crisis. Adding tackling climate change to practitioners' current workload constitutes a brave innovation for social workers and integrates practice into solving major concerns impacting service users.

Green social work: engaging social workers in climate change and other disasters

GSW, a novel paradigm for theory and practice, encompasses caring holistically for people and the ecosystem, enabling practitioners to support life sustainably in an interconnected and interdependent world. It transforms feminist ethics of care (Sevenhuijsen, 1998) into a duty to care for planet Earth alongside caring for people, animals, and plants (Dominelli, 2012). Understanding the implications of climate change for social policy, and humanitarian practice with suggestions for transformative change in social work education and practice provides guidance for addressing extreme weather events, to reverse human suffering and environmental devastation. GSW's holistic, transdisciplinary, inclusive approach to the challenges encountered will co-produce strategies for transformative actions to tackle climate change, strengthen political will and individual resolve to achieve this goal. Supporting practitioners requires the incorporation of climate change knowledge in training and educating social workers at all levels (qualifying, specialisation and doctoral research) to initiate and consolidate the step change necessary to take the profession out of its existing comfort zone of routine practice. A mindset that emphasises psychosocial needs among children, families and older people, and links structural inequalities to personal failings is inadequate in meeting contemporary global challenges that impact daily lives. Altering this mindset requires a positive lunge forward into addressing climate-induced and other disasters as normal. Doing this confidently requires all social workers to be trained in disaster interventions.

Defining green social work

GSW, a holistic, transdisciplinary, human rights and social justice–based model for practice, conceptualises disasters as socially constructed (Homan, 2003; Oliver-Smith, 2022). Disasters occur when risks posed by hazards, natural or human-made, interact with socially created vulnerabilities to produce calamitous events with substantial casualties and damage to local built infrastructures and ecosystems (Dominelli, 2012, 2018). If resources required to re-establish communities exceed their capacity to cope, external actors arrive to rebuild resilience and increase capacity for dealing with future catastrophes. The United Nations differentiates disasters from emergencies as those requiring external personnel and resources to tackle the enormity of calamitous events.

GSW considers inequities generated by neoliberal, fossil fuel–driven economic systems as unsustainable because capitalists derive profits from exploiting nature's resources and human labour. Capitalists also encourage inbuilt obsolescence requiring people to replace appliances regularly, not repair them. GSW rejects anthropomorphic approaches to the physical environment and other sentient beings by arguing that people implement sustainability by recognising their duty to care for planet Earth. This demands a reciprocated sustainable relationship that acknowledges the Earth's right to exist in, for and of itself into infinity. This reconceptualisation of the relationship between people and nature is founded on a forever duty of care. Sustainability is not an exchange transaction whereby people meet the needs of today and tomorrow by continued usage of fossil fuels (Brundtland,1987). Understanding GSW approaches to human–nature interactions requires individuals to hold themselves, governments and multinational corporations accountable for their decisions, promote environmental protection, acknowledge the interdependent nature of all things, and reject fossil fuel–based production and consumption of goods and services that maintain life. GSW provides a step change by caring for nature through a reciprocal integrated relationship promoting health and well-being. Lack of human–nature contact is captured by eco-grief (Cunsolo and Ellis, 2018), a reaction that emphasises the centrality of healthy nature–human interactions.

Generic social work skills encompassing crisis interventions, risk assessments, active listening, and interviewing, underpin disaster responses for eliminating the climate crisis. These skills cover risk assessments, needs identification, resource availability, interviewing people, identifying external resources, investigating situations to ascertain the 'facts' regarding eligibility for aid, implementing crisis interventions, coordinating service delivery, reunifying families, empowering residents as agentic in making decisions, providing residents with psychosocial services, mobilising community energies and resources to 'build back better' (Manyena, 2006), and co-producing innovative solutions to the climate crisis that people will own and implement (Dominelli, 2012). Other elements adapted from daily practice are: empathetic and sensitive engagement to understand lived experiences of disaster-induced hardships; cultural skills attuned to local realities; communication skills and use of traditional and social media; organisational skills to coordinate good relationships between different organisational systems and institutions; critical reflective thinking around concepts, power relations, theories, policies and practice guidelines; active listening; patience when goods and services do not arrive or victim-survivors reject outsider advice; and self-care.

Generic skills are used in all disaster responses throughout the disaster cycle – prevention, immediate relief, recovery and reconstruction (Dominelli, 2012, 2023). They ground daily practice routines in delivering humanitarian aid during a disaster. However, social workers require specific training on climate change and other disasters to provide humanitarian aid with confidence and knowledge of effective interventions. The centrality of adequate disaster training was evidenced in social workers' comments about practice during the 2016 Grenfell Fire in London (Bartoli et al, 2022). While they demonstrated their use of generic skills and learned on the spot, their outcomes would have been better had they known about disaster interventions, and different systems and players with whom they would relate, before arriving. The British Association of Social Workers (BASW, 2019) has initiated round-table discussions for social work experts to produce post-qualifying guidelines and competences for disasters. Accepted by the Local Government Association in England, these are available on BASW's website. Others clarify social workers' roles during disasters (IFRC, 2021).

Disaster-induced challenges to the profession

Climate change has intensified extreme weather events and their frequency across the world (IFRC, 2021). Social workers immediately attend evacuation centres to respond to practical needs, providing food, clothing, shelter, medicines, family reunification and psychosocial support. In its report, IFRC (2021) discussed how to support local communities to handle the consequences of climate change in locality-specific, culturally relevant ways that inform everyday practice with children, families and elders. These embed practice in daily routines, such as resuming children's education; establishing income generation schemes; providing culturally appropriate assistance, as in Mongolia to survive *dzud* (combined drought and severe winter conditions); giving drought-resistant seeds to Ethiopia's drought-stricken communities to grow food; building flood defences in Montenegro; offering psychosocial support to Australia's bushfire impacted communities; and funding storm mitigation measures in Bangladesh. These local initiatives involve volunteers, humanitarian aid workers, social workers, community development workers and health professionals working alongside emergency workers including police, firefighters, military personnel and residents. Transdisciplinary, holistic approaches to climate change require each profession to contribute from its routine practice knowledge and expertise.

Extreme weather events, the consequences of climate change

Climate change, a risk multiplier, activates existing hazards to produce complex social disasters. Some regions are more heavily affected than others: for example, the Asia-Pacific area endures the highest number of climatic events impacting upon people. This is especially worrisome as these locations experience rapid, unplanned urbanisation and socio-economic inequalities disadvantaging those at greatest risk. Extreme weather events accounted for 83 per cent of disasters occurring between 2010 and 2020, killing 410,000 people, and heavily undermining the livelihoods of 1.7 billion (IFRC, 2021). Most victim-survivors reside in low- and middle-income countries in the Global South. For those that survive these disasters, food insecurity, health insecurities and loss of natural habitats have become commonplace. Following Putin's War Against Ukraine, even middle-class people in richer societies have become affected by sociopolitical calamities through cost-of-living price rises in foods and fuel, loss of agricultural production and livelihoods, and unreliability of supply chains in chaotic socio-economic systems. Victim-survivors in low-income countries barely recover from one disaster before another follows. For example, in 2022, Jacobabad, Pakistan had the highest temperature to date. Heavy monsoon rains followed, flooding 10 per cent of the country and affected 33 million people. Yet, Pakistan has contributed little to GHGs (IFRC, 2022). Recovery from widespread, complex disasters is further hindered by inadequate resources including money, insurance and personnel. COVID-19 has complicated national responses regarding people's health and economic opportunities.

In low-income countries, recovering from climate change and the COVID-19 pandemic is a long-term proposition that requires external support to rebuild communities and engage populations in readily accessing green technologies. The funds necessary to achieve this recovery have been estimated to require US$50 billion annually between 2020 and 2030 to meet the adaptation requirements in 50 developing countries. This sum is insignificant compared to the economic devastation caused by COVID-19 which has been calculated at US$10 trillion. In July 2020, EU leaders set aside Euros €750 billion, and the US committed US$2.2 trillion in COVID-19 stimulus schemes to endorse a resilient, green recovery (IFRC, 2021). The realisation of this goal seems remote as none of the 20 countries most vulnerable to climate change have received any such funds (IFRC, 2021). Aid reaching these countries rarely touches their most vulnerable inhabitants.

Some at-risk populations migrate to other countries – usually neighbouring ones, as climate migrants. Their numbers are expected to exceed 1 billion by 2050 if GHGs are not eliminated (Henley, 2020). Migrants requiring social work support lack coverage in international law such as the 1951 Convention. Thus, the countries wherein they seek asylum rarely accord a warm welcome. Green social workers can lobby nationally and internationally through professional associations to secure rights for these climate migrants. Globally, these include the International Association of Schools of Social Work (IASSW), International Federation of Social Workers (IFSW) and International Council of Social Welfare (ICSW). Nationally in the UK, it is the British Association of Social Workers. Learning to intervene at these levels is an area for inclusion in disaster education.

Social workers operate throughout the disaster cycle – preparation, relief, recovery and reconstruction. Supporting people, communities, countries and devastated environments most at risk become major concerns for green social workers and other practitioners having long-term responsibilities for health, well-being and rebuilding communities. IFRC (2021) argues that all stakeholders – governments, donors, humanitarian workers, and those in development, climate and environmental disciplines must prioritise the delivery of aid and funds to the most vulnerable communities. IFRC (2021) argues that the United Nations' Sustainable Development Goals, Paris Agreement and Sendai Framework for Disaster Risk Reduction 2015–30 are integrated into agreed actions to achieve optimal results. Over the next 10–30 years, IFRC (2021) anticipates that weather events exacerbated by climate change, including the displacement of people, food insecurity, loss of livelihoods, damage to property, injury and loss of life, will push those affected well beyond their ability to cope. Responding effectively would require external funds, personnel, expertise and donations. Growing demands on practitioners and volunteers reinforce arguments for training to intervene at any stage in the disaster cycle.

Migration and climate change

Social workers face difficulties in establishing professional credentials and scientific expertise. This long-standing anxiety encompasses its place in the academy. New considerations cover its engagement with the climate crisis. I examine these issues through various scenarios. Climate migration exemplifies a key challenge to human rights–based practice in climate-induced extreme weather events, and war. Climate change, war and migration are interconnected because each element affects the others, as exemplified by South Sudan, a conflict zone that faces regular flooding. Assisting in such situations is extremely complicated because fighting impacts on the logistics of receiving and delivering aid, on transportation routes and on housing (UNHCR, 2022). Risks include lack of safety for workers, aid recipients and practitioners. Warring parties often reject humanitarian workers' neutrality because providing aid to an opposing side is deemed siding with the opposition. Persons forced from homes in South Sudan through flooding are unable to find safe refuge within their community. They would experience difficulty in explaining whether their migration was caused by flooding, war or both. Both calamities would act as push factors compelling them to leave their homeland. Moreover, climate change is affected by the discharge and release of GHGs by military ordinance. Besides destroying built infrastructures including homes, clinics, hospitals, communication systems, power supplies and water supplies, the atrocities of war force people to flee to safety. These comprise both internal and external displacements as exemplified by Ukraine (Sasse, 2020). Poland receives many externally displaced Ukrainians and successfully innovates with anti-oppressive practice to generate acceptance from compatriots.

Social workers responding to these situations encounter serious ethical dilemmas. The ethical principle of 'doing no harm' requiring practitioners to behave ethically is compromised by policies limiting assistance to migrants. In the UK, asylum seekers are rarely allowed to work while their applications remain undetermined. Reaching a decision may take officials years (Vickers, 2012). Moreover, legislative exclusion from earning an income or obtaining full state benefits places enormous pressures on those seeking safety. Social workers may face ethical dilemmas when risk assessments verify that individuals require assistance, but material support is refused unless procured from outside the public sector. Thus, referral to the voluntary sector is common. Some social workers lobby policy makers to pass laws more sympathetic to asylum claims. Green social workers responding to the immense suffering experienced by those displaced by climatic calamities and war enhance inter-country and intergenerational solidarity through sustainable interventions that co-build resilience among individuals, communities and environments locally and internationally. GSW proposes changes to the social work curriculum to prepare practitioners to meet innovative demands for 21st-century practice. These endorse skills and knowledges that support transformative change, human rights, and social justice–based practice in situations of climate change, war, and other disasters.

Climate migrants' vulnerability increases because no country is legally obliged to receive them. The 1951 Geneva Convention is irrelevant for them. Recent immigration legislation explicitly excludes asylum seekers. In the UK, they are denied full benefits and live in dispersed housing because local authorities lack the shelters necessary in communities containing populations from migrant-sending countries. Migrants face a 'hostile environment' from the UK's Home Office which is reluctant to admit people arriving in 'small boats' and threatening to deport such arrivals to Rwanda to discourage migration. Such approaches have not deterred people traffickers from amassing fortunes by exploiting those seeking safer shores. Currently, traffickers crowd people reaching France into small dinghies to cross the English Channel. In 2022, around 50,000 undertaking this perilous journey reached the UK, despite many that died trying. Social workers have responded with assistance despite restrictions imposed on their activities by using voluntary agencies to facilitate practice innovations when dealing with excruciating ethical dilemmas, thereby finding funds and services for needy families in the voluntary sector, defending their human rights, and challenging harsh and inhumane legislation. Social workers have more resources to address the needs of unaccompanied minors (under 18 years of age). However, even these have been squeezed by austerity policies that curtail public expenditures. The British government faces critical questions about why this rich country treats those requesting asylum so poorly. This question is pertinent for climate and other migrants that politicians label 'economic migrants' seeking to abuse the country's welfare system (Shabi, 2019).

War, and climate change: Putin's War Against Ukraine is climatically catastrophic

War, I have claimed elsewhere (Dominelli, 2012, 2023), contributes to the climate crisis by incessantly discharging armaments, running tanks and other vehicles of war, and creating countless migrants. The military is attributed with 5.5 per cent of global GHGs. Moreover, it adds more GHGs into the air, soils, and waters when it destroys built infrastructure including houses, schools, hospitals, medical clinics, power infrastructures and communication systems. It dumps a further payload when these destroyed buildings are rebuilt. Britain's flagship programmes initiated for migrants from Afghanistan, Syria and Ukraine are floundering due to inadequate funding. Those from Ukraine had a groundswell of support from ordinary people who opened their hearts and homes by offering sponsorship through the Home Office's 'Homes for Ukraine' scheme. Social workers criticised these schemes' inadequacies, especially their limited housing availability and poorly implemented vetting procedures to safeguard children and older people (BASW, 2022). Inadequate support for individuals who sponsored Ukrainian individuals or families meant that many did not renew their offers after their six-month period expired. The British government paid £350 monthly as 'thank you' payments to those befriending Ukrainians through the 'Homes for Ukraine' scheme. Initially, payment lasted 6 months, later increased to 12 months. With no end to war in sight as at the time of writing, the period has been extended to 24 months, and monthly payments raised to £500.

The Homes for Ukraine scheme promoted by the Home Office is an innovation for legitimating private sponsorship. Ukrainian forced migrants are allowed to work and receive welfare benefits including healthcare and education. Nonetheless, housing availability does not match need, given UK-wide shortages. Social worker numbers are insufficient to conduct all necessary safeguarding assessments. Consequently, some Ukrainians residing with their 'hosts' cannot rest assured that these homes are safe from such risks. Caring for forced migrants admitted under special schemes, like the Ukrainians and former employees of UK agencies fleeing Afghanistan, can be costly if numbers are significant. The UK government is spending £5 million daily to house forced migrants in hotels due to lack of appropriate housing. Housing shortages intensify concerns about such initiatives.

The social work profession, from Europe to Japan, from Latin America to Africa, responded to those fleeing the War Against Ukraine with donations, training and support for local social workers remaining in Ukraine. This work has been conducted mainly by the IASSW and IFSW and their regional branches. Additionally, Social Work for Peace was formed to attract individuals to donate funds and practical items, develop materials and information about local services, send resources to Ukraine, support social workers inside Ukraine and provide online training workshops for students, practitioners and educators. Furthermore, several GSW academics in the UK successfully applied for funds to recruit Ukrainian colleagues to continue research in this country.

Social workers have intervened in conflict situations and reconciliation endeavours to promote peace between former combatants (Duffy et al, 2022). Duffy et al (2022) highlight social workers' roles in facilitating peace and reconciliation processes, and 'self-care' for those serving in war-torn situations. Some initiatives have been more successful than others, but the skills of building systems for the non-violent resolution of conflicts are practised throughout and remain relevant for current politically based conflicts, despite their seemingly intractable rootedness deep in the historical past. Some conflicts get resolved, only to resurface years, decades or centuries later as occurred in the Balkans following the break-up of the former Yugoslavia. In that conflict, social workers were key in supporting people to rebuild their lives following ceasefire agreements.

This produced innovative, groundbreaking social work practice for supporting women who had been physically and sexually assaulted and gang raped throughout the war (Seifert, 1995). Good practice and lessons learned from the Balkans were rehearsed in the summer of 2022 to address Ukrainian women's sexual and physical abuse by soldiers. This practice exposed the exploitation of women's bodies as symbols of the nation (Yuval-Davis, 1997). Such symbolism turns women's bodies into weapons of war to undermine men soldiers' confidence, thereby perpetrating numerous assaults against women to dishonour men.

Conclusion

Climate change, a dynamic and constantly evolving human-made disaster, impacts on all humanity, as differentiated by socio-economic status and location.

It combines with other hazards including poverty, earthquakes and volcanoes to exacerbate impact and intensify damage. The world's political elites lag behind activists in tackling climate change. Action to mitigate the damage done by extreme weather events must become an everyday concern among politicians, ordinary residents and social work practitioners and educators. Developing social work's academic curriculum to cover all types of disasters, including climate change, is essential. It requires curriculum innovation to incorporate concepts of co-production with victim-survivors of disasters and conflicts to resolve issues and reconcile opposing groups. Practitioners innovate by transferring existing practice skills to new situations and co-producing new knowledges and tools. GSW, an innovative paradigm for overcoming social vulnerabilities in disasters including climate change and war, co-produces new knowledge and tools for analysing and intervening in disasters. Crucially, GSW promotes innovations including caring for planet Earth and critiquing fossil fuel–based production and consumption. Green social workers promote innovative policy changes by lobbying governments for responses that include climate migrants in national and international laws. Demanding the inclusion of disaster interventions in the curriculum and affirming the social dimensions of disasters are other innovations articulated by GSW. As social constructions, disasters highlight diversity in truths and eschew an unchanging nature because hazards pose risks that create disasters when these interact with social vulnerabilities or human behaviour to produce a calamity.

References

Ahmad, M., Yaseen, M., and Saqib, S. (2022) Climate change impacts of drought on the livelihood of dryland smallholders: implications of adaptation challenges, *International Journal of Disaster Risk Reduction*, 80(4): art 103210, https://doi.org/10.1016/j.ijdrr.2022.103210.

Alexander, D. (1993) *Natural Disasters*, New York: Chapman and Hall.

Bartoli, A., Stratulis, M. and Pierre, R. (eds) (2022) *Out of the Shadows: The Role of Social Workers in Disasters*, St Albans: Critical Publishing.

BASW (British Association of Social Workers) (2019) *CPD Guidance on Social Work Roles Undertaken During Disasters*, Birmingham: BASW.

BASW (British Association of Social Workers) (2022) Statement on Ukraine, Birmingham: BASW, https://www.basw.co.uk/what-we-do/internatio nal-work/war-ukraine#:~:text=We%20stand%20in%20solidarity%20w ith,page%20for%20our%20latest%20updates.

Brundtland, G.H. (1987) *Our Common Future. The World Commission on Environment and Development (Brundtland Commission and Report)*, New York: Oxford University Press.

Chou, W.Y.S. and Budenz, A. (2020) Considering emotion in COVID-19 vaccine communication: addressing vaccine hesitancy and fostering vaccine confidence, *Health Communication*, 35(14): 1718–22.

Cunsolo, A. and Ellis, N. (2018) Ecological grief as a mental health response to climate change-related loss, *Nature Climate Change*, 8: 275–81.

Cutter, S.L. (1996) Vulnerability to environmental hazards, *Progress in Human Geography*, 20: 529–39.

de Lange, D. (2018) Building housing on flood plains another sign of growing inequality, The Conversation, 21 August, https://theconversation.com/building-housing-on-flood-plains-another-sign-of-growing-inequality-101552.

Dominelli, L. (2012) *Green Social Work: From Environmental Crisis to Environmental Justice*, Cambridge: Polity Press.

Dominelli, L. (ed) (2018) *The Routledge Handbook of Green Social Work*, Abingdon: Routledge.

Dominelli, L. (2023) *Social Work During Times of Disaster*, London: Routledge.

Duffy, J., Campbell, J. and Tosone, C. (2022) *International Perspectives on Social Work and Political Conflict*, Abingdon: Routledge.

Henley, J. (2020) Climate crisis could displace 1.2bn people by 2050, report warns, *The Guardian*, 9 September, https://www.theguardian.com/environment/2020/sep/09/climate-crisis-could-displace-12bn-people-by-2050-report-warns.

Homan, J. (2003) The social construction of natural disaster: Egypt and the UK, in M. Pelling (ed) *Natural Disaster and Development in a Globalizing World*, London: Routledge, pp 141–56.

IFRC (International Federation of the Red Cross and Red Crescent Societies) (2021) *World Disasters Report 2020: Come Heat or High Water – Tackling the Humanitarian Impacts of the Climate Crisis Together*, Geneva: IFRC, https://www.ifrc.org/document/world-disasters-report-2020.

IFRC (International Federation of the Red Cross and Red Crescent Societies) (2022) Pakistan floods: six months on, humanitarian needs remain dire, 13 December, https://www.ifrc.org/article/pakistan-floods-six-months-humanitarian-needs-remain-dire.

IPCC (Intergovernmental Panel on Climate Change) (2007) Glossary: climate change, https://www.ipcc.ch/sr15/chapter/glossary/.

IPCC (Intergovernmental Panel on Climate Change) (2019) *Global Warming of 1.5°C. An IPCC Special Report on the Impacts of Global Warming of 1.5°C*. Geneva: IPCCC. On https://www.ipcc.ch/site/assets/uploads/sites/2/2022/06/SR15_Full_Report_HR.pdf

IPCC (Intergovernmental Panel on Climate Change) (2021) *Climate Change 2021: The Physical Science Basis, Contribution of Working Group I to the Sixth Assessment Report of the Intergovernmental Panel on Climate Change*, Cambridge: Cambridge University Press.

Lane, S., Odoni, N., Landstrom, C., Whatmore, S., Ward, N. and Bradley, S. (2011) Doing flood risk science differently: an experiment in radical scientific method, *Transactions of the Institute of British Geographers*, 36(1): 15–36. On https://www.researchgate.net/publication/227790320_Doing_flood_risk_science_differently_An_experiment_in_radical_scientific_method

Manyena, B. (2006) The concept of resilience revisited, *Disasters*, 30(4): 433–50.

Oliver-Smith, A. (2022) The social construction of natural disaster: economic anthropological perspectives on the COVID-19 pandemic, *Economic Anthropology*, 9(1): 167–71.

Sasse, G. (2020) War and displacement: the case of Ukraine, *Europe-Asia Studies*, 72(3): 347–53.

Seifert, R. (1995) Mass rapes in Bosnia-Herzegovina and elsewhere: a pattern of cultural destruction, *War Against Women: The Impact of Violence on Gender Relations*, Geneva: Swiss Peace Foundation, pp 15–48.

Sevenhuijsen, S. (1998) *Citizenship and the Ethics of Care: Feminist Considerations on Justice, Morality and Politics*, Abingdon: Routledge.

Shabi, R. (2019) How immigration became Britain's most toxic political issue, *The Guardian*, 15 November, https://www.theguardian.com/politics/2019/nov/15/how-immigration-became-britains-most-toxic-political-issue.

UNHCR (United Nations High Commissioner for Refugees) (2022) Ukraine refugee data, portal, https://data.unhcr.org/en/situations/ukraine.

Vickers, T. (2012) *Refugees, Capitalism and the British State*, Farnham: Ashgate.

Vogel, J., Steinberger, J.K., O'Neil, D.W., Lamb, W.F. and Krishnakumar, J. (2021) Socio-economic conditions for satisfying human needs at low energy use: an international analysis of social provisioning, *Global Environmental Change*, 69: art 102287, https://doi.org/10.1016/j.gloenvcha.2021.102287.

Werndl, C. (2016) On defining climate and climate, *British Journal of Philosophical Sciences*, 67(2): 337–64.

WWF (World Wildlife Fund) (2020) *Living Planet Report 2020*, Geneva: WWF.

Yuval-Davis, N. (1997) *Gender and Nation*, London: Sage.

15

Co-creation of nature-based solutions: guidelines for citizen engagement

Nathalie Nunes, Knud Erik Hilding-Hamann and Isabel Ferreira

Introduction

Nature-based solutions (NBS) are being highlighted as necessarily part of inclusive planning processes for sustainable urban futures, since they constitute important innovations in urban planning, governance and design, by revolutionising current thinking about cities and urban services (UN-Habitat, 2022). They cover a wide range of concepts and practices (European Commission, 2020) related to ecosystem management for sustainability, societal benefit and human well-being (Nesshöver et al, 2017: 1216). In the case of urban areas, NBS is practised by architects, civil engineers and landscape and urban planners, as well as those departments practising land and nature management, such as ecological engineers, bio-tech and farming practitioners (Conserva et al, 2021: 21).

As a novel concept, NBS also bring possibilities for deploying new ways of addressing old problems, new and innovative approaches, and practices that are more inclusive (Egusquiza et al, 2019; Nunes et al, 2021: 1). Therefore, NBS are also characterised as an open innovation process, considering a holistic and integral approach addressing environmental, social and economic challenges, and involving collaboration between government, experts, civil society actors and other professionals (Jeuken et al, 2018: 16–20; Conserva et al, 2021: 20), including social workers both from the public and private or third sectors. Accordingly, broader definitions of NBS (such as URBiNAT's NBS catalogue) integrate solutions inspired by nature that are territorial and technological, including products and infrastructures, as well as participatory and social and solidarity economic solutions, comprising processes and services (Conserva et al, 2021: 21–30).

The European Union (EU) has invested in research and innovation for the implementation of NBS in cities aiming at inclusive urban regeneration of deprived urban districts (European Commission, 2016), and defines NBS as 'solutions that are inspired and supported by nature, which are cost-effective, simultaneously provide environmental, social and economic benefits and help build resilience' (European Commission, 2020: 5). In this context, URBiNAT is a five-year Horizon 2020 project (2018–23), funded by the EU, which tackles urban regeneration in seven European cities (Brussels, Høje-Taastrup, Nantes, Nova Gorica, Porto, Siena and Sofia), as well as the city of Khorramabad in Iran. The international consortium also brings together experts, practitioners, companies, research centres and universities.

URBiNAT's proposition is to develop healthy corridors in the public space connecting social neighbourhoods or deprived urban districts, based on the co-creation with citizens of new urban, social and nature-based relations. URBiNAT's co-creation process has four stages: co-diagnostic, co-design, co-implementation and co-monitoring. It aims to co-plan healthy corridors as an innovative and flexible NBS, by integrating solutions that emerge from community-driven processes (Moniz and Ferreira, 2019), having at its core a multidimensional conception of health as a state of complete physical, mental and social well-being and not merely the absence of disease or infirmity (WHO, 1946).

In this framework, URBiNAT stands for an urban inclusive and innovative nature, as it aims at promoting social cohesion and urban social innovation (Nunes and Caitana, 2018). Social innovation is referred to here as a process, implying changes in social relations and power relations, and a product, by means of the construction of methodologies, artefacts and services, especially those aimed at strengthening the capabilities of the population, the satisfaction of needs and the access to rights (André and Abreu, 2006; Murray et al, 2010; Moulaert et al, 2014). In particular, citizen engagement for the co-creation of NBS may contribute to a paradigm shift in society's relationship with nature by rethinking many aspects of life in the city, in line with the promotion of multisectoral and multidimensional approaches towards healthier cities (Wilding et al, 2017; WHO, 2018; de Leeuw, 2020).

Researchers and practitioners from URBiNAT have carried out extensive research and fieldwork around citizen engagement and the co-creation of NBS of special relevance within the context of inclusive and innovative urban regeneration, that we propose to explore in this chapter. We present developments and findings in relation to understanding local participatory cultures and identifying significant factors impacting citizen engagement. On the one hand, the mapping of local participatory cultures has been established as a research instrument to inform the tailoring of participatory methods and tools to local cultures (Ferreira, 2021; Ferreira et al, 2022). On the other hand, URBiNAT has developed a 'living' framework of guidelines for citizen engagement and the co-creation of NBS that continues to be enriched and fine-tuned, as living knowledge, through sharing and learning with practitioners from the field inside and outside of URBiNAT (Nunes et al, 2021).

These developments and findings have also paved the way to the learning points presented, based on the study of participatory implementations of NBS with relevance to deprived urban districts and the existing designs and implementations in the URBiNAT cities (Hilding-Hamann, 2020; Nunes et al, 2021; URBiNAT, 2022). We particularly analyse how guideline categories addressing core leverages for successful citizen engagement in the co-creation of NBS are combined according to various city cases, with a focus on examples from URBiNAT cities. This alignment will increase the sustainability of citizen engagement in the long run, from which key learning points emerge for other similar NBS development projects.

Finally, we focus on directions to bring further innovation in inclusive urban regeneration, aiming at advancing the science, practice, policy and education of NBS, considering social work practitioners as a fundamental part of the NBS community, in the framework of multi-stakeholder and cross-sectoral partnerships.

Understanding local participatory cultures and identifying significant factors impacting citizen engagement

In the framework of URBiNAT, participation is fundamental to guide the whole process of co-creating NBS within the overall goal of developing healthy corridors in public urban space. It spans the four stages of co-creation by involving citizens and stakeholders of urban regeneration projects from diagnosing to monitoring the NBS that are co-created to respond to needs and ambitions expressed by communities. However, participation is also valuable by itself as a process of promoting active citizenship, that is, it is both a means to achieve the objectives of co-creating solutions and an end aiming at the development of the participants' capacities to engage in collective initiatives (URBiNAT, 2019a: 5–6, 2019b: 12).

The mapping of local participatory culture is used to identify and recognise the diverse participatory cultures of URBiNAT's neighbourhoods, ranging from the formal participation of citizens in urban governance to their participation in other kinds of collective and co-creation process initiatives in a diversity of formats (URBiNAT, 2019a: 7–13; 2019b: 13–24; Ferreira, 2022). As key informants, the ecosystem of stakeholders that was approached and engaged in the mapping process included several municipal departments, schools, non-profit organisations, local associations and champions – local leaders who lead the way and mobilise other citizens (URBiNAT, 2019b: 14–17). At different levels, these stakeholders involve social work practitioners, and play a role in addressing specificities, requirements and limitations experienced by the various groupings of citizens. These are essential to inform the tailoring of participatory methods and tools of the co-creation process, including the assessment of challenges and opportunities for social mobilisation, any issues related to ethics, human rights and gender, and identifying residents as potential participants (URBiNAT, 2019a: 16–33; 2019b: 13–24).

The preliminary results of mapping the local participatory culture (URBiNAT, 2019a: 34–52) have enabled discussing the introduction of elements in the co-creation process focused on improving the quality of participation as a means, to feed the urban regeneration planning, and as an end, to feed a strategy for a municipal roadmap that integrates the local needs, cultures and ambitions of each city (URBiNAT, 2019b: 24–41, 44–8; Ferreira, 2021). Indeed, the co-creation process being tailored and tested in URBiNAT cities is community-driven while focusing on the engagement of citizens and stakeholders in inclusive and innovative city governance models (Ferreira et al, 2022).

Therefore, the strategy of a municipal roadmap has evolved to the proposal of creating municipal committees or local advisory boards, institutionalising the interactions among citizens, municipal decision makers and researchers in a regular and formal governance structure dedicated to making decisions collaboratively that will guide the implementation, production and monitoring of NBS (Ferreira et al, 2022). URBiNAT cities have put in place these advisory boards in different formats, according to their specific contexts, regulations and local participatory cultures. The dialogue with city representatives and local task forces (Moniz, 2021) has been advancing to bring further innovation, based on more in-depth research and assessment on the local participatory processes (URBiNAT, 2022).

In this respect, the local advisory boards also constitute arenas to advance such innovative participatory and governance models in the framework of multi-stakeholder and cross-sectoral partnerships that characterise urban regeneration (Tsenkova, 2002; Carter and Roberts, 2017), namely in the implementation of NBS (Jeuken et al, 2018: 16–20), including key social work actors from the public, private and third sectors. These partnerships are essential to constitute and reinforce the local NBS community around the co-production of processes and services (for example, a solidarity market in Porto). Indeed, social work practitioners have knowledge, experience and networks that contribute to anchoring the co-created solutions in the specificities of each local social context.

Guidelines for citizen engagement and the co-creation of nature-based solutions

URBiNAT's 'living' framework of guidelines for citizen engagement and the co-creation of NBS emerged from URBiNAT's collective and participatory pathway to knowledge on inclusive urban regeneration (production within the context of Nunes et al, 2021). The methodology of developing the guidelines for citizen engagement in NBS co-creation involves three elements:

- the accumulation of insights is based on an ecology of knowledges from partners who brought together different perspectives in the academic, technical and political fields to establish the theoretical and methodological foundations of the project;
- this knowledge has been systematised into categories of significant factors influencing citizen engagement; and
- through sharing and learning with practitioners from the field inside and outside of URBiNAT, the categories of guidelines have been prioritised, enhanced and adjusted to fit with observations of these contributors, including social workers from the public, private or third sectors.

Table 15.1 gives an overview of these categories of guidelines, that, at this stage, are organised into 25 key factors impacting citizen engagement. The participants in workshops and webinars conducted in 2019, indicated that the most critical aspects of citizen engagement in different contexts were communication and interaction, behavioural changes, and trust. Within URBiNAT's framework of guidelines, the categories are detailed into strategic and operational guidelines, and can be organised into necessary preconditions, core enablers plus methods, tools and ways of co-creating NBS in socially disadvantaged neighbourhoods, as highlighted by social work practitioners in URBiNAT cities (Nunes et al, 2021).

These practitioners have deep knowledge in the intervention areas of the URBiNAT project, as employees of the municipality, the agency in charge of the management of social housing and workers of non-profit organisations. In our exchanges, we targeted what was missing in the categories of guidelines and what is most relevant to their practice and cities. As a result, the categories were refined and four more categories on ownership, culture of participation, why participation, and mediation were added.

As 'living' knowledge, URBiNAT's framework of guidelines continues to be enriched in a process of continuously assessing to what extent the categories of guidelines are relevant, complete and useful, and how practitioners can work with these in future work (URBiNAT, 2022). In 2022, the exchanges with city representatives and local task forces confirmed the relevance of the categories of guidelines as factors impacting citizen engagement and the interrelations between them. This framework has also been found relevant for: (1) ongoing assessment of participatory processes, by providing practitioners and participants of living labs with insights for evaluations that will feed the tailoring of participatory processes to local needs and ambitions; (2) advancing the production of living knowledge on citizen engagement and the co-creation of NBS, by promoting the

Table 15.1: Overview of guideline categories addressing core leverages for successful citizen engagement in the co-creation of nature-based solutions

Category	Description	Category	Description	Category	Description	Category	Description	Category	Description
Communication and interaction	Communicating specificities for interacting with citizens.	Behavioural changes	Instigating behavioural adjustments, or changes in behaviour, in some particular respect.	Trust	Improving or creating relationships of trust between citizens, and between citizens and city staff, politicians and other agents.	Co-production	Stimulating and improving co-production of public services, participatory processes and product development.	Inclusion	Having specific guidelines to guarantee the inclusion of all citizens groups.
Regulation	Clarifying rules and regulations for equal rights in the expression of visions and priorities.	Governance	Balancing interactions among citizens, city staff, politicians and other agents.	Innovation cycle	Adopting processes of rupture and searching for alternative solutions to address concrete social problems.	Transparency	Arguments for encouraging efforts to act in a transparent manner.	Intensity and levels of participation	Setting different approaches and levels of participation depending on the goals and real conditions for participation.
Citizenship rights	Broadening the meaning of the appropriation of social, urban, political and cultural rights, both internally in the collective imagination, and externally in rejuvenated relationships with local powers.	Cultural mapping	Articulating and making visible the multilayered cultural assets, aspects and meanings of a place.	Facilitation	Having specific guidelines to address facilitation that include other participatory guidelines.	Quality of deliberation	Setting a meaningful deliberation process.	Where	Having guidelines for the spaces in which the participatory events are held.
When	Identifying the best moment for the participatory events.	Supportive methodologies and techniques	Using specific methodologies and guidelines to support mobilisation and inclusivity.	Integration of participatory process' results	Enlarging the scope of co-creation to validate the ideas developed.	Private sector	Mapping the relevant private sector actors with interests in, and input to, the NBS-targeted area.	Monitoring and evaluation	Addresses monitoring and evaluation of the participatory process.
Risks assessment and mitigation measures	Identifying the factors influencing co-creation processes, as well as those leading to the failure of co-creation and co-production.	Ownership	Citizens having ownership of both problems and solutions.	Culture of participation	Enabling regular interaction with and between citizens and increasing the culture of participation.	Why participation	Being clear as to why we need to engage citizens and support participatory processes.	Mediation	Dialogue and collaboration.

documentation of practices to be shared between cities, but also better connecting knowledge in municipal administrations and private and public organisations to academia.

Ongoing assessment of participatory processes and the production of knowledge on citizen engagement and the co-creation of NBS are key to stimulate the replication and scaling-up of local sustainable citizen-driven initiatives. On this basis, diagnostics can be made, strategies devised and hypotheses tested, paving the way to innovations in overcoming challenges. At the same time, a flexible (or 'living') framework offers room to combinations of guideline categories that ignite inspiration and ownership of the process.

Learning points emerging from citizen engagement

More than 100 participatory implementations of NBS with relevance to deprived areas have been mapped (Hilding-Hamann, 2020), and the existing designs and implementations in the URBiNAT cities have been studied. Additionally, exchanges with European project colleagues through Task Force 6 on co-creation and co-governance have been conducted (NetworkNature, 2022).

From this, several preliminary learning points have emerged that can be linked to the guideline categories for citizen engagement (URBiNAT, 2019a, 2019b; Hilding-Hamann, 2020) and adaptation (Frantzeskaki, 2019). Some examples from the URBiNAT city projects are provided in Table 15.2. The analysis identifies links to a series of guideline categories in these learning points, which make up a possible pathway to successful citizen engagement and the co-creation of NBS.

Conclusion

Under the Horizon 2020 programme, URBiNAT and other NBS projects have been advancing the contribution of the EU to the development of urban policies and urban regeneration practices in its member states. The funding line dedicated to smart and sustainable cities of the Horizon 2020 programme (2014–20) is particularly aimed at new forms and sources of innovation, such as social innovation, also incorporating the social sciences and humanities to better understand and contextualise the development of solutions (European Commission, 2016: 14). In this context, while the novel concept of NBS offers opportunities to deploy new ways of addressing old problems, new and innovative approaches, and practices that are more inclusive, it also raises challenges in terms of operational and technical preparedness, as well as critical issues regarding its transformative potential (Egusquiza et al, 2019; Bulkeley, 2020a; Seddon et al, 2020; Wild, 2020).

Table 15.2: Learning points emerging from citizen engagement in the co-creation of nature-based solutions

Learning points	Overview and discussion	Examples of NBS participatory cases
1. The appeal of NBS to citizens and stakeholders aesthetically, socially, economically and charitably.	NBS need to be aesthetically, socially, economically and charitably appealing to citizens and stakeholders, so that they are encouraged to engage with, further develop, maintain and protect them.	A workshop was conducted at Høje-Taastrup in which huge planter boxes with flowers and berry bushes were co-created to provide an instant reward to co-creators and the inhabitants of the neighbourhood. This was later followed up with plans for further planter boxes and biodiversity enhancements for the enjoyment of the community. Social workers operating in the neighbourhood facilitated the workshop with strong links to an ongoing garden community initiative.

In Porto, a photo exhibition was co-created with citizens to place the city district and people within it on the map and to reinforce the self-esteem of the community and citizens who contributed to the exhibition. A larger exhibition is planned where people from Campanhã district will contribute their own pictures and add their stories for the benefit of community-building. The district social workers support the project by encouraging participation from the community and linking it to ongoing projects. |
| 2. NBS and new urban spaces where people with common interests can regularly gather and engage. | NBS create new urban collective spaces at the neighbourhood level and across the city. This is achieved both virtually, through online platforms, and physically, by creating attractive physical spaces where people with common interests can gather and engage on a regular basis, as part of their daily lives or for special events. | Both in Sofia and in Campanhã in Porto, green markets have been established to facilitate the creation of ingredients and foods as well as offering a place for the community to meet and greet. The markets are used by growers, craft producers, neighbours, tourists and consumers. In Sofia the market is partly organised by a social enterprise with a vision of bringing vulnerable people together. |
| 3. Diagnostics, design and implementation of NBS rely on a community of stakeholders. | For deprived urban districts, NBS diagnostics, design (experiments) and implementation processes rely on and feed into trust, co-ownership, governance and regulation between the five main stakeholders, identified as 'participants' in the URBiNAT model (URBiNAT, 2019a):

1. the municipality (political representatives and public officers of different departments); | In Porto, a task force made up of these five actors has been formed to coordinate and provide project governance to many experiments now being designed in the designated social neighbourhood of Campanhã. The local task force initially brought together municipal technicians, experts and researchers, and has been open to the involvement of citizens and other stakeholders throughout the engagement and co-creation process. This includes NGOs with social purposes.

In Siena, the development of the healthy corridor requires the engagement of private, social and public stakeholders as well as different citizens groups in order to take into account the integration of privately owned land, the needs of schoolchildren from a school nearby and the specific requirements of the local social, church and sports groups. Siena is building its social endeavours on the successful structures of the *contrade* that supports its community through tailored social activities.

(continued) |

Table 15.2: Learning points emerging from citizen engagement in the co-creation of nature-based solutions (continued)

Learning points	Overview and discussion	Examples of NBS participatory cases
	2. housing administrators (responsible for the management of social housing);	
	3. NGOs, businesses and other private and public organisations working in the intervention areas;	
	4. champions/ambassadors and facilitators; and	
	5. citizens, as well as in the experiments themselves. Several other factors also play a role depending on the characteristics of the neighbourhood and the NBS.	
4. Strong common projects between actors with different organisational goals as propellers of social innovation.	Sustainable NBS emerge strongly from the fabric of social innovation at the neighbourhood and urban levels, building success on the back of strong common projects between actors with different organisational goals (link to a sense of co-ownership).	In Nantes, facilities and activities are emerging through social innovation along a green path that connects the deprived neighbourhood with the rest of the city. Pre-existing citizen initiatives plug into the work and help make it a reality. These groups design events and activities to take place along the path of which several become regular features in the neighbourhood and build on the activities of social enterprises and NGOs.

In Sofia, the local cultural centre will play a major role in making a co-designed amphitheatre within the healthy corridor a vibrant cultural event space. Similarly, a swimming pool is being designed with facilities for other cultural activities in addition to the swimming facilities. For this, groups of architectural students have developed proposals by integrating ideas and wishes of different citizens' groups. Social enterprises and NGOs will play a role in organising the events and activities using the new facilities. |
| 5. Inclusive and multi-stakeholder governance as a result of a collaborative approach. | NBS require a collaborative approach that involves and engages all five stakeholders, developing governance that both influences and sets limits for all five, while ensuring that the strengths and weaknesses of each actor are integrated into the division of roles and responsibilities. | In Sofia, the Bread Houses Network, as an NGO and social enterprise, is supported by the other actors and stakeholders to co-deliver the benefits of participation to citizens in the district of Nadezhda. With this multi-stakeholder support, co-production of bread is the basis for cross-cultural exchange, community dinner events, baking education, improved employability and income generation. |

Table 15.2: Learning points emerging from citizen engagement in the co-creation of nature-based solutions (continued)

Learning points	Overview and discussion	Examples of NBS participatory cases
6. Bridging differences through an inclusive and highly attractive narrative.	An inclusive and highly attractive narrative (vision and mission) for the implementation of NBS can help bridge differences between municipal departments, participating businesses, and organisations, and between the different housing blocks in neighbourhoods.	The participatory process in Khorramabad has been particularly targeting the involvement of women. Initially, the local task force focused its efforts on communicating about their rights to the city, and on how they can be influential in the place they live, by giving their opinion about the facilities of the city and asking officials for improvements.

In Khorramabad, the citizen engagement identified a group of men of Roma origin that were excluded from society. Through the co-design processes an art house was developed with the group. The perception and narrative about people of Roma origin may change through artistic activities that communicate their culture to other citizens groups in the city, while earning income from these and other activities. |
| 7. Effectiveness, achievements, scaling-up and replication as a result of monitoring and evaluation. | The design, monitoring and evaluation of NBS need to be arranged so that the effectiveness and achievements can be measured and analysed, enabling successful NBS to be scaled up and repeated in other similarly deprived areas. | In the municipality of Høje-Taastrup, the stakeholders are transferring documented models using URBiNAT co-creation methods from one deprived neighbourhood, Charlottekvarteret, where the quality of life has improved, to another neighbourhood in the city, where there is the potential to achieve similar results. They do this by engaging staff, NGO and business resources who can create the necessary community connections and build the NBS on the same model in other neighbourhoods.

Building upon the results of the previous application of subjective mapping in Neder-Over-Heembeek, the municipality of Brussels (Belgium) has produced an artistic synthesis of the local diagnostic, in the form of a colouring map for all ages, as an innovative baseline of analysis, monitoring and evaluation for the design and implementation of the healthy corridor. This subjective map has proved a communicative impact to present and rediscover the neighbourhood with different audiences and has also transferred through social communities of practice to other cities in Europe. |

In fact, there is still a need to develop the understanding of the economic, social, political and cultural dimensions of designing and implementing NBS, moving beyond seeing the implementation challenge as primarily a 'technical' issue (Bulkeley, 2020b; Wild, 2020).

Analysing local participatory cultures and identifying significant factors impacting citizen engagement have enabled us to access and integrate the ecology of knowledges of a diversity of stakeholders, including the ones specialised in social work. The resulting 'living' framework will be further developed with the contribution of citizens and other stakeholders, based on monitoring and ongoing assessment of actual co-creation mechanisms and activities of participatory implementations of NBS. In this respect, social workers involved with a diversity of specificities (for example, childhood, gender, older adults, race and ethnicity, functional diversity, citizenship status, religious diversity) constitute important partners in establishing communication and interaction with groups and individuals.

Social workers increasingly play a role in engaging citizens in nature-based activities such as managing gardens and harvesting crops for common food production and consumption as part of developing strong community ties and preparing vulnerable groups for participation in society, education and employment. URBiNAT argues that NBS are not only territorial and technological but also participatory, social and solidarity interventions supporting sustainable development of the nature of humanity in coexistence with nature and environments. In this context, social workers are placed at the core of securing the benefits of NBS.

Moreover, the results from mapping local participatory cultures of URBiNAT cities were instrumental to developing community-driven processes. These led to experimenting with local advisory boards that can play a key role in monitoring and evaluating the NBS implementation process, while constituting arenas for cooperation, co-production and consensus-building, as well as to integrate and handle emerging conflicts, dissensus and disagreement (Ferreira et al, 2022). Such innovative participatory and governance models integrate social work actors from the public, private and third sectors in the framework of multi-stakeholder and cross-sectoral partnerships that characterise urban regeneration (Tsenkova, 2002; Carter and Roberts, 2017).

Additionally, the participation experts of the URBiNAT project have, in collaboration with practitioners at city level, produced, shared and made accessible knowledge on citizen engagement and the co-creation of NBS. This knowledge is fundamental to rethink nature-based opportunities and bring further social innovation into living labs at city level. The 25 guideline categories produced are useful for practitioners to think about and plan into the citizen engagement before initiating the co-creation of NBS projects. We see them as essential components to be applied for the best possible social, economic and environmental impact of NBS. By combining the guideline categories in the co-creation of NBS, actors from a diversity of sectors may deliver social innovation that is inclusive in operation and governance, and sustainable economically and environmentally. Furthermore, it builds on proven participatory methods and strengths of relevant stakeholders while considering the fundamental conditions for an effective citizen engagement.

Lastly, we consider the guideline categories for citizen engagement as living knowledge; they continuously evolve as practitioners and researchers jointly come up with new insights on the application, combination and impact of the guidelines. Learning points emerge from participatory processes that lead to innovative NBS and deliver social benefits in terms of improvements through new community facilities and better living conditions for people in the neighbourhoods. As a living knowledge repository, we invite others, namely social work practitioners from different sectors, to join this community of practice and support further development of this framework and these learning points towards improved applicability in real cases, as much as making them more tangible and easier to communicate.

Acknowledgement

This research was funded within the framework of project 'URBiNAT – Healthy Corridors as Drivers of Social Housing Neighbourhoods for the Co-creation of Social, Environmental, and Marketable NBS', by European Union's Horizon 2020 research and innovation programme under grant agreement No. 776783.

References

André, I. and Abreu, A. (2006) Dimensões e espaços da inovação social, *Finisterra*, 41(81): 121–41.

Bulkeley, H. (2020a) Nature-based solutions: towards sustainable communities, in T. Wild, T. Freitas and S. Vandewoestijne (eds) *Nature-Based Solutions: State of the Art of EU-Funded Projects*, Luxembourg: Publications Office of the European Union, pp 157–80.

Bulkeley, H. (2020b) Governing NBS: towards transformative action, in T. Wild, T. Freitas and S. Vandewoestijne (eds) *Nature-Based Solutions: State of the Art of EU-Funded Projects*, Luxembourg: Publications Office of the European Union, pp 181–202.

Carter, A. and Roberts, P. (2017) Strategy and partnership in urban regeneration, in P. Roberts, H. Sykes and R. Granger (eds) *Urban Regeneration*, 2nd edn, London: Sage, pp 44–67.

Conserva, A., Farinea, C. and Villodres, R. (eds) (2021) *Deliverable D4.1 – New NBS Co-Creation of URBiNAT NBS (live)* Catalogue and Toolkit for Healthy Corridor, URBiNAT, https://urbinat.eu/nbs-catalogue/.

de Leeuw, E. (2020) One health(y) cities, *Cities & Health*, 5(S1): S26–S31.

Egusquiza, A., Cortese, M. and Perfido, D. (2019) Mapping of innovative governance models to overcome barriers for nature based urban regeneration, *IOP Conference Series: Earth and Environmental Science*, 323: art 012081, https://doi.org/10.1088/1755-1315/323/1/012081.

European Commission (2016) *Horizon 2020 Work Programme 2016–2017: 17. Cross-cutting activities (Focus Areas)*, Brussels: European Commission, https://ec.europa.eu/research/participants/data/ref/h2020/wp/2016_2017/main/h2020-wp1617-focus_en.pdf.

European Commission, Directorate-General for Research and Innovation, Bulkeley, H., Naumann, S., Vojinovic, Z. et al., *Nature-based solutions – State of the art in EU-funded projects*, Freitas, T. (editor), Vandewoestijne, S. (editor), Wild, T. (editor), Publications Office of the European Union, 2020, https://data.europa.eu/doi/10.2777/236007

Ferreira, I. (2021) Municipal roadmap for a co-implementation and co-monitoring strategy, in G.C. Moniz (ed) Deliverable D4.3: NBS Implementation Strategy, *Part 1 – Introduction*, https://public.3.basecamp.com/p/d1v21TEnkiRH9SQHxZf7cmyR.

Ferreira, I. (2022) Governance, Citizenship and Participation in Small and Medium-Sized Cities: A Comparative Study Between Portuguese and Canadian Cities, PhD thesis, Coimbra: Universidade de Coimbra. https://estudogeral.uc.pt/handle/10316/101712.

Ferreira, I., Caitana, B. and Nunes, N. (2022) Policy brief no. 26: Municipal committees to experiment innovative urban governance in nature-based projects, aimed at inclusive urban regeneration, Visby: Swedish International Centre for Local Democracy, https://web.archive.org/web/20220517130551/https://icld.se/wp-content/uploads/2022/05/ICLD_Policy-Brief_26-web.pdf.

Frantzeskaki, N. (2019) Seven lessons for planning nature-based solutions in cities, *Environmental Science & Policy*, 93: 101–11.

Hilding-Hamann, K.E. (2020) Interesting participatory cases [Basecamp blog on URBiNAT's internal collaborative platform]: Work Package 3 – Citizen Engagement in Support of NBS (unpublished).

Jeuken, Y., Breukers, S. and Karababa, E. (2018) Deliverable 5.2: Citizen and Stakeholder Engagement strategies and tools for NBS Implementation, *Nature4Cities Project*, Brussels: European Commission, https://ec.europa.eu/research/participants/documents/downloadPublic?documentIds=080166e5bfd14c11&appId=PPGMS.

Moniz, G.C. (2021) The local task forces to co-implement NBS, in G.C. Moniz (ed) *Deliverable D4.3: NBS Implementation Strategy, Part 1 – Introduction*, https://public.3.basecamp.com/p/d1v21TEnkiRH9SQHxZf7cmyR.

Moniz, G.C. and Ferreira, I. (2019) Healthy corridors for inclusive urban regeneration, *Rassegna di Architettura e Urbanistica*, 54(158): 51–9.

Moulaert, F., MacCallum, D., Mehmood, A. and Hamdouch, A. (eds) (2014) *The International Handbook on Social Innovation: Collective Action, Social Learning and Transdisciplinary Research*, Cheltenham: Edward Elgar.

Murray R., Caulier-Grice, J. and Mulgan, G. (2010) *The Open Book of Social Innovation*, London: Young Foundation and National Endowment for Science, Technology and the Arts.

Nelson, D.R., Bledsoe, B.P., Ferreira, S. and Nibbelink, N.P. (2020) Challenges to realizing the potential of nature-based solutions, *Current Opinion in Environmental Sustainability*, 45: 49–55.

Nesshöver, C., Assmuth, T., Irvine, K.N., Rusch, G.M., Waylen, K.A., Delbaere, B., et al (2017) The science, policy and practice of nature-based solutions: an interdisciplinary perspective, *Science of the Total Environment*, 579: 1215–27.

NetworkNature (2022) Nature-based solutions task forces, NetworkNature, https://networknature.eu/networknature/nature-based-solutions-task-forces.

Nunes, N. and Caitana, B. (2018) The appropriation of citizenship rights in the promotion of social cohesion and urban social innovation, in URBiNAT (ed) Deliverable D1.2: Handbook on the Theoretical and Methodological Foundations of the Project, Coimbra: URBiNAT, Centre for Social Studies of University of Coimbra, https://urbinat.eu/resources/.

Nunes, N., Björner, E. and Hilding-Hamann, K.E. (2021) Guidelines for citizen engagement and the co-creation of nature-based solutions: living knowledge in the URBiNAT Project, *Sustainability*, 13(23): art 13378, https://doi.org/10.3390/su132313378.

Santos, B. de S. (2018) *The End of the Cognitive Empire: The Coming of Age of Epistemologies of the South*, Durham, NC: Duke University Press.

Seddon, N., Chausson, A., Berry, P., Girardin, C.A.J., Smith, A. and Turner, B. (2020) Understanding the value and limits of nature-based solutions to climate change and other global challenges, *Philosophical Transactions of the Royal Society B: Biological Sciences*, 375(1794): art 20190120. https://doi.org/10.1098/rstb.2019.0120.

Tsenkova, S. (2002) Partnerships in urban regeneration: from 'top down' to 'bottom up approach', in S. Tsenkova (ed) *Urban Regeneration: Learning from the British Experience*, Calgary: Faculty of Environmental Design, University of Calgary, pp 73–84.

UN-Habitat (2022) *World Cities Report 2022: Envisaging the Future of Cities*, Nairobi: United Nations.

URBiNAT (2019a) *Deliverable D3.1: Strategic Design and Usage of Participatory Solutions and Relevant Digital Tools in Support of NBS Uptake*, Aarhus: Danish Technological Institute (DTI). https://urbinat.eu/resources/.

URBiNAT (2019b) *Deliverable D3.2: Community-Driven Processes to Co-design and Co-implement NBS*, Coimbra: URBiNAT, Centre for Social Studies of University of Coimbra (CES–UC), https://urbinat.eu/resources/.

URBiNAT (2022) *Deliverable 3.6: First Assessment Report On Progress, Results, And Insights For The Combination Of Methods, Citizen Engagement, And Usage Of Digital Tools*, Aarhus: DTI – Danish Technological Institute. https://urbinat.eu/resources/.

WHO (World Health Organization) (1946) Constitution of the World Health Organization, adopted by the International Health Conference held in New York 1946 and entered into force on 7 April 1948, https://www.who.int/about/governance/constitution.

WHO (World Health Organization) (2018) Copenhagen Consensus of Mayors: Healthier and Happier Cities for All, Copenhagen: WHO, https://www.who.int/europe/publications/m/item/copenhagen-consensus-of-mayors.-healthier-and-happier-cities-for-all.

Wild, T. (2020) Research & innovation priorities in Horizon Europe and beyond, in T. Wild, T. Freitas and S. Vandewoestijne (eds) *Nature-Based Solutions: State of the Art of EU-Funded Projects*, Luxembourg: Publications Office of the European Union, pp 223–33.

Wilding, H., Gould, R., Taylor, J., Sabouraud, A., Saraux-Salaün, P., Papathanasopoulou, D., de Blasio, A., Nagy, Z. and Simos, J. (2017) Healthy cities in Europe: structured, unique, and thoughtful, in E. de Leeuw and J. Simos (eds) *Healthy Cities: The Theory, Policy, and Practice of Value-Based Urban Planning*, New York: Springer, pp 241–92.

16

Innovating social work practices to better address homelessness: participatory action research with community services in Italy

Marta Gaboardi, Sabina Licursi and Emanuela Pascuzzi

Introduction

In Italy, in 2021 about 5.6 million people lived in absolute poverty (9.4 per cent of the total population). The incidence was higher in southern regions (Istat, 2022a). Homelessness was estimated at 96,000 (Istat, 2022b), while in 2014 it was just over 50,000 (Istat, Ministero del Lavoro e delle Politiche Sociali, Caritas and fio.PSD., 2015). In the Mediterranean welfare system, typical of Italy and of other Southern Europe countries, homelessness has been mainly perceived as a blow of fate managed by public authorities using an emergency-oriented approach, aimed at controlling the phenomenon by delivering basic assistance, rather than at developing social inclusion measures (Ferrera, 1996; Ferrera and Hemerijck, 2003; Pezzana, 2012).

Since the 2010s in Italy the national policy framework has been rapidly changing, due to:

- the introduction of the Housing First approach, commissioned by fio. PSD (see: https://www.fiopsd.org/chi-siamo/) (Italian Federation of the Organisations for Homeless People) and carried out through a network of over 50 organisations that was created in the period 2014–16 (Lancione et al, 2018);
- the release in 2015 of 'Guidelines for tackling severe adult marginality in Italy' (Ministero del Lavoro e delle Politiche sociali, 2015) as the main reference for regions and municipalities to develop actions against extreme poverty, aimed at overcoming the emergency approach and harmonising services, measures and practice within this sector;
- the National Call for Proposals 4/2016 of the Ministry of Labour and Social Policies to plan and implement measures to combat extreme poverty and their first use in the regional territories;

- the adoption of the National Plan of Interventions and Social Services 2021–23 also including combating poverty with specific provisions for homelessness.

The changes introduced at national level have resulted in different interventions, which are more or less coherent with the new policy framework, according to the characteristics of the local welfare systems and of the actors involved. Social practitioners working within public and private social care agencies have a certain degree of autonomy in implementing public policies, and promoting innovation in social work (Hupe, 2019; Aviv et al, 2021). Understanding their point of view and involving them in an iterative process of research and action is important in order to address efforts towards social innovation (Gaboardi et al, 2022a). Community participatory action research (CPAR), as a collaborative, community-based and action-oriented approach, is particularly suited to encourage innovation in both social work practice and research (Parpan-Blaser and Hüttemann, 2010). This chapter describes two CPAR projects carried out with services providers for homeless people. Participants were social practitioners involved in the co-creation and the sharing of the knowledge that fuelled reflection and innovation of practice, taking into account the existing differences in local policies and services for homeless people. Both projects were initiated by universities, engaged in third mission activities aimed at making a contribution to address social issues of the local community (Goddard and Vallance, 2013).

Using a case study methodology (Simons, 2009; Yin, 2014), we analysed experiences in two different cities, the first in the north-east and the second in the south of Italy. Both cases provide some insights into innovation in social services and social work and into the levels at which it may occur (macro-, meso-, micro- and nano-social level; Nicolls and Murdock, 2012; Parpan-Blaser and Hüttemann, 2019). Moreover, this stimulates reflection upon the role of the CPAR in co-constructing innovation, linking science to practice in a cooperative process. Johnson and Cnaan (1995) argued that it is only through research-informed practice that social work will be able to pave the way to fight extreme forms of poverty and alleviate the misery of homelessness. The involvement of social work in the care of, the service provision to or the advocacy of homeless people is varied, extensive and increasingly deemed critical, de pending on several factors such as: social work and social policy approaches to homelessness; sociopolitical contexts and government policy responses to social problems such as homelessness; and organisational frameworks of care providers (Zufferey, 2008; Gaboardi et al, 2022a).

The comparison between the two Italian cases, developed in different local welfare systems, makes it possible to point out the contextual factors of innovation and to highlight what hinders or fosters social innovation in a given place.

Case study Verona

Local context

The first case study was carried out in Verona, a middle-sized town in Veneto, in the north-east of Italy, where local welfare is well structured and organised (Ascoli and Pavolini, 2015; Cersosimo and Viesti, 2022). In particular, the social cooperative involved in this project was the Samaritans Onlus. This cooperative is part of the Caritas Diocesana Veronese and has been active since 2006 with various services to help people in difficulty and marginality. As part of the Housing First Network Italy, the cooperative started a project called Solidarity House, a social housing service that provides single or shared apartments to homeless adults and young adults with the purpose of supporting their autonomy and the social integration. In addition, the cooperative has various services such as dormitories, soup kitchens and occupational workshops.

A number of contextual factors contributed to the success of the project. At the macro level the cooperative is part of the Housing First Network and has participated in national network trainings with other services. At the meso level the cooperative belongs to a network with other local services. At the micro level the manager and the team have a mission to improve services and to work with homeless people (management commitment, organisational structure) as well as to involve users in their improvement (for example through meetings, housing coaching/accompaniment).

The experience with the Samaritans Onlus is part of a larger European project, funded by Horizon 2020 called HOME_EU: 'Homelessness as unfairness' (2016–19) which involved the research group of the Department of Developmental and Socialisation Psychology at the University of Padua as the Italian partner in the EU project together with 11 other partners in nine European countries. The main objective of the European project was to explore the phenomenon of homelessness through separate work packages that captured different perspectives – of professionals, of people experiencing homelessness, of citizens and of public policy. The study we report here is part of the study regarding the social service providers (see Gaboardi et al, 2022a for more information). In order to explore the experience of professionals in homeless services, several third sector organisations working with homeless people were involved, including the Samaritans Onlus.

A group of nine professionals from the cooperative were involved. Four were female and five male. Three of them were social practitioners and six were volunteers aged between 28 and 68.

The method used was the Photovoice, a CPAR methodology that captures aspects of a context – in this case homeless services – from the perspective of the people involved (Wang and Burris, 1997; Wang et al, 2000). The participants led the process as they are considered as the experts in their community, while the researchers were the facilitators. The participants took photos that reflected important aspects of their daily contexts, discussed the photos in groups and then developed proposals to improve their contexts. Overall, the method had three main objectives: (1) to assess the needs and resources of a community; (2) to promote knowledge and critical dialogue on important community issues through group discussions stimulated by the photographs taken by the participants; and (3) to promote social change through collective action.

Process

This project was developed in five biweekly meetings of two hours each from May to June 2017 with a follow-up after one year. The main goal of the project was to explore the factors that hinder or help work with homeless people. In addition, the project aimed to draw up proposals with participants for a programme improvement.

The project participants were professionals and volunteers who were invited to identify, categorise and prioritise work challenges and to propose solutions to these problems. The participants were involved in all the stages of the process: from taking the photographs, analysing the data and developing the proposals for social change, to organising the dissemination of the results and implementing the changes (see Gaboardi et al, 2022a for the results of the larger EU project).

The participants identified both obstacles and resources in their work. In particular, they highlighted three important issues to improve their work. First, the importance of communication, which was sometimes slow and hindered work. One of the participants stated: "Not receiving the necessary information immediately may affect operations, which becomes slower and results in rather long waiting times". Second, the importance of having ongoing team training and support. Third, participants emphasised the importance of individualised pathways that enhance people's resources and respect their privacy.

Starting with the issues discussed through the photos, the participants drew up four proposals for a change in the organisation. The proposals concerned: the internal communications within the organisation; the relationship between professionals and volunteers; the need for constant updates on the clients' process; and the training and psychosocial supervision of the team.

The results and the proposals of the Photovoice were presented during a meeting with the leaders of the organisations and shown in a photographic exhibition associated with a conference titled Not in Words but in Deeds. The conference and the exhibition were attended by citizens and professionals from other services and published in the local media.

Impact

In a follow-up evaluation one year later, the leader of the organisation and the group of participants were interviewed to verify whether the proposals had been implemented.

The participants were satisfied with the project even after one year and the meetings were experienced as moments of reflection and discussion within the team. Most of the proposals identified through the Photovoice had been implemented. First, communication between professionals and volunteers within the service was perceived as smoother and faster thanks to the use of more immediate communication tools (for example, a WhatsApp group). Second, participants organised a monthly meeting between social practitioners and volunteers to discuss clients' recovery paths. Third, volunteers were involved in a training course and project evaluation meetings held every two weeks and one convivial dinner per month; professionals attended two training sessions during the year. Regarding the need for constant updates on the clients' progress, a 'daily diary' was planned to facilitate the circulation of information and updates on the clients, but it had not yet been activated.

This action research project demonstrates the potential of using Photovoice in working environments (that is, in homeless services) to improve the working conditions of professionals (Flum et al, 2010; Gaboardi et al, 2022b). The Photovoice can be an important tool, not only to identify factors influencing providers' work, but also to empower professionals to be more active in improving working conditions, thus facilitating important changes in the workplace (Rahman et al, 2020).

In a bottom-up process, professionals were able to improve their work community by proposing changes both during and at the end of the Photovoice process. In addition, the conference and exhibition were able to offer a space for reflection and discussion not only for those working in services, but also for citizens and local media.

Case study Cosenza

Local context

The second case study was carried out in Cosenza, a province capital city in the Region of Calabria, in the south of Italy, which has very limited public social services, and an extremely weak regulatory capacity (Cersosimo and Viesti, 2022). The municipality is the lead authority of the local social district, but its social services department (SSD) is poorly structured and only in recent years have some new staff been hired, including social workers, albeit on a temporary basis (Pascuzzi and Marcello, 2020).

The National Call for Proposals 4/2016 of the Ministry of Labour and Social Policies, encouraged an activity-oriented local planning. The activities proposed by the Social District of Cosenza were the following: coordination between the SSD and the services for homeless people in the city; activation of low-threshold services (street outreach); and co-creation and management of Housing First and housing-led interventions.

The Foundation Casa San Francesco (CSF) and the social cooperative Strade di Casa (SDC) were selected as partners of the Municipality of Cosenza for the implementation of the proposal. The CSF runs two residential services for adults in poverty, a shelter, a kitchen soup and other services providing basic assistance to homeless people. This agency has been the main point of reference for the SSD in need of emergency accommodation for homeless people applying for help. The SDC is a small social cooperative that has carried out pilot projects for the homeless, participating in the national experimentation of the Housing First programme.

Before starting to implement the activities, the two NGOs involved expressed the need of a space for research, sharing and reflection on the experience, as the latter was developing. To this end, the two NGOs, the Municipality of Cosenza and the Department of Political and Social Sciences of the University of Calabria signed a free agreement for the creation of a multi-session lab for Research and Reflective Learning from Experience (Lab). The agreement, signed in July 2020, ended in the summer of 2021 with activities slowed down by the COVID-19 pandemic.

The multi-session lab adopted the core principles and methodology of the CPAR such as: the collaborative approach to research and the involvement of stakeholders throughout the research project; a research framework aimed at addressing issues, needs and concerns of people of the community; and the development of findings that community members can use to take action and make social changes (Minkler and Wallerstein, 2002; Strand et al, 2004; Chow and Crowe, 2005).

The participants involved in the CPAR were nine social workers: seven women and two men. Four came from the SSD and five from the two NGOs. All were employed on a temporary basis and for some it was their first work experience.

Process

A total of seven sessions were held, all of which were carried out online, due to the restrictions on face-to-face contacts imposed by the pandemic.

Participants were involved in identifying problems and research questions, supported in providing answers and generating action plans based on findings.

Researchers designed research and discussion tools, facilitated sessions, analysed data and disseminated their findings.

All meetings were structured following the 'opening–exploring–closing' phases and each session was opened and closed by rounds of check-in/out, in order to create a trustworthy, supportive and empathetic atmosphere and to foster a sense of connectedness among participants. The opening phase of the meetings was dedicated to data collection. During this phase, participants began to discover the topic at issue, reviewing the events that took place in the period between the meetings and generating insights and understandings.

In the exploring phase, participants were involved in an in-depth investigation that helped to identify positive and negative patterns, already existing, and to highlight areas of potential. Finally, the closing activities focused on the future: after the insights, participants moved on to the planning phase, defining a goal and activities to achieve it.

The topics discussed by the participants included: a better understanding of the national guidelines for tackling severe adult marginality and of Housing First/housing-led approaches; the identification of the essential dimensions of housing (physical space, social space and tenancy); the enhancement of knowledge about the phenomenon of homelessness and its localisation, also through information sharing and understanding gained from practice with service users; the co-creation of shared working tools; the mapping of key stakeholders involved or to be involved in a network of care for homeless people in the local context; and the need and the strategies to leave a trace of the new social work practice in one's own organisations and in the local community.

One year after the conclusion of the lab activities, participants were invited to share their insights on the CPAR-related changes and were also asked to express their level of satisfaction with the overall experience of the CPAR. The follow-up was carried out through a focus group and a short online survey.

Impact

All practitioners were very satisfied with their participation in the CPAR lab, despite the intention of a longer duration. They described the meetings as a 'breath of fresh air' and sharing became a way of not feeling alone in their daily struggles. The multi-session lab was the only opportunity for the operators of the different services and providers involved in the programme to meet and share, since there were no other joint staff meetings, nor meetings of the management committee or steering committee. Poor coordination skills at managerial and interorganisational level resulted in disorientation, frustration and a sense of loneliness and helplessness among social workers throughout the programme. That is why the workshop meetings were important, first of all, to gather participants and then to make them voice out their own dissatisfaction, directing it towards reflection and action. As reported by participants, the CPAR lab fostered the development of the empowerment of professionals, helping them to share feelings, to increase awareness and nurture the belief that they could change circumstances. The meetings improved their deep understanding of societal, political and organisational barriers to the integration of homeless people, and increased their knowledge and ability to analyse critical issues as well as to co-define intervention strategies by drawing attention to particular issues and giving feedback for discussion, templates and concepts for thinking. The multi-session lab also enabled the improvement of transversal skills, especially the ability to work in situations with high risk of burnout, not only due to the complexity of social needs and work overload, but also to the weakness of local welfare and to the lack of integration between social and health services.

The impacts of the CPAR activities were observed in the social service delivery and at social work practice level, too. The SDC's street outreach unit worked to build a trustworthy and supportive relationship with homeless people and to involve them in accessing local services, as well as working hard to open up ways to access basic rights (such as a registered address, without which people cannot register for a general practitioner, renew identity documents or access welfare provisions); the outreach service also worked with neighbourhoods, informing and engaging shop owners, office employees and residents in the support process. The SSD developed a new procedure to facilitate homeless people's access to formal aid, by building collaborative practice with the street outreach service and designing new tools and forms not previously used by the Social Secretariat Office. The CSF focused its interventions on rapid rehousing much more than in the past, on one hand, through several interviews with the users for a personalised assessment of needs and circumstances, to increase their motivation to move forward; on the other hand, through mapping available living solutions in the locality and building relationships with landlords and real estate agents in order to facilitate homeless people's access to housing.

At the organisational level, the impact was different in the three agencies. As mentioned, the SSD had only recently been provided with staff, funds and a new regulatory framework. The struggle to replace the old institutionalised and welfare culture was under way, with traditional positions difficult to overcome. Social workers participating in the CPAR could only make new arrangements within the Social Secretariat Office without being able to fully involve the Adults Social Services Office in the design of care plans for the person and, overall, to affect the organisational settings. As in its long history and vocation, the CSF core activities remained focused on providing basic and emergency assistance to people in extreme poverty, and the housing programme did not become permanent. Thanks to its younger age and vocation for innovation and social inclusion as well as its cooperative nature, the SDC was, instead, open to incorporate new forms of service delivery and organisational approaches. However, in the end, insufficient financial resources made their services economically unsustainable.

Finally, interorganisational coordination and networking have remained limited, more often conveyed by relationships among professionals.

The suspension of funds and the lack of full investment of the SSD management in the new service did not make it possible to preserve the newly introduced social work practice. The expiry date of the employment contracts of some practitioners or their relocation to other services or agencies contributed to the extinction of the experience in Cosenza, which nonetheless left some traces. As participants pointed out, most of them brought learnings, relationships, core practice and some tools to other programmes for homeless people they were subsequently involved with. Their agencies kept collaborating on an informal basis, while the SSD agreed to submit a new proposal in order to access new national funds and activate a low-threshold intervention for homeless people, working in partnership with the SDC.

Discussion

The case studies presented questioned some aspects of social innovation in social work, illustrated now, along with the main findings.

Is innovation triggered by bottom-up and/or top-down factors?

In both experiences it is possible to identify top-down factors (broader strategies, actors, resources) promoting changes. In Verona's case, the opportunity to develop the CPAR project was, in fact, part of the wider Horizon 2020 project HOME_EU: 'Homelessness as unfairness'. In Cosenza's case this was linked to the implementation of a local project, funded by the National Call for Proposals 4/2016 aimed at experimenting with social inclusion interventions for homeless people.

However, innovation also occurred through bottom-up factors that in both cases were related to the involvement of NGOs and public authorities in CPAR projects whose activities were directed towards the participative development of knowledge, skills and strategies aimed at improving social services and social work for homeless people. This involvement could not be presumed and showed at least an initial willingness to engage and experiment the adoption of new models and practice of help.

What are the specific aspects of innovation presented?

For both cases, the specific aspects of innovation can be attributed to two co-existing conditions:

1. The involvement of universities, which have built alliances with public and third sector entities to encourage participatory research, and have animated and facilitated the meetings with social practitioners, supporting a reflective and empowering process and fostering cooperation between practice and theory.
2. The use of the CPAR and, thus, of a methodological approach that encouraged equal inclusion and collaboration of social professionals in the identification, research and resolution of community issues, while additionally supporting the group re-elaboration of their own experience working with homeless people.

At what aggregate level does the innovation operate?

The two CPAR projects have mainly produced changes at nano and micro levels, which can be traced back to a new person-centred and inclusion-addressed approach to social work with homeless people, to the improvement of targeted professionals' skills, to the co-creation and introduction of new practice and procedures in each organisation involved, to collaborative relationships established among professionals from different agencies and services.

The two experiences indicated that the involvement and the empowerment of social workers is a necessary step to promoting change in particularly complex fields of social work such as that of extreme poverty. Nonetheless this does not always seem to be sufficient to generate enduring innovation. Other conditions were found to be important to this extent. These relate to dimensions such as: the political will to change; the functioning of public administration; the organisational structure of service providers and the culture of care; as well as management commitment to innovation.

Conclusion

The case studies showed that contextual factors can be critical in social innovation. In Verona, a number of factors fostered social change:

- an institutional culture open to change and training;
- a team willing to engage in internal reflection;
- resources from the European project that enabled the organisation of meetings and the final exhibition;
- a high level of management commitment;

- the cooperative's connection with other local and national services;
- the involvement of the political level in structuring services and disseminating the results of the CPAR project.

In Cosenza the previously described positive impact was attenuated by some factors such as high precariousness of employment for social workers both in the public sector and in the NGOs, poor commitment of management, organisational structures and cultures not fully open to embrace changes, and a lack of political will to reform social services for homeless people in the local welfare system.

The case studies also showed how CPAR can contribute to the co-creation of innovation in social work, at least at the nano and micro levels. In fact, the Photovoice in Verona and the multi-session lab in Cosenza have promoted analysis, discussion and knowledge-sharing and the identification of factors and strategies needed to make changes in services for homeless people. However, social innovation needs to move beyond the initial phase of growth among a small group of committed supporters, to spread and gain wider support and then to scale up and disseminate, in order to consolidate itself. To this end, it is essential to have a communication strategy designed to capture the imagination and the consensus of a broad community, as well as the creation of strong alliances. The visual methodology used in Verona facilitated communication and community engagement, while in Cosenza participants did not involve the local community.

Both in Verona and Cosenza, during the follow-up phase of the two projects, a claim was made for permanent spaces for co-research, discussion and reflection, based on the CPAR methodology. The presence of such cooperative processes over time may support social change even within the most difficult and resistant contexts.

References

Ascoli, U. and Pavolini, E. (eds) (2015) *The Italian Welfare State in a European Perspective: A Comparative Analysis*, Bristol: Policy Press.

Aviv, I., Gal, J. and Weiss-Gal, I. (2021) Social workers as street-level policy entrepreneurs, *Public Administration*, 99(3): 454–68.

Chow, J.C.C. and Crowe, K. (2005) Community-based research and methods in community practice, in M. Weil (ed) *The Handbook of Community Practice*, Thousand Oaks, CA: Sage, pp 604–19.

Cersosimo, D. and Viesti, G. (2022) Il welfare italiano da Nord a Sud, in C. Giorgi (ed) *Welfare: Attualità e prospettive*, Rome: Carocci, pp 307–22.

Ferrera, M. (1996) The 'Southern model' of welfare in social Europe, *Journal of European Social Policy*, 6(1): 17–37.

Ferrera, M. and Hemerijck, A. (2003) Recalibrating Europe's welfare regimes, in J. Zeitlin and D.M. Trubek (eds) *Governing Work and Welfare in a New Economy: European and American Experiments*, Oxford: Oxford University Press, pp 88–128.

Flum, M.R., Siqueira, C.E., DeCaro, A. and Redway, S. (2010) Photovoice in the workplace: a participatory method to give voice to workers to identify health and safety hazards and promote workplace change – a study of university custodians, *American Journal of Industrial Medicine*, 53(11): 1150–8.

Gaboardi, M., Santinello, M., Disperati, F., Lenzi, M., Vieno, A., Loubière, S. et al (2022a) Working with people experiencing homelessness in Europe, *Human Service Organizations: Management, Leadership & Governance*, 46(4): 324–45.

Gaboardi, M., Santinello, M., Lenzi, M., Disperati, F., Ornelas, J. and Shinn, M. (2022b) Using a modified version of Photovoice in a European cross-national study on homelessness, *American Journal of Community Psychology*, 70(1/2), 139–52.

Goddard, J. and Vallance, P. (2013) *The University and the City*, Abingdon: Routledge.

Hupe, P. (ed) (2019) *Research Handbook on Street-Level Bureaucracy: The Ground Floor of Government in Context*, Cheltenham: Edward Elgar.

Istat, Ministero del Lavoro e delle Politiche Sociali, Caritas and fio.PSD (2015) *Anno 2014. Persone senza dimora*, Available from: https://www.istat.it/it/files//2015/12/Persone_senza_dimora.pdf.

Istat (2022a) *Rapporto povertà, Anno 2021*, Rome: Istituto Nazionale di Statistica, https://www.istat.it/it/files//2022/06/Report_Povert%C3%A0_2021_14-06.pdf.

Istat (2022b) *Popolazione residente e dinamica demografica, Anno 2021*, Rome: Istituto Nazionale di Statistica, https://www.istat.it/it/files//2022/12/CENSIMENTO-E-DINAMICA-DEMOGRAFICA-2021.pdf.

Johnson, A.K. and Cnaan, R.A. (1995) Social work practice with homeless persons: state of the art, *Research on Social Work Practice*, 5(3): 340–82.

Lancione, M., Stefanizzi, A., and Gaboardi, M. (2018) Passive adaptation or active engagement? The challenges of Housing First internationally and in the Italian case, *Housing Studies*, 33(1): 40–57.

Ministero del Lavoro e delle Politiche sociali (2015) Linee di indirizzo per il contrasto alla grave emarginazione adulta in Italia, Available from: https://www.lavoro.gov.it/temi-e-priorita/poverta-ed-esclusione-sociale/focus-on/Poverta-estreme/Documents/Linee-di-indirizzo-per-il-contrasto-alla-grave-emarginazione-adulta.pdf

Minkler, M. and Wallerstein, N. (eds) (2002) *Community-Based Participatory Research for Health*, San Francisco: Jossey Bass.

Nicolls, A. and Murdock, A. (eds) (2012) *Social Innovation: Blurring Boundaries to Reconfigure Markets*, Basingstoke: Palgrave Macmillan.

Parpan-Blaser, A. and Hüttemann, M. (2010) Key issues and dimensions of innovation in social services and social work, in K. Müller, S.R. Steffen and M. Žák (eds) *Social Dimension of Innovation*, Prague: Linde, pp 183–94.

Parpan-Blaser, A. and Hüttemann, M. (2019) Social innovation in social work, in J. Howaldt, C. Kaletka, A. Schröder and M. Zirngiebl (eds) *Atlas of Social Innovation: A World of New Practices, Vol 2*, Munich: Oekom, pp 80–3.

Pascuzzi, E. and Marcello, G. (2020) La riforma mancata: Cronache del ritardo, deficit e tracce di innovazione nel welfare sociale in Calabria, *Politiche Sociali / Social Policies*, 2020(3): 419–38.

Pezzana, P. (2012) Control and contain: a 'hidden strategy' where a common strategy is lacking: perspectives from Italy, *European Journal of Homelessness*, 6(1): 125–41.

Rahman, R., Ghesquiere, A., Spector, A.Y., Goldberg, R. and Gonzalez, O.M. (2020) Helping the helpers: a Photovoice study examining burnout and self-care among HIV providers and managers, *Human Service Organizations: Management, Leadership & Governance*, 44(3): 244–65.

Simons, H. (2009) *Case Study Research in Practice*, London: Sage.

Strand, K., Marullo, S., Cutforth, N., Stoecker, R. and Donohoe, P. (2004) *Community-Based Research and Higher Education: Principles and Practices*, San Francisco: Jossey-Bass.

Wang, C. and Burris, M.A. (1997) Photovoice: concept, methodology, and use for participatory needs assessment, *Health Education & Behavior*, 24(3): 369–87.

Wang, C., Cash, J.L. and Powers, L.S. (2000) Who knows the streets as well as the homeless? Promoting personal and community action through Photovoice, *Health Promotion Practice*, 1(1): 81–9.

Yin, R.K. (2014) *Case Study Research: Design and Methods*, 5th edn, Thousand Oaks, CA: Sage.

Zufferey, C. (2008) Responses to homelessness in Australian cities: social worker perspectives, *Australian Social Work*, 61(4): 357–71.

17
Challenging the power status quo: paradoxes in grassroots social innovation

Luc de Droogh and Jeroen Gradener

Introduction

Most practices of social innovation acknowledge that alternative arrangements between state, market and civil society are called for if innovations are to be sustainable (Ibrahim, 2017; Budd et al, 2015). However, seldom is social innovation explicitly set up as a strategy to address structural economic, cultural or political inequities vis-à-vis dominant bureaucratic, professional and market discourses; in other words, social innovation being set up as a bottom-up approach, stimulating citizens' agency (see Chapter 1 in this volume) to take control of the narrative, processes and goals of practices of social innovation. In this chapter, we will address this bottom-up approach as a grassroots-led process of innovation, in which social workers engage to establish an antidote to structural power disparities between market and state forces and citizens' needs. Social workers are often driving forces in innovations that lack effectiveness and sustainability, to correct violations of fundamental social and professional values and to promote democratic practices in social work (Spierts et al, 2021). Social innovation in this sense is set up as a social work strategy for critical inquiry of the status quo, for democratisation and for the promotion of agency of actors whose voices in social innovation, such as the design of new social arrangements in care and welfare, are needed. This chapter explores these cornerstones for grassroots-led social innovation and evaluates its tensions and the dilemmas that can occur in practice, especially for social work professionals and engaged citizens. What happens when an innovation strategy aims to flip the position of people in poverty from subjects to actors in the process of policy making and service provision? With this focus we address two of the principal questions guiding this book: first, is social innovation a process or a result or both and, second, how do factors outside of the innovation process work? Especially, in this case social innovation as a participative, grassroots approach was set up with an ambitious end: not only to address the structural causes of poverty through participation but also to yield concrete and sustainable improvements in the lives of people living in poverty. Our exploration draws upon Ibrahim's (2017) work on grassroots development as social innovation strategy. We will outline the model, clarify paradoxes that occur in social innovations as political practice exemplified by Flemish grassroots-led social innovation project Where People in Poverty Speak Out (WPPSO), which will be introduced later in this chapter, especially in the relation between grassroots-led initiatives and social workers.

Central to Ibrahim's model of social innovation is the concept of grassroots-led development (GLD). It considers social innovation as an 'improvement in one or more aspects of human well-being brought about by people acting as initiators and agents of change (in collaboration with other development actors/institutions) at the grassroots' (Ibrahim, 2017: 199). GLD is an approach to foster behavioural change of individuals, nurturing their capabilities to act and become agents in their own right, collective agency of all stakeholders in social innovation and institutional reforms to allow innovations at the grassroots level. Central to the GLD approach are three processes:

1. Conscientisation, or citizens' critical examination of the status quo and development of their 'capacity to aspire'.
2. Conciliation, or the resolution of particular interests of stakeholders in social innovation to favour collective interests.
3. Collaboration as a political practice, scrutinising power disparities in existing social arrangements and replacing them with a level playing field one.

In what follows, we will examine how these three processes of GLD took shape in organisations where people in poverty speak out (hence WPPSO) – self-organisations of people in poverty – and afterwards critically evaluate its ambitions and results. But first, we will introduce the case of the GLD project WPPSO as our central case.

Introducing 'Where People in Poverty Speak Out'

Flanders, one of the three regions of Belgium, has seen, since the publication of *The General Report on Poverty* (Santkin, 1994), a revival of grassroots community initiatives, under the name WPPSO.

The preparation of the report was and still is considered a landmark in the history of Belgian poverty policy, as for the first time the poor themselves were invited to speak out about poverty – not (only) social policy makers or social scientists (Vranken et al, 2004; Smeyers, 2020). Two self-advocacy organisations together and under the guidance of the

King Baudouin Foundation, Belgium's most prestigious philanthropical organisation, worked with the poor themselves to prepare the *General Report on Poverty*. Since the publication of the report a poverty policy has been developing in which the participation of people in poverty and people with lived experience and the organisations WPPSO are framed as being crucial partners in the development, implementation and evaluation of poverty policy (Degerickx, 2020). But there are also more and more critical voices to be heard about this participatory poverty policy. The question is whether WPPSO as grassroots social innovation in fact generated emancipatory policy and transformational practices based on empowerment of individuals and promoting inclusive practices.

Belgium is a highly developed and rich country, placed 13 in the Human Development Index in 2021. In contrast, however, using the EU Standard for Poverty, around 16 per cent of the population in Belgium live in (relative) poverty. In 2003, a Flemish Decree on Poverty was voted in parliament, formally recognising self-organisations of people in poverty. This Poverty Decree requires that self-advocacy organisations fulfil six diverse criteria to be subsidised:

1. enable people in poverty to form an organisation;
2. give a voice to people in poverty;
3. work towards their social emancipation;
4. change social structures;
5. create dialogue and training activities to enhance the solidarity of people in poverty and the non-poor;
6. continue to seek out people in poverty.

Currently, there are 59 WPPSO groups in Flanders, coordinated by one umbrella organisation, the Network Against Poverty.[1] In almost all WPPSO, paid practitioners like social workers take on the overall responsibility for shaping daily practices. However, exceptionally, volunteers also take on this responsibility due to the choices of the WPPSO organisation in dealing with their limited resources or their historical background. With the decree the Flemish government accepts a responsibility to develop a participatory policy to combat poverty and subscribes to a construction of poverty as a structural problem.

Process 1: conscientisation

The first process in Ibrahim's model of GLD is conscientisation. It refers to a developmental process of critical inquiry where participants examine and evaluate their lives. It draws upon the critical pedagogy of the Brazilian pedagogue Paulo Freire (1970) and rests upon the tenet that collective inquiries lead to the identification of systemic and enduring obstacles people experience in their quest for a meaningful and valuable life. Becoming conscious of factors, such as exclusion, stigmatisation and lack of access to resources, such as education and other opportunities, is key to social change, according to Freire. Margaret Ledwith, one of Freire's foremost adepts, formulated it as a process 'by which people become aware of the political, socio-economic and cultural contradictions that interact in a hegemonic way to diminish their lives' (2001: 178). Hegemony refers to the dominance that political, socio-economic and cultural actors have in determining the conditions and norms through which people live their lives.

According to Freire and other pedagogues, social work scholars and practitioners after him, this dependency also creates a kind of self-fulfilling prophecy. Because of their dependence on help and support, people have often been told that their experience and opinion do not matter. Consequently, people living in poverty often are seen to adapt their world views and, even more, their aspirations based on the dominant discourses; in the case of poverty this is, for instance, on individual shortcomings.

This encapsulation in expert and elitist views of their evaluations about culpability and responsibility for being poor predominantly results in so-called 'adaptive preferences' (Begon, 2015: 246), or fixed expectations about what people think they are entitled to, based on social views they ultimately did not participate in creating.

Freire's pedagogy of conscientisation is an active endeavour to address and correct these 'adaptive preferences' and free themselves of dominant discourses about, for instance, the origins of poverty and the solutions brought about by policy makers and experts. The WPPSO organisations explicitly refer to Freire as a source of inspiration. They are very carefully and scrupulously working to realise processes of conscientisation. They aspire to working in the safe space of their organisation to collectivise the experiences of people through dialogue – to make their shared experiences visible and then strive for action. So these associations[2] create a stage for speaking out about the struggles of people in poverty and against poverty. Based on their stories, common themes – or generative themes in Freirean terminology – can be identified as a grassroots-developed discourse and thus as a starting point for discussions with welfare organisations and policy makers.

The WPPSO organisers are playing a pivotal role in 'flipping the coin': from a hegemonic policy and expert poverty-led discourse about people in poverty, towards a critically examined experience-based discourse by people in poverty. What can be learned from self-advocacy organisations and even critically addressed about the way the process of conscientisation is being applied (Schiettecat, 2016; Boone, 2019; Degerickx, 2020)?

First, grassroots organisations aim to offer safe spaces that allow people to express themselves freely and unfettered. This requires social workers to perform complex balancing acts, between recognition, support and challenge. In the organisations, people in poverty will find recognition in similar experiences, understanding the daily struggle with poverty from within. Building support and challenging the status quo, many hurdles must be addressed by social workers.

An important hurdle remains to transcend paternalistic tendencies of professionals. This requires a robust ability of social workers to take the stories of people in poverty seriously. Often, social workers outside the organisations handle an implicit agenda that poor people need to transcend victimhood and acknowledge many of their ideas and behaviours are irrational. If people in poverty first must become conscious of the structural and institutional causes of the problem of poverty, this at least simply neglects the value of the everyday stories, and how the poor developed their views based on their experiences of what it means to be poor. It demands respectful treatment from social workers. People in poverty should not be seen, as is still often the case, as passive victims of their situations. What is needed is a recognition of the different kinds of agency – from getting by in their daily lives as individuals to forms of resistance and getting back at the situation through the bending of rules, all kinds of manipulation and so forth, they are using to try to deal with the situation. Middle-class people, including many social workers and social researchers, often do not 'see' these kinds of agency or label them as 'irrational behaviour' because it is a poverty-generating or poverty-reinforcing behaviour. From an external point of view – the dominant perspective – this might be irrational behaviour but in the specific situation and the context the behaviour can be perfectly rational adaptations to the challenging situations in which the poor are making their lives (Calnitsky, 2018). Therefore, it is so crucial that the voices of people in poverty are heard and listened to, unscrutinised and in a co-creative manner. There is a lot to learn for social work by carefully listening to people in poverty, about their creativity and inventiveness in adapting to demanding situations. In other words, it requires social workers to be able to relate to people in poverty as equals and empathically, and resist adopting the role of 'saviours', the latter being an often-preferred role in the world of welfare and social work.

The second hurdle for social workers consciously relying on principles of critical pedagogy, is being attentive for processes of exclusion. Is living in poverty simply living in poverty and is there no relation – except for individual differences in, for example, character and intelligence – to mechanisms of exclusion, starting from the cradle one is born into to exclusion processes in education, in the labour market, the housing market and so on? The complexities involved in bringing the experiences into dialogue in the WPPSO and linking them to processes of exclusion and injustices in society are described in Boone et al (2019) in a very nice and fine-grained way. Being attentive to macro processes of exclusion requires social workers to be conscious of economic injustices and the division of opportunities and wealth in society, but also to be aware of the subtle exclusionary processes that occur at the level of micro relations between people, and in and through the relations between institutions and the people living in poverty. Inequality is deeply relational. And we should keep this in mind when we discuss the second C in Ibrahim's model – conciliation of interests.

Process 2: conciliation

The second process pivotal to grassroots-led innovation is conciliation – or the development of 'new social relations, social networks and collaborations' (Ibrahim, 2017: 217). It requires social workers to support people to gain access to decision-making forums that can realise structural improvements in their living situations. These forums are often very diverse and can be found in policy development and in local political debate and in the realms of consultation by professional social service providers. Each of those forums has divergent motives and instruments to tackle social problems. Sociologists, such as Freidson (2001) speak of disparate 'logics' of service provision: the bureaucratic logic of government, fostering equality and due diligence; the logic of the professional, which aims at quality of service provision and doing the right thing based on professional values such as social justice; and, finally, the logic of the market, which cultivates efficiency, choice and organisability of social services for citizens. The question is how to bridge or transcend these divergent interests, and ways of thinking and doing – starting from the assumption that conciliation is always the appropriate goal. Is a consensus really always the best thing when we are confronted with structural inequalities?

Ibrahim refers to this process of transcending interests and strategies as 'conciliation', or the bridging of interests through deliberative and joint decision-making. According to the urbanist Flyvbjerg (2001), in this exploration of disagreements and possible shared interests, a collective 'value-driven' dialogue can emerge in which participants often find that – even though they have a different position, interests and socialisation, common visions can be created (Gradener and de Kreek, 2019). It is important here that the various actors experience the added value of their own contribution, and where possible also receive support to realise that contribution.

But next to the tradition of consensus-seeking, a second deliberative tradition and type of practices must be considered: the agonistic tradition (Rancière, 2005; Mouffe, 2005) that acknowledges the existence of fundamentally opposing interests and disagreement. The focus on the public interest in both traditions invites politicians, policy makers, social workers and citizens to engage in dialogue. But is this dialogue a forum in which we try to realise a formal level playing field – realising conditions of equality only to be able to participate as equals in the dialogue? The first tradition assumes that a consensus is in principle always possible and the best possible result, therefore all parties need to be prepared to transcend their own interests. A fundamental conflict of power in society does not exist.

The second tradition starts from the assumption that there will always be inherent structural tensions and conflicts in society and that we should recognise this. This is what politics is about: the recognition of conflict as the essence of politics and the political. The dialogue is not taking place on a forum, the dialogue takes place in an arena. Power differences and inequalities are inherent to every form of society. Assuming that agreements can be reached across a great variety of stakeholders runs the risk of ignoring deep, contradictory interests and social distrust built up over decades.

With the Flemish Decree there is in principle a shared goal for all parties: the fight against poverty. There even seems to be a consensus on a common vision on the problem of poverty. Poverty is seen as a structural problem of society. The self-organisations in Flanders succeeded in realising in principle a participation-oriented policy towards policy making about poverty on the regional Flemish level as well as on the communal level. A lot of new instruments were developed to ensure that people can make their voice heard on many different policy levels. There exist many formal and informal places where people in poverty can make their voices heard.

If we look at the practices of WPPSO from the perspective of conciliation, we see that on the level of professional organisations there are some successes. The experts by experience (people in poverty with two years of training to function as a kind of interpreter between two worlds) manage to bridge the perspectives of clients and professionals. Their mediation between the lifeworld of people living in poverty and professional social workers and their organisations is sometimes successful. Also on the local level there is some success. In cities like Ghent and Kortrijk there is a place, a forum or an arena, where the city and WPPSO organisations meet and discuss about the local policies on poverty. We can observe that there are direct and indirect effects of the introduction of people in poverty or the creation of networks between organisations of people in poverty (Boone, 2018) and professional organisations. Some crucial barriers to social and medical care are removed. We help them to better negotiate their lives in poverty. But do we combat poverty or deal with the social exclusion processes that cause poverty?

Critical voices about participation, such as Degerickx (2020), describe the *General Report on Poverty* as the practice through which the participation paradigm was produced. During the working process on the *General Report* there were already a lot of discussions between the different partners. There was a lot of distrust, prejudices and practical issues between policy makers, professionals and people in poverty and their organisations. Different expectations, the issue of taking time to work on the rhythm of people in poverty and not following the dominant culture of policy makers was a very important one. The concept of participation itself was also a very important – its meaning shifted a few times during the process. For some policy makers it was the mobilisation of society, for others the consultation of people in poverty was central. Some experts and organisations stressed the confrontation between different forms of knowledge but the dominant one until today became participation as social inclusion of people in poverty (Degerickx, 2020). This means that the structural message about the processes of social exclusion did not become the central issue at that moment and that this logic of participation remains the more dominant. 'Combating poverty equals participation' became the central message of poverty policy and a logic of conciliation based on consensus became dominant.

Process 3: Collaboration

A third motive at the grassroots of social innovation is to improve the structural position of marginalised groups to create level playing field practices of collaboration. According to Ibrahim, collaboration between grassroots-led initiatives and other social actors is essential to promote institutional reform at the grassroots level. It introduces the perspective of the 'subjects' of social innovation in the development, provision and evaluation of new social arrangements, first of all allowing them to bargain with policy makers and service providers about how to more effectively address communities' needs. In addition, sustainable social innovations at the grassroots 'need to challenge the unequal power relations between them and other development actors' (Ibrahim, 2017: 210). In collaborative practices at the grassroots the existing power disparities between grassroots actors and all other actors have to be scrutinised, 'to enhance the bargaining power of local communities vis-à-vis other actors' (Ibrahim, 2017: 210).

Did the WPPSO organisations succeed in handling both hurdles to authentic processes of conscientisation – where lived experiences are taken seriously, and met by firm efforts to battle processes of exclusion? The first hurdle is to transform social participation into political action. Becoming a member and active in such an association can be regarded as an awareness of the necessity of a collective resistance against poverty and thus as a breaking through of hegemony (Lister, 2004; Schiettecat, 2019). More than 20 years in existence, indeed, organisations for the poor have been able to establish safe spaces where people share their experiences, identify injustices done to them and empower each other in surviving in poverty. Converting this social empowerment into transformative political action, to convert safe spaces into brave spaces, however, remains a challenge. More and more organisations and people question the possibility to fundamentally realise transformative political action. Organisations like Welzijnsschakels (Bridts and De Pril, 2021) question whether this is leading us somewhere since the numbers on poverty do not seem to go down (Jaarboek Armoede en Sociale Uitsluiting, 2022). Some of the organisations WPPSO are retreating from the policy level, certainly on the Flemish level and see their role more and more mainly as 'safe space' (Boone, 2018).

The second strategy to make the risks of inequalities in the process of conscientisation reflective is to deconstruct any hidden knowledge hierarchy between experts based on a social analysis and the insights of people in poverty based on their experiences. Both the experts and the people in poverty have insights into poverty situations that make a fundamental contribution to understanding what poverty is. Ignoring this specific form of the contribution of people in poverty is what Fricker (2007) calls 'an hermeneutical injustice'. This contribution might be valued in the organisations, but their knowledge is often not valued in institutional settings.

In these settings, all too often there is still a hierarchy installed, because the 'experts' track down the contradictions and then turn them into the cornerstone of a training programme. This seems in contradiction to Freire's original message. Oppression is, in Freire's conceptualisation, not a matter of one group exercising power over another but a situation of alienation. One cannot become a full, autonomous human being when in poverty or when someone else 'liberates' us from this situation of oppression (Freire, 1970).

In other words, this process risks also realising an inequality ingrained between the common people, in this case the poor and the training workers. Research into the work of the associations shows that people in poverty do indeed often have a great understanding of their living situation and deepen this by becoming active in the associations. It also appears that people are not resigned to their poverty, but on the contrary actively deal with their living situation in various ways and are therefore not only or not just victims who resign themselves to their fate (Lister, 2004; Schiettecat, 2019). They deal in different ways and exercise agency through different kinds of actions, including so-called small acts of resistance that clearly point to a certain awareness of the unjust situation the poor are faced with in their everyday lives (Scott, 1985). However, understanding the situation does not necessarily lead to transformative political action that produces structural changes. The ascertainment that having a structural view on poverty does not automatically lead to transformative social action was also found in research in Israel (Krumer-Nevo, 2015).

More and more voices state that in addition to this approach a more fundamental, structural approach is also needed. Three of the most important poverty experts in Flanders stated in interviews that this approach is needed (Cantillon and Marx, 2022; Gordts, 2022). Another voice, Wim Van Lancker

(2014) suggested a structural, more redistributive approach to children's allowances at the moment that Flanders became responsible for these allowances and could develop its own policy. He calculated how important this approach could be for people with children living in poverty, starting from the existing budget. The Flemish government chose to develop another policy, giving each child the same amount of money, even children in families for whom this barely makes a difference. The fundamental causes of poverty are not addressed. Many reformations in society in our neoliberal times go in the opposite direction of what is needed for people living in poverty: a decent income and a decent house to live in. Many politicians believe there is no support base for a more redistributive policy. Is this really the case, or do these politicians just want to believe that redistribution policies are not popular?

When we look from the perspective of the two antagonistic logics through which the contemporary politics of participation takes shape, we can see both logics at work in Flanders. The dominant one, the socialisation view, confronts the consensus democracy and the failure to bring everyone onto the deliberative playing field of democracy. The other, antagonistic, logic starting from equality also questions the underlying set of rules of the game, and questions the structural dimensions of poverty in a more profound way. The idea that one can bracket these dimensions and, for the purpose of dialogue, create an equal playing field hides the very uneven slope of that playing field.

Conclusion

This chapter examined grassroots-led processes of social innovation in the field of poverty in Flanders, inspired by Ibrahim's (2017) model of GLD. Two principal questions were addressed. The first, whether GLD social innovations such as WPPSO aimed to improve the voice of people in poverty can rely upon the quality of the process of GLD social innovation, we explored along the lines of processes of conscientisation, conciliation and (level field) collaboration. The second was if other factors, outside of the innovation process, also need to be considered, even in radical bottom-up approaches such as GLD? While stressing the importance of a process-oriented approach as a necessary condition for social innovation, it became apparent here that the democratisation of policy processes such as WPPSO not necessarily creates the conditions for concrete enhancements of the living conditions of people in poverty. Indeed, mere reorganising the decision-making processes might lead us to forget that as many or even more people live in poverty since the development of WPPSO.

Finally, regarding our second principal question, whether factors outside of the process of grassroots-led social innovation of WPPSO should be considered, we must answer this question affirmative. A key external factor was that of encapsulation tendencies in policy production. The specialisation of policy domains vis-à-vis the division of political-administrative responsibilities within current day governance, tends to the 'silofication' of social issues without considering underlying mechanisms, in this instance the relationship between poverty and broader macro-economic policy. This isolated WPPSO as an endeavour to deal with poverty issues, while avoiding the fundamental question about how we as a free market–led welfare society in fact constantly produce and reproduce social inequalities. The participative way of policy making about poverty with the grassroots organisations of people in poverty has brought about a separate domain of poverty policy. Questioning the neoliberal logic of stressing the personal responsibility of the poor for their poverty is an important corpus of knowledge, but that does not add up to more bargaining power for the poor to question the logic of the market. Cynics might even think that this kind of participatory policy making is but a small price to pay because the organisations of the poor are now also responsible for the continuing reproduction of poverty. The poor were not liberated but captured in an institutional arrangement that from the beginning was in great need of being scrutinised.

Notes

[1] See http://www.netwerktegenarmoede.be/

[2] The founder of one of the first self-advocacy-organisations in Flanders worked for a long time in Latin America in Freirean practices. After coming back to Belgium, he was shocked that poverty and functional analphabetism could exist in a rich country as Belgium and he founded this organisation at the beginning of the 1980s – working along the methods he had learned in Latin America.

References

Begon, J. (2014) What are adaptive preferences? Exclusion and disability in the capability approach, *Journal of Applied Philosophy*, 3: 241–57.

Boone, K. (2018) Social Work, Poverty and Parity of Participation: A Search for Social Justice, PhD thesis, Ghent: Ghent University Press.

Boone, K., Roets, G. and Roose, R. (2019) *Sociaal werk als armoedebestrijder, Zoektocht naar een participatieve benadering*, Oud-Turnhout: Gompels & Vansina.

Bridts, C. and De Pril, L. (2021) *De kansendans: Woede over armoede*, Antwerp: Halewijn.

Budd, C.H., Naastepad, C.W.M. and Van Beers, C. (2015) *Introduction: Deliverable D1.1 – Report on Institutions, Social Innovation & System Dynamics from the Perspective of the Marginalised*, CRESSI Working Paper 1/2015, https://web.archive.org/web/20161229231848/http://www.sbs.ox.ac.uk/sites/default/files/research-projects/CRESSI/docs/CRESSIWorkingPaper1D1.1Chp11Nov182014.pdf.

Calnitsky, D. (2018) Structural and Individualistic Theories of Poverty, *Sociology Compass Online*, 12.

Cantillon, B. and Marx, I. (2022) Dienstencheques zijn een perfecte illustratie van hoe verwend onze hogere middenklasse is, *Humo*, 4920: 25–33.

Coene, J.c.s. (2022) Armoede en sociale uitsluiting, Jaarboek 2022, 13-496, Leuven, Acco.

Degerickx, H. (2020) Participation of people in poverty in social policy making: a historical study off the rhetoric of self-advocacy organisations, PhD thesis, Ghent: Ghent University.

Flyvbjerg, B. (2001) *Making Social Science Matter: Why Social Inquiry Fails and How It Can Succeed Again*, Cambridge: Cambridge University Press.

Freidson, E. (2001) *Professionalism: The Third Logic*, Cambridge: Polity Press.

Freire, P. (1970) *Pedagogy of the Oppressed*, New York: Herder and Herder.

Fricker, M. (2007) *Epistemic Injustice: Power and the Ethics of Knowing*, Oxford: Oxford University Press.

Gordts, P. (2022) Professor Griet Roets: 'Armoede bestrijden? Daar is gewoon te weinig draagvlak voor', De Morgen, 10 October, https://www.demorgen.be/nieuws/professor-griet-roets-armoede-bestrijden-daar-is-gewoon-onvoldoende-draagvlak-voor~bcc5ff74.

Gradener, J. and de Kreek, M. (2019) Negotiating consent in neighbourhood community development work, in S. Banks and P. Westoby (eds) *Ethics, Equity and Community Development*, Bristol: Policy Press, pp 83–102.

Ibrahim, S. (2017) How to build collective capabilities: the 3C-model for grassroots-led development, *Journal of Human Development and Capabilities*, 18(2): 197–222.

Krumer-Nevo, M. (2015) Poverty-aware social work: a paradigm for social work with people in poverty, *British Journal of Social Work*, 46(6): 1793–808.

Ledwith, M. (2001) Community work as critical pedagogy: re-envisioning Freire and Gramsci, *Community Development Journal*, 36(3): 171–82.

Lister, R. (2004) *Poverty*, Cambridge: Blackwell/Polity Press.

Mouffe, C. (2005) *On the Political*, New York: Simon & Schuster.

Rancière, J (2005) *La haine contre la démocratie*, Paris: La Fabrique.

Santkin, J. (1994) *Algemeen Verslag over de armoede*, Brussels: King Bauduin Foundation.

Scott, J.C. (1985) *Weapons of the Weak: Everyday Forms of Peasant Resistance*, Cambridge, MA: Yale University Press.

Schiettecat, T. (2016) Trajectories of Poor Families in Child and Family Social Work, PhD thesis, Ghent: Ghent University.

Schiettecat, T. (2019) Hide and seek: political agency of social workers in supporting families living in poverty, *British Journal of Social Work*, 48(7): 1874–91.

Smeyers, T. (2020) Confronterend: 25 jaar oud verslag over de armoede brandend actueel, Sociaal.Net, 22 01 2020.

Spierts, M.J., Cools, P., Gradener, J. and Raeymaeckers, P. (2021) Democratische professionaliteit in het sociaal werk, in P. Raeymaeckers, J. Gradener, S. van Dam, S.J. Botman, K. Driesens, J. Boxstaens and M. Timions (eds) *Denken over Sociaal Werk*, Leuven: ACCO, pp 339–60.

Van Lancker, W. (2014) Kinderbijslag hervormen in functie van armoedebestrijding, *Basis*, 14: 8–10.

Vranken, J., De Boyser, K. and Dierckx, D. (red) (2004) Armoede en Sociale Uitsluiting, Jaarboek 2004, 13–553, Leuven, Acco.

THEME D

Social entrepreneurship: inclusive and regenerative models of social business and innovation for sustainable impact

18

Social entrepreneurship as social innovation: what about social work?

Leendert de Bell, Zsolt Bugarszki and Geof Cox

Introduction

Traditionally, social work professionals are some of the people best prepared to address the needs of marginalised and disadvantaged groups. The scale and complexity of today's social challenges (including climate change, forced displacement, poverty and inequality), however, often call for more creative and innovative solutions. Social workers are increasingly experiencing difficulty tackling these issues effectively with current means and approaches (Germak and Singh, 2009). Since the late 20th century, social workers across Europe have also been increasingly confronted with a shift in the balance between public and private provision of social and community services (Gray et al, 2003). Alongside funding reductions in social welfare, philanthropic donations and charities have also declined in since the early 2000s. In practice, social workers are asked to do more with less (Neal, 2015).

In response to these unsolved or inadequately met social problems and needs, there has been a spectacular global growth and development of social enterprises that address market and government policy failures and transform lives (Sepulveda, 2015). Although there is a wide diversity in the social aims (such as poverty-related issues, homelessness, social isolation and distance from the labour market) and in the business models of social enterprises, their main objective is to generate market revenues in order to create social or environmental benefits. Social enterprises either provide goods and services for the market and use their profits to achieve social objectives or may serve social objectives directly with their products and services. Social enterprises challenge the accepted perception of 'the profit motive' as the central impetus and aim of business activity. Often described as hybrid organisations, social enterprises achieve both financial sustainability and social and/or environmental impact, and use innovative governance structures (Battilana and Lee, 2014; Doherty et al, 2014). Those social enterprises that have developed strategies to achieve financial sustainability as well as social impact have more independent economic capabilities compared with non-profit organisations (Chang et al, 2021). Successful social enterprises generally also tend to be more successful social innovators (Phillips et al, 2015; Hagedoorn et al, 2022).

In terms of social innovation, social enterprises have to work closely with stakeholders in order to determine the best way of directing limited resources to design products and services that are sensitive to market demand and responsive to the needs of beneficiaries (Pache and Santos, 2012). In some impact areas such as 'fair trade' or 'green' social enterprises, the main objective is to replace more damaging products or services in a market. Their financial and social/environmental aims are aligned: the more they sell, the better they do. In other areas such as work integration, achieving a balance between economic sustainability and social impact may be more challenging. In trying to maintain quality levels and adhere to ethical standards while dealing with strict legal boundaries, bureaucracy, funding shortages and market competition, social enterprises are forced to provide new and smarter solutions (including new products or services, process innovation, new organisational structures and business models) that meet social needs more effectively than existing solutions and make better use of assets and resources (Pot and Vaas, 2008; Biggeri et al, 2017).

Despite a natural overlap in mission and potentially complementary approaches (Bent-Goodley, 2002), the growing movement of social enterprise is still notably absent in social work practice (Berzin, 2012). This has partly to do with long held misconceptions. A market-oriented approach and talk about profit may still make some social workers uncomfortable. This chapter aims to provide several compelling arguments that, in order to address the complexity of current social problems more adequately, there is still much to be gained when social workers better understand and embrace important elements from the 'toolbox' of social enterprise. We will focus our attention mainly on evidence of social innovation practices in social enterprises that focus on work integration – the most common type of social enterprise in Europe – and which play a central role in reintegrating the economically and socially marginalised into mainstream society (Cameron, 2010). In the following section, we will first go a bit deeper into the background of these specific types of social enterprises. Then we will briefly discuss several case studies from the European context that provide a good overview of how to achieve financial sustainability as well as social impact, along with some more experimental linkages of social work and social enterprise. We will conclude with some recommendations for social work professionals.

Social enterprises and work integration

Social enterprise has experienced explosive growth over recent decades. Existing businesses and new start-ups increasingly tackle problems that were traditionally addressed by the public or non-profit sectors (Burfield,

2018). In 2015 the Social Business Initiative of the European Commission estimated that 1 in 4 new businesses set up in the European Union were social enterprises, and up to 1 in 3 in France, Belgium and Finland (European Commission, 2015: 3). Within this broad movement many social enterprises engage in areas relevant to social work, especially in facilitating employment and social inclusion for people that would otherwise suffer exclusion, for example people with physical or mental disabilities, people with little formal education, refugees, ex-offenders, substance abusers and so on. The benefits of employment for these marginalised groups are multiple. Work not only provides financial independence, but also helps to provide (daily) structure, access to social networks, a sense of purpose and belonging, increased self-esteem and personal development.

This particular type of social enterprise, often referred to as 'work-integration social enterprise' (WISE), mostly operates in the same field that was long covered by 'sheltered employment'. The origins of the sheltered employment model go at least as far back as the 17th century, when Thomas Firmin established a factory to create jobs for destitute workers in England. This model became very widespread in the 20th century in both Western and communist societies, as it was seen as a crucial rehabilitation and employment support arrangement for the millions of veterans injured in both World Wars, and in the form of 'industrial therapy' was an aspect of institutional care. In the UK, the best known sheltered employment provider was the Remploy chain of 90 factories, which employed 6,000 disabled people (Holroyde, 2020). However, challenged by social developments and the counterculture movements of the 1960s – not least in psychiatry – the sheltered employment model came to be seen as based on fundamentally conservative practice, both in terms of its organisational and its disability model. In essence, a small number of non-disabled managers were employed to provide support and supervision to a large disabled workforce. Often, this focus on disability across the whole shop floor led to generalised low expectations, resulting in the allocation of work in an institutionalised environment, regardless of both changing market opportunities and individual workers' abilities, often for only a few hours a day, and with little relationship between production and compensation.

Today's social enterprises build on more democratic approaches such as the Italian 'social co-operative model', or the more generic 'social firms' as they became known in the UK, creating employment for people with mental health issues and other disadvantages in the labour market in workplaces that are both participative and supportive, but in real, viable enterprises. The radical nature of the social innovation involved in these approaches deserves emphasis. In contrast to sheltered employment, the focus is on the inclusion and empowerment of disadvantaged and disabled people, for example using organisational structures with employee directors – including directors that may have mental health issues or learning disabilities. Unlike traditional sheltered workplaces, these social enterprises enable participants to be treated as valued staff team members, rather than 'welfare clients', thus facilitating integration in society. Jobs are usually structured around workers' abilities, not their disabilities. As such, these social enterprises challenge both the conventional business view of people as interchangeable 'human resources', and the assumption that people with disabilities cannot fit into regular jobs – and they create an example for other employers to follow (Gidron and Monnickendam-Givon, 2017).

Case studies from the European context

There are no reliable figures for the total number of work-integration social enterprises across Europe – mainly because not all of the firms that aim to create jobs for disadvantaged groups think of themselves as part of an identifiable type or sector – but there is abundant evidence that their numbers are growing rapidly. Specific institutional and labour market contexts influence the numbers and the diverse ways social enterprises are organised and operate. The chapter now focuses on a few specific examples from the UK and the Netherlands to demonstrate the variety of ways in which social enterprises have managed to contribute to social innovation. These case studies will illustrate important aspects of social innovation that the social work professional may want (or need) to add to their toolbox.

In some countries, favourable tax treatments or job subsidy schemes have facilitated large numbers of similar social enterprises, but in the UK there is no significant long-term state support for social enterprises employing disabled or disadvantaged people, which has tended to produce smaller numbers, but perhaps more experiment and variety. A typical social entrepreneurial story arising directly out of frontline social work in the UK is that of Exchange Supplies. Just as conventional entrepreneurs spot a commercial opportunity and develop a business model to exploit it, social entrepreneurs see a social problem and develop a business model to solve it. Andrew Preston was a frontline UK drugs worker in the 1990s. Observing first-hand that many of the health and social problems associated with drug abuse did not stem from the drugs themselves, but the harmful way they were administered and policed, Andrew became an evangelist for the 'harm reduction' approach to drug abuse. He wrote a number of practical guides to safe injecting and addiction management – for both drug users and professionals in the field – then went on to organise the supply of safe drug-taking paraphernalia. In this process he negotiated the first agreement with local police to 'turn a blind eye', even though some of the supplies were at that time illegal in the UK (Andrew was subsequently active in getting the law changed). Unsurprisingly, given this dubious legality, conventional medical supply businesses refused to help him, so he founded the social enterprise Exchange Supplies simply as a natural extension of what he was already trying to do as a frontline drug worker. Naturally, the workers he took on were drawn from among unemployed drug users. Some 20 years later most of them (over 40 now) still are former, or indeed current, drug users. Exchange Supplies has grown continuously, is now expanding its sales internationally, and is still committed to evangelising the 'harm reduction' philosophy and disseminating safe practice and equipment.

More common routes for the establishment of social enterprises in the UK are initiatives by disabled people themselves, often supported by family and friends, and sometimes also by voluntary and community organisations. These inputs have been evident, for example, in the development of Viewpoint – a research agency that trains and employs disabled people in telephone survey work. Viewpoint started in Sheffield in the north of England in 2008, and now also operates in nearby cities Doncaster and Leeds. The Doncaster office was established in partnership with a housing association, and trains and employs tenants that have faced multiple barriers to employment; the Leeds office was a partnership with the large UK visual impairment charity RNIB, and employs blind and partially sighted people. The Viewpoint model is typical of many in the UK in offering both training and employment to a target group. Trainees move on to permanent employment either within Viewpoint itself or for other employers. The business model is in fact one generally only seen in large companies: two business activities within the shell of a larger enterprise – one selling training, and the other telephone surveys and research. The two businesses work in synergy, thus enabling the whole enterprise to remain competitive even though, because it provides exceptional support for its staff, some of its costs might be higher than competitors. It is the combination of a business activity that is not a barrier for wheelchair users, visually impaired people and others, with an innovative business model, that makes Viewpoint viable – and the fact that it has grown to branches in neighbouring cities is evidence not only of the viability of the model, but also its replicability.

In the UK public sector, the administrative division of health and social services into 'purchaser' and 'provider' arms has enabled more experimental social enterprise on the provider side, and indeed the 2014 Care Act enabled local authorities to take the commissioning role only, and to outsource social work delivery to external organisations.[1] One social enterprise, People2People, had already been established in Shropshire, taking the 'community interest company' form – a UK legal structure format specifically for social enterprise – and following the 2014 Act this inspired a national pilot project involving nine local authorities looking at similar developments. For several years, People2People delivered most community-based adult social work and occupational therapy in parts of Shropshire, and claimed improved outcomes for local people, a more motivated staff team and significant efficiencies for the local authority – in part by capitalising on the local knowledge of frontline social workers to exhaust available community support and act preventively before drawing on public service provision. A crucial strength was the presence of both frontline social work staff and service users on the board of directors. Unfortunately (for reasons we will discuss later) People2People and most of the other pilot social enterprise social work developments ultimately remained, or were taken back under local authority control – although a small number are still thriving, still demonstrating the benefits of running social work in a social enterprise contracting with, rather than directly controlled by public service purchasers. An example here is Focus, another community interest company providing the whole range of core social work functions in Lincolnshire, now employing 160 social workers and support staff as at the time of writing.

Similar lessons emerge from what is probably the most socially innovative of UK social enterprises in social work: the miEnterprise project. miEnterprise also takes the UK community interest company form, and was also spun directly out of a local authority service – in this case not community-based social work, but a day centre for people with learning disabilities. In itself, this is not unusual: there have been many service transformations to social enterprise, but most have been in services already customer-facing and trading to some extent, for instance therapeutic activities in gardening or cookery. But miEnterprise started in a general day centre for severely disabled people, in which most individuals were pursuing their own individual activities. When a new day centre manager with previous experience of self-employment was appointed, he could see that some of the centre users could earn from their activities, and he was also aware that earnings from self-employment need not be caught in the 'benefits trap' – the operation of welfare benefits and employment regulations rendering it impossible to enter employment without working regular, full-time, well-paid hours. He designed a support structure to provide both front-end (marketing and contract negotiation) and back-office services (accounts and so on), so that severely disabled people can become self-employed just doing what they are good at, and earning as little or as much as they like. miEnterprise works with the individual budgets allocated by care commissioners – either in the form of direct payments or service funds – but instead of buying 'care' (as they did in the old day centre), people buy the business support. Because their work is in itself fulfilling, that is generally all the support they find they now need – so they get to keep most of their earnings. miEnterprise was seen very favourably by the UK government, which in 2010 undertook a pilot project to replicate it nationally. However, as with the planned social enterprise social work roll-out, it was soon found that more conservative local authorities were resistant to the use of individual care budgets to buy support outside the normal range of publicly controlled or commissioned services. miEnterprise has been working successfully in Herefordshire since 2007, and has inspired a number of similar initiatives. People2People and the other social enterprises it inspired, like Focus, have also worked successfully for many years. But there is a clear lesson to be learned from the fact that despite the well-recognised achievements of these innovative social work social enterprises, risk-averse public sector managers have made it difficult to systematically replicate either model.

In the Dutch context, 'sheltered employment' ceased to be subsidised by the government with the introduction of the Work and Social Assistance Act in 2004. As it turned out, this left large groups of people outside the labour market. The 2015 Participation Act was intended as an instrument to encourage (regular) employers to hire more people with an occupational disability or distance from the labour market, but instead there has only been a growing number of (work-integration) social enterprises that address the needs of these vulnerable groups. Following the implementation of the Participation Act, Confed – a technical service provider that focuses on the development, production and assembly of a wide range of electrical and electronics products, including cabling systems and printed circuit boards – acquired several workplaces for sheltered employment, and – thanks to the entrepreneurial mindset of its owner – managed to turn these into a profitable social enterprise with €26 million turnover in 2022. Confed does not retail any products itself, but produces to contract for third parties. Thanks to a good balance between automation and manual production, Confed can offer a one-stop service concept to its customers, which is one of its competitive advantages. Confed's customers are very diverse, but are mainly in the form of long-term partnerships. Because Confed deliberately focuses on the production of expensive, high-end products, there is no need to constantly negotiate prices, which allows more people from different target groups to be structurally employed, with decent working conditions. Confed operates with the philosophy that the talents and competences of its employees are essential and necessary for the company. This requires good coordination between competences and the supply of work, which is mostly task-oriented instead of function-oriented. At the time of writing, the company operates from three locations, two in the Netherlands and one in the Czech Republic, and employs about 480 people, of which 40 per cent are people from different target groups. The scale and scope of this social enterprise is unique in its market, but there are still many opportunities for growth and replication of the concept.

Another pioneer in the field of social entrepreneurship for people distant from the labour market in the Netherlands is The Colour Kitchen. The Colour Kitchen offers everyone who is willing and able to work the opportunity to develop their skills and find a job in the catering industry. The needs of the individual are always the starting point of their journey 'from couch to job'. The methodology of The Colour Kitchen is to set aside the individual's past, and to focus on the future from day one, in a real business environment. All participants of The Colour Kitchen go through several stages, but the duration per phase is determined individually. This provides participants with a clear structure and enables them to build stability, self-esteem, self-confidence and resilience. The coaches above all make sure that the participants are seen and heard, which allows them to take steps that they were not able to make previously. Since its inception in 2008, The Colour Kitchen has gone through a number of course changes in the search for a financially sustainable business model, including bankruptcy. What started as a catering company focused on the retail market has subsequently migrated to the business to business market via the operation of company restaurants. After its restart in 2019, The Colour Kitchen has been characterised above all by strategic partnerships with a number of commercial clients and other partners. In addition to the five locations of their own, at the time of writing they are now operating as a facility service provider in ten other commercial partner locations. Through this collaboration, The Colour Kitchen are currently growing very fast and are now also thinking of expanding their model to other sectors.

A final example is Specialisterren, a Dutch social enterprise in which the majority of employees have a diagnosis on the autism spectrum. Specialisterren is based on the Danish example of Specialisterne, which is now working in 17 countries around the world (including the UK). It came out of its founder's realisation that his autistic son, though disabled by the everyday world in which he lived, actually had unique abilities which could be a competitive advantage in areas of new technology like software testing and data entry. Specialisterren is a social enterprise that provides IT services for governments, the financial sector, e-commerce and e-health companies. These services are mainly provided by people on the autism spectrum. They have excellent qualities such as the attention to detail required to test software and provide business intelligence and robotic process automation services. This allows Specialisterren to deliver high-quality work for its customers, while providing well-paid, permanent jobs to people who have experienced difficulties in finding decent employment in the regular job market. At present, Specialisterren employs over 50 people who have some form of autism; the company offers a workplace that is adapted to the specific needs of its employees, which means, for example, that the office is quiet with few distractions. Moreover, project managers offer a filter between the testers and the customers, allowing their employees to focus on what they are good at and avoid losing energy on direct communication and interaction with customers. The ambitions of Specialisterren are big – such as getting 1,000 people into work – but are not necessarily to be achieved via endogenous growth but through collaboration with other organisations.

Conclusion

The experience of social enterprises addressing social problems holds clear lessons for both social work professionals and those active in social enterprise. The central insight here is that social work and social entrepreneurship have complementary aims, and when successfully brought together, this could result in truly impactful social innovation. However, the generally very different organisational contexts, cultures and associated mindsets of these different practices still present formidable barriers to cooperation.

We feel the most significant barriers follow from the fact that social work is generally embedded in public bodies, or NGOs contracting with public bodies. Public sector management is fundamentally different from entrepreneurialism. In part because they expect policy direction to be set elsewhere (by elected members), and partly because they are sometimes subject to hostile media coverage, managers in public bodies often see their function as the careful administration of delivery, rather than undertaking risk or innovation. Risk management strategies in the public sector are often concerned with blame attribution, and seek to 'cover' decisions from public scrutiny or accountability. This is a preventive, or at best responsive approach to risk management (Osborne and Brown, 2011). But while the public sector tends to view risk simply as something to be minimised, in enterprise risk is sensibly managed, but also embraced as one of the keys to success. Moreover, experiment and failure are seen much more positively in the world of enterprise – histories like that of The Colour Kitchen, featuring failure on the way to greater success, are common.

A further result of social work being embedded in public bodies is the adoption of public sector approaches to evaluation, whereas social enterprise must have regard to business viability criteria, even if using these measures to ultimately achieve wider social benefits. Performance measurement and management is a growing phenomenon in the public sector, and has also been developing in social enterprise, with the integration of financial metrics like revenue, costs and surpluses with the measurement of social impact (sometimes monetised in measurements like 'social return on investment'). Social enterprises generally now think in terms of a 'triple bottom line' – financial sustainability, social impact and environmental impact (Bengo et al, 2016).

Both social workers and social enterprise activists tend not to be fully aware of these cultural and organisational differences, leading to frustration on both sides. This might be addressed via social work training and education (Linton, 2013). We can find examples of social work programmes embracing social entrepreneurship in the curriculum (Shier and Van-Du, 2018), but entrepreneurial education for social workers is still rare. We would like to see joint, multidisciplinary development courses at universities and colleges including students from different fields and using project-based learning techniques in order to develop the entrepreneurial skills and contacts of social workers. In cities with a vibrant social enterprise start-up ecosystem it is also worth considering involving local innovation hubs, participating in or organising social hackathon events and so on (Toros et al, 2022).

Perhaps the most important lesson here is that people with direct experience of social exclusion often develop the most successful social enterprises. Their main purpose is to create employment and/or products or services that enable people to use and develop their abilities, instead of feeling limited by disabilities. A priority must be raising awareness among social workers of this potential to introduce previously untapped entrepreneurial resources that might address the very social problems they are working on. There is hard evidence, in fact, that disabled people tend to be more entrepreneurial than the population at large (possibly through necessity; Kitching, 2014).

Instead of conventional public sector risk management, a conscious risk governance approach is recommended. This requires an inclusive process with broad political, interorganisational and internal debate about the acceptable level of risk for innovations. The core of these processes is not 'how safe is safe' but rather how much uncertainty the different stakeholders are willing to accept in exchange for the expected benefit of innovation (Renn, 2017). Similarly, the adoption of the kind of broad range of impact measures used in the 'triple bottom line' and monetisation of social outcomes metrics used by social enterprise should help make performance measurement more relevant to entrepreneurial approaches to social work.

Finally, but perhaps most importantly, more 'out of the box' thinking is needed. Often we see that the only way social workers can engage with entrepreneurial activities is by leaving the public sector for innovative start-ups, for their own enterprise or for jobs in other sectors. While social work is a profession that can be practised in different settings, it is also important to create a path for social entrepreneurship and innovation within public services (Nandan et al, 2015). In order to embrace social entrepreneurship in social work and to encourage social workers to participate in innovation a new approach is needed, extending the existing professional standards and traditions of social work. This new 'out of the box' way of thinking and acting should open up cooperation with business professionals, embracing some of their metrics and vocabulary, should explore links with social entrepreneurs, most of whom will be found willing to share their knowledge, should look for entrepreneurial potential among service users, and should develop new perspectives on risk, experiment and failure.

Note
[1] https://www.legislation.gov.uk/ukpga/2014/23/contents/enacted

References

Battilana, J. and Lee, M. (2014) Advancing research on hybrid organizing: insights from the study of social enterprises, *Academy of Management Annals*, 8(1): 397–441.

Bengo, I., Arena, M., Azonne, G. and Calderini, M. (2016) Indicators and metrics for social business: a review of current approaches, *Journal of Social Entrepreneurship*, 7(1): 1–24.

Bent-Goodley, T.B. (2002) Defining and conceptualizing social work entrepreneurship, *Journal of Social Work Education*, 38(2): 291–302.

Berzin, S.C. (2012) Where is social work in the social entrepreneurship movement?, *Social Work*, 57(2): 185–8.

Biggeri, M., Testi, E. and Bellucci, M. (2017) Enabling ecosystems for social enterprises and social innovation: a capability approach perspective, *Journal of Human Development and Capabilities*, 18(2): 299–306.

Burfield, E. with Harrison, J.D. (2018) *Regulatory Hacking: A Playbook for Startups*, New York: Portfolio/Penguin.

Cameron, J. (2010) Business as usual or economic innovation? Work, markets and growth in community and social enterprises, *Third Sector Review*, 16(2): 93–108.

Chang, Y., Peng, X. and Liang, C. (2021) Transforming nonprofit organisations into social enterprises: an experience-based follow-up study, *VOLUNTAS: International Journal of Voluntary and Nonprofit Organizations*, 32(1): 3–12.

Doherty, B., Haugh, H. and Lyon, F. (2014) Social enterprises as hybrid organizations: a review and research agenda, *International Journal of Management Reviews*, 16(4): 417–36.

European Commission (2015) The Social Business Initiative of the European Commission, Ref. Ares(2015)5946494, https://ec.europa.eu/docsroom/documents/14583.

Germak, A.J. and Singh, K.K. (2009) Social entrepreneurship: changing the way social workers do business, *Administration in Social Work*, 34(1): 79–95.

Gidron, B. and Monnickendam-Givon, Y. (2017) A social welfare perspective of market-oriented social enterprises, *International Journal of Social Welfare*, 26(2): 127–40.

Gray, M., Healy, K. and Crofts, P. (2003) Social enterprise: is it the business of social work?, *Australian Social Work*, 56(2): 141–54.

Hagedoorn, J., Haugh, H., Robson, P. and Sugar, K. (2022) Social innovation, goal orientation, and openness: insights from social enterprise hybrids, *Small Business Economics*, 60(1): 173–98.

Holroyde, A. (2020) Sheltered employment and mental health in Britain: Remploy c.1945–1981, in S.J. Taylor and A. Brumby (eds) *Healthy Minds in the Twentieth Century: In and Beyond the Asylum*, Cham: Palgrave Macmillan, pp 113–36.

Kitching, J. (2014) Entrepreneurship and Self-Employment by People with Disabilities, OECD Background Paper.

Linton, K.F. (2013) Developing a social enterprise as a social worker, *Administration in Social Work*, 37(5): 458–70.

Nandan, M., London, M. and Bent-Goodley, T. (2015) Social workers as social change agents: social innovation, social intrapreneurship, and social entrepreneurship, *Human Service Organizations: Management, Leadership & Governance*, 39(1): 38–56.

Neal, A.A. (2015) The intersection of social work and social enterprise, *Journal of Social Work Values & Ethics*, 12(2): 1–9.

Osborne, S.P. and Brown, L. (2011) Innovation in public services: engaging with risk, *Public Money & Management*, 31(1): 4–6.

Pache, A.C. and Santos, F. (2012) Inside the hybrid organization: selective coupling as a response to competing institutional logics, *Academy of Management Journal*, 56(4): 972–1001.

Phillips, W., Lee, H., Ghobadian, A., O'Regan, N. and James, P. (2015) Social innovation and social entrepreneurship: a systematic review, *Group & Organization Management*, 40(3): 428–61.

Pot, F. and Vaas, F. (2008) Social innovation, the new challenge for Europe, *International Journal of Productivity and Performance Management*, 57(6): 468–73.

Renn, O. (2017) *Risk Governance: Coping with Uncertainty in a Complex World*, London: Earthscan.

Sepulveda, L. (2015) Social enterprise, a new phenomenon in the field of economic and social welfare?, *Social Policy & Administration*, 49(7): 842–61.

Shier, M.L. and Van-Du, B. (2018) Framing curriculum development in social work education about social enterprises: a scoping literature review, *Social Work Education*, 37(8): 995–1014.

Toros, K., Kangro, K., Reimann, K., Bugarszki, Z., Sindi, I., Saia, K. and Medar, M. (2022) Co-creation of social services on the example of social hackathon: the case of Estonia, *International Social Work*, 65(4): 593–606.

19

The growing rhetoric of entrepreneurship in times of crisis: future challenges of social work in the case of Portugal

Antonela Jesus and Maria Inês Amaro

Introduction

Entrepreneurship is a structured process between different actors predetermined to change, based on market principles such as profit and individualism. However, when we move to entrepreneurship in its social dimension, it is possible to identify some links with social work values, namely: empowerment, democracy and the satisfaction of social needs. Undeniably, we can trace social entrepreneurship back to the origins of the profession, either with Jane Addams and the Settlement Movement or Mary Parker Follett with 'direct democracy', which by engaging the power of creative individuals for collective action, compares to what we now call social entrepreneurship (Jesus, 2019).

Furthermore, other understandings of entrepreneurship can be found in the literature. For example, the largest study of entrepreneurship in the world – the Global Entrepreneurship Monitor (2012) – also distinguishes two types of entrepreneurship activity: (1) by necessity, referring to entrepreneurs who seek self-employment to ensure their subsistence; and (2) by opportunity, referring to those entrepreneurs who identify and explore market opportunities.

It follows that entrepreneurship is an activity that may be determined by personal, organisational, sociological and environmental factors.

Thus, it is with the reconfigurations in the labour market, which have occurred mainly since the late 1990s, that the narrative of entrepreneurship becomes dominant, accentuating the neoliberal logics rooted in the development of a generalised employment crisis, a rhetoric based on freedom and individuality, which requires an 'attitude', a 'spirit', an innovative and differentiating 'way of being' capable of solving 'individual' problems (Campos and Soeiro, 2016).

In the specific case of Portugal, the omnipresence of the 'more entrepreneurship, more jobs' narrative acquires particular attention in public discourse at the time of the subprime crisis in the US, which shook the entire global banking system. At the time, Portugal followed the fall and in 2011 a memorandum of understanding was established by the Portuguese government with the European Commission, the European Central Bank and the International Monetary Fund, and in 2013 the country reached the highest peak ever in its unemployment rate, 17.8 per cent (EUROSTAT, 2013).

Without being immune to these transformations, Amaro (2009, 2015), a Portuguese social worker, in her doctoral thesis presented entrepreneurship as one of the challenges that social work faces today within the structure of contemporary society and naturally the profession itself. Not only do professionals face challenges in their own integration in the labour market, but there is also an urgent need to explore possibilities for activity in the private or non-profit sector.

This chapter analyses the configuration of entrepreneurship in the European Union agenda, followed by a particular look at those reproductions in Portugal, trying to point out if that 'appearance' is conditioned by the socio-economic and political contexts, but also some of its implications in the employment and social intervention sphere. For that purpose, we develop a documental analysis of the European measures and national government programmes since 1997, year when the entrepreneurship concept was introduced for the first time in the European policies with the launch of the European Employment Strategy. Here it is worth noting that the government programmes are a 'map' of intentions and concerns, which do not necessarily reflect the measures implemented by the respective governments.

As mentioned previously, we consider that the procedures and goals of social work are not free of the winds of change in contemporary social policy (Branco and Amaro, 2011). Thus, we conclude a critical analysis of social work's participation in processes of (social) entrepreneurship, not only because it takes part in the historical path of the profession (with the response to social problems from innovative solutions or the replication of existing social responses), but also because it is recognised that it is not a cure-all for social problems. In fact, the success of entrepreneurship depends on a combination of factors – (the access to) financial resources, business skills, contact network – that are not only not accessible to all, but also seem to call into question the conception of work as a human right.

Entrepreneurship on the (super)national agenda

After 'glorious' decades of economic growth, low unemployment and general prosperity, the 1990s brought economic stagnation in Europe not seen since the Second World War. As a result, the EU was forced to devise a new strategy to increase economic growth and job creation. It was in this context that entrepreneurship emerged as a central element of European policy and was therefore strongly associated with the transformations in the dynamics of the economy and employment. While these discourses were becoming dominant, Audretsch et al (2009) argued that societies abandoned a vision of work as a collective activity and began to transform everyone into a company and responsible for themself.

The promotion of entrepreneurial spirit is presented as an attempt to adapt to the principles of profit growth, competition and individual initiative, which postulate the sovereignty of the market. More specifically, it is a central element for the revitalisation of the economic structure, capable of creating a new momentum for the economy (Saraiva, 2011; Campos and Soeiro, 2016). As a paradigm for employment, the logic underlying entrepreneurship is that the risks associated with market instabilities are transferred to the workers themselves.

'Europe needs more entrepreneurs' (European Commission, 2013: 4). This was the statement of the European Commission that came forward with the aim of resuming growth and higher employment levels. Such declaration stems from the scenarios of instability motivated by the social, economic and financial crisis of 2008. This was the premise underlying the Entrepreneurship 2020 Action Plan, presented in Brussels in 2013: 'Entrepreneurship is a powerful driver of economic growth and job creation ... it fosters the development of new skills and capabilities ... it increases the competitiveness and innovativeness of economies' (European Commission, 2013: 4).

Although this attention around entrepreneurship and the concern for (un)employment[1] issues has been mediatised or intensified since 2008, in 1997 the Luxembourg European Council had already introduced the European Employment Strategy (EES). This highlighted what is a common cohesion policy, that is, although the countries had different problems and different employment, protection and health systems, they faced common problems.

The EES was implemented in 1998, supported by four pillars that, in turn, were formulated into a set of guidelines. Entrepreneurship and 'an entrepreneurship spirit' appear in the EES together with employability, adaptability and equal opportunities. The entrepreneurship pillar, placed for the first time at the top of the European agenda, aimed at reducing the costs and administrative burden associated with business, especially for small and medium enterprises (SMEs), looking at all opportunities for job creation, including the social economy and the creation of start-ups. Also included in this pillar was the goal of making the tax system more employment-friendly by seeking to reduce non-wage costs.

The EES went through different stages of development and in the first quarter of 2000 it was integrated in the Lisbon Strategy. A set of 24 new guidelines for growth and jobs was established. Entrepreneurship stood out in the integrated guidelines at number 15 ('Promote a more entrepreneurial culture and create a more favourable environment for SMEs') and number 23 ('Expand and improve investment in human capital'), as it aimed to integrate entrepreneurial competence in education policies (European Council, 2005; Rodrigues, 2009; Varela, 2013). These guidelines served as a basis for each Member State in the configuration of national action programmes (Audretsch et al, 2009). There was indeed an increase in the growth rate of potential GDP in the eurozone and the creation of new jobs, which was around 65 million. However, with the 2008 crisis, these figures were called into question. With GDP falling and unemployment rising, public finances were affected, and debt was forecast to exceed 80 per cent of European GDP in 2011. However, in 2010, at the end of the EES, the Commission's assessments concluded that Europe was a more favourable place for entrepreneurial activity compared to 2000. Furthermore, one third of EU Member States were included in the World Bank's list of the 30 most business-friendly countries (European Commission, 2011). The Lisbon Strategy was followed by the Europe 2020 Strategy, presented by the EU in March 2010, with the aim of invigorating the EU's economy in the decade 2010–20, were it not for its priority commitment to 'smart, sustainable and inclusive growth' (EAPN, 2011).

The case of Portugal

If in 2008 the unemployment rate in Portugal and in the EU was between 7 and 8 per cent, in 2012, during a period marked by the intervention of the Troika (the European Commission, the European Central Bank and the International Monetary Fund), the same rate reached 16.5 per cent in Portugal and 10.4 per cent in the EU28 (PORDATA, 2022). In 2013 the country reached the highest peak ever in its unemployment rate, 17.8 per cent (EUROSTAT, 2013). The same happened with the rate of risk of poverty and social exclusion, which rose from 26 per cent in 2008 to 27.5 per cent in 2014 and 2015; the rate of poverty intensity reached its peak in 2013 with 30.3 per cent opposed to 23.2 and 23.6 per cent in 2007 and 2008, respectively.

Within this time frame, has entrepreneurship effectively gained a stage in the public and political agenda?

Once supported by the government programmes, it was also considered worth examining the 'valorisation' attributed to entrepreneurship as an expression, through the analysis of the frequency with which the word 'entrepreneur' (and all the words that derive from it), appear and with what framework (Table 19.1). We have chosen the constitutional programmes that cover the year 1997, the year in which the EES was launched, up to the current one as at the time of this writing, the XXIII Constitutional

Table 19.1: Frequency of the word 'entrepreneur(ship)' in government programmes

Government programme	Time frame	Political party	Entrepreneur(s)	Entrepreneurship
XIII	1995–99	Socialist Party (PS)	0	0
XIV	1999–2002	PS	3	0
XV	2002–04	Coalition PSD-CDS/PP[a]	2	1
XVI	2004–05	Coalition PSD-CDS/PP	6	2
XVII	2005–09	PS	1	2
XVIII	2009–13	PS	2	12
XIX	2013–15	PSD	0	10
XX	2015	Coalition PSD-CDS/PP	9	21
XXI	2015–19	PS	10	18
XXII	2019–22	PS	5	13
XXIII	2022–	PS	2	14

Note: [a] Alliance by the Social Democratic Party (PPD/PSD) and CDS – People's Party.
Source: Own elaboration, based on Government Programmes XIII–XXIII.

Programme. It is important to highlight that these documents, presented by each of the governments, give an account of a set of concerns and intentions, without necessarily being reflected in measures, strategies and/or policies developed.

Next, we will present some aspects that we think deserve to be highlighted in each of the programmes.[2]

In the XIII Government Programme there is no mention of the entrepreneur. This result can be easily understood within the supranational context since it includes the year in which the EES was launched. In the following government a new approach to entrepreneurship begins, an effect of what are also the European guidelines. An integrated youth policy stands out, aimed at stimulating young entrepreneurs and creatives in the economic, cultural and technological areas. Here is also demonstrated the intention to develop an action that facilitates the appearance of innovators and entrepreneurs, and that materialises the transformation of ideas into economic opportunities.

With the XV Constitutional Government the role of the private entrepreneur is considered primordial and irreplaceable, namely regarding the development of business strategies guided by innovation and by the complementarity between production and distribution strategies.

The XVI Government intended to continue to focus on innovation, training and qualification of the Portuguese, considering them as strategic elements for the affirmation of a modern, dynamic and entrepreneurial Portugal. Another added objective was at the level of 'Science and Training'. The intention was to promote an entrepreneurial spirit in the scientific-academic environment, leading to the strengthening of the connection between both and the needs of companies and society.

The XVII Government, marked by a period of strong economic and financial constraints, framed the entrepreneurial spirit in an articulation between the promotion of quality education and the development of a youth policy. In short, it proposed to support youth entrepreneurship through the gradual introduction of entrepreneurship in the curricular structure of the different levels of education.

As a result of the whole socio-economic context, entrepreneurship emerged with different contours in the XVIII Constitutional Programme. It was developed between 2009 and 2013, a period contiguous to the 2008 crisis, marked by the request for external aid and the consequent climate of austerity. In this context, entrepreneurship emerged in nine dimensions. The 'Modernising Portugal' measure stands out, in which one of the lines indicated by the government for the country's structural modernisation was the boost to entrepreneurship, through initiatives aimed at promoting an attitude of initiative and innovation. Also, for the first time, a specific dimension was dedicated to entrepreneurship, within the scope of the integration of immigrants and the deepening of support mechanisms for female entrepreneurship.

The XIX Programme was guided from the outset by the challenge of change, arising from the difficulties faced by all sectors of Portuguese society. The strengthening of the entrepreneurial spirit is placed side by side with the strengthening of democracy, prosperity and social cohesion.

With the XXI Constitutional Government, the premise of turning the page on austerity was set as a priority. As such, the fight against precariousness and the promotion of employment were an important dimension of this governance proposal. Encouraging entrepreneurial activity is presented in axes related to supporting small businesses, but also the creation of new ones in sectors considered emerging and innovative. The rationale here is to create national networks that promote co-operation and the sharing of resources. Also noteworthy is the promotion of entrepreneurship as (i) a mechanism for social reintegration, increasing the supply of work in prisons; (ii) a way of stimulating forms of organisation such as agricultural cooperatives and creating a mechanism to support the internationalisation of agricultural and regional products; (iii) a strategy to guarantee the conditions for creativity to take place, assuming the commitment to invest in culture.

The XXII Government Programme came into force in 2019 and was planned to be concluded in 2023. It was presented with an optimistic narrative by considering that with the recovery of incomes, the economy, employment and public finances, Portugal would enter a new cycle.

The entrepreneurial activity is referenced with particular focus on the domain of social inclusion, from the implementation of specific programmes to support immigrants, as well as with the presentation of innovation instruments in the labour market for the integration of people with disabilities. In this scenario, Portugal is referenced as a business hub, based on a set of public policies that support this activity, but also the visibility of events such as the Web Summit (a technological event hosted in Lisbon annually).

Under the motto 'Good Governance', the XXIII, current, Government Programme arises from a process of early elections motivated by the resignation of the previous government due to the leadership of the proposed state budget. It introduces concerns associated with the effects of the pandemic on Portuguese families and companies.

It is noted that the programme does not bring an exponential growth in terms of the reference to entrepreneurial activity, as was demonstrated to us in a previous crisis period. The reference to entrepreneurship in the following areas stands out: in the boost to the social and solidarity economy; in the training and empowerment of leaders and workers for innovation and creativity; in the decentralisation strategies and strengthening of investment incentives in low density regions; in the support and encouragement to senior entrepreneurship, with an endogenous base; in business innovation and investment in disruptive technologies, with the start of a new cycle of the National Entrepreneurship Strategy 2022–24.

(Social) entrepreneurship as a strategy for social integration?

As we have analysed, the socio-economic collapse led to an increased attention on entrepreneurship, being considered, in several public speeches – different political decision-makers, media, industry leaders –, a central strategy in the face of the perverse effects of unemployment. But how has this been experienced by people? And what about the social workers who work at the interface between user/institution and citizen/social policies?

Thus, we will focus on how these reconfigurations have been reflected in the trajectories of individuals who have experienced (social) entrepreneurship processes in Portugal. To this end, we take as main reference the study conducted by us within the scope of the PhD in social work (Jesus, 2019), which not only involved in the empirical part participants in (social) entrepreneurship processes, but also social workers linked to academia and involved in social interventions.

Regarding the first category of research participants, we found that access to entrepreneurial activity is more effective the more educated the subjects are. Regarding the motivation to attend training, the acquisition of new knowledge, personal development and integration into the labour market stand out. However, this motivation is determined by the labour market situation – if for short- or long-term unemployed people, the entrepreneurial activity seems to be a possible way to reverse this situation, for employed participants, regardless of their employment relationship, it is the personal development and the acquisition of new knowledge that stand out. This data can be crossed with what Campos and Soeiro (2016) present about entrepreneurship as a way out of the unemployment crisis, but a way out that emphasises neoliberal logics, with a rhetoric based on freedom and individual autonomy, making each person feel solely responsible for their situation.

The subjects also recognised post-training challenges related to operationalisation and the need for financial investment; it was confirmed that attending training is often associated with the payment of an enrolment fee, so that most participants in this specific training modality had a university degree, were integrated in the labour market and, when unemployed, were not in long-term unemployment situations.

As for the relationship between social work and entrepreneurship processes, we saw, on the academics' side, entrepreneurship being conceptualised as a postmodern rhetoric, which emphasises the individual and their competencies, but also individual trajectories in response to social needs. Here, we intersect with some of the social work–(social) entrepreneurship divergences suggested by Bent-Goodley (2002). The first refers to the focus of entrepreneurship on business/profit, which in fact clashes with the core values of social work. On the other hand, it places social entrepreneurship as a form of undertaking that is not focused on profit, but rather on new ways of identifying and applying resources. A second divergence has to do with the conceptual understanding of entrepreneurship, since for Bent-Goodley a narrow definition of entrepreneurship could aggregate social entrepreneurship into the 'hat' of private for-profit organisations. In this logic, they would be considered a minority of professionals since the 'dominant' professional sectors are the public and private non-profit sectors.

From the perspective of social interveners, entrepreneurship is associated with a process of restructuring and adaptation to reality, without necessarily producing profit. The potential and limits of the social work–(social) entrepreneurship relationship are highlighted: while on the one hand there is a sense of complementarity through the orientation towards solving problems neglected by society, through the capacity to manage resources and attention to the sustainability of the intervention and through the potential for innovation, on the other hand there are some limits to this relationship, namely the profit orientation of 'pure' entrepreneurship, which can lead to a vision of a commercialised profession.

Reflection

From our analysis of the macro-social perspective, the data show the path taken by the EU to respond to the challenges of (un)employment and the maintenance of the social welfare state, namely in a conciliation between economic competitiveness and social cohesion.

In Portugal we see that the frequency of the term 'entrepreneur' or 'entrepreneurship' is increasing, which in practice translates into a greater appreciation of this type of activity, but also in a plurality of fields, sectors and applications. There is an abrupt rise, especially when we look at the XVII and XVIII Constitutional Governments, resulting from the whole conjunctural framework experienced. Transversally, we then see that entrepreneurship figures in the official government discourses, without being restricted to a particular ideology or party-political orientation.

Therefore, we ask ourselves, is this emphasis on entrepreneurship the result of a change of socio-economic paradigm, guided by a (new) view on the economy or by ideals of collaboration and creativity? Or, is it an approach seen as a solution, with the primacy of combining the logics of individuation and disengagement of the state?

The concept of entrepreneurship acquires importance as a 'spirit' that associates innovation and risk. At the same time, it seems to place the responsibility for their fragile situation and its resolution on the individuals; it is also here that work seems to be no longer seen as a social right and entrepreneurship is apparently presented as a strategy accessible to all of us, as a panacea for the 'evil' of unemployment and labour precariousness.

However, when we talk about social entrepreneurship we expect an obliteration of individualistic logics, which responds to the gaps left by the state and the market. It reinforces the importance and urgency to innovate, as a 'privileged' way to respond to social needs. As such, the research shows that social entrepreneurship is configured as a new strategy or intervention of social workers with socially more vulnerable groups, promoting logics of empowerment and capacity-building, insofar as it promotes the acquisition and/or development of essential competences for their social (re)integration, especially when this is based on workfare logics. Such an explanation is in line with the proposal of the European Commission (2006, 2018) when it points to entrepreneurship as one of the key competences for lifelong learning: 'Entrepreneurship competence has become a priority in policy agendas of modern economies … investing in entrepreneurship education is one of the highest return investments Europe can make' (European Commission, 2018: 57, 58).

Innovation is the specific tool of entrepreneurs (Drucker, 1985). So, if we want to innovate in social work, its relationship with social entrepreneurship must be effective, not only because of the potential that the social economy and the third sector represent for the profession, but in the private sector, for example in the field of corporate social responsibility.

As Bent-Goodley (2002) points out, with the technological advance and the introduction of new lifestyles, social work is challenged to (re)allocate resources, allowing them 'universal' access. We recall that all people have the right to work, to freely choose what it should be and to favourable conditions to perform it (Art. 23, Universal Declaration of Human Rights[3]). Then, as agents committed to the defence of human rights, it should be our role to stand, above all, 'small entrepreneurs', who face challenges in accessing resources and capital. This could be by reactivating services in the community or by mentoring on project planning. This work can also be transposed to a more macro level, in the advocacy for public policies promoting more equitable business and work environments.

Hence, we suggest a reopening of paths that have already been walked by a centenary profession and it is urgent to understand and analyse them in the light of what is contemporary. In this sense, it is worth recalling the legacies of: (1) Mary Richmond, who with her work in the Charity Organisation Society and with her call for attention to the deficient coordination between services and users established the basis for what today is called case management (Santos and Nunes, 2013), but also for a political practice of the social worker, thus establishing the conception of the case manager far from the one examined today – guided by metrics and quantitative indicators of evaluation; (2) Jane Addams, who showed us early on the entrepreneurial sense of the profession by creating a new sustained social response and by making a commitment to political practice giving meaning to the ethos of the profession; and (3) Mary Parker Follett who introduced us to theories for the administration, management and organisation of services, which are today referenced by other social sciences and apparently somewhat neglected by social work.

Conclusion

This chapter analysed the emergence and acknowledgement that has been given to entrepreneurial activity in the EU and, particularly, in Portugal.

Based on the Portuguese case, it allowed us to verify, similarly to what the literature suggests, that entrepreneurship gains stand in a context of neoliberal policies, focused, in the first instance, on the production of a 'healthy economy' regardless of which political party is governing – more left or more centre.

This macro landscape brings aspects which we consider to be an important frame of reference for social work, namely under the influence of neoliberal social policies, which expect citizens to play a 'proactive role' in changing their situation of vulnerability or fragility.

Social work is not immune to these influences and faces challenges that also relate to social workers' employability. In other words, associated to the profound mutations of the liberal market, marred by scenarios of instability and greater difficulty of insertion, social workers are increasingly faced with the need to face the possibilities of professional exercise through the free market or the third sector.

But these challenges do not stop here. As Tan (2004: 87) states: 'in a rapidly changing world, social entrepreneurs innovate and create social value. Social workers today need to redefine their roles to include that of the social entrepreneurs'. As such, we must not fail to be critical of this focus on the individual, on competitiveness and on market forces, which are natural to a neoliberal vision. We therefore advocate an engagement of social work with policy makers, community organisations and other stakeholders, which supports entrepreneurship both as a means of economic development and as a means of social justice. It seems to us that a more community-oriented approach is needed to respond to structural problems.

Moreover, at a time when the idea of self-employment or freelancing work is romanticised, we find ourselves re-entering a deep crisis of uncertainty – the wake of a pandemic, the existence of a war in Europe or even the rise of far-right forces.

As social work develops within the spectrum of political orientations and contextual forces, it seems to us, then, that it is time for social work to step up again and reinforce in more macro-oriented paths and defend the notion of work as a human right, dignified and protected.

Notes
[1] Batista and Thurik (2007) relate unemployment with entrepreneurship: unemployment leads to increase in entrepreneurial activity (refugee effect), and, on the other hand, entrepreneurship decreases unemployment (entrepreneurial effect).
[2] Programmes of the consequent Constitutional Governments of Portugal: https://www.parlamento.pt/sites/EN and https://www.portugal.gov.pt/en/gc23
[3] https://www.un.org/en/about-us/universal-declaration-of-human-rights

References
Amaro, M.I. (2009) *Urgências e Emergências do Serviço Social Contemporâneo: Contributos para a discussão dos fundamentos da profissão (Tese de Doutoramento)*. Lisboa: Universidade Católica Portuguesa.

Amaro, M.I. (2015) *Urgências e Emergências do Serviço Social: Fundamentos da profissão na contemporaneidade*, 2nd edn, Lisbon: Universidade Católica Editora.

Audretsch, D.B., Lehmann, E.E. and Plummer, L.A. (2009) Agency and governance in strategic entrepreneurship, *Entrepreneurship Theory and Practice*, 33(1): 149–66.

Batista, R. and Thurik, R. (2007) The relationship between entrepreneurship and unemployment: is Portugal an outlier? *Technological Forecasting & Social Change*, 74(1): 75–79. doi: 10.1016/j.techfore.2006.04.003.

Bent-Goodley, T.B. (2002) Defining and conceptualising social work entrepreneurship, *Journal of Social Work Education*, 38(2): 291–302.

Branco, F. and Amaro, I. (2011) As práticas do 'Serviço Social activo' no âmbito das novas tendências da política social: uma perspetiva portuguesa, *Serviço Social & Sociedade*, 108: 656–79.

Campos, A. and Soeiro, J. (2016) *A Falácia do Empreendedorismo*, Lisbon: Bertrand Editora.

Drucker, P.F. (1985) *Innovation and Entrepreneurship: Practice and Principles*, New York: Harper Business.

EAPN Rede Europeia Anti-Pobreza – Observatório de luta contra a pobreza na cidade de Lisboa (2011) Estratégia Local Integrada Combate à pobreza Lisboa: Roteiro. Lisboa: EAPN.

European Commission (2011) Industrial policy: reinforcing competitiveness. Communication from the Commission to the Council, the European Parliament, the European Economic and Social Committee and the Committee of the Regions. COM (2011) 642 final, 14 October 2011. Retrieved from https://eur-lex.europa.eu/legal-content/EN/TXT/PDF/?uri=CELEX:52011DC0642&from=EN

European Commission (2013) *Entrepreneurship 2020 Action Plan. Reigniting the entrepreneurial spirit in Europe*, Brussels: European Commission. LexUriServ.do (europa.eu).

European Commission (2018) *Proposal for a Council Recommendation on Key Competences for Lifelong Learning*, Brussels: European Commission, https://www.eumonitor.nl/9353000/1/j4nvgs5kjg27kof_j9vvik7m1c3gyxp/vkl58h3b78m1/f=/5464_18.pdf.

European Council (2005) Lisbon Strategy, 1–11. Retrieved from http://www.eurocid.pt/pls/wsd/wsdwcot0.detalhe?p_cot_id=1079&p_est_id=5266.

European Parliament and Council (2006) Recommendation of the European Parliament and of the Council of 18 December 2006 on key competences for lifelong learning. *Official Journal of the European Union* (2006/962/EC).

EUROSTAT (2013) Estatísticas Taxa de Desemprego 2013. Luxembourg: Publications Office of the European Union, https://www.gee.gov.pt/pt/en/daily-indicators/list-gee-daily-indicators/4555-eurostat-taxa-de-desemprego

Global Entrepreneurship Monitor (2012) *Global Entrepreneurship Monitor: 2012 Global Report*, Babson Park, MA: Babson College, https://www.gemconsortium.org/report.

Jesus, A. (2019) *Inovação em Serviço Social: Potencialidades e limites do empreendedorismo (social) como estratégia de integração social*, doctoral thesis, Lisbon: ISCTE-IUL.

PORDATA (2022) *Estatísticas sobre Taxa de Desemprego: total e por grupo etário*, Paris: PORDATA. Retrieved from https://www.pordata.pt/Portugal/Taxa+de+desemprego+total+e+por+grupo+et%C3%A1rio+(percentagem)-553

Rodrigues, M.J. (2009) *Europe, Globalization and the Lisbon Agenda*, Cheltenham: Edward Elgar.

Santos, C.C. and Nunes, V.C. (2013) Desafios da gestão social no serviço social, in C.C. Santos, C.P. Albuquerque and H.N. Almeida (eds) *Serviço Social: Mutações e Desafios*, Coimbra: Universidade de Coimbra, pp 87–102.

Saraiva, P.M. (2011) *Empreendedorismo: Do conceito à aplicação, da ideia ao negócio, da tecnologia ao valor*, 2nd edn, Coimbra: Universidade de Coimbra.

Tan, N.T. (2004) Social entrepreneurship: challenge for social work in a changing world, *Asia Pacific Journal of Social Work and Development*, 14(2): 87–98.

Varela, N. (2013) O empreendedorismo na União Europeia: da estratégia de Lisboa à economia do empreendedorismo (Dissertação de mestrado em Políticas de Desenvolvimento dos Recursos Humanos). Lisbon: ISCTE-IUL. Retrieved from https://repositorio.iscte-iul.pt/handle/10071/7626.

20

Unlimited incubators for belonging, cohesion and impact: nurturing 'what is already there'

Sarah Prosser, Ole Pedersen and Rosa Engebrigtsen Bye

Introduction

Community incubators are spaces for social innovation through both the interpersonal processes that occur within them and from the individual and collective outcomes that result. The results of research presented in this chapter show how these spaces could be a natural home for social work – combining the topics of this book in a natural, effective and innovative manner. We present evidence that incubators, if designed well, can support individuals and communities to achieve a stronger sense of belonging, greater cohesion and increased inclusion. In addition, they can catalyse innovative solutions to local, national and global challenges. The field of social work can be broadened to include these kinds of community incubators and the direct and indirect impact they bring.

The specific approach to social innovation, social work and community development presented in this chapter is the 'Unlimited incubator model' and can be referred more generically as one kind of 'community incubator model'. The Unlimited model has grown, matured and been replicated four times in Norway since 2016 when the first incubator (Tøyen Unlimited) started to emerge in an unused room in a municipal building in the Tøyen neighbourhood of Oslo. Norway Unlimited was established in 2022 as a linking network organisation, functioning as a learning platform between incubators and as a driver for systems change and transformation (see Chapter 2) to bring about stable supportive cultures and structures for this way of working.

Tøyen Unlimited was established by the first author in the spirit of asset-based community development, social enterprise support structures (such as UnLtd in the UK) and co-working hubs (such as the global network of Impact Hubs). The approach took inspiration from Umberto Crenca's question:[1] 'What if we considered that the talent and creativity we need to create [and maintain] a vibrant place already exists locally, it just needs the conditions to grow and be nurtured?'

In the context of this chapter, we explore how a community incubator such as Tøyen Unlimited can contribute with respect to nurturing such a place. In particular, we examine what activities and approach the incubator should prioritise and what professional skills are required to deliver impact based on Crenca's premise. We consider how to identify indicators of change that document the relationship between the incubator, its participants and the conditions from which a vibrant place where people thrive can emerge. Throughout we consider how this approach relates to social innovation and social work.

We first describe the principles and structure of the Unlimited incubator model. We then further examine the model based on (1) structured research (Engebrigtsen Bye, 2022), (2) insights from a participant (Pedersen, co-author of this chapter) and (3) external evaluation. After that, we give some reflections, specifically regarding the relevance for the future of social work, community development and social innovation. We end with conclusions regarding the type of innovation delivered through the case of the Unlimited incubator, and some recommendations for those who want to use the approach to combine social work and social innovation.

The case of the Unlimited incubator

The Unlimited incubator can be most simply described as a physical space to nurture what is already there. It consists of support services where local residents can develop ideas into social economy enterprises that improve the quality of life in the neighbourhood and beyond. It is a place where people are seen, believed, listened to and recognised for their insights and abilities to find solutions that benefit others, usually through lived-experienced, proximate, leadership. The incubator aims to provide a supportive pathway to participatory and democratically inclusive processes that both start and finish with local residents themselves owning and leading change.

The first Unlimited incubator in Norway grew from idea to reality in the Tøyen area of east Oslo. This has since been joined by three more: Storhaug Unlimited in Stavanger, and Søndre Unlimited and Romsås Unlimited in south and north Oslo respectively. These four incubators, and future additions, are organised into a networked learning collective supported by a registered association called Norway Unlimited.

The Norwegian Unlimited incubator model was inspired in part by UnLtd in the UK – a national programme for social entrepreneurs running since 2000, underpinned by major capital investment from leftover millennial funds. The Norwegian model lacks any such national funding, its origin depending upon the intrapreneurial (innovation initiated while working within a larger sector or organisation) aspect of setting up a proto-incubator in an empty room of a municipal building and looking for new forms of partnerships outside of the sector for project-based funding. The Norwegian model also varies from UK UnLtd by introducing the terminology 'Unlimiter' for members of the incubator.

Two comprehensive booklets have been written describing the Unlimited incubator model: 'How to Start a Community Incubator' in your area and 'How to Support Unlimiters'; both publications are available for free download but are currently only available in Norwegian (Prosser and Pedersen, 2019; Prosser, 2022).

Founding principles

Anyone contacting an Unlimited incubator will find the following common foundational principles governing how it is run (Prosser and Pedersen, 2019):

- The focus is on the person, not the idea. In contrast to many pitch- and profit-driven innovation and start-up spaces, the business idea is not central to leading to further engagement. The person can change their idea partly or completely after exploring it in the early stages. Closeness to the social challenge and (an often quiet) passion to make change alone and as a collective are typical factors in becoming an Unlimiter (being granted membership and support services through the incubator).
- There is a collective place-based approach. The person and the social impact must have a previous connection to the local neighbourhood. Unlimited is not there to help external social entrepreneurs bring their innovations to a new community. Additionally, being open to work with social innovators from the same neighbourhood is key. The aim is to lock in value (social, financial and human capital) that already exists in the area – it just needs to be nurtured and brought to the surface. Peer-peer support and a collective impact ethos among local residents is central.
- The social purpose always comes first. The main mission of the enterprise must be to deliver social or environmental impact. This is expressed in the way the idea is developed into a social enterprise, and through an asset-lock (profits cannot be taken out by owners or small groups of shareholders) legal form – or as close as one can come to that in the available options for entity registration in Norway.
- Cooperation with and closeness to the public sector. The Unlimited incubators were all established with a degree of self-autonomy but close formal connection to the public sector. This provides a valuable contact interface between incubator staff, Unlimiters and the strong welfare service providers in Norway – a relationship that would otherwise be hard for early-stage entrepreneurs to develop. Each incubator-public sector collaboration model is different according to local context and opportunity.

The 'How to Support Unlimiters' booklet (Prosser, 2022) is divided into two sections (1) the human aspect and (2) how to start and run a social enterprise – combined the sections span aspects more usually associated with social and community work, and aspects more recognisable in innovation contexts. Selected examples (five from a total of over 40 topics in the handbook) of what is included in each section are as follows:

1. Human aspect tools ('being valued')
   - Mattering: mattering as a concept (Prilleltensky, 2019) combines the importance of being valued and giving value. In the incubator being valued is implemented by the support roles actively seeing and believing in every Unlimiter, irrespective of what idea they might bring.
   - Strength-based and capability approaches: the incubator staff are encouraged to use techniques such as appreciative enquiry and strength-based cards (as used by Ung Invest, Ness, 2021) to explicitly discover and describe the unique perspective and insights of the Unlimiters, with the aim of proving these strengths are the agency to positive and appropriate change.
   - Power: a deep awareness of power and equity, where it is and how it expresses itself, and open discussions about these, can be used to give confidence to the Unlimiters and clarity about how to deal with what can all too often be met as barriers to the success of their social enterprises.
2. Social enterprise tools ('giving value')
   - Planning for and documenting social impact: the Unlimited incubators have developed an online tool called Vis det! [Show it!] (Marano, 2023) to guide Unlimiters along a user-friendly route to defining the change they want to make, identifying how they will know they are getting there, and knowing how to communicate the results.
   - Collective impact partnerships and alliances: a major element in the incubator is the mutual support from peers, as well as working alongside other community groups in the neighbourhood. The collective impact principles of Kania and Kramer (2011) are applied, with the goal of building collective agency by all incubator members. Weekly and monthly meetings are deliberately designed with equity in mind.

Research, insights and evaluation

The questions posed at the start of this chapter ask what kind of support works when it comes to supporting thriving communities for all, and where relevant indicators for related outcomes may be found. Three approaches are presented: a research case by Engebrigtsen Bye (2022), an insight piece by author Pedersen and an evaluation case by Rogaland Revisjon (2021). These are then comparatively analysed in the subsequent section.

Insights from research

Research undertaken by Engebrigtsen Bye (2022) sought to examine if support for community-based social entrepreneurship contributes to wider outcomes of social inclusion, particularly in areas such as Tøyen, Storhaug and Søndre Nordstrand, all of which are characterised by complex socio-economic challenges, diverse populations and underinvestment in physical and social infrastructure. The research focused on the Unlimited model and the experience of the Unlimiters as its central case. Engebrigtsen Bye's research methodology of semi-structured interviews was designed to enable the Unlimiters to have the room to fully understand and share their subjective experiences and to express self-perceived views, this as opposed to a methodology based around measuring social inclusion based on questionnaires with quantitative pre-determined indicators.

Six interviews were conducted with Unlimiters from diverse backgrounds, two from each of the three Unlimited incubators (full transcriptions and analysis in Engebrigtsen Bye, 2022). The resulting material was originally analysed along the axes of the five aspects of social inclusion of Saarinen (2019) and Olesen (2019): belonging, influence, participation, access and relations/support. The results showed a positive correlation on all five fronts. For the current chapter we re-examine the responses to additionally look for insights and outcomes directly relating to social work and social innovation. These can subsequently be used to answer what works to nurture local assets to create local social impact.

Indicators of outcomes typically associated with social work and community development include factors such as improved individual and collective quality of life and well-being, greater participation and more awareness of rights-based services and opportunities.

Improved mental health, often relating to self-worth, self-confidence and belief in one's own abilities is a key indicator of quality and life well-being, and often rooted in degree of social capital. The interviewees clearly described how much they recognise the incubator as important in this type of dimension:

> 'It was a place where someone believed in us and our idea, and wanted to help us succeed. That made me even more confident in our idea. Personally, receiving support and guidance has been really important for me to sort out the mental part, it's been of great value.'

> 'The first time I met my supporter [employee who supports the Unlimiters], it was like paradise. When they told me about the support and help I would receive from Unlimited, I was in shock, I couldn't believe that this existed! And they have helped me so much, they have pushed me, made me believe in my own abilities and skills. And I have learned so much, to pitch my idea, I've learned words and expressions in

the system [public system and innovation/startup] and my Norwegian language skills have improved.'

'At Unlimited, there is no discrimination, we are all equal, everyone is welcome, and taken care of. No matter where you come from, what the colour of your skin is, what's your religion, everyone is welcome and treated as equals. And everyone is nice and inclusive. They [Unlimited incubator] have created a space where we can all meet, exchange experiences, work together and expand our network.'

Being able to participate in meaningful leisure activities and find opportunities for participation in work-related arenas, and thereby develop a sense of being a valued part of local community and wider society, was expressed by the interviewees in two distinct ways. One related to the impact on themselves as social innovators, the other for the target groups they have established social enterprises to make a difference for, for example:

'To me, social inclusion is about the opportunity to participate in society, in those arenas that you wish to participate in. And that those arenas are available to you, that you feel welcomed. Many of them [immigrants] want to participate, but they do not feel like they can. The work that we do is very much about removing some of the barriers, so that they [immigrants] can participate on equal footing with others, regardless of their background.'

A social worker may be tasked to find ways for vulnerable and excluded people to access education, employment and housing. These objectives can be very similar to the missions of the social enterprises run by the Unlimiters. The next quotation makes it clear that their lived experience, combined with the support and skills they gain at the incubator, can be an effective way of reaching shared goals of social worker and social entrepreneur:

'I have been able to create my own place of work, but I have also been able to give jobs to many who have been unemployed for many years, and who never thought they would be able to get back to work. Giving jobs to individuals who really need it is important to me, that they are able to see that the experiences they have can be of value to others, to see them blossom when they get to work, that has been really rewarding for me personally.'

Data from the research revealed indicators of social innovation as a process, for example through being included in processes citizens have access to and can be engaged in new forms of partnership, governance, relationships and support.

"Through Unlimited I have got to know so many people, and expanded my network. Many of us [Unlimiters] have also developed relations outside of work, and we cooperate a lot. We offer support and guidance to each other."

Insights from a case example

Nedenfra [From Below] is a social enterprise that was established at Tøyen Unlimited incubator by author Pedersen. Its mission is to explore and create opportunities for democratic and direct participation in urban development. One of several outcomes of this work has been the creation of a local and social housing construction cooperative, Tøyen boligbyggelag (TBBL). TBBL is established as a formal housing construction cooperative with a cross-disciplinary project group working to include local residents in construction of housing and influencing housing policy and decision-making.

The insights from this case are not the result of an external researcher determining what questions might uncover new knowledge, but rather about topics self-selected by an Unlimiter as important regarding the role the Unlimited incubators can play, and reveal topics relating to the wider Norwegian context of social and community work and of innovation not expressed in the other cases.

Pedersen reflects that community work as a whole has not been recognised in the Norwegian welfare system since the 1980s and believes there is a serious lack of recognition and understanding of the approach taken by community-led initiatives such as TBBL and Nedenfra. This expresses itself in practice through a lack of opportunity in procurement processes which tend to ask for user participation on lower levels of the ladder of participation (Arnstein, 1969), rather than co-creation, partnership, distribution of power or citizen control. Pedersen states that: "Tøyen Unlimited is a rare contribution in the Norwegian context in that it bridges the innovation and start-up scenes with social work and welfare systems, bringing citizens up the ladder of participation".

A consequence of this contextual factor is that Nedenfra has had to shift its financing strategy, originally focused on business and procurement opportunities, towards identifying opportunities to work in ways that are relevant for public sector grants. A knock-on effect of this strategic shift, while still exploring social business opportunities, has been that it opened up for working with symptoms innovation (Chapter 2, addressing visible experiential issues) but also for targeting systems change at deeper root-cause levels.

The systems innovation work undertaken by Nedenfra has had tangible outcomes in an increase in the degree of awareness among politicians and the general public for the potential of new housing solutions in the 'third sector' (Prosser, 2020), and in particular how to increase bottom-up agency to co-create these solutions. The incubator could therefore be seen as supporting entrepreneurship for systems change as well as the more common social enterprises working at symptoms level.

Social change takes time, and TBBL is an example of how, by establishing a new housing cooperative, residents can gradually become involved in the development of housing that is suitable for the local needs of their neighbourhood rather than the general housing market as a whole. It awaits to be seen how the municipality and state choose to support TBBL beyond offering encouraging words. The long-term success will be measured when TBBL is empowered through partnership to engage in concrete housing projects in the Tøyen neighbourhood and beyond. Meanwhile, the increased level of access for residents to engage in developing appropriate local housing solutions, while also contributing to systemic shifts in national housing policy and awareness of alternative solutions, can be considered social innovation in process, if not yet in outcome.

Insights from evaluations

Two formal evaluations were commissioned from external consultancy companies on behalf of the municipalities associated with Storhaug and Tøyen Unlimited (Agenda Kaupang, 2021; Rogaland Revisjon, 2021). These provide a third form of insight and knowledge relevant to the topic of this chapter.

The resulting reports highlighted the high number of people (over 100 Unlimiters have been supported to date) and the broad spectrum of social issues they address. Both evaluations concluded that the incubators brought a positive impact to the neighbourhoods (and that their localities in disadvantaged areas were important) and that the municipalities could save money long term on welfare services by supporting them. They highlighted the Unlimited incubators' unique ability to mobilise under-represented groups to engage in social entrepreneurship (in particular women with an immigrant background), giving new role models, opening new networks and building trust. Their evaluations also included feedback from the Unlimiters who had reported that the incubators had been extremely important to them and had led to increases in local employment, inclusion, increased participation and heightened levels of security.

The form of the two evaluations was more structured through the use of questionnaires than the other approaches in this chapter. This meant less room for the Unlimiters to provide additional information in their own words about what they perceived to be of importance. This may mean that some of the goals of the incubator were under-evaluated – for example in building self-confidence or generating collaboration effects that in turn to increased social cohesion.

Reflections

The topic of this chapter was to describe the model of the Unlimited incubator and to consider if a place-based community incubator can provide the necessary conditions to nurture what is already present in the community in such a way that this contributes to enabling everyone to thrive and experience increased well-being, and what the indicators of change in this direction might look like. The collective findings already presented provide a positive answer to this question. We summarise some findings and share some reflections.

The overwhelmingly positive responses from Unlimiters interviewed through the research, insights and evaluation suggest the incubator activities have made fundamental positive contributions to themselves, those they aim to serve through their social enterprises and potentially the wider community. We believe this is due to the fact the Unlimited model was designed to go further than superficial nods to equity and inclusion, and make these a core priority to embed what these mean in practice. Over 40 individual potential activities and approaches applied in the incubators have been described in the 'Unlimited Supporter Handbook' (Prosser, 2022), summarised as a balance between human-directed methods and building social enterprise competencies.

The skills required in incubator employees with 'supporter' roles must be those that can address individual and groups on both human and enterprise aspects (Prosser, 2022). Start-up accelerator and incubator environments often prioritise business skills when recruiting staff. The Unlimited model is also dependent on skills more associated with social workers – something that is reflected in the social outcomes being generated by the incubator – in addition to entrepreneurial competencies.

Data from the research, presented earlier, indicate the value of the Unlimited incubator. Unlimiters reported that the incubator had supported them to make tangible positive change, and also led to increased personal self-worth and well-being, in addition to acquiring new skills. The insights from the case example of Nedenfra unveiled that when a participant is given room to self-select how to describe the importance of the incubator to them, a new narrative appeared about support that had led to a change of mission toward more systemic forms of innovation. The structured evaluations gathered important quantitative data and gave the municipalities formalised indicators of the positive impact Unlimited incubators contribute with, though they may have failed to capture aspects from the first two (the research and evaluation cases) methodologies.

On an individual level, an Unlimited style of incubator demonstrably leads to increased levels of well-being, quality of life, mental health and access to jobs. This is true both for the participating early-stage social entrepreneurs (the Unlimiters) and the individuals they reach through their social enterprises working at a symptom level of innovation (see Chapter 2).

On a collective level, the Unlimiters as a group achieve greater amounts of social impact than they would do working alone. This is the result of developing new networks and increased collaboration and peer support inside and outside of the incubator setting.

On a societal level, systemic innovation (see Chapter 2) was highlighted as an outcome for individual Unlimiters. Norway Unlimited, representing all of the incubators and their members, is also changing understanding in municipalities and beyond regarding the benefits for the welfare system in Norway if more community incubators are supported.

Recommendations

The overwhelming positiveness expressed by those involved, and by those researching and evaluating Unlimited incubators, suggests strong recommendations should be made to increase the presence of such spaces across Norway, and beyond, on a global level. Different strategies for different depths of intervention are recommended, corresponding with the symptoms, systems and transformation innovation presented in Chapter 2.

Recommendations for symptoms level of innovation in neighbourhoods

Addressing the visible problems experienced by residents in a community is the motivation for social entrepreneurs. Lived experience is key to the passion and knowledge behind the services and products they offer through social enterprises. Innovation to address these will take many forms depending on the target group and the entrepreneur. If impact is to be significant, we recommend that in creating and replicating neighbourhood incubators:

- all core principles of the Unlimited model should be adhered to (person-focused, place-based, social purpose first and partnership with public sector);
- the balance of investing in the human aspect as well as social enterprises is respected. In other words, 'mattering' (being valued and being able to add value) matters;
- employ social workers with social innovation mindsets, and/or skilled innovation and entrepreneurial trainers with social work mindsets as support-staff in local place-based community incubators; and
- interested parties should take advantage of the existing knowledge and experience, and take learnings from other incubators through Norway Unlimited. And if in Norway, join the collective.

Recommendations for systemic and transformational innovation

Systems change is urgently needed to enable the Unlimiter incubator model to become the norm in every municipality, within reach of every citizen. To achieve this there must also be an increase in awareness of the importance of the localised social and solidarity economy in general, and how it can be implemented through activities such as the incubator in particular.

To prepare for, and make it possible to establish, incubators in every neighbourhood we recommend investing in education of future and current professionals:

- Social work and community development students should be educated on the potential role of the community incubator to act as a powerful catalyst for social outcomes, both for incubator participants and the target groups they work to reach. This aspect of higher education has been part of bachelor and master's programmes at VID Specialised University, Oslo since 2018, but it would do great good to deliver compulsory modules on social innovation and community work for all students and all staff levels to make universities more relevant to our contemporary problems and sufferings.
- Capacity-building courses should be held for public sector employees to increase their absorptive capacity to invest in, and develop policy for, social innovation and community work initiatives such as the Unlimited incubator. This includes showing that current common methods of service design are often working at a symptoms level only, such as improving user journeys, without addressing root and systemic causes behind the problems experienced in society today.

The Unlimited incubators depend on a working context that understands the potential of social enterprise, the social and solidarity economy, social capital (including bonding and bridging) and community ownership (Sacchetti and Campbell, 2014). The importance of these topics together as an important value-creating sector is gradually becoming more visible in Europe and globally. In Norway such thinking is lagging behind, partly due to the dominant systems of profit-driven businesses, top-down public services and a highly organised charity sector. The following description summarises why we should be paying more attention to a new context for local incubators:

> In SSE [the social and solidarity economy], ordinary people play an active role in shaping all of the dimensions of human life: economic, social, cultural, political, and environmental ... SSE is not only about the poor, but strives to overcome inequalities, which includes all classes of society. SSE has the ability to take the best practices that exist in our present system (such as efficiency, use of technology and knowledge)

and transform them to serve the welfare of the community based on different values and goals. (RIPESS, 2015: 2)

A transformation strategy for innovating around a third horizon (Chapter 2) that lifts social and solidarity initiatives to a dominant position in society should be part of supporting neighbourhoods for change. This should be done by recognising and investing in local system-changing social entrepreneurs as well as organisations representing them. National and municipal governments as well as funders should embrace this thinking.

Conclusion

We started this chapter by asking if we had evidence of what role an incubator that supports local residents can have in contributing to thriving communities and creating vibrant places. Through combining research, insights and evaluation, we have documented positive indicators that suggest Unlimited-style incubators can indeed play a central role in such a context. We can surmise that these spaces support individuals and communities to achieve a stronger sense of belonging, greater cohesion and increased inclusion, rooted in strategic facilitation for equity and participation.

The core principles behind running relevant and impactful incubators combine many well-known aspects of social work (which can be related to feeling valued) with flexible use of tools and tips for establishing social enterprises (which can be related to giving value back). These incubators work best in a context of public sector collaboration, and when they are co-financed for stability and firmly located within the neighbourhoods they strive to create well-being in. If this approach is fully embraced, positive change and well-being will flourish in the community. The signs indicating this will be found through open and structured methodologies that when combined unveil the ultimate indicators: the voices of the people themselves.

Social work, community work and social innovation are intertwined in Unlimited incubators. It is this that gives them a unique position that could, with careful replication, have major impact on the long-term future well-being of individuals, the communities they are embedded within and multiplied and interconnected on a national and even global scale.

Note
[1] Cited from: https://norgeunlimited.no/nabolagsinkubatorer/

References
Agenda Kaupang (2021) *Evaluering av Tøyen Unlimited og partnerskap med Bydel Gamle Oslo*, Report number R1021510, https://www.oslo.kommune.no/getfile.php/13449081-1651494125/.

Arnstein, S. (1969) A ladder of community participation, *Journal of the American Institute of Planners*, 35(4): 216–24.

Engebrigtsen Bye, R. (2022) Community based social entrepreneurship contribute to social inclusion: a case study exploring the Unlimited model and the experience of the Unlimiters, Internal Publication, Rosa International.

Kania, J. and Kramer, M. (2011) Collective impact, *Stanford Social Innovation Review*, 9(1), https://doi.org/10.48558/5900-KN19.

Marano, L. (2023) Guide on Impact Measurement for the NGO Sector, Oslo: Fundraising Norge, https://fundraisingnorge.no/content/uploads/2023/02/Guide-on-Impact-Measurement-for-the-NGO-sector_Eng.pdf.

Olesen, E. (2019) NABO – Unges opplevelse av sosial inkludering i Norge, TemaNord, 2019:545, Copenhagen: Nordisk Ministerråd, http://norden.diva-portal.org/smash/record.jsf?pid=diva2%3A1351893&dswid=-2013.

Prilleltensky, I. (2019) Mattering at the intersection of psychology, philosophy, and politics, *American Journal of Community Psychology*, 65(1/2): 16–34.

Prosser, S.D. (2020) Den tredje boligsektor: Hva det kan bli, og hvorfor vi trenger det. *A third housing sector in Norway: what it could be and why it is needed.* Tidsskrift for boligforskning, 3(3): 180–92.

Prosser, S.D. (2022) *Håndbok for støttespillere i Norge Unlimited, Kunnskaps- og erfaringsbaserte tips til hvordan man kan støtte lokale ildsjeler gjennom å satse på felleskap og ideelt sosialt entreprenørskap*, Oslo: Norge Unlimited, https://norgeunlimited.no/wp-content/uploads/2022/11/Ha%CC%8Andbok-for-stottespillere.pdf.

Prosser, S. and Pedersen, O. (2019) *Håndbok for Norge Unlimited: Hvordan å starte nabolagsinkubator for sosialt entreprenørskap*, Oslo: Norge Unlimited.

RIPESS (2015) *Global Vision for a Social Solidarity Economy: Convergences and Differences in Concepts, Definitions and Frameworks*, RIPESS, https://www.ripess.org/wp-content/uploads/2017/08/RIPESS_Vision-Global_EN.pdf.

Rogaland Revisjon (2021) *Evaluering av Storhaug Unlimited, Stavanger kommune 2021*, [online] Available at: www.rogaland-revisjon.no/Userfiles/Upload/files/Rapport%20RR%202021%20Evaluering%20av%20Storhaug%20Unlimited.pdf.

Saarinen, Y. (2019) Vilka ska med? *Ungas sociala inkludering i Sverige*, Växjö: Myndigheten för ungdoms-och civilsamhällesfrågor.

Sacchetti, S. and Campbell, C. (2014) Creating space for communities: social enterprise and the bright side of social capital, *Journal of Entrepreneurial and Organizational Diversity*, 3(2): 32–48. DOI: 10.5947/jeod.2014.012

21

Developing the innovative power of social work: synthesis and future directions

Erik Jansen, Anne Parpan-Blaser, Suzan van der Pas, Sarah Prosser and Jean Pierre Wilken

Introduction

The chapters in this book provide exciting insights about the crossroads between social work and social innovation. These insights show that there are at least two angles to consider: the innovative power of social work in the human service domain, and the role and meaning of social work in all kinds of innovations in other areas (economy/entrepreneurship, digitalisation, ecology, housing), raising the question of what the human value of these innovations is.

The first angle considers how social work can be innovative itself, as a field of practice and an academic discipline. It includes the competencies of social workers and the innovative character of social work research. In other words: this angle highlights social workers *as* social innovators. The second angle brings to the fore the critical-ethical role social work can play regarding the added value of so-called 'social innovations' for human well-being, applying the normative framework as expressed in the international definition of social work. Another aspect considers how social work can help in creating this value by bringing in its knowledge about human needs, social relations and social quality. In other words: this highlights social workers as critical evaluators of social innovation.

Bearing in mind these perspectives on social work and social innovation, several motives emerge from the 20 chapters in this volume. These motives are:

- social complexity and contextuality
- social workers as change and transformation moderators
- participation, social inclusion and collaboration
- social innovation as a learning process

In what follows we briefly elaborate and reflect on these motives. We then conclude our reflections with some future directions for practice, research and education.

Social complexity and contextuality

Social innovations refer to changes and improvements related to social hotspots, tensions and problems. When it comes to tackling social problems, social work plays a crucial role: it involves identifying, researching and addressing these social problems. Accordingly – and this is shown in various chapters in this volume – social work is or can be involved in the emergence of social innovations. The range of topics is broad. If we assume that the biggest and most urgent problems correlate highly with the United Nations' Sustainable Development Goals[1] it becomes clear that social work is already addressing many of these issues (such as poverty, health and well-being, inequalities, peace and justice, working environment, education) and should therefore also play a role in their further development at all levels.

Waldenfels (1991: 92) states that he understands productive action to be 'action that is itself involved in creating the order in which it operates and in formulating the questions to which it responds' (translation by the authors). From this it follows that fundamental and lasting changes also imply addressing the structural conditions and the causes of complex social problems. This too becomes clear in several contributions, as well as how interdependent the different levels of the social system are for social innovations.

For social work to have a transformative effect requires not only profound descriptions of conditions and contexts by research and novel methods, concepts, programmes and forms of organisational structures that relate to them, but also broad alliances and cooperative approaches between stakeholders in those settings where changing contextual conditions is at stake. Social workers are (or should be) methodologically equipped for these tasks. To use the social work repertoire of methods in the sense of innovative literacy, social workers need to be linked with and well versed in creative thinking and effective collaboration with heterogeneous actors, and be comfortable with using such methods in a way that can generate leverage, for example by pursuing a critical mass of political pressure.

One comment on the use of models and frameworks is presented in this book. Many authors throughout this book express their findings and ideas about how social innovation and social work can be categorised, summarised, distilled and put into matrices and frameworks – each of them hoping that readers will be inspired to absorb this and implement at least some of these frameworks in their own work. Moreover, using models and frameworks is a potentially strong way of dealing with social complexity. In this regard, we would like to note the following: striving for change does not necessarily lead to novel outcomes. On the one hand, because innovation processes are complex and fundamentally open-ended. Failure to innovate can also be part of it. On the other hand, because the degree of innovation of a change can only be assessed in retrospect, with some distance and in comparison. It is therefore more realistic to assume that the chapters of this book promote a way of thinking that is aware of the importance of social work skills for social innovation. This also includes meeting change projects that are brought to social work and development pressure with appropriate scepticism, because sometimes it is also about saving money under the label of innovation, shortening processes, increasing efficiency under conditions of reduced resource allocation and irrespective of professional considerations.

Social workers as change and transformation moderators

Social workers appear in several chapters as moderators or facilitators of change and transformation, rather than as the initiators of change themselves, and therefore become involved in the social innovation once change processes have already started. This is often a challenging role since it requires operating in a complex and dynamic field of interactions, with many stakeholders and differing interests and perspectives as is common when it comes to the wicked problems that are faced. Social workers (and social work action researchers) are by default part of this complex field, since they always work in an embedded way, as part of a social ecosystem. This requires not only a clear and firm position and motivation on their behalf, with sufficient professional autonomy (the 'frontline freedom' of street-level bureaucrats), but also a lot of know-how on the actual wicked issues and their intricacies. Thus, social workers often face serious ethical dilemmas that emerge while the social innovation unfolds. They might find themselves in unwanted positions in between parties engaged in a power struggle. They can get stuck in between the demands of authorities in control of policies, legislation and funding, and the actual needs and demands of the population, whose members are often in a marginalised or subordinate position. In this sense, it is important that social workers organise good back-up and support, both from social work colleagues and from the leadership of the organisations they work for.

In the chapters in which this issue was brought up, however, it is considered a distinguishing characteristic of social workers that they know how to connect, and connect with, people and how to work on bottom-up change and empowerment considering democratic and socially just values. One way that this is emphasised appears in different chapters highlighting the ways in which social workers engage with co-creation and participatory approaches. Moreover, social work core concepts such as empowerment, cohesion and collectiveness are at the heart of any type of innovation on all levels from the local to the global. One of the main commonalities between different actors working on different levels is a sense of weaving relational-based networks for change, both horizontally, on a peer-to-peer basis, but also vertically, weaving relationships and impact between levels, sectors and disciplines.

Thus, social innovation does not merely enhance the participation of people in the current social practices that matter to them, but it generally also pursues change in these practices for the better, and perhaps new practices that may not yet exist. This increases or enhances the agency of persons and groups in their everyday lives. One way to conceptualise this is using Rutger Claassen's distinction between participational agency and navigational agency (Claassen, 2018). The former concept refers to agency in the existing practices, whereas the latter refers to the autonomy and freedom to criticise, change, swap or exit existing practices that one is involved in. As such, navigational agency explicitly refers to the capacity to induce and pursue lasting and fundamental social change, either for oneself or for a group. Hence, social innovation of the sort that is relevant to social work may be viewed as involving the enhancement of navigational agency of individuals and groups, and social workers fostering this aspect of human flourishing.

Several of the chapters refer to this core concept of 'change' in both social innovation and social work. To bring about change implies that a 'change-maker' role exists somewhere behind the strategies and programmes that have been designed to intentionally introduce new elements into a current, unsatisfactory, context. Although innovations in social work are mostly the work of a team, a project group or a community of interest, it is not uncommon to have a change-maker as the driving force. This can be a social or community worker, a leader of public services, or a citizen passionate about improving the situation for themselves or their neighbours and family. These key persons can best contribute their lived experiences, and/or their education and subsequent professional development, when supported with relevant knowledge and skills development. Challenges arise in matching or building suitable knowledge on change processes in social innovation with the people that should use it to establish effective and sustainable substantive change. This book addresses that by providing a way of increasing anyone's social innovation literacy as a fundamental skill in their social work research and education. A raising of the level of social innovation literacy should lead to an increase of the absorptive capacity of organisations and individuals to contribute to better ways of making collective impact for increased well-being.

A danger that may indeed lurk in some social innovations (as for instance demonstrated in Chapter 9), is that social innovators (not being social workers) may strive for (radical) social change on the basis of well-intended paternalism while developing a blind spot for other social aspects such as the systemic partnerships that are necessary to sustainably embed their social innovations, or ethical issues arising from indirect unintended consequences of the innovation. In other words: these innovators may think that they know what is best for other people. This particularly necessitates a strong role for social workers as change moderators, in that they can provide a countering voice by keeping an eagle-eyed view on the plural social values to be safeguarded.

Participation, social inclusion and collaboration

Social work is traditionally aimed at supporting participation and inclusion of people in vulnerable or marginalised positions. Since the first two decades of the 21st century, a shift has become visible: from working (only) on an individual level to (also) working on a collective level. Community social work is reinvented and regenerated, as is demonstrated in several chapters in this volume. Social work turns around the quality of social relations. Precisely this is essential in social innovation, conceived as a collaborative process of social capitalisation, next to working on solutions for societal problems.

Social workers are experts in working in a participative, collaborative way, as well as promoting participation in different domains of life (work, education, sport and leisure) and different types of communities. As such, they can play important roles in social innovation. One of the roles appearing in the contributions in this book is the role of community worker or, more specifically, the role of 'weaver' or 'incubator'. Another term is 'social entrepreneur'. All these terms metaphorically express a value that social workers can add by creating spaces and social settings where people can flourish and supporting the search for answers to societal challenges such as poverty and the consequences of climate change and other disasters.

The involvement of people in marginalised situations in social innovation processes is essential, as is emphasised by many chapter authors. Their lived experiences form a source of knowledge that fuels understanding and developing solutions. This involvement can be considered the heart of co-creation and co-production. It requires the acknowledgement of the methodological, ethical and epistemic values of personal and collective experiences, as a cornerstone for grassroots initiatives: equal collaboration contributes to better working methods, more just processes and more societally relevant and diverse knowledge, respectively. Social workers practise the art of strengths-based work, to work in a horizontal way on bottom-up innovation. Innovation and empowerment are intertwined. This requires many competences that are currently not always addressed in the curricula of social work education.

Competences include connecting to multi-actor perspectives, mediating, applying methods to elicit voices of people and support empowerment. What also seems important when it comes to social innovation is to connect the micro level to the meso and macro level. Reigning organisational and policy frameworks may hinder or facilitate social quality. Social workers should feel obliged to mediate between the different levels, supporting persons and communities to be heard and to participate on the level of institutions and authorities.

Also, the role of social work researchers is discussed. In particular, participative forms of research and co-design research methods are highlighted in several chapters. And again, participation and collaboration are key here. Several contributing authors demonstrate how research can elicit the value of certain social innovation methods and support positive developments by taking an active role in innovation processes. Thus, social work research can not only demonstrate successful approaches, providing scientific evidence, but also help to design solutions for societal problems, as well as better ways of working on well-being.

Social innovation as a learning process

In several chapters social innovation is explicitly regarded as a learning process, and particularly a process of collective learning and development. In the overwhelming majority of the chapters, however, learning at least implicitly plays a role in the social innovation at stake. Learning together particularly enhances the quality of connections and collaboration between the actors involved. However, learning can take on various forms, such as the explicit organisation of learning circles, communities of practice and learning networks, but also implicitly by way of reflection, emancipation and change processes with the persons or groups involved.

The focus in learning networks in social work practice is not only on strengthening the personal skills and competencies of social workers but also on an organisational level of learning and the connection between policy and implementation practice. Learning in such networks then forms a crucial element of social innovation and in most cases the process of learning becomes more important than its tangible substantive result. To facilitate such learning, opportunities for exchange play an eminently important role in the context of innovation: only outside of current (thinking) routines and in contact with heterogeneous people who share an interest for the same topic something new or innovative can truly emerge.

The transformative power of social work can be utilised to its full potential if one imagines a shift towards a conception of 'social work' not as the exclusive domain of social workers, but rather as a collective capacity of the system. It should not (only) be viewed as a profession, but as a capacity or function of society at large, requiring the participation of many stakeholders and actors in change-oriented networks initiated and sustained from within society. Such a conceptualisation reflects not only the rediscovery of an early understanding of social work but also highlights that at all levels of social work there is a need for competent actors to 'organise' social innovation processes.

Learning communities in higher education are one way of doing this, as their structural characteristics and areas of tension align with those of innovation processes. In learning networks many other actors than merely social workers are involved in social innovation regarding issues that are at the core of the social work field. For all these actors, the focus in these learning communities is on not-knowing versus clarity, friction versus harmony, structure versus freedom, process versus result. Students (and lecturers) who learn in learning communities thus acquire innovation skills and learn about the agency of other stakeholders but also contribute to the solution of so-called wicked problems and to the transformation of the social system. Working with learning communities in higher education matches with the paradigm shifts Biesta (2014) describes as a shift from the instruction paradigm to a learning paradigm and the education paradigm to a paradigm of life-long learning.

Conclusion

Human well-being is what matters to all of us. People want to be happy and healthy. Children want to grow up in a safe and healthy environment. Adults want to develop and use their talents, to lead a decent life, to be connected in a meaningful way to others. Although all human needs are basically the same, fulfilment of these needs, desires and aspirations is often frustrated. Persons normally face setbacks and hardships as part of their lives. One can fall ill or may need to cope with a disability, or the loss of a loved one. Traumatic events may happen, caused by human factors and, more and more due to our neglect of the earth, by natural factors. Furthermore, people are complicated beings who often get into conflict as the only living beings on the planet that harm or violate each other systematically and at mass scale. But people also create systems that are supposed to be facilitating and enhancing well-being but, in reality, may turn out to be counterproductive for prospering. We seem to keep getting seriously entangled in complexity on personal, local and global scales.

One could say that social innovation is in many ways finding our way back to the essence of what it means to be a human being among other human beings. From a more critical perspective, it is up to us to renovate our societies and regenerate social and other forms of non-financial capital as essential resources for valued and dignified lives. This implies restoring basic conditions, or capabilities – as phrased in the capability approach – for human existence. Thus, social innovation may partly, or sometimes predominantly, be social renovation, first, because it always involves a critique of existing conditions and, second, because it points to novel ways based on relevant knowledge. In order for these to achieve their transformative potential, effective ways are needed that go beyond the professional context to lead to social change. Putting social capital in the centre and connecting this to other forms of capital like ecological capital, will connect the social with all other challenges we are facing.

We think that the value of this book is that it demonstrates in many ways how these connections can be constructed, and which roles social workers can take. Social work – both as practice and as research discipline – in different fields is, as yet, not well-articulated and therefore undervalued. Many social workers still appear to lack a basic social innovation literacy. A growing awareness of the connection between social innovation and social work is therefore quite necessary to understand the amplitude of contemporary challenges and the potential of the social work discipline. Many promising developments are already happening, as numerous examples in this volume show. In these examples, social professionals are already actively involved and contributing greatly, but in many other cases they are not yet involved. Thus, fantastic opportunities are not taken up to play a central role and make a difference, particularly where people and communities are marginalised and suffering or otherwise at risk of being compromised in the lives they aspire or deserve to live. Increasing social quality, in connection to the quality of our material resources, is at the heart of social work and social innovation.

One question arises as to the impact of social innovations. We believe that a critical appraisal of social innovation as it is used in a general way in many fields, especially when it comes to businesses and products, is needed. Whenever the word 'social' is employed, as a social work discipline we must critically assess how the word is used and if this is compatible with values of social quality.

When the social is put at the heart of innovation, this may bring about many challenges. For instance, different actors may have contradictory ideas or agendas. Innovation might be spurred by external pressure such as national policies and austerity measures. This can be counterbalanced by keeping a firm orientation towards the values of social work as expressed in the global definition of social work. As we have discussed, social innovations should be based on human rights and social inclusion, on well-being and equal opportunities for all people, if they are to be relevant to social work. However, many social innovations focus on local issues that do not always clearly reveal these larger dimensions. As noted, this may be solved with conscientisation such as in joint learning processes. However, it will continually remain a task to make these insights adaptable and transferable to other local or national contexts, or other fields of practice. Thus, inevitably social innovation will involve some sort of politicisation, albeit in varying levels of intensity.

Further research can help to strengthen the profile of social work regarding social innovation. This can, first of all, be done by continuing to participate in social innovation projects, and to further refine methods of participatory action research and design research. It is evident that the value and role of social work should be demonstrated more clearly. We encourage professional associations on a national and international level to include and emphasise these in their policy documents and communication. We recommend schools of social work to include 'social innovationship' in their curricula to enhance social innovation literacy among future practitioners.

Second, we think it could be highly useful to develop knowledge and insights on a more overarching level in the nexus between social innovation, social change and social work. As the chapters of this volume clearly show, there is considerable overlap between these three concepts and their associated practices, but differences also appear. More research could yield better demarcations and thereby better role positioning for the actors involved, with the social worker in the first place.

In closing, to achieve innovativeness beyond local contexts as a profession and a discipline (this means to identify opportunities for innovation, to develop and test new approaches, and scale successful interventions to maximise their impact) it takes exchange and networking in the respective subject areas (and beyond) and across the regions of Europe (and beyond). This not only allows us to discuss opportunities and limitations for social work in relation to social innovation, but also to work collaboratively towards a future in which persons and groups can live the lives they aspire to live.

Note
[1] https://sdgs.un.org/goals

References
Biesta, G.J.J. (2014) *The Beautiful Risk of Education*, Boulder, CA: Paradigm.
Claassen, R. (2018) *Capabilities in a Just Society: A Theory of Navigational Agency*, Cambridge: Cambridge University Press.
Waldenfels, B. (1991) *Der Stachel des Fremden*, Frankfurt: Suhrkamp.

Index

A

Abma, T.A. and Widdershoven, G.A. 126
academic discourses of social innovation 13
academic knowledge 117
adaptive preferences 239
Addams, Jane 48–9, 263, 272
agency 55, 62, 64
AI (artificial intelligence) 92–3
Amaro, M.I. 264
ARI 92
Arnold, G. 43–4
Ashoka 30, 31, 35, 36
asset-based collaboration 100
assets 76
assisted technologies 91
asylum seekers 202
Audretsch et al 265
Austria 171
autism spectrum 258
Avans University of Applied Sciences 150, 152, 161
    see also learning communities

B

backbone organisations 30
Balkans 204
BASW (British Association of Social Workers) 199, 201
Beck et al 16
Belgium 237–8
    Flemish Decree on Poverty 238, 242
    grassroots social innovation see GLD (grassroots-led development)
    poverty 237–8, 242–6
    redistribution policies 245
benefits trap 256
Bent-Goodley, T.B. 270, 272
Beresford, P. 75
Biesta, G.J.J. 151, 152
big data 105–6
Bindkracht10 58
bioregion (case study) 30–2
Blue Neighbourhood Economy 127
Boden, M. 45
bonding 180, 181, 187–8
Boone et al 240–1
Boschma, R. 117
bottom-up processes 33, 34
Bourdieu, Pierre 182
BPU model 143
Brandsen et al 14
bridging 180, 181, 188
Brooks, David 29
building bridges 187–8
Bulletin of the Atomic Scientists 24
BWL (Bioregional Weaving Lab) 30–2, 36
    Waterford bioregion 31–2
Bye, Engebrigtsen 280–2

C

CA (capability approach) 54, 126
    agency and plurality of well-being 62
    basic capabilities 76
    capability, notion of 54–5
    capability sets 55
    conversion factors 55
    criticisms of 76
    good life 56, 62, 63, 64, 65
    macro level 55
    meso level 55
    normative framework 57–8
    paradigm-like qualities 57
    personal level 55
    philosophical nature of 57
    social innovation and 56–7
        capabilities and functionings 56, 64
        focus on individuals 56
        pursued functionings and means 56–7
        valued life 56
    social work practice and research 57–8
    valued functionings 55
    valued life 55
    see also Capability Cards
Campos, A. and Soeiro, J. 270
capability approach see CA (capability approach)
Capability Cards 58–61
    deliberative questions 64–5
    lessons for practitioners 62–3
    observations from 61–2
    PO model 59–61, 62, 63
capability sets 55
capitalist exploitation 198
carbon storage 196
Care Act (2014) 255
care innovation 91
Caritas Diocesana Veronese 225
catalysts 101, 102
China 196
citizen engagement (URBiNAT) 209
    learning points 214–18, 219
    living framework of guidelines 211–14, 218
    categories 215–17, 218–19
    core leverages 212
    living knowledge 212, 219

Index

social workers and 218
stakeholders 218
Claassen, Rutger 76, 292
climate change
  COP26 196
  definition 195
  dialogue 197
  extreme weather events 200–1
  fossil fuel consumption 196
  heatwaves 195
  inaction of political elites 204–5
  migration and 201–3
  net zero target 196, 197
  vulnerable countries and regions 200–1
  war and 203–4
  see also disaster(s); GSW (green social work)
climate crisis 195
  generic social work skills 198–9
  impact of war 203
  snail's pace climate action 195–6
climate migration 201–3
  hostile environment 202–3
  vulnerability of migrants 202–3
Co-Crea-Te project 100
co-creation 17, 71
  collaboration 99, 109
  of community 181–2
  conceptualising 72–6
  dark side of 75
  definition 72, 98
  effective practice 74
  equality 99–100
  hard-to-reach citizens 108–9
  instruments of
    design thinking and social hackathons 106–8
    digital solutions or applications 106
    lived experience storytelling and community reporting 103–4
    living labs 104–5
    Luuppi tool 105–6
    power relations 104–5
    social media 106
  as a moral endeavour 74
  New Public Governance 74
  non-linear and unpredictable 108
  normative theory of value 75–6
  phases of 101–2
    co-design 102
    co-evaluation 103
    co-implementation 103
    co-initiation 102
    co-management 103
    personalisation 102–3
    stakeholder engagement 102
  policy for 76–7
  professional behaviour 99–101
  social innovation 77, 78–9

strength-based approaches 75
sustainability 109
unpredictability of 108
URBiNAT 209, 210–11
as a value-led practice 98–9
see also CoSIE (Co-creation of Service Innovation in Europe); NBS (nature-based solutions)
co-creation ladder 72
Co-creation of Service Innovation in Europe *see* CoSIE (Co-creation of Service Innovation in Europe)
co-design 102
co-evaluation 103
co-implementation 103
co-initiation 102
co-management 103
co-production 72, 76–7
  definition 72
co-teaching 113
cognitive distance 117–18
cognitive proximity 117
cohesion 25, 37, 291
  see also social cohesion
collaboration 94, 99, 100, 109, 293–4
collaboration in GLD 237, 243–5
collaborative innovation 27
collective impact 27
collectiveness 25, 37, 291
The Colour Kitchen 258
common good 13
Commonland 30, 31
commons 182
community 179
  bonding, bridging and linking 180, 181, 187–8
  local 180–1
  mobility issues 189
  notions of 179–81
  objective dimension 180
  polarisation of 189
  political and institutional context 189
  rediscovering 180
  social connections 180
  subjective dimension 180
  tensions and challenges 188–9
  undemanding sociality 185
  well-being 180
community-building 179, 181
community capacity 75
community development 179
  asset-based 182–3
  co-creation 181–2
  community connector 183
  innovation requirements 181
  need for 189–90
  practice of 182–3
  research 179
  social capital 181–2

social inclusion
  Estonian project 183–6
  'First a Home' project 186–8
  strengths-based approach 182–3
community incubators 276–7
  see also Unlimited incubator model
community learning 183
community places 184
community reporting 103–4
community social workers 182–3
community work 27
community workers 179
  challenges of 189
  important role of 189–90
  main task of 188
  social inclusion 188
conciliation in GLD 237, 241–3
Confed 257
conscientisation in GLD 237, 238–41
construction paradigm 151
CoSIE (Co-creation of Service Innovation in Europe) 71–2, 76
  activities
    catalysts 101
    mapping core values 101
    systemic questions 101
  Co-Crea-Te project 100
  design thinking and social hackathons 106–8
  facilitated events 78
  lessons learned 108–9
  Luuppi tool 105–6
  new knowledge and insights 109
  pilots 77, 78–9, 98, 101
  service innovation 100–1
  sites and target populations 73
  social media 106
  Turku 100
CoSIE Roadmap to Co-creation (CoSIE Consortium) 98, 99, 101
COSMOS (Co-creation Service Modelling System) 105
COVID-19 pandemic 19, 194, 200–1
CPAR (community participatory action research) 224
Cosenza (case study) 231
  contextual factors 233
  CSF (Foundation Casa San Francesco) 228, 230–1
  impact 229–31
  importance of workshop meetings 229–30
  lack of funding 231
  local context 227–8
  multi-session lab 228, 229, 230, 233
  National Call for Proposals 4/2016 228, 231
  NGOs 228
  process 228–9

SDC (Strade di Casa) 228, 230, 231
Social Secretariat Office 230
social services department (SSD) 228, 230–31
social innovation findings
  aggregate level 232
  bottom-up factors 231
  co-creation in social work 233
  involvement of universities 232
  methodological approach 232
  top-down factors 231
Verona (case study) 231
  contextual factors 232–3
  impact 227
  local context 224–5
  Not in Words but in Deeds conference 227
  Photovoice methodology 226, 227, 233
  process 226–7
creativity 41, 44–5, 49
Crenca, Umberto 276
CRPD (United Nations Convention on the Rights of Persons with Disabilities) 164
  Article 9 165
  CRPD Committee 165
  equal access to information 165
  innovation potential of 165
  see also EL (Easy Language)
CSF (Foundation Casa San Francesco) 228, 230–31

D

data, in social services innovation 87
deep listening 34
deep personalisation 74–5
Degerickx, H. 242–3
descriptive research knowledge 47
design thinking 78, 106–8
Dewey, J. 49, 50
dialogue seminars 115–16, 117, 120
digital solutions/applications, instruments of co-creation 106
digital tools 94–5
direct democracy 263
disability 253–4
  see also CRPD (United Nations Convention on the Rights of Persons with Disabilities); EL (Easy Language)
disaster(s) 193–4, 205
  claimant-induced 193
  definition 194
  generic skills 198–9
  socially constructed 198
  survivors of 200
  see also climate change; GSW (green social work)
discretion 45–6, 51

Doroud et al 184, 185
doughnut economies 33
drug abuse
  harm reduction approach 254–5
  safe drug-taking paraphernalia 254–5
Duffy et al 204

E

Easy Language *see* EL (Easy Language)
eco-grief 198
economic innovation 12
education
  added value 118–19
  involvement of service users in 113–14
  three models 114–15, 117, 118, 121
education paradigm 151, 152
EES (European Employment Strategy) 264, 265–66
effectiveness 89
Einfach leicht verstandlich *see* Just Easy to Understand project
EL (Easy Language) 164
  disseminating knowledge about 172
  implementing materials in practice 169
  individual initiatives 173–4
  as an innovation in practice 165–7
  Just Easy to Understand project *see* Just Easy to Understand project
  origins 166
  political will 173–4
  purpose of 166
  recognisable text 166
  reducing barriers to communication 171
  research and use of 171
  target group 166
emergencies 198
empathetic listening 99
empowerment 16, 37, 119, 120, 121, 182, 230, 253–4, 291
end users 99
entrepreneurial discourses of social innovation 13
entrepreneurialism 43
entrepreneurship 12
  (super)national agenda 264–6
  EES 265–6
  innovation 272
  paradigm for employment 265
  in Portugal *see* Portugal
  social dimension 263
  types of 263
environmental injustice 194
environmental justice 193
environmental stress 196
equal opportunity 55
equality 99–100
ERSISI (Enhancing the Right to Social Inclusion through Service Integration) 89–90

ESN (European Social Network) 84, 85, 90
Estonia 183–6
EU 2020 Strategy 86
EU (European Union) 89, 94, 200, 214, 264–5, 271
  investment in NBS 208–9
European Commission 41, 181
  co-creation 77
  entrepreneurship 265–6, 271–2
  Entrepreneurship 2020 Action Plan 265
  social experimentation 42–3
  social innovation 42–3
European Conferences of Social Work Research (ECSWR) 1
European Economic and Social Committee 77
European Quality of Life Survey (EQLS, 2016) 105
evaluative quantitative research 47
Evers et al 14–15
evidence-based practice 47, 47–8
Exchange Supplies 254–5
experiential knowledge 17, 113–14, 115, 117
experimentation, in social services innovation 87
extreme weather events 200–1

F

family coaches 91
Firmin, Thomas 253
Flanders 237, 238
  grassroots social innovation *see* GLD (grassroots-led development)
Flyvbjerg, B. 241
Focus 256, 257
Foley, R. 44–5, 49
Follett, Mary Parker 263, 272
fossil fuels consumption 196, 198
Fox et al 98
freedom 76
Freidson, E. 241
Freire, Paulo 238–9, 244
frontline freedom 41

G

GDP (gross domestic product) 266
The General Report on Poverty (Santkin) 237–8, 242–3
Geneva Convention (1951) 202
Gewirth, A. 76
GHGs (greenhouse gases) 200, 201
  failure to reduce 196–7
  military attribution 194, 195, 202, 203
GLD (grassroots-led development) 237
  collaboration 237, 243–5
  deconstructing knowledge hierarchy 244
  living situation of people in poverty 244
  marginalised groups 243–4

structured approach 244–5
valuable insights of people in poverty 244
conciliation 237, 241–3
  agonistic tradition 241–2
  dialogue 242
  disparate logics of service provision 241
  transcending interests and strategies 241
conscientisation
  empathy to people in poverty 240
  listening to people in poverty 240
  processes of exclusion 240–1
  safe spaces 239–40
  transcending paternalism 240
  voices of people in poverty 240
global community (case study) 32–3
global crises 24
Global Entrepreneurship Monitor (2012) 263
globalisation 181
Goffman, E. 44
good knowledge 48
good life 18, 56, 62, 63, 64, 65
good practice 49–50
Goscha, R.J. 184
governance structures 12
governmental discourses of social innovation 13
GPMH (Good Practices in Mental Health) 49–50
grassroots innovation 16–17
grassroots-led social innovation 236–7
  grassroots-led development *see* GLD (grassroots-led development)
  WPPSO (Where People in Poverty Speak out) 237–8
Gray, M. 75
green social work *see* GSW (green social work)
green social workers 201
  interventions 202
  promoting innovative policy changes 205
green technologies 197
grounded knowledge 48
grounded theory 170
group reflection 50
GSW (green social work) 193, 195
  approaches to human-nature interactions 198
  defining 198–9
  engaging social workers 197–9
  promoting innovations 205
  sustainability 198
  theory and practice of 197
  training for social workers 202
  transdisciplinarity 194
  see also climate change

H

hackathons 78–9
Häfeli, C. 166–7
HAN University of Applied Sciences 58
hazards 193–4, 198
hegemony 239
home care services 92
HOME_EU: 'Homelessness as unfairness' (2016–19) 225, 231
homeless people 186–8
homelessness 223
  social work 224
  see also CPAR community participatory action research
AS Hoolekandeteenused 183–6
Horizon 2020 71, 77, 214, 225, 231
  see also URBiNAT
Horizon Europe 77
horizontal creativity 41–2, 44–5, 46, 48, 51
  criticisms of 49–50
horizontal military innovation 44–5
Housing First Network Italy 225
Housing First programme 88
'How to Start a Community Incubator' (Prosser and Pedersen) 278, 279
HR (human resources) 254
Hull House Settlement 48, 49
human services 46
Hvinden, B. and Halvorsen, R. 55

I

IASSW (International Association of Schools of Social Work) 201, 204
Ibrahim, S. *see* GLD (grassroots-led development)
iceberg metaphor 25–6
ICSW (International Council of Social Welfare) 201
IFRC (International Federation of Red Cross and Red Crescent Societies) 199, 201
IFSW (International Federation of Social Workers) 201, 204
Ilie, E.G. and During, R. 13
improvement 89
inclusion paradox 188
India 196
individual agency 76
individualism 180, 181
informal learning 152, 161
innovation 1–2, 77
  bottom-up 231
  empirical insights 173
  hackathons 78–9
  process of 173
  in social services *see* social services innovation
  social work and 14–15

Index

top-down 231
user participation 173
innovation processes 168
innovation strategy 35, 37
institutions of higher education 151–2
instruction paradigm 152
Involving Service Users in Social Work Education, Research and Policy: A Comparative European Analysis (Driessen and Lyssens-Danneboom) 113
IPCC (Intergovernmental Panel on Climate Change) 195, 196–7
IPG (integrated process supervision of groups) model 143
Italy 223–5
 CPAR projects *see* CPAR (community participatory action research)
 homelessness 223
 national policy framework 223–4
 poverty 223

J

Johnson, A.K. and Cnaan, R.A. 224
Just Easy to Understand project 164–5, 166, 167
 adult protection brochure 168, 171, 172
 aim and implementation of 167
 creating texts in EL 168
 dissemination of results 171–2
 essential effects 172–3
 evaluating the effects 170–1
 evaluating the processes 169–70
 innovation 172–3
 networking 173
 outcomes 172–3
 training validators 168–9
just-in-time education 152, 161

K

Kania et al 27
Kania, J. and Kramer, M. 27
KI-I (Competence Network Information Technology to Support the Integration of People Disabilities) 169, 171
Kierkegaard, Søren 116
King Baudouin Foundation 237–8
knowledge 121
 forms of 47–50
knowledge exchange 37
KOKES (National Conference for Child and Adult Protection) 168
Kowalk, H. and Wetterling, J. 116–17

L

labour market 270
 issues 124
 unemployment 124
Lancker, Wim Van 244–5
Lane et al 194
language barriers 165
Leadbeater, C. 74
learning communities 150, 161–2, 295
 dualities
  friction versus harmony 158
  group versus individual(s) 160–1
  not-knowing versus clarity 157–8
  process versus results 159–60
  structure versus freedom 159
 as an emerging model 150–3
  institutions of higher education 151–2
  wicked problems 151
 equality 154
 examinations 153
 examples of 154–5
 positioning educators in 155
 in practice 153–5
 principles of 153–4
 reflection groups 155–6
 schedules 154
 sensitising concepts 156–61
 in social work education 152–3
 stages
  Blue Monday 156–7
  Digging Deeper 156
  Reaping the Harvest 157
  Testing the Waters 156, 159
 uncertainty 157
 versions of 151–2
 wicked problems 150–1, 154–5, 156, 161–2
Learning Community Stages 156
Learning from Learning Communities project 150
learning networks 294, 295
learning paradigm 151, 152
Ledwith, Margaret 239
lifelong learning 151, 152, 271–2
Lindholm, C. and Vanhatalo, U. 166
linking 180, 187–8
Lisbon Strategy 265
lived experience storytelling 104
living labs 104–5
local innovation 49
Lund University 113
Luntley, M. 49
Luuppi tool 105–6
Luxembourg European Council 265

M

Meadows, D.H. 36
mental health 183–6
 neighbourhood and surroundings 185
 reciprocal relationships 185–6
miEnterprise 256–7
migrants
 from the Ukraine 203–4
 housing shortage 204
migration 201–3

Mintrom, M. 43
MISSION (Mobile Integrated Social Services) 90–1
modus 2 knowledge production 117
Moore et al 172
Mulgan, G. 25
multi-stakeholder ecosystems 37
Municipality of Cosenza 228
Murray et al 12, 181

N

navigational agency 64, 292
NBS (nature-based solutions) 208–10, 214–19
  characteristics of 208
  definitions of 208
  dimensions of 218
  EU investment 208–9
  practitioners of 208
  social innovation 218–19
  URBiNAT *see* URBiNAT
Nedenfra 282–3, 284
neighbourhood incubators (case study) 29–30
  human aspect practices 30
  social enterprise 30
neoliberal individualisation 179
Netanyahu, Benjamin 195
Netherlands
  'First a Home' project 186–8
  learning communities *see* learning communities
  Ministry of Health, Welfare and Sports 140–1
  Participation Act (2015) 257
  regional learning networks *see* regional learning networks
  Social Support Act (SSA, 2007) 140
  social work 151
  Work and Social Assistance Act (2004) 257
Network against Poverty 238
New Public Governance 74
New Public Management 74
Nicholls et al 25, 33, 124–5
NJA (Neighbourhood Job Agency) (case study) 125
  context specific 126
  methodology: responsive evaluation 125–7
  as a new practice for job activation 127–8
  philosophy 132
  local work 131–2
  social innovation 133–4
  social workers 133–4
  sustainability projects 132
    capability voice 132–3
    commitment 133

confusion 133
needs 133
overstated expectations 133
social outcomes 133
user-driven innovation 127–8
users and non-users 128–32
  accessibility 129–30
  confusion 130
  dream jobs 128
  freedom of choice 129
  inclusion 129
  job opportunities 130
  local businesses 131
  local work 130
  municipality 131
  network of employers 131
  voluntary work 130
normative theory of value 75–6
Norway 276
  community incubators *see* Unlimited incubator model
NU (Norway Unlimited) 29, 30, 35, 36, 276, 277, 285
Nussbaum, M.C. 54, 58

O

OECD (Organisation for Economic Co-operation and Development) 33
OECD Skills Outlook (2013) 165
open innovation 77
Open Innovation 2.0 77
Orman model 156
Osborne et al 73–4
Osborne, S. and Strokosch, K. 72
outreach support 90–1

P

Pakistan 200
paradigmatic thinking 46
Paris Agreement (2015) 201
Parpan-Blaser, A. 15, 112
participation 293–4
Participation Act (2015) 124
participatory agency 292
participatory research methodologies 118
Pedersen, O. 282
People2People 255–6, 257
People's Voice Media 103
personal autonomy 91–3
  artificial intelligence 92–3
  robots 91–2
personal business models 128
personalisation 74–5, 102–3
perspectives, alignment of 18
Phillips, C. and Shaw, I. 117
policy entrepreneurs 43–4
Portugal 263–4, 268
  entrepreneurship 266–9, 271, 272–3
    Modernising Portugal measure 268

as a panacea 271
plurality of fields 271
social inclusion 269
research study 269–70
  education of subjects 270
  entrepreneurship and social work 270–1
  labour market 270
unemployment 266
XIX Government Programme 268
XV Constitutional Government 267–8
XVII Constitutional Government 268, 271
XVIII Constitutional Government 268, 271
XXIII Government Programme 266–7, 268, 269
postcode lottery 85
poverty 223
  in Belgium 237–8, 242–6
  in Italy 223
  see also CPAR (community participatory action research); GLD (grassroots-led development); WPPSO (Where People in Poverty Speak out)
power 188
power relations 104–5, 119
practical knowledge 48
practice 47
pragmatism 48–9
Presencing Institute 31
Preston, Andrew 254–5
Price et al 75
Problem Tree tool 27, 28
professional behaviour 99–101
  changing working routines 99–101
  thinking for others 100
professional knowledge 48
Prosser, S.D. 30
public administration 73–4
  New Public Management 74
  traditional 74
public sector management 259
public spending 85
Putnam, Robert 180, 181–2

Q

quantitative descriptive research 47
quantitative evaluative research 47, 48, 51
quantitative research 47

R

randomised controlled trials 87, 89, 90, 95n1
reciprocity 185–6
reflection 50
regional learning networks
  action research 141, 143, 145
  agenda formation 139, 144

BPU model 143
definition 139
embedding conditions of learning 146
establishment of 139
funding for 147
IPG model 143
learning facilitators 139, 144
learning process 144
local stakeholders 147, 148
national working group 142
neighbourhood-based teams 147
network facilitators 144
objective 145
operationalisation of principles 145
organisation of 142
participatory process 145
practical tools and activities 142–3
practice-based framework 146
programme approach 145
sense-making 148
social innovation 147–8
social transformation 146–7
in the social welfare domain 140–2
SSA 140
substantive aims of national policies 147
survey 142–3
  deliberation and emancipation as learning 145–7
  findings 143–5
  transformative questions 145
universities of applied sciences 140–1, 144
wicked challenges 141
Regional Networks for the Social Welfare Domain (RNSWD) see regional learning networks
relational networks 180
relevance, in social services innovation 87–8
Remploy 253
renewable energy technologies 196
research 18–19
  experiential knowledge 117
  service user involvement 114–16, 117
  in social work 121
  student career options 38
responsive evaluation 125–7
Richmond, Mary 272
RIPESS (2015) 286–7
risk management 259
Rittel, H.W.J. and Webber, M.M. 151
RNIB (Royal National Institute of Blind People) 255
RNSWD (Regional Networks for the Social Welfare Domain) see regional learning networks
Robeyns, I. 57
robots 91–2
Romsås Unlimited 277

Russia 195, 196, 203–4
Ryan, R.M. and Deci, E.L. 159

S

Samaritans Onlus 225
SARS-COV-2 194
scientific knowledge 47
SDC (Strade di Casa) 228, 230, 231
SEIN 91
Sen, A. 54, 55, 76
Sendai Framework for Disaster Risk Reduction (2015–30) 201
service delivery 104
service user involvement 112
  added value 118–20
  dialogue seminars 115–16, 117, 120
  in education 113–14, 120
    collaboration 118
    models of cooperation 113–14
  empowerment 119, 120
  equal partners 119
  experts by experience 113–14, 116–17
  helpful assistance 116
  implementation guide 116
  knowledge capture 115
  mobilisation course 113
  new or newly combined knowledge 116–18
  participatory research methods 118
  in research 114–16
  social problems 118
  transformation of social relations 119–20
  useful help 116
service users 99, 100
Settlement Movement 263
shallow personalisation 74
Sharpe et al 36
Shaw, Ian 19
sheltered employment 253, 257
silos 94
situational contracting 46
situational knowledge 49
Sixth Assessment Report (IPCC) 196–7
small entrepreneurs 272
social capital 17, 180, 181–2, 188, 190, 296
  Bourdieu 182
  efficacy 181–2
  engagement 181
  homogeneity, lack of 182
  Putnam 180, 181–2
  trust 181
social change
  bioregion as unit of 30–2
  global community as unit of 32–3
  levels of innovation strategy 35
  neighbourhood as unit of 29–30
  spatial and cultural context 37
social cohesion 16
social complexity 290
social empowerment 16
social enterprises 127
  case studies
    The Colour Kitchen 258
    Confed 257
    Exchange Supplies 254–255
    Focus 256, 257
    miEnterprise 256–7
    People2People 255–6, 257
    Specialisterren 258–9
    Viewpoint 255
  disadvantaged and disabled people 253–4
  experiment and failure 259
  financial metrics 259
  financial sustainability 251–2
  growth and development of 251, 252, 253
  innovative solutions 252
  lessons 259–60
  objectives 251
  'out of the box' thinking 260
  risk governance approach 260
  social co-operative model 253
  stakeholders 252
  triple bottom line 259, 260
  work integration and 252–4
social entrepreneurs 13
social entrepreneurship 43, 132, 254–60, 263, 269–71, 271, 273
social experimentation 42, 44, 87
social firms 253
social hackathons 106–8
social inclusion 16, 88–91, 183–6, 280–1, 293–4
  building bridges 187–8
  community workers 188
  discovering connections 185
  empowering niches 184
  ERSISI project 89–90
  MISSION project 90–1
  reciprocity 185–6
social innovation 295–6
  aligning perspectives 18
  capability approach and 56–7, 64
  co-creation and 77, 78–9
  community participation *see* CPAR (community participatory action research)
  concept of 12–14
  core elements 13
  critical appraisal 296
  decline in trust 125
  definitions 2, 12, 25, 85, 125
  discourses of 13–14
  elements of 16–18
  frameworks for 25–9
  global problems 12
  governmental discourses of 13

Index

grassroots-led *see* grassroots-led social innovation
interpretations of 42
as a learning process 294–5
literature 12
macro level 25
NBS and 218–19
NJA and 133–4
non-relational types of innovation 12
place-based approach 37
regional learning networks and 147–8
research and 18–19
social change for the common good 13
social cohesion and empowerment 182
types and styles of 25
vertical *see* vertical social innovation
see also innovation; social services innovation
social innovation community incubators 29–30
Social Land Programme 105
social media 106
social needs 12, 127
social practice 86
social problems 118
social quality 15–16, 20
social relations 119–20
social robotics 91–92
social services
postcode lottery 85
social change and development 86–7
social services innovation 84–5
approaches 85
collaboration 94
criteria 85–6
defining 85–6, 88
funding 94
improvement 89
key concepts 86–8
data 87
experimentation 87
relevance 87–8
transferability 88
professional training 95
promoting personal autonomy 91–3
artificial intelligence 92–3
robots 91–2
scaling up 93–4
silos 94
social inclusion 88–91
ERSISI project 89–90
MISSION project 90–1
technology and digital tools 94–5
social values 15
symptoms level 30
social welfare *see* regional learning networks

social work
activistic stream 14
career and research opportunities 38
challenges 193
community development 179
connecting different forms of capital 17
decentralisation 151
definition of innovation in 112
definitions 2–3, 25
embedded in public bodies 259
entrepreneurship 264
frameworks for 25–9
innovation and 14–15
learning process 17
place-based approach 37
research 121, 296–7
users and 114–15
see also GSW (green social work)
Social Work for Peace 204
social workers
as change and transformation moderators 291–3
citizen engagement 218
community-building 190
complexity of challenges 251
conflict situations 204
disaster cycle 201
'doing no harm' principle 202
driving innovation 236
entrepreneurial education 260
ethical dilemmas 202, 291
helping migrants 203
responding to climate change disasters 199–200
risks in military conflicts 201–2
securing benefits of NBS 218
self-care 204
skills of 290
see also green social workers
socio-economic security 16
Solidarity House 225
Søndre Nordstrand 280
Søndre Unlimited 277
South Sudan 201–2
Specialisterren 258–9
SSA (Social Support Act, 2007) 140
objectives 140
'participation law' 140
stakeholder engagement 102
Stam, M. and Wilken, J.P. 157
Storhaug 280
Storhaug Unlimited 277
storytelling 103–4
strength-based approaches 75
sustainability 90, 198
Sustainable Development Goals (SDGs) 201, 290
Switzerland
Child and Adult Protection Act (2013) 166

CRPD *see* CRPD (United Nations Convention on the Rights of Persons with Disabilities)
EL (Easy Language) 166
Federal Chancellery 172
Federal Office for the Equality of Persons with Disabilities 167, 172
national disability policy, lack of 165
symptom innovation 34–5
systemic innovation 117
systems change approach 27
systems innovation 25, 35–6

T

Tan, N.T. 273
Task Force 6 214
TBBL (Tøyen boligbyggelag) 282, 283
technological innovation 12
technology 94–5
third horizon thinking 27
Three Horizon Tool 27, 29, 36
Torfing et al 72
Tøyen 280
Tøyen Unlimited 276–7, 282
traffickers 202–3
transdisciplinarity 194
transferability, in social services innovation 87–8, 88, 90
transformative innovation 27, 36
Turku 100

U

Ukraine 195, 200, 203–4
  Homes for Ukraine scheme 203–4
United Nations Framework Convention on Climate Change 195–6
universities of applied sciences 140, 144, 147, 152
University of Calabria 228
University of Padua 225
University of Tartu 179, 183–6
Unlimited incubator model 276–8
  evaluations 283
  founding principles 278–80
  'How to Start a Community Incubator' (Prosser and Pedersen) 278, 279
  insights 282–3
  recommendations
    innovation in neighbourhoods 285
    systemic and transformational innovation 286–7
  reflections 284–5
    on a collective level 285
    employees' skills 284
    on an individual level 284–5
    on a societal level 285
    value of 284
  research 280–2
  social inclusion 280–1

structure of 277–8
Unlimited Supporter Handbook 284
UnLtd 277–8
Upper Austria 171
Upper Austrian Equal Opportunities Act (2014) 171
urban regeneration 209
  see also URBiNAT
URBiNAT 209–10, 218
  advisory boards 211
  citizen engagement *see* citizen engagement (URBiNAT)
  co-creation process 209, 210–11
  developing community-driven processes 218
  local participatory culture 210–11
  participation experts 218
  partnerships 211
  proposition 209
  research and fieldwork 209
  social innovation 209
US (United States of America) 196
useful help concept 116
Utrecht 186–8
Utrecht University of Applied Sciences 179

V

value 98–9
valued functionings 55
van der Have, R.P. and Rubalcaba, L. 13
Van Ewijk, H. 187
vertical social innovation 41, 42–4, 45–7, 50–1
Viewpoint 255
voluntary work 130
Voorberg et al 72, 125

W

Waldenfels, B. 290
wars 194, 201–2
  climate change and 203–4
weavers 31–2
well-being 55, 61–2, 76, 180, 295
Wellbeing Economy Alliance 33
Welzijnsschakels 244
wicked problems 150–1, 154–5, 156, 161–2
  definition 151
  transformation of the welfare state 151
Windrum, P. 117
WISE (work-integration social enterprise) 253
work integration 252–4
WPPSO (Where People in Poverty Speak Out) 237–8, 239, 242, 245–6
Wrocław Guide to Social Experimentation 42
WSF (World Social Forum) 32–3, 35

www.ingramcontent.com/pod-product-compliance
Lightning Source LLC
Chambersburg PA
CBHW051527020426
42333CB00016B/1811